327.098
L34

102139

DATE DUE			
Nov 30 '84			
Apr14 '83			

LATIN AMERICA:
THE SEARCH FOR A NEW INTERNATIONAL ROLE

LATIN AMERICAN INTERNATIONAL AFFAIRS SERIES
Sponsored by the **CENTER FOR INTER-AMERICAN RELATIONS**

Volume I. Latin American International Affaris Series
Sponsored by the Center for Inter-American Relations

LATIN AMERICA:

The Search for a New International Role

Edited by:
RONALD G. HELLMAN and H. JON ROSENBAUM

SAGE Publications

Halsted Press Division
JOHN WILEY & SONS
New York—London—Sydney—Toronto

327. 098

L 34

102139

Sept. 1977

Distributed by Halsted Press, a Division of
John Wiley & Sons, Inc., New York

Printed in the United States of America

Library of Congress Cataloging in Publication Data
Main entry under title:

Latin America: the search for a new international role.
  (Latin American international affairs series; v. 1)
    1. Latin America—Foreign relations—Addresses, essays, lectures. 2. United States—Foreign relations—Latin America—Addresses, essays, lectures. 3. Latin America—Foreign relations—United States. I. Hellman, Ronald G., ed. II. Rosenbaum, H. Jon, 1941-   ed. III. Series.
F1415.L37   327'.098   75-692
ISBN 0-47-36917-5

FIRST PRINTING

CONTENTS

PREFACE

This volume is the first in a series devoted exclusively to Latin American international relations and sponsored by the Center for Inter-American Relations. However, all views expressed in this publication are purely those of the individual authors and do not represent the opinions of the Center.

The purpose of the publication coincides with the Center's, which is to build in the United States an understanding of the other nations in the Western Hemisphere. The series is intended to provide a regular vehicle for detailed and relatively current comment on Latin American international relations. At present, serials devoted to Latin American studies and other journals provide only infrequent commentary of this kind.

Each volume of the series will contain both commissioned and unsolicited articles by leading authorities as well as by promising younger writers. Scholars, journalists, government officials, and businessmen from the United States, Latin America, and elsewhere are encouraged to participate in this publishing venture. The hope is to stimulate greater discussion and consideration of the foreign relations of the Latin American region and the countries that comprise it.

Forthcoming volumes, which will appear biennially at first but later appear more frequently if reader and contributor interest is demonstrated, will have two features in common. First, each volume will be introduced by an article summarizing developments that have occurred since the appearance of the previous issue. Second, every volume will conclude with a section devoted to short commentaries. Other than these two features the format of the series will not conform to any set organization. Rather, individual issues will be devoted to themes that appear to be particularly crucial at the time of publication. Although under the general editorial direction of the Series Editors and the International Advisory Board, these volumes will be produced by invited guest editors.

The current volume covers the period from 1972 through mid-1974. Manuscripts were received during August 1974 and therefore in most cases the contributions have not taken into account events transpiring after that date.

Volume I examines the Latin American countries' increasing efforts to assert their sovereignty more aggressively in the global as well as the regional contexts. Yale H. Ferguson, in a survey of hemispheric relations from 1972 to mid-1974, suggests at the conclusion of Chapter 1 that future ties between the United States and Latin America will be shaped significantly by a more interdependent global picture characterized by increasing tensions between the developed Northern hemisphere and the less developed Southern half of the world. The essays which follow in Part I of the volume (Kalman H. Silvert, Irving Louis Horowitz and Arthur Schlesinger, Jr.) explore the relationship of Latin America's assertion of sovereignty in world affairs to the interplay between national and international politics. Part II illustrates Latin America's search for a new global role by focusing on some conceptual (Edward S. Milenky) and concrete developments (Robert H. Swansbrough and Alexandre Barros) in recent intra-Latin American relations. The essays in Part III concentrate on the role of the United States in the development of present and future bilateral (Robert Anderson and Thomas E. Skidmore) and multilateral (Ben S. Stephansky) inter-American ties. Finally, Part IV looks at the nations of the region as world actors affecting and affected by such global issues and problems as the energy crisis (Pedro-Pablo Kuczynski); mining, exploration, navigation and other dimensions of the law of the sea (E. D. Brown); and international finance, credit and trade (Carlos Fortin).

It has been extremely gratifying to be able to assemble such a distinguished group of contributors for this initial effort. The authors have studied their subjects in depth. The essays in the volume appear in substantially the form in which they were submitted by the authors. The Series Editors confined themselves to standardizing style in order to attain as much consistancy as possible throughout the collection.

We would like to express our appreciation to A. Denman Pierce-Grove for her editorial assistance. We also extend our gratitude to Sara Marie August and Nora Schinnery both of whom went beyond the call of duty at the Center to help assure the success of this project. Rhoda Blecker, Senior Editor of Sage Publications, deserves special mention for her cheer and fine patience. Finally, the deepest appreciation goes to our wives, Diana and Betsey, for the ideas, support and loyalty they have given to us, especially during the entire time we worked on this project.

—Ronald G. Hellman
—H. Jon Rosenbaum
May 1975

Chapter 1

TRENDS IN INTER-AMERICAN RELATIONS:

1972–MID-1974

YALE H. FERGUSON

During the past two and a half years, some of the most dramatic newspaper headlines have been about domestic political events in several western hemisphere countries. In the United States, Watergate revealed the sort of pervasive corruption more often associated with the south-of-the-border stereotype. Also in the United States economists have been discussing the feasibility of a "Brazilian" solution to an inflation of "Latin American" proportions. Coups in Chile and Uruguay transformed South America's two oldest democracies into unusually repressive, rightist military-dominated regimes. In mind-boggling succession, Argentina saw a conservative military dictatorship give way to a freely elected *Peronista* government, the triumphant return to power of Juan Perón, and the death of Perón.

It is significant that to date these developments have had only a marginal impact upon the general course of inter-American relations. Obviously, worldwide, regional, and subregional forces are at work, minimizing the importance of instability within and diversity among particular domestic political systems.

Recent trends in inter-American relations must be viewed against a background of the divergent paths of the United States and Latin America over the last decade (for further details and documentation through 1972, see Ferguson, 1972; 1973). Whatever substance remained to the historic "special relationship" steadily evaporated. The Nixon Administration completed the process, begun by President Johnson when he entered the Vietnam quagmire, of moving Latin America from near the top to near the bottom of the list of U.S. foreign policy concerns. Most important for Latin America, the Nixon Administration scaled down the U.S. estimate of the security threat, which has always been the principal rationale for U.S. involvement in the area. With the decline of Castroist subversion and the increase of Latin American nationalism, U.S. policy-makers have felt it prudent to strive for a "low profile" in the hemisphere. They could thus devote their major attention to trouble-spots like Southeast Asia and the Middle East, and to the related, primary task of reshaping U.S. relations with the Soviet Union, China, Europe, and Japan. Henry Kissinger's conception of an emerging multipolar world has clearly assigned only residual significance to the developing countries, Latin American ones included. For their part, Latin Americans have come to the inescapable conclusion that their national dignity and development require greater cooperation among themselves and with extra-regional developing countries, as well as the cultivation of a broader network of political and commercial ties with Europe, Japan, and Communist governments.

This background notwithstanding, there seems to be some evidence of a modest revival of United States' interest in Latin America and the English-speaking Caribbean countries: former Secretary of State Rogers made a Latin American tour (May 1973), Mrs. Nixon traveled to presidential inaugurations in Venezuela and Brazil (March 1974), and Secretary of State Kissinger undertook a highly publicized "new dialogue" with hemisphere foreign ministers at meetings in Mexico (February 1974) and Washington-Atlanta (April 1974). Rediscovering hemisphere sources of primary commodities as the energy crisis loomed, the Nixon Administration apparently decided that it was time at least to address itself directly to some Latin American complaints. At the Atlanta General Assembly of the Organization of American States, Mr. Kissinger invoked the hoary "Western Hemisphere Idea" and the "Spirit of Tlatelolco" that had supposedly emanated from the Mexico City conference, pledged the United States to a vague "Good Partner Policy," and expressed his confidence that a continuing dialogue among "equals" could remold the special relationship "to meet the new conditions of our time."

Whether the new dialogue initiated by Secretary Kissinger will represent a turning point in the deterioration of United States-Latin America relations— or is too little, too late—remains to be seen. In any event, the following simple survey of recent developments regarding key issues will suggest that the obstacles to a reinvigorated special relationship are formidable indeed.

"POLITICAL" ISSUES

U.S. Security Policies: The Not-So-Low Profile

As we have noted, the Nixon Administration decision to seek a low profile derived mainly from its assessment that no security threat of major proportions was likely to emanate from Latin America. This generally optimistic forecast rested, in turn, upon the presumed intentions of Moscow and Peking to establish "respectable" links with Latin American nationalist governments rather than to support revolution, and upon the apparent failures of Latin American rural guerrillas. Latin American urban terrorism, kidnappings, and hijackings have been increasingly interpreted as byproducts of social unrest in specific countries, not as manifestations of cross-national subversion. Nevertheless, the low profile has been frustrated partly because it did not involve a drastic overhaul of certain pre-existing, high-profile security policies, in which the United States government and various domestic groups now have a considerable stake.

Among these policies, of course, is the continuing boycott of Cuba (for discussion, see especially Domínguez, 1973). For several years the Nixon Administration adamantly opposed any change in the status quo regarding Cuba. However, after the breakthrough in U.S. relations with Peking and especially since the conclusion of the 1972 hijacking pact with the Cuban government, some observers have expected to wake up one morning to find Kissinger in Havana breakfasting with Fidel Castro! Speculation that an accommodation might be near gained further impetus when, in conjunction with the recent inter-American conferences, Kissinger agreed (1) to leave the question of inviting Cuba to participate in the next round of the new dialogue entirely to a poll of the OAS membership, and (2) to license three subsidiaries of U.S. automobile manufacturers in Argentina to export cars and trucks to Cuba. Significant though it was, however, the second decision should probably be regarded more as a concession to the Perón regime and to beleaguered U.S. companies in Argentina than as a gesture to Cuba. The first decision was particularly interesting for what it was *not*. That is, it did not express U.S. support for ending the boycott. Indeed, State Department sources quickly indicated that if the invitation came to a vote, the United States would not support it. Predictions are always hazardous, but it seems doubtful whether an invitation will be forthcoming without U.S. active support. Only a dozen or so countries, led by those who already have defied the OAS ban on relations with Cuba—Mexico, Peru, Argentina, and the English-speaking Caribbeans— are reported to be favorably inclined. On the other hand, Brazil and Chile can be expected to rally a determined conservative opposition.

Be that as it may, the prevailing attitude within U.S. official circles to date has apparently been that there is little or nothing to be gained from an accommodation, and at least something to lose. The Castro government is a financial burden for the Soviets. Moreover, Cuban influence has been on the wane in the hemisphere. There is also a politically significant constituency in the United States—including conservative Congressmen, businessmen still bitter about confiscations, sugar importers, and the Cuban exile community—to whom Castro remains anathema.

Thus, no dramatic change in U.S. Cuban policy would seem to be likely in the near future. However, should a bandwagon start rolling in the OAS or should the administration desperately need a foreign policy "coup" to steal the headlines from bad news, an accommodation could happen.

Events do seem to be moving inexorably toward an eventual accommodation in any case. Several members of the Senate Foreign Relations Committee and four Congressmen have formally "requested" the executive to take a "new look" at the Cuba issue; and at this writing Pat Holt, the Senate committee's staff director, is visiting Havana—a trip long blocked by the State Department. Commenting on Holt's visit, Castro stated that he would also be willing to meet with Kissinger—whom he termed a "realistic man" and "not a negative figure in United States foreign policy"—but only after the U.S. economic embargo had been "unconditionally lifted."

While Cuba's status within the hemisphere continues unresolved, the Castro government has been formalizing international relationships in other quarters. The "Sovietization" of the Revolution proceeded to such an extent that Cuba was officially accepted as a member of COMECON (Council for Mutual Economic Assistance, the Communist equivalent of the Common Market) in July 1972. Castro's frank alignment with the Soviets has threatened Cuba's role as a participant (beginning in late 1971) in the so-called Group of Seventy-Seven (a group of developing countries—now over 100 members—within the United Nations Conference on Trade and Development). The Cuban Premier's ringing praise of the Soviet Union in his address at a September 1973 meeting of nonaligned states in Algiers drew bitter criticism from Colonel Qaddafi of Libya and from Cambodian Prince Sihanouk.

Cuba aside, abatement of the Cold War and movement toward multipolarity has not made U.S. decision-makers any less concerned about the prestige implications of adverse developments in this country's traditional sphere of influence, Latin America. In this connection, until Watergate made the possibility seem remote under Nixon, one could not absolutely rule out another U.S. military intervention were civil war again to break out in a small Caribbean country like Haiti or the Dominican Republic.

The Nixon Administration also repeatedly warned the Soviets that it would not tolerate the use of Cuba as a base for missile-carrying submarines—in Washington's interpretation, such a base would violate the agreement that resulted from the 1962 Cuban Missile Crisis. President Nixon asserted that the Soviets accepted this interpretation after the United States expressed concern over unusual Soviet naval activity in the Cienfuegos harbor in late 1970.

However, in May 1972, the Defense Department protested as contrary to the spirit of the "understanding" the visit of a Soviet diesel-powered submarine carrying three missiles to a port on Cuba's northern coast.

Elsewhere in Latin America: the election of Salvadore Allende to the Chilean presidency in 1970 presented a major challenge to U.S. policy. Later we will advance the interpretation that the Nixon Administration's hostility during the three years of the Allende government was *primarily* a function of the threat it posed to U.S. private economic interests. But students of inter-American relations may want to speculate as well about the extent to which Washington's attitude represented a defense of U.S. prestige, a simple visceral reaction to "Marxism," and/or an expression of genuine fear about a security threat to Chile's Latin American neighbors.

U.S. security policies also have continued to involve close ties (attachés, training, aid, etc.) with the Latin American military.[1] As part of its low profile, the Nixon Administration initially planned to phase out U.S. permanent military missions and to discontinue grant military aid. These preliminary decisions were reversed, not coincidentally, after Allende's election. Washington pointedly continued military assistance to Chile while other aid dried up. In June 1973, the administration went a step further and authorized the sale of F-5E supersonic jet fighter planes to Argentina, Brazil, Chile, Colombia, and Venezuela. Congress had consistently attached the Conte-Long and Symington amendments to aid legislation. These amendments mandated a withholding of funds equivalent to the amount spent by individual Latin American countries on "sophisticated" weapons. However, the amendments included an "escape clause" to the effect that the President could waive the restriction in the interest of national security. President Nixon seized upon this loophole, both to further U.S. influence over the Latin American military and to reserve a share of the lucrative arms market for U.S. suppliers who are facing increasing competition from European (especially French) firms. It is perhaps needless to say that Washington has given little support to Peru's proposal for a ten-year moratorium on arms purchases, and the perennial threat of a Latin American arms race persists.

Like its predecessor, the Nixon Administration viewed military rule in Latin America as generally consistent with U.S. interests and attempted to cultivate a particularly close relationship with Brazil. The President's 1969 declaration that the United States would deal on an individual basis "realistically with governments in the inter-American system as they are" has been useful in this regard as a means of bypassing the moral issue raised by repression. Nevertheless, the administration quietly expressed concern about some of the excesses of the Chilean military after the September 1973 coup, and the Senate voted a cutoff of aid pending the restoration of "human and civil rights." It is interesting to note, in passing, that the Labour Government in Britain reacted to the situation in Chile by suspending arms sales and economic aid.

Asylum

Rightist military takeovers in Chile, Uruguay, and Bolivia have severely strained the right of asylum traditionally recognized by most Latin American governments. Previously, in 1970-1971, the Organization of American States General Assembly grappled with the institution of asylum as it related to control of political terrorism. The OAS at length produced a convention which defined only the kidnapping of diplomats as an international "crime" and maintained the right of governments to refuse extradition if they judged that the act committed was essentially "political" in nature. Several rightist governments (including Brazil) found the document inadequate and boycotted the session that approved it. However, the current problem involves not so much small groups of fugitives but large numbers of political refugees (an estimated 40,000 from Chile alone), who have flooded mainly into Mexico, Argentina, and Peru. Peru has generally refused permanent visas, and beginning in January 1974, Mexico closed its doors to most exiles except Chileans who had already found asylum in the Mexican Embassy in Santiago. To avoid charges of serving as a base for armed assaults on neighboring regimes, Argentina has prohibited exiles from engaging in various forms of political activity.

The Panama Canal

Domestic pressures for a settlement have been mounting on the Torrijos government in Panama for some time, but negotiations with the United States appeared to be stalemated until Panama managed to persuade the United Nations Security Council to meet in Panama in March 1973. [2] This meeting generated substantial sympathy for the Panamanian position and forced the United States to veto a resolution calling for a new treaty that would give Panama sovereignty over "all its territory." [3] Subsequent talks, with Ellsworth Bunker representing the United States, produced a declaration of principles governing future negotiations, and Secretary Kissinger signed it in Panama in February 1974. The agreement involves real movement on the U.S. side, providing as it does for Panamanian sovereignty over the Canal and abandonment of the concept of perpetuity (the new treaty will have a fixed termination date). On the other hand, the United States will retain the "rights necessary" to "regulate the transit of ships" and to "operate, maintain, protect and defend" the Canal.

It remains to be seen whether the rights reserved by the United States will be sufficient to gain the Senate's approval of a final treaty. A month after the declaration was signed, 32 Senators—only two short of the number required to defeat a treaty—declared themselves adamantly opposed to surrender of U.S. sovereignty over the Canal.

Rivalry Between Brazil, Argentina, and Mexico

Additional political tensions are currently arising from the open competition of these three countries for a Latin American leadership role. Brazil obviously aspires to world great power status as well (see Rosenbaum, 1972), one symbol of which is its refusal to sign the Nuclear Non-Proliferation Treaty and its highly qualified acceptance of the Treaty of Tlatelolco, which made Latin America a nuclear-free zone. Moreover, Brazil's impressive economic boom, its 1971 decision to embark on a substantial foreign aid program involving numerous Latin American countries, its goal of nearly doubling its population by the 1990s, and its policy of opening up its vast interior with projects like the Trans-Amazonian Highway—all combine to make Brazil a focus of speculation and concern.

Neighboring countries worry about Brazilian influence over the Banzer and Stroessner governments in Bolivia and Paraguay respectively, and over the new conservative military regimes in Chile and Uruguay. Bolivia has received a disproportionate share of Brazilian aid, and the pro-Brazilian faction in the military there now appears to have the upper hand. President Banzer was almost deposed when he considered selling more Bolivian oil and natural gas to Argentina rather than to Brazil. This was doubtless a factor in his agreement in May 1974 to the construction of a massive pipeline that will carry natural gas to São Paulo. That same month, Brazil concluded an agreement with Paraguay to construct the world's largest hydroelectric plant on the Paraná River. The arrangement was made despite strenuous Argentine objections that the project would divert waters from its territory (see Rosenbaum, 1973). For its part, Peru fears that Brazil may eventually seek an outlet to the Pacific, perhaps by supporting Bolivia's ambition to regain the corridor to the sea it lost in the nineteenth-century War of the Pacific.

Under these circumstances, it is not surprising that President Nixon's remark upon the occasion of Brazilian President Medici's visit to the United States in December 1971—"We know that as Brazil goes, so will go the rest of that Latin American continent"—prompted protests from Argentina, Peru, and Venezuela. President Lanusse of Argentina rejoined when he visited Brazil, "We Argentines, we Latin Americans, will not accept under any conditions a second-rate destiny." He and Medici signed a communiqué that, among other things, pointedly condemned spheres of influence dominated by major powers. Partly to counter Brazil, Lanusse paid calls on all South

American countries during his term in office, and the Argentine government under Perón announced its own program to double Argentina's population by the end of the century.

Argentina's divergent diplomatic course can be seen in its recognition of China and the trip to the Soviet Union that Perón before his death planned for the fall of 1974, its 1971 subscription with the Allende government to the "Declaration of Slata" that proclaimed the acceptability of "ideological pluralism", and its support for Allende's successful bid to host UNCTAD (United Nations Conference on Trade and Development) III (April-May 1972) over the opposition of Brazil and the United States. It has been considered likely that Argentina would ultimately seek formal association with Bolivia, Chile, Colombia, Ecuador, Peru, and Venezuela in the Andean Common Market (ANCOM). However, with Bolivia and Chile increasingly receptive to Brazil, and facing political turmoil and chronic economic difficulties at home, a "second-rate destiny" may yet prove to be the *best* that Argentina can hope for.

Mexico meanwhile has been attempting to establish its influence in Central America and the Caribbean and cultivating closer relations with Argentina and the ANCOM countries to offset Brazil. President Echeverría has been the most-traveled Latin American head of state. He has made visits to several Central American and Caribbean countries, and to Japan, Canada, the United States, the United Kingdom, Belgium, France, the Soviet Union, and China as well.

We should mention that oil-rich Venezuela, too, is making a bid for greater prominence in hemisphere affairs. President Pérez pledged in his inaugural address that his country's enviable bargaining position based on oil would be put to the service of Latin America generally. Most notably, he vowed to use a portion of Venezuela's oil profits to set up a veto-free special trust fund within the Inter-American Development Bank (IDB), to ease the plight of hemisphere countries hard hit by the energy crisis. Venezuela has also joined several other members of the Organization of Petroleum Exporting Countries (OPEC) in making expanded contributions to the World Bank and the International Monetary Fund (IMF).

ISSUES OF DEVELOPMENT

Foreign Investment

Perhaps *the* most widely discussed issue in inter-American relations during the past few years has been the multinational corporation (see for example, Sunkel, 1973; Diebold, 1973; Lodge, 1973; Müller, 1973-1974; Vernon, 1973-1974). The concept of *dependencia* has made a decided impact on the thinking of many Latin American policy-makers. Although specific policies toward foreign investment differ from country to country, there seems to be an emerging consensus that it must be limited to certain sectors of the economy and assume appropriate forms if it is to serve the interests of the nation. Joint ventures, for instance, are common even in the relatively free-wheeling investment climate of Brazil.

The most ambitious code regarding the treatment of foreign capital to date is that enacted by ANCOM in mid-1971 (see Oliver, 1972). In general, the code restricts new foreign investment to sectors not competitive with domestic industry, decrees the establishment of local majority control and ownership of all enterprises within fifteen to twenty years (varies by country), and limits the repatriation of capital to the original investment when foreigners disengage from an enterprise. Companies which export 80 percent or more of their output are exempted from the provisions relating to local majority participation. The code also includes provisions permitting member countries to make a limited number of exceptions to the rules.

How successful the Andean code will be over the long haul, of course, is hard to predict. Foreign business concerns actively tried to defeat or substantially modify the code when it was being negotiated, and only time will tell whether new investment from abroad will be forthcoming in the amounts desired by individual countries. The argument is often made that foreigners will continue to invest wherever there is a profit to be made and the rules of the game are reasonably clear and stable. However, particularly insofar as the code leaves implementation mainly up to member governments, the clarity and stability of the Andean rules of the game are still open to question. Governments have been making liberal use of discretionary clauses, and domestic political changes over time could make for critical shifts in policy. For example, the coup in Chile brought to power a government whose continued participation in the Andean Pact is itself uncertain (though probable, until and unless Chile moves decisively into the Brazilian orbit), and whose eagerness to reattract foreign capital after the Allende period may lead to agreements that are difficult to reconcile with the code.

Early in 1974 President Pérez in Venezuela had to confront public demands from the outgoing Social Democrats that he speed up the nationalization (with book value compensation) of the Venezuelan oil industry. The nationalization was originally scheduled for 1983 and 1984, when existing concessions expire. Pérez promised that he would reach a decision on this question within the first two years of his five-year term. Meanwhile, Venezuela is reaping windfall profits in the wake of the energy crisis, based on ever-increasing oil prices and the substantial tax hikes levied on the industry by the previous Caldera government. Caldera required foreign oil firms to deposit large sums of money as a guarantee against a decline in the oil industry prior to takeover, and set minimum production rates with fines for insufficient output. However, with prices continuing to rise, some Venezuelan oil experts (including OPEC architect Juan Pablo Pérez Alfonso) are now insisting that production should be cut in half to protect reserves and to keep profits from rolling in faster than the country can invest them wisely.

Outside of the Andean region: in January 1973, Mexico added teeth to its longstanding policy of "Mexicanization" by providing that foreigners generally may not control more than 49 percent equity in any newly established business venture (a national commission is empowered to change the percentage somewhat as circumstances may require). The Mexican government also took over the sulfur industry, ended foreign dominance of the tobacco industry by creating Tabamex (52 percent government-owned), acquired a majority holding in the telephone company, and decreed the necessity of 60 percent local ownership in auto-parts manufacturing. Finally, President Echevarría announced plans to limit the amount of technology that may be purchased abroad by companies in Mexico, reportedly to ensure that Mexicans will not purchase outmoded technology and to force them to develop their own.

Early in the Nixon years, expropriations with the threat of little or no compensation in Peru, Bolivia, Ecuador, Chile, and Guyana touched off a bitter internal dispute in the U.S. executive branch as to the appropriate response. State Department officials held that efforts to protect private business abroad would have only marginal success and might do irreparable damage to U.S. relations with Latin American governments. The State Department opposed especially any policy that would involve automatic withholding of aid to the governments in question. On the other hand, Treasury Secretary John B. Connally, backed by Exim Bank President Henry Kearns, argued for an automatic cutoff on the grounds that protection of private interests is a legitimate national interest of the United States, which Latin American governments ought either to respect or to suffer the consequences of not respecting. In their view, punishment of errant governments would serve as a lesson to others that might be tempted to a similarly "irresponsible" course of action. According to Mr. Connally, they should be told: "You don't negotiate just with American business enterprise. You negotiate with the United States Government." He commented bluntly with specific reference to Latin America, "We don't have any friends there anyway" (*New York Times,* August 15, 1971: 6).

From mid-1971 to early 1972 the hard line gradually gained the ascendance, and the position eventually dictated by the White House stopped just short of the automatic cutoff desired by Treasury. On January 19, 1972, the White House issued the following statement:

Under international law, the United States has a right to expect that the taking of American property will be nondiscriminatory; that it will be for a public purpose; and that its citizens will receive prompt, adequate and effective compensation from the expropriating country.

Thus when a country expropriates a significant United States interest without making reasonable provision for such compensation to United States citizens, we will presume that the United States will not extend new bilateral economic benefits to the expropriating country unless and until it is determined that the country is taking reasonable steps to provide adequate compensation or that there are major factors affecting United States interests which require continuance of all or part of these benefits.

The statement also confirmed that in such cases the United States would "withhold its support from loans under consideration in multilateral development banks," a policy that Congress subsequently incorporated into the Gonzalez Amendment to foreign assistance legislation (see Inter-American Economic Affairs, 1973). The phrase in the statement referring to "major factors affecting United States interests which require continuance of all or part of these benefits" was a concession to the State Department's position that the U.S. response should be tailored to the particular situation at hand.

At the outset, the Nixon Administration denied any new authorizations of bilateral development aid or military aid to Peru, Bolivia, Ecuador,[4] Chile, and Guyana pending satisfactory settlement of outstanding claims. The Hickenlooper Amendment[5] was not invoked, and aid already "in the pipeline" continued to flow. Treasury also ordered U.S. officials in the World Bank, the IDB, and other international credit institutions to oppose or abstain on further loans to these governments for the time being. The White House made it clear to the Chilean government that the administration would regard the terms offered to the copper companies—rather than the matter of Chilean Marxism per se—as the principal initial test of Allende's desire for amicable relations with the United States. When Allende refused to pay and went on to nationalize other U.S. companies, United States-Chilean relations degenerated into open hostility. Symbolically, as we have noted, Washington then decided to continue aid to the Chilean military while other funds dried up.

Several incidents regarding the investments of the International Telephone and Telegraph Corporation (ITT) in Chile have recently been under scrutiny. Hearings by the Senate Subcommittee on Multinational Corporations and the work of other investigators have shed additional light on U.S. policies in this period (see Gil, 1973; Sampson, 1974: ch. 11; Sigmund, 1974). Although to date no hard evidence has surfaced which directly links the Nixon Administration with the coup that overthrew Allende,[6] it is clear that U.S. officials gave careful consideration to various schemes advanced by ITT and that the

CIA tried to enlist ITT's support for a scheme of its own. ITT President Harold Geneen on at least two occasions offered the administration large sums of money to be used to stop Allende from coming to power. The administration demurred. However, in late September 1970, William Broe, the CIA's chief for clandestine activities in Latin America, came back to ITT with a plan to create economic chaos in Chile prior to the upcoming congressional runoff elections there. ITT reluctantly turned down this plan, mainly because of doubts that other companies could be persuaded to cooperate. A year later, in October 1971, ITT submitted to the State Department a "Chile White Paper," proposing an escalation of U.S. economic sanctions against Allende. The paper apparently received a "mixed" reception at a meeting that Secretary of State Rogers convened with the principal U.S. companies having investments in Chile, and existing U.S. policies were not modified. Over the entire two-year period of contacts between ITT and the government, ITT officials grumbled particularly about the State Department's attitude, which they felt belied Rogers' assurance "that the Nixon administration was a business administration, in favor of business and its mission was to protect business" (Sampson, 1974: 275). ITT memos singled out for criticism Assistant Secretary of State for Inter-American Affairs Charles Meyer, who was frankly opposed to the hard line.

The issue of protection of foreign investment has subsided somewhat in the last year, with the coup in Chile and an agreement concluded by the United States and Peru in February 1974 that provides a modest $76 million compensation for five expropriated U.S. companies. However, there was one new incident in Argentina in the summer of 1973, when bills concerning restrictions on foreign capital and the nationalization of several foreign-owned banks were under consideration in the Argentine Congress. The U.S. Embassy handed the Argentine government a series of memorandums warning that Washington viewed the bills as ill-advised. The Argentine Foreign Minister denounced the memorandums, saying they contained "veiled threats" that constituted "improper intrusion in the internal affairs of our country," and the Argentine Senate suggested that the embassy official involved might be declared persona non grata.

No doubt with such incidents and particularly the thorny Chilean case in mind, Kissinger pledged at the OAS conferences in Mexico City and Atlanta that the United States "will not intervene in the domestic affairs of its Western Hemisphere neighbors." Nevertheless, the Nixon Administration did *not* regard vigorous protection of U.S. private investment as "intervention," and further clashes are virtually inevitable as long as the hard line remains in effect.

Action at the multilateral level to establish comprehensive norms relating to foreign investment might help to dampen future conflict. The United

States and several Latin American countries—led by Mexico, Peru, Argentina, and Colombia—have expressed their support for negotiations on this subject, and the recent OAS meeting created an OAS working group charged with developing principles for the "conduct of transnational enterprises." But all-embracing, substantive agreements are probably beyond the capacity of member governments at this stage of history.

Territorial Waters and the Environment

The United Nations Conference on the Law of the Sea is meeting in Caracas in the summer of 1974, but the agenda is so overcrowded that resolution of many key issues may have to await the "second phase" of the conference, tentatively scheduled for Vienna in 1975.

The territorial waters issue arose originally mainly from the claims of what soon came to be nine Latin American countries[7] to the exercise of some form of jurisdiction 200 miles from their shores—Brazil, Ecuador, and Peru claim total sovereignty. Persistent seizures of private fishing vessels transgressing the 200-mile limit off Ecuador and Peru have proved a serious nuisance to the United States. The Nixon Administration cross-pressured by the Pentagon and the offshore fishing industry on the one hand, and the inshore fishing industry and nervous U.S. companies in affected countries on the other, earnestly cast about for a compromise formula. In May 1972, the United States managed to conclude a temporary shrimping agreement with Brazil under which the Commerce Department would license a maximum of 325 shrimp boats, with only 160 allowed to operate in Brazilian waters at any one time (see Morris, 1973).

Negotiating positions established prior to the present conference seem to indicate that a likely compromise may emerge along the following lines: (1) the extension of sovereign jurisdiction from three to twelve miles, with international guarantees of the traditional right of free passage; and (2) the establishment of an additional "coastal zone" ("patrimonial sea" or "economic zone") of up to 200 miles, providing for coastal state exercise of yet-to-be-defined special rights over such possible matters as fishing, pollution and safety regulations, and the exploitation of natural resources. This is the essence of the position of the world's major maritime powers, including the United States and the Soviet Union, as well as that embodied in the "Declaration of Santo Domingo" issued by ten Latin American and Caribbean governments in June 1972.[8] Deciding exactly what rights the coastal state should exercise will be quite an undertaking. Moreover, none of the original 200-mile claimants (except Nicaragua) were parties to the Santo Domingo document, and their position and the extreme position of Brazil, Ecuador, and Peru—with apparent support from China—may yet prove insuperable obstacles to agreement.

The closely related issue of the exploitation of the seabed and subsoil, which the United Nations General Assembly in 1970 declared to be "the common heritage of mankind," may be even more divisive. In question are not only rights beyond continental shelves within the projected 200-mile zone but also those in the ocean depths beyond 200 miles. Copper-producing countries, including Chile and Peru, are fearful that mining of undersea copper resources will drive the price of copper down. They are therefore troubled at the prospect of any agreement in this area. Many poor countries, including 31 landlocked states, want undersea resources to be exploited directly only by a strong United Nations authority (no private companies), with the proceeds devoted to international development assistance. For their part, the developed countries are anxious to reserve a leading role for their corporations, operating under a weak U.N. authority.

Finally, there are major divisions over marine pollution and—though for obvious reasons it is not on the current conference's agenda—over nonmarine forms of industrial pollution as well. As early as 1972, Brazil established itself as a "leader" in arguing that the developing countries often cannot afford the luxury of pollution controls sought by those nations who are already substantially developed and whose very past development is largely responsible for present-day environmental problems.

Aid

The developing countries have been increasingly conscious of the shortcomings of aid in recent years. They note its uncertain future, political implications and links to multinational enterprises, the repayment burden, and traditional emphasis on economic growth over social change. Most of these nations have therefore long ceased to view aid as a panacea for development, and country development plans are giving ever-greater stress to the generation of domestic capital (see for example Sloan, 1973). Nevertheless, the developing countries have been reluctant to forgo whatever capital aid programs can still provide. At their insistence, UNCTAD III strongly endorsed the U.N. Second Development Decade target of a minimum of one percent of GNP for public and private capital transfers from the developed countries (.07 percent for "official development assistance," which is food aid plus bilateral and multilateral assistance).

Few developed donor nations have reached this goal, and partly because of the worldwide inflation that has accelerated with the energy crisis, "real" aid to the developing countries actually declined in 1974. It is now less than it was three years ago. The United States bears a large share of the responsibility for this trend, as statistics illustrate. Although the United States still provides more public aid funds than any other single donor, its total contribution has been only about .03 percent of GNP in recent years, ranking the United States in an estimated fourteenth place among sixteen major donor nations in early 1974.[9]

The United States aid program has lately been in the throes of fundamental change. Since the late sixties, development aid has been gradually multilateralized, as the United States has channeled more and more of approximately the same total through international lending agencies. In 1973 this pattern reached a point at which the Nixon Administration's request for Agency for International Development funds was the lowest in two decades. The AID component is itself in evolution as a result of an administration-supported Congressional initiative in 1973.[10] The new legislation emphasizes the needs of the poor majority in the developing countries and the importance of their participation in the development process. One antecedent is Title IX attached to the Foreign Assistance Act in 1960, calling for maximum popular participation in development. This emphasis is becoming current among development theorists (see Grant, 1973) and aid programs worldwide. In recent years, AID has ostensibly stressed "social" programs in the fields of agriculture and education. Other antecedents for the new legislation are the Pan American Development Foundation, the Inter-American Foundation, and President Nixon's abortive 1971 plan (based on the Peterson Report) for a reorganization of U.S. bilateral assistance. Congress has now directed AID to focus its attention determinedly away from large-scale capital transfers for infrastructure and industry toward programs aimed primarily at rural development and food production, population and health, education, and human resources development. In this new effort, AID is to make greater use of private organizations such as voluntary agencies and universities, rather than directly administering so many programs. Lastly, under the policy guidance of the Secretary of State, AID will have the "responsibility for coordinating all United States development-related activities."

How AID will perform in its new role is, of course, yet to be established. The coordinating function will be particularly difficult to operationalize, given the interests that other executive bureaucracies have in matters like private foreign investment, trade, and monetary reform. An even more pressing question is whether Congress will provide the funding required to allow the new emphasis a fair test.

Congressional support for most forms of U.S. aid has continued to decline in the seventies. In the past, bilateral programs of both military and development assistance had had the bipartisan support of moderates, and a voting majority had been constructed on the basis of trade-offs between liberals and conservatives. Liberals voted for military aid bills with various ceilings and the Conte-Long and Symington amendments attached. Many conservatives, who decried "waste" and the "ingratitude" of the Latin American governments on the security and private investment issues, nevertheless voted for development aid with the addition of restrictions like Hickenlooper. The situation facing the Nixon Administration was unique in the hardening of conservative opposition to development aid because of expropriations and, most recently, because of the energy crisis. The ranks of liberals and moderates also showed growing dissatisfaction with both military *and* bilateral development aid. Liberals and moderates have become increasingly uneasy about bilateral programs that, they believe, identify the United States too directly with repressive and unprogressive regimes in the Third World. This attitude in Congress has been partly responsible for the multilateral trend in U.S. aid.

Considering this climate, most observers agree that the aid program has managed to survive only because of the large stake that the business community still has in it. Nevertheless, aid has indeed been in trouble in Congress, and will likely continue to be for the foreseeable future. In 1972 the Senate startled the world by temporarily killing the administration's aid bill. Aid came back from the grave on that occasion, but it is sobering to note that in December 1973 the Senate approved the latest aid bill (incorporating the shift for AID) by a margin of a mere three votes. Likewise, U.S. pledged contributions to multilateral programs have customarily been delayed for a year or two or more, lagging well behind those of other donor states. Congress still has provided only $50 million toward a pledge of $100 million for the soft loan program of the IDB that was made five years ago. In January 1974, the House voted down a U.S. contribution of $1.5 billion over four years to the International Development Association (IDA), the soft loan window of the World Bank. The contribution was finally approved seven months later when its supporters hit upon the device of attaching a provision to the bill that allows Americans to buy, sell, and own gold!

Changes have also been underway at the World Bank under the presidency of Robert McNamara (see Reid, 1973). Several years prior to the U.S. Congress's latest initiative on AID, McNamara began reorienting a major part of World Bank lending toward programs (especially rural development) directed at the poorest two-thirds of the peoples in the developing countries. This emphasis has not yet been reflected in actual lending for a variety of reasons—the long lead-time for processing applications, the dearth of imaginative programs to assist, traditionalism in the Bank's staff, etc.—so it will doubtless be some years before the new policy can be assessed. Another interesting development is that several governments in OPEC (including Venezuela) have used some of their energy-crisis profits to sharply increase their contributions to the Bank.[11] The Bank reportedly hopes to be able to borrow $1.5 to $2 billion a year from OPEC sources in the future.

The OPEC countries played a prominent role in the United Nations special economic assembly in April-May 1974, which was convened upon the initiative of President Boumédienne of Algeria primarily to discuss natural resources. One of the issues was the possible establishment of an emergency fund to aid those countries adversely affected by the energy shortage. The Nixon Administration was initially convinced that the U.N. session was a relatively meaningless exercise engineered by the oil-producing countries to deflect criticism from higher prices. Kissinger was preoccupied with the Middle East; and outgoing Treasury Secretary Schultz, it was rumored, also raised objections to any U.S. pledge. Hence the United States, when it began to take the meeting more seriously, presented only a hastily contrived proposal for a $4 billion assistance program at the eleventh hour. In a clear diplomatic slap at the United States, the delegates from the developing countries brushed aside the Kissinger proposal and adopted a funding program of their own devising.

The United States and the developing countries have been at odds, as well, over IMF Special Drawing Rights (SDRs), the new paper reserves for international monetary transactions. A central demand by the developing countries at UNCTAD III was that SDRs not be allocated as in the past, on the basis of national income and trade, but be "linked" in some way to their requirements to finance imports for development—that is, SDRs should become essentially another kind of aid. The Nixon Administration has been exceedingly skeptical of this concept, although the United States did support another UNCTAD resolution to the effect that the developing countries should have an active role in the current talks about reform of the international monetary system. In fact, beginning in 1972, increased developing-country representation (to nine seats) on the Committee of Twenty of the International Monetary Fund forced the United States to soften its opposition to the SDR "link." This was one concession Treasury Secretary Simon had to make to get the June 1974 interim accord that launched the present "managed float" arrangement for international currencies. The accord also provided (1) a new "oil facility" of the IMF, financed at the outset by pledges from seven oil-producing countries (including Venezuela and Canada), to lend money to those countries suffering severe balance-of-payment difficulties derived from the energy crisis; and (2) a new IMF "extended loan facility," designed primarily for the benefit of poorer countries, to make loans—in larger amounts and at longer terms than previously—in the form of monetary reserves that (unlike other aid) can be spent on virtually anything.

Ironically, the SDR question is somewhat academic at this stage, since there is no sure indication that the IMF will ever create any new SDRs. In any event, long-term reform of the international monetary system will need the support of the developing countries (see Bergsten, 1973: 116-119). Amendments to the IMF's Articles of Agreement require a weighted majority vote of 80 percent and the concurrence of 60 percent of all member countries, and the developing countries (prior to the oil-producing members' stepped-up contributions) held 27 percent of the weighted vote and well over half of the total membership.

Another aid-related issue is the matter of repayment. The debt burden already incurred by many Latin American and other developing countries has reached staggering proportions, and they were united at UNCTAD III in arguing for relief. Donor countries have been receptive to the idea of some rescheduling, mainly out of fear that the developing countries will, in effect, give themselves a sudden, massive shot of "aid" by repudiating debts entirely. At UNCTAD, the United States promised to assume a leadership role in negotiating a general rescheduling and to use its influence to attain a reversal of the World Bank's policy of opposition to such a course of action. Washington promptly negotiated a rescheduling of debts owed by the Allende government, witnessing the extent to which the United States was prepared to go to avoid the opening up of a possible Pandora's Box. No worldwide agreement on general rescheduling is in sight, but thus far individual countries threatening repudiation, like Chile, have consistently succeeded in getting action.

Integration and Trade

The Latin American Free Trade Association (LAFTA) peaked at a very low level of integration, and the Central American Common Market (CACM) has never recovered from the 1969 "Soccer War" between El Salvador and Honduras. Honduras withdrew from CACM in 1970, and the latest effort to settle outstanding issues failed in December 1973.

ANCOM hence remains the most interesting experiment in Latin American integration.[12] However, it is too early to predict ANCOM's full success. Intra-regional trade has continued to increase, but for most countries it has not surpassed trade with other members of LAFTA, and the problem of unequal sharing of benefits may yet arise. The intra-regional multinational enterprises that are envisaged as the future "grid" of the system are still in the planning stage, and partly for this reason the Andean Development Corporation (CAF) has barely begun to play its envisaged role as entrepreneur for projects that bridge national boundaries.

Prospects for ANCOM improved considerably in 1972 with the conclusion of its first sectoral agreement, which provides for the complementary division and assignment among member countries of some 73 basic metal-mechanical industries. Another significant boost was the long-delayed entry of Venezuela in 1973. Also, the Marañon dispute of many years' standing between Ecuador and Peru seemed to vanish almost overnight when Ecuador realized that the existing division of territory left it in control of extensive oil reserves. On the debit side, as we have noted, the coup in Chile threatened ANCOM's foreign investment code, and the Banzer government's ties with Brazil raised questions about Bolivia's future orientation. Moreover, the controversy between Colombia and Venezuela over the right to resources in the Gulf of Venezuela grew a little more heated in April 1973, when Venezuela rejected Colombia's suggestion that the two countries take it to the World Court.

Another relatively new integration scheme is experiencing some difficulties too. In August 1973, the four Caribbean states of Barbados, Jamaica, Trinidad and Tobago, and Guyana formally converted the Caribbean Free Trade Area (CARIFTA) into the Caribbean Community (CARICOM); and Belize, Dominica, Grenada, Monserrat, Antigua, St. Lucia, and St. Vincent joined CARICOM in May 1974. However, CARICOM has been hard hit by higher fuel prices and acute agricultural shortages. The former have placed oil-producing Trinidad and Tobago in an awkward position, and the latter are threatening delicate reciprocity arrangements.

Turning to extra-regional trade: the attention of the developing countries has focused on the issue of U.S. noncompliance with the system of generalized preferences for their manufactures and semi-manufactures that was agreed upon in 1970 at UNCTAD II. Europe and Japan quickly implemented partial preferences, and the European Economic Community in mid-1974 was seriously considering additional concessions. Yet a protectionist-minded Congress has made virtually no headway on the Nixon Administration's proposals that are contained in the Trade Reform Act of 1973.[13] With the energy crisis aggravating the situation, the best that Kissinger could offer the Atlanta OAS meeting was a pledge that "we will do our utmost to avoid new restrictions on Latin America's access to our markets." Other significant provisions languishing in the trade bill are reductions in U.S. nontariff barriers to trade with the developing countries, and authorization for the President to negotiate additional reciprocal reductions in tariff and nontariff barriers with major trading partners of the United States on a "most favored nation" basis. Going beyond the U.S. legislation, some observers (see Erb, 1974) maintain that active participation by the developing countries in multilateral trade negotiations is essential, both to obtain reductions in items not covered by preferences and because preferences themselves may be withdrawn at any time.

In quite a different direction from preferences, we are now entering a new

era in world trade in raw materials and other commodities, for which the
energy crisis acted as something of a catalyst. *How new* an era is the question
of the hour. There is considerable debate at to whether OPEC is or is not the
precursor of numerous developing-country cartels and whether they are likely
to work anywhere nearly as well as the one that brought the developed
countries to their knees in 1973 and early 1974 (see for example Bergsten,
1973; Mikdashi, 1974; Krasner, 1974; Bergsten, 1974; Levy, 1974).

Commodity agreements based on management of supply have been discussed for many years, but the prospects for them have not appeared bright.
Three existed prior to 1973, governing coffee, tin, and cocoa—the last
negotiated in 1972 upon the urging of UNCTAD III. All three had the
participation of some or all of the consumer countries. Only the International
Coffee Agreement had United States support and proved reasonably satisfactory, and that broke down in 1973 when the United States and principal
producers could not agree on a price.

However, it was the OPEC model—a cartel of producing countries acting
jointly against consumers—that the developing countries overwhelmingly
endorsed at the Algiers meeting and the U.N. special economic assembly. The
U.N. resolution constituted a defiant reply to Kissinger's stern warning
against the "politics of pressure and threats," which he said would undermine
the domestic base of support for the transfer of developed-country resources
to the Third World.

There are clear signs that the developing countries are beginning to
practice what they preach. Three major coffee producers—Brazil, Colombia,
and the Ivory Coast (total 56 percent of world production)—are boosting
prices through Café Mundial, a multinational coffee-marketing corporation
they created in September 1973. Seven bauxite-producing countries—
including Jamaica and Guyana and, incidentally, Australia (total 63 percent)
—formed a permanent organization in March 1974. In May, Jamaica, which
currently has 60 percent of the U.S. market, forged ahead of its associates to
triple the taxes and royalties it charges to mining companies. The Inger-
governmental Council of Copper-Exporting Countries—Chile, Peru, Zaire, and
Zambia (80 percent total)—met to set prices in April 1974. Earlier, in late
1972, the organization had boycotted Kennecott in retaliation for the company's attempts to prevent the sale of Chilean copper in Europe.

Where international commodities go from here is anyone's guess, although
it is certain that things will never be quite the same again. A great deal
depends upon how much unity is achieved and *sustained* among producers of
how many commodities, and particularly how successful producers of certain
different commodities are in avoiding destructive competition. Bergsten has

commented (1973: 111): "Concerted action by copper, tin, and bauxite producers would sharply reduce the risk to each that cheaper aluminum or tin would substitute for higher-priced copper, or vice versa. An alliance among the producers of coffee, cocoa, and tea could preempt substitution by drinkers around the world." Bergsten believes there is real potential along these lines:

> All that is needed to permit political cooperation is increased knowledge of the market and the potential gains from concerted action, self-confidence and leadership. Whether such action actually eventuates would seem to depend quite importantly on the policy milieu of the future. The countries involved will certainly be more likely to act if the industrialized world frustrates their efforts to achieve their goals more constructively, and if they are barred from participating effectively in global decisions which vitally affect their own destinies. They are more likely to act against the United States alone if the United States is the most obstinate or neglectful of all.

As Bergsten cautions, however, confrontation is a high-risk strategy for all concerned, from which there may emerge "no winners." Developed and developing countries alike would be losers if a series of confrontations were to lead to worldwide economic collapse, or if "drinkers of the world" were to turn exclusively to soda pop.

Even apart from the cartel question, the current world shortage of basic foodstuffs leading to the World Food Conference in late 1974 also has important implications for the development of hemisphere countries. Almost all are suffering some shortages, but every agricultural commodity produced in the area is enjoying boom market conditions. This situation means more financial resources for some countries to pursue industrialization, ironically at a time when agricultural production suddenly seems almost more profitable. In any event, the Prebisch "terms of trade" argument for industrialization seems a little less compelling than it did some years ago.

Indeed, if a single conclusion emerges from our survey, it is that there are precious few "givens" in current inter-American relations. As was stated at the outset, worldwide, regional, and subregional forces are minimizing the impact of domestic political shifts; however, it is difficult to predict the eventual outcome of the interplay of various trends. We seem to be on the brink of a new era, in the light of which the "mature partnership" will ultimately prove to have been merely a transitional phase. But a transition to what? The answer is obscured by all the imponderables in the rapidly evolving North-South relationship, that is itself only one dimension of an increasingly interdependent world.

NOTES

1. Congress abolished U.S. assistance to Latin American police forces in 1973.

2. The Nixon Administration had already resolved two other "colonial" issues in United States-Latin America relations. In 1971 the United States ended its lease over the Swan Islands and returned them to Honduras. The Bryan-Chamorro Treaty, giving the United States rights to a canal in Nicaragua, was terminated in 1972. Later, prior to the Mexico City OAS meeting, the United States settled a longstanding dispute with Mexico over Colorado River salinity.

3. Australia, Austria, China, France, Guinea, India, Indonesia, Kenya, Peru, Sudan, the USSR, and Yugoslavia voted for the resolution and the United Kingdom abstained.

4. The Nixon Administration reportedly responded even more directly to ITT's pleas for protection in Ecuador, following expropriation of its properties there, than it did in the Chilean case. Aid was withheld in 1971 and 1972 until a satisfactory settlement was reached (*New York Times*, August 10, 1973: 37,40—following up on a *Business Week* article).

5. The Hickenlooper Amendment requires the President to suspend aid if "adequate" compensation is not paid within six months after an expropriation—subject to presidential waiver on the basis of overriding national interests.

6. Senator Fulbright commented on September 27, 1973, "The U.S. Government has flatly denied any involvement in the coup and I have not seen any credible evidence to the contrary at least as far as direct involvement is concerned" (quoted in Hanson, 1973: 72).

7. Argentina, Brazil, Chile, Ecuador, El Salvador, Nicaragua, Panama, Peru, and Uruguay. See Edmonds, 1973, for an interesting discussion linking Peru's position to import tariffs in the developed countries.

8. Colombia, Costa Rica, Guatemala, Haiti, Honduras, Mexico, Nicaragua, Dominican Republic, Trinidad and Tobago, Venezuela. See *American Journal of International Law*, 1972.

9. Statistics drawn from Howe, 1974: 26-27. This book is a valuable collection of essays and tables on current issues relating to the developed countries.

10. For discussion see Paolillo, 1974. Congress defeated a proposal for an Export Development Credit Fund, which would have provided about $1 billion annually to finance exports of U.S. goods and services to the developing countries.

11. Ecuador is also a member of OPEC, but is still a small producer and has not yet joined in the contributions that several other members are making to international organizations.

12. See especially Milenky, 1973; Parkinson, 1973. I have drawn interpretations from both of these articles. For an analysis of ANCOM in terms of integration theory, see Avery and Cochrane, 1973.

13. President Nixon also failed to exempt Latin America from the 10 percent surcharge he imposed on all exports beginning in August 1971.

REFERENCES

American Journal of International Law (1972) "Specialized conference of Caribbean countries concerning the problems of the sea: declaration of Santo Domingo." 66,5 (October): 918-920.

AVERY, W. P. and J. D. COCHRANE (1973) "Innovation in Latin American regionalism: the Andean Common Market." International Organization 27, 2 (Spring): 118-124.

BERGSTEN, C. F. (1974) "The threat is real." Foreign Policy 14 (Spring): 84-90.

——— (1973) "The threat from the Third World." Foreign Policy 11 (Summer): 102-124.

DIEBOLD, J. (1973) "Why be scared of them?" Foreign Policy 12 (Fall): 79-95.

DOMINGUEZ, J. I. (1973) "Taming the Cuban shrew." Foreign Policy 10: 94-116.

EDMONDS, D. C. (1973) "The 200-miles fishing rights controversy: ecology or high tariffs?" Inter-American Economic Affairs 26, 4 (Spring): 3-18.

ERB, G. F. (1974) "The developing countries in the Tokyo round," pp. 85-94 in J. W. Howe (ed.) The U.S. and the Developing World: Agenda for Action. New York: Praeger.

FERGUSON. Y. H. (1973) "The final decline of the Western Hemisphere idea and its implications for Latin America: consequences of current United States policies," pp. 262-311 in Y. H. Ferguson and W. F. Weiker (eds.) Continuing Issues in International Politics. Pacific Palisades, Cal.: Goodyear.

——— (1972) "An end to the 'special relationship': the United States and Latin America." Revista/Review Interamericana 2, 3 (Fall): 352-387.

GIL, F. G. (1973.) "Socialist Chile and the United States." Inter-American Economic Affairs 27, 2 (Autumn): 29-47.

GRANT, J. P. (1973) "Development: the end of trickle down?" Foreign Policy 12 (Fall): 43-65.

HANSON, S. G. (1973) "Kissinger on the Chilean coup." Inter-American Economic Affairs 27, 3 (Winter): 61-85.

HOWE, J. W. [ed.] (1974) The U.S. and the Developing World: Agenda for Action, 1974. New York: Praeger.

Inter-American Economic Affairs (1973) "Government documents: . . . the Hickenlooper Amendment." 27, 2 (Autumn): 92-96.

KRASNER, S. D. (1974) "Oil is the exception." Foreign Policy 14 (Spring): 68-84.

LEVY, W. J. (1974) "World oil cooperation or international chaos." Foreign Affairs 52, 4 (July): 691-713.

LODGE, G. C. (1973) "Make progress the product." Foreign Policy 12 (Fall): 96-107.

MIKDASHI, Z. (1974) "Collusion could work." Foreign Policy 14 (Spring): 57-68.

MILENKY, E. S. (1973) "Developmental nationalism in practice: the problems and progress of the Andean group." Inter-American Economic Affairs 26, 4 (Spring): 49-68.

MORRIS, M. (1973) "Trends in U.S.-Brazilian maritime relations." Inter-American Economic Affairs 27, 3 (Winter): 3-24.

MULLER, R. (1973-1974) "Poverty is the product." Foreign Policy 13 (Winter): 71-103.

OLIVER, C. T. (1972) "The Andean foreign investment code: a new phase in the quest for normative order as to direct foreign investment." American Journal of International Law 66, 5 (October): 763-784.

PAOLILLO, C. (1974) "Development assistance: where next?" pp. 107-123 in J. W. Howe (ed.) The U.S. and the Developing World: Agenda for Action, 1974. New York: Praeger.

PARKINSON, F. (1973) "Power and Planning in the Andean Group." World Today 29, 12 (December): 527-536.

REID, E. (1973) "McNamara's World Bank." Foreign Affairs 51, 4 (July): 794-810.

ROSENBAUM, H. J. (1973) "Argentine-Brazilian relations: a critical juncture." World Today 12, 29 (December): 537-542.

——— (1972) "Brazil's Foreign Policy: Developmentalism and beyond." Orbis 16, 1 (Spring): 58-84.

SAMPSON, A. (1974) *The Sovereign State of ITT*. New York: Stein and Day.

SIGMUND, P. E. (1974) "The 'invisible blockade' and the overthrow of Allende." Foreign Affairs 52, 2 (January): 323-340.

SLOAN, J. W. (1973) "Colombia's new development plan: an example of post-ECLA thinking." Inter-American Economic Affairs 27, 2 (Autumn): 49-66.

SUNKEL, O. (1973) "Transnational capitalism and national disintegration in Latin America." Social and Economic Studies 22, 1 (March): 132-176.

VERNON, R. (1973-1974) "Does society also profit?" Foreign Policy 13 (Winter): 103-118.

PART I

DOMESTIC FACTORS OF INTER-AMERICAN
FOREIGN POLICY-MAKING

Chapter 2

THE KITSCH IN HEMISPHERIC REALPOLITIK

KALMAN H. SILVERT

The world did not wait while the United States disentangled itself from Vietnam, experienced Watergate, and entered into stagflation. Even the Latin American states—"static," "chronically unstable," "militaristic"—continued on their increasingly rapid evolutionary ways. Now, in the mid-1970s, American policy-makers are facing a different Latin scene from the one that they saw as a gray sameness when the "low profile" was announced in the first months of the Nixon Administration in 1969. Cuba is back as an active participant in hemispheric affairs. The Mexican government has broken its diplomatic isolationism of over forty years and is seeking collaborative political relations with its sister republics. The Organization of American States and its dependent agencies have shriveled, the Economic Commission for Latin America has lost its gloss, and the Inter-American Development Bank is pursuing "safe" financial policies, but the foreign policies of individual Latin American countries are becoming more adventurous.

Perhaps most important of all in the international scene is the Latin attempt to organize for the purposes of diplomatic collective bargaining. Whether through some formalized heir of the regularized foreign ministers' meetings, or another device yet to be created, the search is on for a common set of political interests that can be pursued jointly by Latin American governments themselves. Obviously, it will be difficult to stitch together such disparities as those represented by Chile and Cuba, Peru and Nicaragua, or Argentina and Brazil. However, domestic political scenes—which will determine external stances as Latin governments continue to grow more national and thus more powerful—will not remain unchanged. The roots of a common interest lie in desires to control the national fates. To gain this control, Latin American countries are working to assert sovereignty; contain multinational corporations; promote national development; and confront problems associated with population, urbanization, and international marketplaces which are brokered by the powerful and bereft of the self-policing of supply and demand. The reasons for combination exist; the vessels and the ideas are as yet embryonic.

The new presidency in Washington will have to stir itself belatedly to recognize the latency and the actuality of change in Latin America. What the United States government can "see" in Latin America, and what it can possibly imagine doing in terms of what it thinks it sees, are related to its past perceptions and policies and to its generalized view of the world and how one practices diplomacy within it. I do not wish to enter into debate as to whether or not in recent American history we have had a single and self-consistent policy toward such a diverse area as Latin America, or even any policy at all. The reason I evade the debate is not a matter of empirical determination; that task could be accomplished readily enough. Rather, my avoidance of the theme has to do with doubt concerning the definition of the word "policy." If we mean that within the decade from 1965 to 1975 we have had a firm definition of our own national interest, an application of that interest to a realistic assessment of the situations of the Latin American states, a categorization of those states by type for differential policy application, and then an evolved set of mechanisms for the pursuit of our interests— then, of course, we have had no policy. If, on the other hand, by that word, we refer to a generalized posture, an attitude, a vaguely followed set of instrumental guides, and organized interests pressing for certain goals—then, indeed, we have had a policy. The "low profile" is as appropriate a title as any for that bundle of traditions, attitudes, and practices.

The substance of the "low profile" has been a mechanistic and eclectic issue-by-issue approach to Latin America that is of the essence of contemporary American foreign policy in general. Indeed, our past stance toward Latin America can be taken as a possible preview of what we can expect elsewhere as "normalization" is designed by the managers of the political systems of the major nations and power blocs. The fact that Latin America poses no threat to vital American interests means, in the minds of the crisis managers, that it is a stable area that needs little attention. In this view of the world, the decency or indecency of domestic political doings has no place in international affairs. Only if internal factors seriously threaten primary or secondary interests will "appropriate" reactions fitting to each case be taken. The discipline and predictability of overtly defined policy about anything other than national security are absent; order and sense are to be inferred from watching what the United States does, and not from what its leaders say. This style of diplomacy may be a foretaste of international-politics-to-be everywhere as America discards its role of global policeman and faces "realities."

Whatever past administrations' motives may have been, an international politics of "realism" (*Realpolitik*), supported by a vague and situationally undefined willingness to employ military might (*Machtpolitik*), has led to a crass and ineffective foreign policy (*Kitschpolitik*) in the hemisphere. The proponents of "realist" politics invariably content themselves with the "concrete" and "positive" facts of social life. Natural resources, population size, urbanization, military preparedness, and industrial development are for them "hard" facts: the "real" ones. Ideologies, norms, values, personal crotchets, and ethics are "soft": the claptrap in utopian minds. It follows, then, that an efficacious politics flows from accepting the physical bounds of situations, and seeing those bounds as inelastic parameters, or fixed limits, constants for the purpose of working out given policy problems. Consequently, values are to be shunned, and an effective politics must be "pragmatic." This construction turns night into day; it is hardly pragmatic in the philosophical sense of that term, and it is fiercely, if pessimistically, ideological. This idea, like many others in our contemporary political armory, will have to be taken off its head and put back on its feet before we can go on to make sense out of our situation.

Cleaning up ideas about international politics is of particular urgency at this time, for the domestic tensions of all industrial and industrializing societies are increasingly flowing over onto the international scene. It used to be held that that United States should break out of isolationism because all nations are interdependent. This postulate is based primarily on benefits expected from trade and economic specialization, and secondarily on the cultural fruits of international ties. A contemporary version of the same view emphasizes ecology, "spaceship Earth," scarce resources, swelling populations, earth-threatening weaponry, and other goads to global applications of reason and planning. Not so often mentioned, but certainly more perturbing to national politics and thus more threatening, are the direct effects of the international order on the tug-and-pull between privilege and equality that is the stock-in-trade of all domestic politics. There are many ways of putting this dynamic. In developing countries the craglike class structures stand opposed to the creation of national community, to the continued incorporation of populations into equalitarian participation in the full institutional panoply. The class-nation disharmony of Latin America is most nearly replicated in the United States by its race-nation split. For many years, however, U.S. foreign policy was intellectually divorced from domestic politics precisely on the grounds that the former involved a *status* (security) on which all could agree, and the latter involved a *process* (the distribution of values, ostensibly toward an expanding equality of opportunity) concerning which legitimately expressed disagreement was the motor force of politics. Therefore, foreign policy was justifiably bipartisan, domestic politics necessarily partisan.

The distinction will no longer serve. As the wars of nation-states have long since involved total populations, with correspondingly growing costs and increasingly intimate effects on the creation, use, and distribution of domestic material and attitudinal values, the international economy is also increasingly able to affect power distributions within developed as well as developing states. The most notorious instruments of these changes are the multinational corporations, of course, one of whose principal immediate effects is to threaten the position of organized labor in the older industrial societies. Politically organized international economic structures, such as common markets, also contribute to a cross-national rationalization that tends both to stabilize and to destabilize internal systems of power allocations, the effects depending on the natures and types of political-economic systems of the nations concerned. Even though the major difference between intra- and international politics remains the absence of social and political community in the latter, both arenas now are scenes for playing out the same problem— the grounds on which individual and group differences are maintained or eroded.

Bipartisan foreign policy-making thus is anachronistic because international affairs now involve as many ethical, ideological, and moral determinations affecting personal and national interest as does domestic politics. Latin American developmentalists have long recognized this commonality and have created theories to explain it. North Americans have been laggard in this respect, however, preferring to keep international affairs separate from domestic politics, and to think of relations among nations as somehow involving only formal structures and manifest "leaders," not the people who follow leaders and give them their power. This antiseptic and asocial approach has greatly contributed to the creation of empty ideas and linguistic distortions— euphemisms which cover the carnal facts of death, corruption, sacrifice, and heroism. As we proceed now to attempt to clear away some verbal problems in understanding international affairs, we will also be dealing with domestic happenings in both Latin and North America. We should not want it otherwise if we have any pretenses toward respect for all persons, or toward the application of reason to the solution of problems that are increasingly world-wide and, thus, the problems of every man as well as of every state.

Let us look at some aspects of hemispheric politics in which domestic and international affairs have become twisted, and illogically related.

Isolationism and internationalism, unilateralism and multilateralism. The

United States has been dealing with Latin America on a country-by-country and case-by-case basis. A small genuflection has been made in the direction of Brazilian hegemony, indicating the "realistic" acceptance of that country's potential power and hinting that it may become the surrogate for the United States in policing South America. Actually, Brazil has a limited capacity for such a role, and other Latin American republics are organizing themselves to inhibit the possibility. In the meantime, the U.S. government is encouraging to Mexico, broadly hostile and punitive to Cuba, puzzled about and increasingly ineffective in influencing internal Argentine events, defensively protective of the Chilean junta, quietly worried about Venezuela but content with its two major parties, eclectic about the Caribbean islands and too abstracted to pressure them severely, and so on and on. While the multilateral agencies are withering, as was said earlier, we go on thinking by ourselves about Latin America, we alone deciding with whom we shall tango, with whom we shall rumba, and whom we shall snub.

The forgers of this approach call themselves internationalists, and accuse those who disagree with them of being neo-isolationists. Yet unilateral moves into unbalanced bilateral relations, and a shunning of multilateralism, add up to nothing more than isolationism practiced overseas. The functional distinction which should interest us is between acting alone and acting in concert with others, and not the misleading words "isolationism" and "internationalism." The former involves working abroad with no entangling alliances. It does not accept the mutuality of obligation, feels no need to compromise, and has no desire to establish a community of interests involving the happiness of living and sharing together. Conversely, to act multilaterally implies attempting to *create* interests whose sharing can generate a complex and broad basis for international comity, in much the same way as one seeks to create national community within one's own borders.

These behavior patterns are not, of course, specific only to hemispheric relations. Solitary internationalism has characterized the way in which the present American government has treated Chinese and South and Southeast Asian politics, to the dismay of Japan and most other nations friendly to the United States. The monetary crises of recent years provide an even starker example of our style of international sociability.

The ideology of value-free "pragmatism." Among the unhappier legacies of the complacent fifties is the idea that industrial, democratic societies had solved their basic problems, and needed only to continue to administer into existence for others the better world past whose threshold we had already stepped. No overarching questions about the total system remained to be asked. Only subversives, malcontents, and the emotionally disturbed still insisted on the need for explicitly held ideologies. The proponents of this "pragmatic" argument acted in unwitting ideological good faith as utopian democrats. They did not know, did not foresee, and very few have subsequently admitted that their views have served to usher in not an age of expanded participatory democracy, but an ideology and a practice of technocratic management that profoundly threatens free institutions.

Events of the past decade have clearly demonstrated that in the formal institution of the American state as well as in the informal workings of the polity, there are underlying structural problems which tap the ethical and moral roots of beliefs and thus are *necessarily* ideological in implication. But the notion that techniques alone can solve our problems remains with us in both international and domestic affairs. The pretense is made that politics can be understood and administered in an essentially value-free way, as a play of effective desires among participants in the "game." In this construction, balance-of-power politics abroad are the same as interest-group politics at home. One must simply accept the rules of play, and let power plus perceived interest work themselves out—all the while making certain that one's own power and explicit recognition of interest are maintained at as high a pitch as possible. If the system and its rule remain unchallenged, then it is indeed possible to act without questioning basic premises, thus pretending to amorality and ethical neutrality, to "practicality" and "pragmatism" without asking what we are being "practical" and "pragmatic" about. Certainly it is sometimes useful to assume an amoral position within a value-freighted system, but that contained neutrality is not possible when systems are themselves in contention. Fundamental choice is unavoidable, and thus amorality is impossible when the survival of societies and their systems of behavior and beliefs are at stake. Under such conditions, neutrality slides into either morality or immorality, depending on one's values. There are no *technical* solutions to basic *policy* problems, only political ones. And *all* political solutions are seated in ideologies—systems of belief that interpret the past, justify present behavior, and seek to control the future in desired ways.

The more advanced Latin American countries have the historical opportunity to attempt many alternative ways of organizing their societies. No longer held in the firm grip of Iberian tradition, freed from slavish dependence on foreign models whose attractiveness diminishes every day, and with goodly numbers of urban, literate, and reasonably educated persons who can be recruited to active civic life, perhaps a dozen countries have the opportunity to move effectively and firmly toward structuring new ways of going about social life. At issue are patterns of participation, the nature of political-economic relations, the kinds of national consciousness that will be forged, the nature of and restraints on state power, the building of appropriate legal and educational institutions, and the many other fascinating problems that must be solved to build the structures and articulations of complex social life. Obviously, there are also stern limitations on the freedom of choice of these countries. Needed are intelligence, capable administrators, support and not hindrance from overseas, a willingness to be playful and experimental, increased economic productivity and equity in distribution, stable international markets, and ideologies supportive of both rationalism (a way of thinking) and rationalization (a way of organizing). All these elements are in short and irregular supply. Particularly lacking are models, physical and ideological. Arid technocracy and mechanistic balancing are no substitute for the satisfying excitement of systems of thought that directly address themselves to how people do and should go through their lives. If those idea-systems deal with participation, belonging, and dignity within a frame of secular rationalism, they can establish an ordered relation among goals, expectations, and means in creating the power that comes from public agreement with political policies. This consensus helps to provide the political wherewithal to assure sufficient success in ordering social events to warrant continued public enthusiasm as the difficult processes of development proceed. The decay of democratic idealism is not merely the loss of an old and sentimentally cherished ideology, or of the power of moral leadership; it is also the loss of a moral reason for working toward development with efficiency and dignity.

Because systems themselves are at issue in Latin America, a truly realistic hemispheric policy will need to make its moral basis clear. To continue a pretense of "pragmatic" amorality is only to invite self-delusion, unreason, and hence failure. Bertrand Russell put it more elegantly in *A History of Western Philosophy* (New York: Simon and Schuster, 1945, p. 494):

> The power conferred by technique is social, not individual. . . . Scientific technique requires the co-operation of a large number of individuals organized under a single direction. Its tendency, therefore, is against anarchism and even individualism, since it demands a well-knit social structure. Unlike religion, it is ethically neutral; it assures men that they can perform wonders, but does not tell them what wonders to perform. In this way, it is incomplete. . . . The men at the head of the vast organizations which it necessitates can, within reason, turn it this way or that as they please. The power impulse thus has a scope which it never had before. The philosophies that have been inspired by scientific *technique* are power philosophies, and tend to regard everything non-human as mere raw material. Ends are no longer considered; only the skilfullness of a process is valued. This . . . is a form of madness. It is, in our day, the most dangerous form.

Nationalistic anti-nationalism. The United States, from the heights of its development and its history of democratic sophistication, is beset by the same fundamental political problem that the more advanced Latin American states encounter as they push to choose the corner of the modern estate in which they will live. The primary public question of countries like Argentina, Chile, and the United States has to do with the form and content of national community—with the nation and with nationalism. In contention are two opposing views of proper and feasible national organization:

—A national society organized to provide equality for all before its diverse institutions. A society whose power is molded from the positive consent of the governed. A relativistic, secular, and rational society in which a contained and accountable government is accepted, for the immediate purposes of conflict-resolution, as being the ultimate mundane arbiter of secular dispute. A society which attempts to mitigate the effects of social class through merit selection and equality before the laws, and which attempts to guarantee a minimum decent level of existence for all its citizens. Or,

—A national society organized to maintain hierarchy and existing privilege. A society which exhorts its people to support the state for reasons of grandeur, mystical or otherwise, while at the same time assuming the necessity and righteousness of the uses of overt coercive power, sometimes in massive doses. An absolutist state which demands that it be taken on faith as the legitimate ultimate arbiter of secular dispute. A society which justifies the effects of social class, equates achievement with moral worth, and applies moral, ideological, class, personality, and ethical criteria in its selection procedures. A society which at best defines social decency in only material terms, and prefers the argument that God helps him who helps himself.

A curious anomaly describes the relation between belief in the value of an open national community, and most consciously held ideologies of nationalism: the two attitudes are usually held as opposites through the Americas. North American liberals and Latin American center-leftists who espouse the value of an equalitarian national community have ceded nationalist appeals to the jingoists who praise the value of hierarchically stable, class-bound authoritarian organization. In other words, the self-professing nationalists in both culture areas of the hemisphere oppose the extension of the national community on conditions of equality to all citizens, while the ashamed nationalists want a complete social nation, but blush to exhort the loyalty that supports legitimacy.

The contradiction between belief in the value of building a national community and the current ideologies of nationalism has served to weaken national communities and therefore to make the democratic solution of problems difficult, and sometimes impossible. Anti-national nationalist governors demand loyalty from everybody, but in turn extend their own loyalty only to citizens of proper "standing" and beliefs. The more nationalistic in ideology political leaders are, the more prone they are to disown some of their own citizens as heretic, and to make common cause with their ideological breathren across national boundaries. (International military and police activities in the western hemisphere are clear day-to-day proof of the primacy these ideologists give to their political values over their loyalties to fellow nationals.) The results are as clear in Argentina, Uruguay, and Brazil as they are threatening to become in the United States: nationalistic governors erode the power of the social nations they lead, weakening states in their international relations both politically and militarily, and crippling their ability in domestic affairs to identify and deal flexibly and equitably with problems surging up from rapidly changing economic, technical, and demographic factors.

A Committed International, Nationalist Policy

This article is, among other things, an attempt to revive the forgotten half of a famous pair of articles that appeared in *Foreign Affairs* over twenty years ago, signed by one Mr. X. There the argument was advanced that containment of Soviet expansionism might well be necessary as a temporary expedient, but that the long-run *justification* for the immediate behavior of this country must ultimately rely on the quality of its national life, on its worth as a decent society per se. Because Latin America does not threaten North American security in any military sense, containment or its analogues are not at issue; the justification for behavior certainly is.

In a time of the increasing entanglement of domestic with international affairs, we have no sound choice but to want for others what we want for ourselves. We should not expect any immediate equalization of physical conditions; such a desire is impossible to fulfill readily, and in any event flies in the face of cultural, ideological, and historical differences. Therefore, that which we can rationally desire in common has to do with a process—the procedures by which societies can satisfy material wants for their populations, and find ways to organize themselves so they can constantly expand their capability to reduce alienation and free creative talents of all kinds. If that commitment is rejected, another must be taken—its opposite, perhaps. Such a policy might seek to institute those procedures which assume that socially created hierarchy is an eternal necessity, given innate human corruption, and that the good society will be attained when classes are stabilized, everyone knows his place and is made content with it, and status can be transmitted through the generations. Yet a third alternative is to seek order and efficiency within existing frames through the establishment of a merit-based technocracy. Political leaders and managers would no longer be selected by election, nepotism, or buddyism, but by objective tests of capacity, and they would run the present structures, although somewhat more efficaciously than now. Regardless of the option selected—whether participatory democracy, corporatism, or technocracy—certain trends will have to be faced by everyone. Among others, they are:

—The increasing unity of national and international politics, already stated.

—The increasing unity of political and economic power. Unhappily, the time of a clean differentiation between the economy and the polity is over in erstwhile liberal western, capitalistic societies. In most other countries, the idea never gained ideological or structural hold. How to maintain economic incentives in a time of general collectivization is a critically important issue for us all. How to maintain democratic mechanisms in a time of economic gigantism is an even more important issue.

—The increasing intimacy of global communications. The possibility of a world television network promises potential access to cultural richness and variety. Yet it also contains threat of the opposite: the swamping of cultural uniqueness, with a concomitant loss in the ability to judge among viable alternatives and a resultant impoverishment of values.

—The increasing power of governmental authorities to control individuals. The days are numbered of the traditional authoritarianism, in which the dissident can withdraw from politics and remain safe, hidden inaccessibly in many institutional nooks and crannies. Now, even in tiny Central American republics, the total control governors had over illiterate populations can be extended by modern techniques to individuals, bypassing institutional protections. Totalitarianism is no longer a threat only to developed countries.

—The increasing independence of industrial development from education. Capital-intensive industries using imported technicians no longer need draw on skilled and semi-skilled populations for their work forces. The productive side of industrial society needs many fewer educated persons than it did even thirty years ago. Education will increasingly have to do with consumption, a fact which deeply affects the distribution of power as well as goods, and which permits us to raise questions about the intrinsic functions of an educational system, its role in the development of individuals for their own sakes, instead of for a series of economic roles.

This list could be much longer, of course. The point, however, should be clear: there are constraints stemming from pressing problem areas that everyone will have to consider. Each ideological group, however, will define its own problems into existence—for, after all, a problem is brought to life only by our heads and our passions.

Problems in the Definition of a Hemispheric Policy

The contradictions described in this article impregnate the recent history of United States-Latin relations. We have a quiet and static policy for a rapidly changing hemisphere, a policy offhandedly seen as a part of our general defense of raw national security, against which no important threats come from the lands to our south. Otherwise, we have no statement of our interests. There is a vague feeling that American private investments should be defended, and that somehow Venezuela is more "important"—or more easily influenced—than is Argentina, say. Even our ideas about what we do *not* wish to see in the hemisphere have become muddy. This policy of misplaced concreteness cannot last much longer. Because it is unrealistic, passively reactive, and out of intellectual control, it can satisfy no group—whether business, governmental, academic, or the country writ large.

If we are to act on the assumption that many Latin American nations are soon going to take their places in the world as viable powers of the second and third rank, then the United States must prepare itself to compete in the hemisphere as it does in Europe. The ends for which this country competes, the means it will permit itself to use, and the ways in which it attempts to give structure to the conditions of the competition depend primarily not on inputs from the hemisphere, but rather on domestic political dynamics. In short, some of the contradictions on the home front need resolution before policy, deeds, and words can be brought together on foreign fronts.

If the line of argument so far has any validity, and if we search for an effective policy because to search for an ineffective one would be madness, then the basis for recreating a Latin American foreign policy should in the first instance be to strengthen the national community of the United States. This task should be guided by an ideology that insists that rationalism be applied to measure the proper balance between means and defined ends. This writer, then, has made some value commitments: he believes rationalism is possible in human affairs; that it is preferable to irrationalism; that the play of rationalism requires self-correcting, relativistic, and free social institutions; and that from this combination flows the power to pursue rational purposes, including increased power through time to pursue such objectives. To be consistent with the analyses above, the internal conditions for the creation of such a foreign policy involve:

—A reinforcement of America's social nation. That is, the incorporation into participating, ordered, and creative social life of as many persons in this society as possible. No social task is more important than this one, given my values. No social sacred cow is worth preserving if it inhibits the growth of nationalism of this kind.

—The recognition that acting as an isolate abroad is as inefficient and eventually self-defeating as it would be in national social life. A concomitant understanding is the realization that internationalism depends on social nations, and the two can be mutually reinforcing. They are opposites only when made so, an act to the detriment of both. Even etymologically, it is impossible to imagine fruitful relations among "nations," if there are only states, but no nations. In other words, the fecund participation of individuals and groups at international levels depends upon a prior assembly of individuals into groups within their cultures. This statement has been clearly true of cosmopolitan elites for centuries. Let it also become true for the humblest among us.

—The conscious creation of systems of understanding and explanation, backed by adequate information subject to test in a competitive market of ideas—what the Latin Americans call *concientizacion,* an arousal of consciousness. If these ideas are to support secular national community and interacting participation, then they must also be pragmatic in the true sense of the word. Secrecy must be abandoned, information made freely available, the grounds for governmental decisions made public, and ends and means conceptually laced together.

And what should be our hopes for Latin America as a result of our interaction with them? Why, that Latin Americans should develop the same general values, of course, and find their own ways to work toward them within their particular cultural contexts. If some Latin American governments do not pursue such ends, what should we do? Do not support those trends, as we do now, but also do nothing which would damage the integrity of our national interest by doing to others what a decent person would not do to his fellow citizens. If some Latin American governments do pursue such positive ends, we should help them in any reasonable way, avoiding paternalism or any other attitude or action that may impede the development of autonomous, interactive, cooperative, self-sustaining national/international life.

Chapter 3

UNITED STATES POLICIES AND

LATIN AMERICAN REALITIES:

NEIGHBORLINESS, PARTNERSHIP AND PATERNALISM

IRVING LOUIS HOROWITZ

I

When most governmental and academic circles examine United States policy toward Latin America, they assume that there is in fact an entity called United States Policy in Latin America. I find slender evidence to support the thesis that there is a consistent United States policy in or toward or about Latin America. From the "Good Neighbor" policy of Franklin Delano Roosevelt in the 1930s to the "Hemispheric Partnership" approach of Richard M. Nixon in the 1970s, the rhetoric of an integrated policy toward the hemisphere has only served to disguise the facts of a fragmented policy. It is true that there have been a series of major decisions which have drastically, and at times dramatically, affected affairs in Latin America. However, such policy decisions do not flow from an overall grand design and certainly do not emanate from any hemispheric posture.

What does one do with conflicting interpretations of the same events? How does one measure such factors as dependence and independence, investment made from altruistic motives and investment based on egoistic motives? The analyst of United States foreign policy is first faced with the problem of two types of analyses: one is structural analysis which places the blame for Latin American underdevelopment squarely on the external variable called imperialism; the other model places the blame for underdevelopment on internal variables such as religion, traditionalism, climate, and race (cf. Portes,

1974; Graciarena, 1965). Nor does it suffice to say that the truth is some admixture of the two. This form of question-begging does not come to terms with the existence of special problems affecting Latin American relations with the United States. If imperialism is ubiquitous, why is there such a differential response, country by country? If cultural and sociological factors like race and religion are so powerful, why does there seem to be such a strong connection between the problems of Latin America as a whole and the penetration of United States capital as whole.

The answers given seem to depend more on the interests of the examiner than on the nature of what is being examined. There are few areas of the world in which ideological determinants play so central a part in the analytical scheme. This ideological persuasion is a function of the presumed overall importance of Latin America to the United States (especially since the latter's share of the imperial market is shrinking). The geographical proximity of the two continents may be the key variable; or perhaps it is a common background in constitutional regimes and republican forms of government. Whatever the explanation, we are nonetheless obliged to assess these competing claims of hemispheres and empires.

The issues generated by United States foreign policy in and toward Latin America are of a magnitude calculated to increase frustration and ferocity, but hardly reason or relaxation. For one economist, the United States is simply the center of an imperial domain. It is, moreover, under growing pressure by the international monopolies to formulate and implement political and economic policies which will create an attractive investment climate in Latin America and the Third World. Economic development is thus promoted by the United States as a means for anxiously seeking outlets for its economic surplus (Frank, 1972, 1974). For another economist, the United States effort to aid development is an experiment in selfless giving, an attempt to help create enough stability to ward off the thrusts of inflation and totalitarianism (Carlson, 1963). Thus, foreign aid as an instrument of United States foreign policy is the most mature expression of the American corporate belief in itself—in capitalism.

United States foreign policy toward Latin America is often not only filtered through a grid of Soviet and Chinese aspirations, but also shaped by entrepreneurial aspirations within the United States government. The result is conflict at the policy-making level. Military sectors believe in the need to respond always and everywhere to socialist and communist challenges; State Department sectors tend to advocate a benign, détente approach based upon tolerance and respect for sovereignties as long as business interests are not menaced; and the Department of Defense views intervention as a subtle matter based on generating civic action and counterinsurgency programs. In short, the complexities of interest factions within the United States, no less than of the world order, make the various formulators of United States policy toward Latin America either substantially or downright self-contradictory.

II

The idea of a unified United States policy in Latin America derives from an ideological inflexibility and a rhetorical consistency that has reflected a profound separation from the realities of policy decisions throughout twentieth-century United States history. To the same extent that our actual policy toward the hemisphere has been inconsistent and incongruous, our ideology and rhetoric have fostered the idea of a consistent and congruous posture. The beginning of all wisdom about United States hemisphere policy is an awareness of the schism between action and doctrine. This schism becomes exceedingly dangerous to both North and Latin Americans when it is forgotten that foreign policy serves national interests and that, in fact, whatever moral imperatives exist, they derive precisely from such highly selective interests.

The *ideological* posture of the United States toward Latin America is indicative of a generalized policy schizophrenia. The policies are far more rigid in theory than in fact. The State Department situation with respect to Argentina is both evocative and indicative. We are informed that the United States opposes any yielding to guerrilla claims or any subjugation of the American government to blackmail or pressure. This is often followed by pained corporate statements about packing up and leaving the whole country where kidnapping and ransom are presumably commonplace. In practice, however, United States policy is quite flexible. It worked with the Juan Perón government to curb kidnapping; offered assurances of maintaining physical plants supplied and intact; and even worked out arrangements with the host country for counterinsurgency measures.

Quite beyond operational measures, there is a tacit understanding that the activities of guerrilla movements have been counterproductive. First, terrorist tactics have badly split the trade union movement and isolated its followers from the socialist framework. Second, even the radicals have become seriously divided on the merits and demerits of random terrorist approaches. Finally, regimes such as the Perónist government were compelled to move far to the right; indeed, beyond the wildest expectations of American foreign policy experts, who expected Perón's resumption of power to result in a strong left wing and ultimately, an anti-American position. The kidnapping of several dozen minor officials and $14 million must appear an inexpensive price indeed to pay for the reabsorption of Argentine political life into the

American orbit. All these beneficial results took place without a United States foreign policy initiative.

American foreign policy is often dignified by the term "pragmatism." Its defenders speak of pragmatism as the equivalent of a semisecret operational codebook intended to disguise imperialist aggression. Either as a pedestrian concept or as a sophisticated one, the claims to a pragmatic foreign policy collapse under the weight of scrutiny. First of all, how can pragmatism serve as a doctrine of imperialism when not one of its three chief American advocates was in favor of imperialism? William James was the vigorous founder and sponsor of the anti-imperialist league opposing United States intervention in Cuba and the Philippines; John Dewey was perhaps the most traditionalist opponent of United States involvement in European affairs, arguing that the curse of the world is European machinations, and claiming that even membership in the League of Nations would be untenable and unjustifiable; and Charles Sanders Peirce, who can be accused of many sins, but not imperialism, was the least political of men—at least in the larger sense of politics.

The term "pragmatism" is used by American foreign policy makers to indicate a simple doctrine of expedience, of doing what is ostensibly best for the survival of the United States. Such a doctrine is not a particularly explicit or meaningful foundation for policy. Indeed, an ideological rigor mortis has combined with a functional and tactical immaturity to produce a certain crudity in American foreign policy. How could the situation have been otherwise? The United States is a society that did not choose pluralism; rather it dignified its plethora of doctrines after the fact. Unlike the Soviet Union, or socialist states in general, the capacity of the American system to generate a foreign policy of any consistency is limited. And it is these limitations rather than policies that are consecrated with the word "pragmatism." Whether consistency is a virtue or not is beside the point; rather the point is that pragmatism has been used not as a doctrine or an ideology, but as a device revealing the absence of both.

Understanding what is known as United States foreign policy is complicated not only by the emergence of the Third World as an independent force, but by the murkiness of motives and the decision-making itself. For example, to what degree is United States foreign policy shaped by fear of the loss of its $16 billion in corporate assets throughout the Third World, and to what extent by fear of Soviet Communist militancy? In the case of Latin America at least, the preponderant evidence would suggest that the investment portfolio is dominant. Further, the behavior of the Soviet Union has been either revisionist or counterrevolutionist, and therefore the "threat of communism" either muted or blunted. Ironically, the requirements of its own foreign policy have compelled the Soviet Union to pursue a conservative approach serving as a major brake on radical social change. However, the Chinese Communist movement has stepped into the void left by the Soviets, and has radicalized Latin American Communist behavior in such diverse political systems as Brazil, Uruguay, Peru, and Chile.

The schism within the Communist movement has assisted United States policy aims even in the absence of United States policy initiatives. Hence, the rise of guerrilla insurgency under the banner of Maoism has proven more counterproductive than productive to revolutionary ends. Indeed, in most of the aforementioned countries, the rise of para-military units, the emergence and growing fear of the creation of a parallel army of workers resulted in coups d'etats that in the short run at least signified the collapse of left-wing postures. In this sense, the American position was inadvertently and indirectly strengthened. It is worth noting again that such political movement occurs quite independently of any entity called United Staeates policy for the hemisphere.

The presumed cornerstone of United States policy toward Latin America has, in effect, been an anti-policy—namely, anti-communism. Between Roosevelt's hemispheric neighborliness and Nixon's hemispheric partnership, this nation managed to sandwich a policy posture that had no essential vision beyond that of a crash program in a poverty area of Appalachia. Even the Alliance for Progress had that essential ex post facto quality, and this factor permitted its dismantling on the same grounds and even in the same way as, in domestic affairs, the Office of Economic Opportunity programs for the poor were phased out.

At the Tenth Inter-American Conference, which met at Caracas in March 1954, the United States, intervention into Guatemalan affairs was anticipated on the basis of forging "a clear-cut and unmistakable policy determination against the intervention of international communism in the hemisphere." The U.S. Congress later ratified intervention in Guatemala on the grounds of "the existence of strong evidence of intervention by the international communist movement in the State of Guatemala." Somewhat later, in August 1960, at the foreign ministers' meeting of the Organization of American States at San Jose, it was noted that "all members of the regional organization are under obligation to submit to the discipline of the Inter-American system." And in January 1962, at the Punte del Este meetings of the OAS, this discipline was spelled out: "The adherence by any member of the Organization of American States to Marxism-Leninism is incompatible with the Inter-American system, and the alignment of such a government with the communist bloc breaks the unity and solidarity of the hemisphere." The assertion of such broad-ranging jurisdictional rights provided the rationale for unqualified intervention in the affairs of Cuba, just as it had earlier for Guatemala, albeit with far different consequences.

Despite the seeming ideological consistency of United States hemispheric policy, the diversity of Latin American politics created serious problems at the policy level: Cuba became the first socialist regime in the hemisphere; Peru has now declared strong nationalist aims counter to United States policy. The smashing force of political pluralization has struck the hemisphere. Sometimes the thrust is left, at other times right; inevitably it is military. The United States response has been to attempt to adjust realities to its ideological posture. At least in part, this response accounts for American advocacy of interventionist policies. However, it is extremely doubtful that the same sort of interventionist maneuvers can be maintained in this decade.

The 1974 OAS meetings indicate how far the United States has moved from its hemisphere posture during the 1960s. The new position, while hardly serving as a rally to the oppressed, nonetheless took seriously the notion of partnership, economic independence, and the rights of all nations to self-determination. The United States delegation even made the first steps, haltingly to be sure, toward reconciliation with Cuba. Indeed, the Castro regime appeared more reluctant than the Nixon government to move toward accommodation. This attitude of the United States indicates a new flexibility in the practice of American foreign policy and, quite beyond that, the independence of that policy from domestic partisan affairs. In other words, in Latin America, as elsewhere, the so-called conservative Republican Party moved further toward accommodation with anti-imperialist regimes than did the liberal Kennedy government in the early 1960s. This points strongly toward increasing autonomy of foreign policy from domestic party politics. Beyond that, the policy must respond to contingencies having little or nothing to do with the democratic way of life or the needs of capitalism within that way of life.

With respect to Latin America, United States foreign policy is and has been adjudicative at the ideological level, but it has managed to be relatively accommodating at the institutional level. In Mexico, Guatemala, Cuba, the Dominican Republic, and Brazil, where efforts to end colonialism and institutionalize nationalism took place, the United States applied economic sanctions and military intervention in defense of corporate interests.

Latin American policies toward the United States have accommodated this dangerous polarity in United States policy-making. Mexico is a bourgeois one-party state, relatively friendly but clearly nationalistic. Cuba is a peasant proletariat one-party state, flatly hostile to the United States, nationalistic, anti-imperialistic, and friendly to the Soviet Union. Chile, under Allende, represented a socialist front coalition, nationalistic, anti-imperialistic, but maintaining strict neutrality with respect to the Cold War. Most Latin American states maintain a national policy rather than a hemispheric policy toward problems of economic development. During Juan Perón's first and second regimes, Argentina witnessed a coalition between middle-echelon officer corps, trade-unionist and declassé elements. The country is nationalistic, but quite ready to cooperate with the imperial powers of Europe and America by playing them off against each other. In general then, Latin Americans recently have carefully avoided offending North American ideological sensibilities, but have nonetheless gone about their business without giving much thought to United States views.

III

Confusion between foreign policy and foreign aid is widespread. The United States does engage in heavy dosages of foreign aid—at both the civilian and military levels. Whether such aid adds up to a foreign policy is something else again. Foreign aid has been designed to serve many and diverse purposes. In the 1940s its primary purpose was European recovery along capitalist and democratic lines. In the 1950s foreign aid was meant to serve mutual security; this was the period during which most aid and trade pacts were negotiated with Latin American countries. In the 1960s foreign aid was tied to the tasks of economic development, specifically to making the UN Development Decade successful. In Latin America this meant that certain activities in the public sector, such as the Alliance for Progress, were underwritten as a countervailing force to private sector imperialism. In the 1970s aid programs are increasingly being linked to an improved human and physical environment. Moreover, the programs are performed in the context of mixed ownership trans-national corporations, rather than in that of direct federal aid. It is probably correct to say that in each period foreign aid was more often spent to satisfy the desires of what is euphemistically termed the cosmopolitan center of the client nations than to advance the interests of their colonized peripheries.

Justification and rationalization of foreign aid differ in each period. In the forties, aid was to create a world safe for capitalism. In the fifties, it was to make a world safe for democracy, or at least safe from Soviet expansionism. In the sixties, foreign aid was justified primarily as a tool to narrow the gap between wealth and poverty. And as the seventies unfold, it is clear that the orientation is toward problem areas rather than national ones, and aimed toward middle-class solutions rather than populist revolutions. For example, more attention is being directed to problems of demography and urban explosion than to issues affecting the masses within overseas nations as a whole. These shifts in emphasis have been responses to national situations, not part of an overall grand plan to deepen the penetration of overseas holdings. In fact, so little federal programing is directed toward specific private sector needs in foreign lands, that one must wonder whether the tasks of managing overseas holdings have not been given over, once again, to the North American corporate sector.

The Nixon program of Action for Progress for Latin America follows closely the recommendations of the Rockefeller Commission of 1970. Basically, the commission's report argued that business and private investment funds should once more become the main instrument for promoting development. After $20 billion and an Alliance for Progress program that failed to alter any fundamental relationships, Washington is turning once more to private rather than public sector solutions; even the rhetoric of partnership reflects this change of emphasis. However, as the Special Latin American Coordinating Commission (CECLA) made clear in its Vina del Mar meetings of 1970, the problem is neither private nor public funding, and therefore the solution is something else again. In fact, listing what CECLA holds to be the main problems makes clear that the tactic of emphasizing private sector over public sector investment may have as many hurdles to overcome as the programs being replaced.

Among the major obstacles blocking Latin American efforts to carry out a coherent, progressive series of reforms in economic and trade relations with the United States, CECLA lists the following: (1) restrictions which seal off equitable or favorable access for Latin American exports to other world markets; (2) the continuing deterioration of the volume, conditions, and means of international financial assistance, a problem which is aggravated by the need to repay high interest charges on existing debts; (3) imposed difficulties which impede the transfer of technology to the nations of Latin America, thus delaying the modernization of its research and development facilities; (4) the discouragement of multinational trade and aid pacts that would break the cycle of dependence inculcated by bilateral pacts.

In many ways, the United States government has avoided dealing with these and other obstacles by going backward rather than forward; that is to say, by putting the entire matter of foreign aid back in the hands of entrepreneurs doing business in Latin America. The United States has abdicated what little policy leverage it once had (which was precious little indeed), and is returning the hemisphere to the source of its ills, private investors, rather than addressing itself to the cure of such ills.

The matter of perception and perspective is crucial. The United States has rarely had any real appreciation of the extent of Latin American nationalism. Only the Castro revolution seems to have shaken the American faith that

Latin American nations are little more than an additional twenty states which, added to the fifty already in existence, make a greater United States of seventy states. To be sure, Latin Americans speak Spanish and they are not as natty and neat as Protestants up North; but notwithstanding these differences, the Latin American nations have come to be treated as states. Lyndon B. Johnson, in particular, tended to put his arm around Latin American presidents as if they were governors, with appropriate and respectful back slapping, before the inevitable question: what can I do for you today? It was as if dignitaries of Ecuador or Mexico were simply state representatives sent from the folks back home with petty squabbles needing arbitration. That such paternalism is finally breaking apart is more a consequence of Latin American militarism and its newfound sense of purpose, than it is a function of American policy initiatives.

A vocabulary of motives that no amount of revision of foreign policy on either side can or will remove divides Latin America from the United States. What for the United States is the containment of communism is for most Latin American governments pure and simple intervention. What the United States sees as dangerous tendencies toward communism indicated by expropriation, may for Latin Americans simply be a half-way house of nationalization of basic industry. What the United States sees as assistance, Latins see as containment or even intervention. Thus, the vocabulary of motives imprints its diachronic series of words upon the facts, causing an escalation of rhetoric and response far beyond the actual problems which may exist. There is a further complication over understanding what Latin Americans want: the products and results of development or the control of the actual process for gaining development. More simply: do Latin Americans want a first-rate set of pots and pans made in the United States, or do they want a second-rate set that are of domestic manufacture? Is national production or national pride the key to their attitudes and the basis of their foreign policy posture?

Such questions are largely beyond the scope of cost-benefit techniques or input-output tables based upon political and economic infrastructures (see Ilchman and Uphoff, 1969: 256-286). For what is involved are decisions that, however well or poorly they work, will have different consequences for different social classes and interest groups. Any powerful nation, whatever its motivations, will find it difficult to convince the recipients of aid or trade that a special nobility permits one nation to be in a superordinate role, while twenty nations remain in a subordinate role. In one sense the fundamentals of social psychology, rather than the fundamentals of economics, hold the key to foreign policy and its reception. What we are dealing with is the undulation of power and discontent, of superordinate and subordinate relationships. And it is hard to deny the conclusion that as long as nations behave as surrogate

persons, assuming the characteristics of power and powerlessness, no complete resolution of the policy questions can occur.

Once again, we must understand that the problem is one of size as well as
perception. Can any small or medium-sized nation feel secure and in a
condition of equity when confronted by a superpower such as the United
States? Can any set of actions or pronouncements by a superpower be greeted
with anything less than universal suspicion?

The emotive drive behind the charges of imperialism and dependency
stem, in considerable part, not from the conduct of specific policies, but from
the implicit power behind the nation asserting such policies. In this, we have
ample precedent, not just in the history of European colonies, but in the
present period as well. There is Cuba's hostility to China, Algeria's response
to France, Rhodesia's response to England, Yugoslavia's response to the
Soviet Union. The negative response of Latin America to United States
interests is part of a worldwide mosaic of nationalisms—especially of small
nations in the Third World context against powerful blocs in the advanced
industrial sector. There is real oppression as well. The outbursts of small
powers against big powers are often based on hard fact; for example, the
violations of territorial waters in Latin America (Martinez, 1973: 213-223).
Further, all superpowers are not the same; and small powers' claims are of
varying magnitudes. Claims to our sympathies and support cannot be eliminated by an awareness of big-power chauvinism. The point is entirely beyond
that: as long as superpower exists, resentments based on disequilibrium of
power and wealth will remain a constant fact of political life.

IV

The rise of the multinational corporation illustrates how limited the
federal foreign policy role has become. Although still largely dominated by
United States industrial units, international combines in the fields of petroleum, chemistry, and electrical energy stimulate direct contacts between the
corporate structures and the political leadership of Latin American nations
(Vernon, 1971). Venezuela makes agreements with Standard Oil, Chile deals
directly with Anaconda Copper, Peru arranges meetings with the Council of
the Americas (a collectivity of more than two hundred United States firms
representing more than 30 percent of our investments in this area). The
Nixon Doctrine of maintaining a "low profile" in the hemisphere is directly
connected to the reemergence of the entrepreneurial hard sell. Whatever this
might signify in the larger context—a return to neo-isolationism or simply a
faith in the supremacy of capitalism with or without democracy—it is evident
that at this juncture official United States foreign policy counts for consid-

erably less than at any time in the twentieth century, or certainly since the presidency of Herbert Hoover.

The impact of United States foreign policy is limited by the rise of nationalism politically, and the emergence of multinational corporativism economically. The increased pressure within Latin America for national control of the industrial base reflects a double tendency: the maturation of a domestic bourgeoisie rather than a foreign-controlled economic consortium. This limitation on United States policy-making has been accelerated by the withdrawal of industrial linkages generally from the political field. In the past economic domination has been used for political ends. However, with the rise of the multinational corporation, economic relations have instead been subjected to technical personnel and fiscal considerations.

If imperialism could have been ended by diplomatic maneuver or popular acclaim, United States interests in Latin America would long since have been eliminated. The process of nationalizing industry, however, raises as many problems as it resolves. Compensating the former owner may simply not be worth the costs, and as in Chile, mixed companies might be superior. Yet seizure without compensation may so alienate the former colonial power that it may deny the Latin American nation access to United States and European banking credit. The power may cut off the supply of capital goods and technology as well, and pressure the other advanced countries to deny the expropriating nation any international development loans. What adds salt to the wound in the case of Chile, for example, is that the denial of the copper yield to the United States may prove meaningless—since Chilean copper mainly supplies the needs of Western Europe and Japan. Just what United States foreign policy can do in such a situation is problematic. At the most, it can support the claims of its own capitalist entrepreneurs, and at the least, it can work out equitable grounds for the transition from foreign to domestic ownership. Of course, in the absence of a policy, the United States can do nothing, and this is its usual type of "action."

United States foreign policy toward Latin America is widely believed to be both more rigorous and more extensive than it is toward other parts of the Third World. Adherents of this belief claim that there is a special tutelary relationship between the United States and Latin America, and this results in a much tougher stance toward our hemispheric neighbors than toward other areas. I would submit that this is not entirely true. What does in fact exist is a tough corporate policy of American giants of industry toward Latin America. That is to say, after years of struggle against foreign corporate interests, the United States emerged as the strongest of foreign investors in the private sector. General Motors has prevailed over Fiat and Peugeot in the automobile sector, Pratt & Whitney has ousted Rolls Royce in the aircraft engine market,

Ford-Philco dominates the television field over Phillips of the Netherlands, Colgate-Palmolive is supreme in the bathroom utensils field, etc. However, this may change with the penetration of Japanese and German products expressly geared to Latin Americans' purchasing power. The situation may also be altered by the multinationalization of American corporate investments; i.e., new connections may be made among the leading industrial powers doing business in Latin America.

The federal foreign policy sector has been a tail wagged by the corporate dog. United States foreign policy in general has little to it, but its scantiness in Latin America is downright notorious. At every turn, United States policy has been dictated to and overrruled by United States corporate interests. Oil interests so far dictated United States foreign policy in Mexico that the Good Neighbor Policy of the New Deal period collapsed. International Telephone and Telegraph anger over attempts to expropriate its interests in Brazil hardened the United States attitude toward the Goulart regime in the early 1960s. Similarly, the Anaconda and Kennecott copper interests more than any other single influence, dissuaded the United States government from establishing friendly relations with the Allende regime in Chile. Thus foreign policy is made, more by the private corporate sector than by the federal public sector, although there are limits to this too. When ITT sought to financially undermine the Chilean regime, United States policy clearly diverged and sought accommodation, if not support, with the socialist regime.

The relationship between the United States and Latin America is special, and foreign policy is difficult in this area of the world. One of the reasons for these problems is that many Latin Americans identify more strongly with the Western world than with a Third World. The interests of Latin America, Asia, and Africa coincide far less frequently than revolutionary rhetoric claims. To say that they all suffer from imperialism and colonialism is simply insufficient, especially if imperialism is itself a differential response revealing changing tactical requirements. Latin America has a long tradition of constitutionalism, bourgeois economic control, ultra-nationalistic quests, and countervailing demands for world power. It also has raw materials in an energy-hungry world. These make Latin America far from the subordinate hemisphere that it once was. Whether individual regimes are bourgeois or socialist, democratic or undemocratic, Latin America displays a much more powerful clustering of nations, a more forceful presentation of national self-interests, than do other parts of the Third World. In all of this, one would have to say that the stalemating of the United States military in Southeast Asia has had the uniform effect of hardening attitudes, and of making it clear to Latin America that the age of gunboat diplomacy is over. In this sense, United States intervention in the Dominican Republic in 1965 ended a chapter of American military history that began with the invasion of Nicaragua in 1912. The war in Vietnam has profoundly underscored this fact. The United States which could only manage to achieve a draw in Korea in the fifties and which lost in Vietnam in the sixties, can no longer expect acquiescence even from the most subservient Latin American regime. The bottleneck that Vietnam represents for the United States has served to emphasize the absence of an overall United States policy, and overextension in the Asian conflict has necessarily shrunk its commitment to Latin America.

V

The end of World War II, and the Chapultepec Conference that followed, failed to signal the end of Latin American distrust of the United States. Moreover, the end of the war brought to the surface differences that had been buried for the duration, and stopped the profits Latin American businessmen made from it. Differences of opinion emerged on every major policy front after World War II and remained unresolved. Problems arose about areas such as tariff protection, foreign capital domination in Latin American enterprises, government intervention in economic affairs, and the need for multilateral finance mechanisms in place of existing bilateral mechanisms. In addition, there was a strong difference of emphasis on the crucial subject of planning and the public sector.

The aim of every American president, from Truman to Johnson, was the same: to abolish Latin American economic dependency on non-American producers, and, in the same process, to establish Latin American dependence upon the United States. Insofar as this is a policy, then the United States has a policy. In establishing such a model of dependency, however, certain tactical problems arose. Should the United States base its foreign policy on an economic model of free enterprise and private property, or should it place its bets on a military model of government assistance? Private enterprise versus the military appropriations approach has become the crucial divide among policy makers interested in formulating a Latin American policy. Obviously, such problems will ever remain unresolved, to the extent that Latin America has moved beyond a dependency model to begin with.

In the past, State Department officials like Spruille Braden and John Foster Dulles ranked the institution of private property alongside religion and the family as the bulwark of civilization. Needless to add, their beliefs were translated into the cornerstones of American foreign policy. In contrast, George C. Marshall, Bernard Baruch, Will Clayton, and Averell Harriman began to note that the real problem was military control and not economic control. As the military situation tightened up throughout the Third World, the Pentagon began to win out over the Brookings Institution in forming a strategy for Latin America. Agreements such as the Rio Pact began to stress the role of the military—not as an international check against communism, but as an internal check against unsponsored social change. The Bogota Conference of 1948 went even further toward securing political concessions from Latin America in exchange for slender economic concessions from the United States.

After World War II, elite groups asserted independence in Latin America, and therefore nationalism reemerged in Bolivia in 1952, Guatemala in 1954, Cuba in 1959, the Dominican Republic in 1965, Peru and Bolivia again in 1968, and Chile in 1970. As a result, the idea of imperial military solutions or military solidarity between Latin and United States officers broke down. The Latin American military increasingly became attached to middle-class nationalist aspirations and decreasingly attached to overseas American commitments. Because of this, Nixon's Action for Progress looked much like the earlier Roosevelt Good Neighbor Policy with its emphasis on private investment and private initiative. United States foreign policy, whatever its overall consistency at the level of principles, is badly polarized at the tactical level between economic laissez-faire doctrine and military interventionist policies. The resolution of this policy dilemma no longer lies within the power of the United States government. Instead it depends upon the internal dynamics of Latin American social classes and political movements on one side, and upon the changing character of industrial ownership and management on the other.

This regional approach has always added a special dimension to United States relationships with Latin America. Every rebellion has appeared as treason, and every revolutionary nationalist seemed to come across as a Robert E. Lee seeking to take his state out of the Union. The very proximity in geography and history has led to a special sort of policy-response—a response based on the assumption that what Latin America did was part of domestic policy. It has taken Castro in Cuba, Allende in Chile, and the military golpistas of Peru and Bolivia to make it clear that things have changed in the Western hemisphere and in the world, and that the nations of Latin America do not wish to become part of a statehood or commonwealth program. Even little Puerto Rico, long a United States satrapy, has become restless. Indeed, the shock of recognition that Latin America, left, right, or center, is not part of the United States may finally lead to an appropriate foreign policy posture.

In converting the realities of foreign *affairs* into a conviction of foreign *policy*, the Nixon-Kissinger posture toward Latin America at least had the advantage of revealing the very considerable liabilities the United States must seek to remedy if it is to be taken seriously. Perhaps for the first time in the twentieth century, American military power is not exaggerated (or to put it more carefully, there is an appreciation that political problems are not easily solved by military means). Beyond that, there is a new-found recognition that the military of Latin America, under a Bonapartist-Nasserist formula, is more interested in national claims than in overseas economic holdings. The United States carefully maintained the "hands off" policy with respect to the Chilean administration of Allende, despite all kinds of unproven charges to the contrary. The United States government was unwilling to go along with International Telephone and Telegraph and CIA efforts to overthrow Allende. These reactions offer convincing evidence of this turn toward realism and positivism and away from the moralism of the Cold War èpoch.

Still, the Nixon and the Ford administrations share a continuing problem with their predecessors, a myopic inability to link problems of social equity to those of conflict resolution among the Latin American nations. The gap between social equality and conflict resolution stems from that ubiquitous notion called the Nixon Doctrine. If such a doctrine exists and has been articulated, it relates far less to the Third World of Latin America than to the stability required in big power relationships, especially American-Soviet affairs. In other words, even if there is an entity known as American foreign policy, that policy relates primarily to equilibrium among the powerful nations. It is based upon adding a note of tranquillity to foreign affairs by reducing the margin of "adventurism" (otherwise known as revolution) available to smaller militant liberation movements throughout the hemisphere. The unreported aspect of the Nixon Doctrine of hemispheric partnership is its essence: multinational diplomacy in an era of trans-national corporations. This again deprives American foreign policy of an essential hemispheric focus, since it must establish priorities based on the political and diplomatic obligations of the First World with respect to the Second World, rather than long-range hemispheric integration along democratic and autonomous developmental lines.

The Nixon-Kissinger approach to the hemisphere is based upon military self-reliance for all parties concerned. However, this new emphasis profoundly underestimates the connections between the new Latin American military and the emerging bourgeoisie of such nations as Brazil, Chile, Argentina, and Mexico. United States policy toward the hemisphere assumes that a Pax Americana is a likely consequence of military self-reliance. In fact, available evidence now suggests that such a peace would be the least likely outcome to hemispheric militarism. Indeed, the transformation (and not just evolution) of the 1960s to the 1970s is characterized by the extent to which the military pivot within Latin America undercuts rather than underwrites the United States' economic presence in Latin America (Baer, 1973; McNicoll, 1973). As a result, the United States may have a more modest, and at the same time a more restrictive outlook toward the hemisphere. It is, however, still incapable of generating a foreign policy position with any sense of overall consistency.

A marked danger in this period is the emergence of neo-isolationism in the United States policy. With this attitude, policy-makers tend to accept a truly formalist arrangement and lose sight of the historical proximities between North America and Latin America. My own feelings are that those proximities and feelings of closeness are real; and that only the perseverance of support for conservative (and even reactionary) regimes, has created strains and animosities at both policy and intellectual levels. Hence, at the time when United States foreign policy seems to be developing a more modest and realistic appraisal of Latin America, it may be more feasible to establish contacts that are personal as well as professional and based on a sober and genuinely mutual sense of shared interest (see Kissinger, 1974).

There is something preposterous in an American Left which automatically and unthinkingly places the blame for any and all collapses and lapses of Latin American radical regimes at the doorstep of United States imperialism. It would be absurd to expect the United States to applaud efforts that would expropriate its own massive holdings and impair its huge volume of business transactions. It would be a mistake to equate the new spirit of partnership with a position of support for radical sectors. Indeed, American policy in general has been based upon and continues to be based upon the ideal that most people in Latin America prefer the United States to the Soviet Union, urbanization to rural violence, modernization to traditionalism, electoral politics to barracks revolts, bourgeois life-styles to folklorism as a way of life. I am not suggesting that any or all of these surmises and premises are ethically correct. I am suggesting that Latin America has increasingly become an "open turf," a place where differences in social systems in the advanced sectors of the world test each other and the localistic and nationalistic strains of social order.

Whatever the impulses which have created such an open-ended "business-like" approach, it is now conceivable that the United States could develop a policy toward Latin America based on its general principles of foreign affairs, and away from the primitive, imperial vision of Latin America as a North American satellite. Nor is this a product of benevolence. Rather, it is a consequence of a general sentiment through Latin America—left and right, civilian and military sectors, middle and working classes—that national sovereignty and economic independence are perquisites and not gifts. In the face of such a massive Latin American consensus, the North American colossus must either adapt to the new realities or fall.

Years ago and in a different context, the extraordinary George Kennan made a remarkable statement. It is herewith offered both as the necessary assumption of sound policy, and as a statement of our seeming inability even at this late date to move beyond subjects to citizens in the treatment of Latin America's peoples and nations.

One is moved to wonder whether our most signal political failures as a nation have not lain in our attempts to establish a political bond of obligation between the main body of our people and other peoples or groups to whom, whether because we wished it so or because there was no other practical solution, we were not in a position to concede the full status of citizenship. There is a deep significance in the answer to this question. If it is true that American society is really capable of knowing only the quantity we call "citizen," that it debauches its innermost nature when it tries to deal with the quantity called "subject," then the potential scope of our system is limited . . . the ruling of distant peoples is not our dish . . . there are many things we Americans should beware of, and among them is the acceptance of any sort of a paternalistic responsibility to anyone, be it even in the form of military occupation, if we can possibly avoid it [Kennan, 1951: 19].[1]

NOTE

1. An impressive article detailing essentially the same point as mine, albeit using different examples, appeared after my piece was submitted for publication. But this is no reason that this illustration of "multiple discovery" should not be acknowledged. See Christopher Mitchell, "Dominance and Fragmentation in U.S. Latin American Policy," in *Latin America and the United States: The Changing Political Realities,* edited by Julio Cotler and Richard R. Fagen; Stanford: Stanford University Press, 1974, pp. 176-204.

REFERENCES

BAER. W. (1973) "The Brazilian boom 1968-1972: An explanation and interpretation." World Development 1 (August): 1-15.
CARLSON, R. E. (1963) "The economic picture," pp. 86-120 in H. L. Matthews (ed.) *The United States and Latin America.* Englewood Cliffs, N.J.: Prentice-Hall.
FRANK, A. G. (1974) "Dependence is dead, long live dependence and the class struggle." Latin American Perspectives 1 (Spring): 87-106.
——— (1972) "The development of underdevelopment," in J. Cockcroft, A. Gunder, F. Johnson and D. Johnson (eds.) *Dependence and Underdevelopment.* New York: Doubleday-Anchor.
GRACIARENA, J. (1965) "Algunas consideraciones sobre la cooperacion international y el desarrollo reciente de la investigacion sociologica." Revista Latinoamericana de Sociologia 2 (July): 231-242.
ILCHMAN, W. F. and N. UPHOFF (1969) *The Political Economy of Change.* Berkeley: University of California Press.
KENNAN, G. (1951) *American Diplomacy.* Chicago: The University of Chicago Press.

KISSINGER, H. (1974) "Good partner policy for the Americas." Society 11 (Sept.-Oct.): 8-10.

MARTINEZ, A. D. (1973) "The politics of territorial waters." Studies in Comparative International Development 8 (Summer): 213-223.

McNICOLL, R. E. (1973) "Peru's institutional revolution." Latin American Studies. The University of West Florida.

PORTES, A. (1974) "Trends in international research cooperation: the Latin American case." Unpublished manuscript.

VERNON, R. (1971) *Sovereignty at Bay: The Multinational Spread of U.S. Enterprises.* New York: Basic Books.

Chapter 4

THE ALLIANCE FOR PROGRESS:

A RETROSPECTIVE

ARTHUR SCHLESINGER, JR.

The year 1961 was a very long time ago, a golden time when all the world seemed young and all dreams capable of fulfillment. I exaggerate, of course. But those of us who came to Washington with John F. Kennedy did feel for a moment that there were profound longings at home and abroad for a better life, that it was possible to use reason as an instrument of social change, and that we were moving in the grain of history. It was in this spirit that the *Alianza para el Progreso* was launched. In later and darker times, our illusions, if such they were, have fallen under a more somber light. In the disenchanted perspective of the mid-1970s, the Alliance for Progress is dismissed as at best, a classical example of liberal good intentions overpackaged, overpromised, and oversold; at worst, as neocolonialism, "an instrument of the imperial mission of the United States" (Fairlie, 1973: 273), designed "to make the region perpetually safe for private U.S. investment" (Bodenheimer, 1971: 177). Such judgments imply, among other things, the false premise that the Alliance was a unified undertaking throughout the decade of the 1960s. In fact, there were two Alliances for Progress; or, to put it more accurately, there was the original Alliance and another program by the same name that struggled on after the political and social components of the original Alliance—i.e., its heart—had been removed.

I

Let me begin discussing these two Alliances by recalling the mood in which the original one was launched. It is first essential to note that the men in Washington who conceived the Alliance genuinely liked and cared about Latin America. The point may seem simplistic. It is not. One of the more conspicuous hypocrisies of the (North) American way in foreign affairs is the combination of ritualistic solicitude about the inter-American system with visceral indifference to the Latin American ordeal. On ceremonial occasions United States leaders talk lavishly about hemisphere solidarity. When a United States company is nationalized or a United States diplomat kidnapped, Latin America creates a brief stir in the newspapers. But one cannot resist the conviction—certainly Latin Americans don't—that deep down most North Americans do not give a damn about Latin America. Only two presidents in half a century, Franklin Roosevelt and John Kennedy, have shown convincing interest in the western hemisphere. Our politicians, professors, and journalists expend endless emotion on remote parts of the planet, Indochina, say, or India, or the Middle East. Invited to contemplate the fascinating problems of the western hemisphere, too many heads nod and eyes glaze over.

I am not clear on how John Kennedy had become involved in Latin America. Perhaps his Catholicism had something to do with it; perhaps it was a feeling that the mansion on the hill owed a concern to poor neighbors in the shanties below. In any case, his interest was of long standing. He had made his first visit—a long one—to Latin America more than twenty years before he became President. His basic instincts were those of a historian, as against those of a lawyer, a businessman, or a general; and, along with his (and my) generation, he had been educated to the historical assumption—which some in a later time saw as sentimental and therefore pointless—that history had somehow united North and South America in a common destiny.[1] He believed, in addition, that Latin America was uniquely the western part of the underdeveloped world, and that if the United States could not help in development there, it could not help anywhere. He had been thoroughly disgusted by the vulgar Latin American policy of the Eisenhower Administration, with its solicitude for private investors and its medals for dictators.

No doubt the rise of Fidel Castro, who had seized power in Cuba in 1959, did more than anything else to make Latin America a campaign issue in 1960. Certainly Kennedy, like most Americans at this stage in the cold war, saw dangers to the security of the United States if further Latin American countries started "going communist." Also, like all Democrats, he remembered the unscrupulous diligence with which the Republicans a decade before had converted the "loss" of China into an issue in domestic politics; for a moment in 1949 he had been shaken by this attack himself. He greatly regretted this in later years; and afterward, as President, he was determined to protect his political flanks from damaging assault as a consequence of "losing" anything in Latin America, even the Dominican Republic or British Guiana.

I have the strong impression, derived from conversations with Kennedy in 1960, that without these reasons, even had there been no Castro and no cold war, he would have felt keenly about Latin America, although he might not have made it such an issue in the campaign. His essential critique of the Eisenhower policy, as set forth in his Tampa speech on October 18, 1960, had independent sources and expressed other concerns. Time, he said, was running out for the United States in Latin America. "Our historic ties are straining to the breaking point under American failure to understand the rapidly changing hopes and ambitions of the people to the south." Our "failure to identify ourselves with the rising tide of freedom" was persuading Latin Americans "that we are more interested in stable regimes than in free governments; more interested in fighting against communism that in fighting for freedom; more interested in the possible loss of our investments than in the actual loss of the lives of thousands of young Latins who have died fighting dictators." He called for a new approach to Latin America—"the good neighbor policy is no longer enough"—and laid out his idea of an Alliance for Progress, "not merely directed against communism, but aimed at helping our sister republics for their own sake."

Of course he meant for the sake of the United States too. But he had a new conception of the United States interest in Latin America. The Eisenhower Administration, nearly to the end, believed that the United States interest lay in backing Latin American governments that would protect U.S. private investment, no matter how vicious they might be toward their own people. Kennedy argued that the United States interest lay in the extension of popular government. "We must give constant and unequivocal support to democracy in Latin America. We must end our open and warm backing of dictators. Our honors must be reserved for democratic leaders, not despots." And popular government, if it were to endure, had to be based on social and economic change. "We must encourage and aid programs of land reform." In this regard too he went beyond the Good Neighbor policy. Though it had distinguished between the interests of United States business and the interests of the United States, the older policy had displayed no great concern about dictatorships or regressive economic structures. The promotion of democracy and reform, Kennedy added, was "the ultimate answer to Castro and the Communists," but answering Castro was a by-product, not the purpose, of the Alliance (1961: 1160-1166).

He staffed his Latin American effort in accordance with these convictions. Adolf Berle, whom he made chief of the post-election task force on Latin America and later his special adviser on Latin American affairs, was the personal link between Good Neighbor days and the 1960s. Berle had long contended that the logic of the Good Neighbor policy called for the strengthening of democracy in Latin America; he was also a vigilant warrior in the cold war. Douglas Dillon, Kennedy's Secretary of the Treasury, had got religion about Latin America when, as Under Secretary of State for Economic Affairs in the Eisenhower Administration, he had attended the Inter-American Economic Conference at Buenos Aires in 1957. Richard Goodwin had had friends among Latin American democratic exiles in Washington during the fifties when he served as clerk to Justice Frankfurter. Ralph Dungan entered more accidentally when, encouraged by Kenneth O'Donnell and Lawrence O'Brien, he took on a watching brief after the manifest failure of Kennedy's Latin American advisers before the Bay of Pigs; but he soon developed a strong and informed concern. As for myself, I had actively followed Latin American affairs since I had written about hemisphere matters for *Fortune* in 1946 and gone to the first meeting of the Inter-American Association for Democracy and Freedom at Havana in 1950.

II

Berle in particular, and I to a lesser extent, had had some personal association with the leaders of the progressive democratic parties in the Caribbean area—especially with Romulo Betancourt in Venezuela, with Alberto Lleras Camargo in Colombia, with Jose Figueres in Costa Rica, and above all with Luis Muñoz Marin in Puerto Rico. These bright, confident, determined, admirable men united idealism and experimentalism in fine New Deal style. They fought both the oligarchs and the communists; their goal was to improve the life and release the energies of the workers and *campesinos*. They saw the United States as essentially democratic rather than as essentially capitalistic, Roosevelt and Kennedy as more representative of the U.S. ethos than the United Fruit Company. They therefore believed in the possibility and necessity of collaboration with liberal administrations in Washington. They were physically fearless and intellectually indefatigable. And they were friends, comrades, skilled propagandists on each other's behalf. The eloquence and faith they displayed on the firing line helped convince us that the demand for modernization in Latin America was indeed irresistible and that with such leadership the revolution would be democratic and peaceful.

Their writings in the 1950s had deeply colored the expectations of the New Frontiersmen of 1961. Figueres wrote (1955: 11),

The Latin American people are ripe for democracy. They have heard so much for such a long time about representative government, free elections, respect for the dignity of man, division of governmental

powers, and all that goes with the democratic creed, that you could no
more erase those political aspirations than you could eradicate the
Christian faith.

Muñoz said (1956: 12):

> Let us solemnly declare that our essential goal—the goal of all Amer-
> icans, North and South—is the abolition of extreme poverty, in the
> areas of misery remaining in the regions of the U.S. and in the altiplano
> of Bolivia, the plains of Venezuela, the coffee lands of Puerto Rico and
> Central America, the sierras of Mexico—to wipe out extreme poverty in
> this Hemisphere within the lifetime of children already born.

These were the goals: the enlargement of democracy and the conquest of
poverty. We all knew how Puerto Rico had been transformed under Muñoz's
leadership from the "stricken land" that Rexford G. Tugwell had written
about in 1946 into a bustling and self-respecting community. In 1954 I
visited Costa Rica in the company of Adolf Berle and was much impressed by
the dash and imagination with which Pepe Figueres pursued democratic
objectives. The program of *Accion Democratica* in Venezuela after the
overthrow of Perez Jimenez in 1958 confirmed our hope.

No doubt we should have noted more carefully the special advantages that
Puerto Rico, with its ties to the United States; Costa Rica, with its homogeneous population and wide distribution of land ownership; and Venezuela,
with its oil, enjoyed over most of Latin America in the struggle for development. We were marginally aware of this, but in the late 1950s we were more
impressed by the fact that dictators were falling around the continent—not
only Perez Jimenez but Odria in Peru, Rojas Pinilla in Colombia, and soon
Batista in Cuba—and that the democratic left seemed everywhere rising in
strength. In 1958 John J. Johnson in his persuasive book on *Political Change
in Latin America* instructed us in the political implications of the growth of
the "middle sectors." Tad Szulc in *The Twilight of the Tyrants* (1959)
portrayed the decline of the dictators. Robert J. Alexander, a member of
Kennedy's Latin America task force, celebrated the democratic left in
Today's Latin America (1962). In the early sixties progressive democracy
seemed to be surging forward in Latin America and the United States
simultaneously. And in Latin America what we saw as the betrayal of the
democratic Cuban revolution by Fidel Castro defined, we thought, a sharp
continental choice: whether the supposedly irresistible movement toward
modernization woudl fulfill itself through democracy or through dictatorship.

Without the rise of the democratic left (perhaps rather of the legend of the
democratic left) there would have been no Alliance. For the democratic left was
to be the lever through which United States aid could make a difference.

Kennedy had few illusions about the ability of the United States to solve the problems of other countries by itself. As he put his essential view of things on November 16, 1961:

> We must face the fact that the United States is neither omnipotent nor omniscient—that we are only six percent of the world's population— that we cannot impose our will upon the other ninety-four percent of mankind—that we cannot right every wrong or reverse each adversity— and that therefore there cannot be an American solution to every world problem [1962: 726].

He had applied this generalization to Latin America in the speech of March 13, 1961, announcing the Alliance:

> Only the most determined efforts of the American nations themselves can bring success to this effort. *They and they alone* can mobilize their resources, enlist the energies of their people and modify their social patterns so that all, and not just a privileged few, share in the fruits of growth. If this effort is made, then outside assistance will give vital impetus to progress; without it, no amount of help will advance the welfare of the people [1962: 172, emphasis added].

Kennedy's Latin American policy was thus a wager on the capacity of the progressive democratic governments and parties of Latin America, with properly designed economic assistance and political support from the United States, to carry through a peaceful revolution. It was thus a gamble, but, as we saw it, a necessary one. In our view, if progressive democracy disappeared in a Latin American country, the country would move on to authoritarian government, whether of the right or of the left. The later history of the decade proved the general accuracy of this premise. Unlike those who followed us after 1963, we did not assume that right-wing authoritarian governments would necessarily be friendly to the United States. Trujillo had already demonstrated this point at the start of the decade, as Perón was to demonstrate it again in the early 1970s.

The informal alliance between progressives north and south therefore seemed the key to the problem. The first mission Kennedy sent to Latin American countries was headed by George McGovern, then director of Food for Peace, and by me; the next was headed by Adolf Berle. This choice of emissaries, the President explained to me, was to make clear to our Latin American neighbors that the United States was turning a new, and progressive, face to the hemisphere and that they should get used to the fact that, however essential the role of private investment might be to the success of the Alliance and the development of Latin America, Washington's top concern was no longer the profits of North American corporations doing business in

South America. In a speech in Mexico City in October 1961, Chester Bowles emphasized the strict limitations "on what any foreign nation can do for others, regardless of the extent of its resources and good will. Neither prosperity nor freedom can be bestowed on one people by another." He warned the Latin Americans that economic development would "fail in its purposes if its benefits go primarily to a wealthy elite" (Bowles, 1961).

At times Kennedy even thought it might be useful to convene a "club" of democratic presidents for regular meetings in Puerto Rico or Florida. He hoped that the less democratic presidents might be stimulated to work on reform in order to make the club; but the idea presented obvious problems, and nothing came of it. He expressed his preferences forcefully, however, when he welcomed Betancourt to the White House in 1963 and, praising his "companionship with other liberal progressive leaders of this hemisphere," said, "You represent all that we admire in a political leader" (1964: 184).

III

In its ideas the Alliance was essentially a Latin American product. A glance at its origins shows that it was hardly, as some later writers have claimed, an "arrogant" North American effort to transform Latin American countries into "mirror images" of the United States (Harrison, 1971-1972: 169). It drew from Raul Prebisch of Argentina and the United Nations Economic Commission on Latin America, from Juscelino Kubitschek of Brazil and Operation Pan America, from the ten eminent Latin American economists, among them Prebisch, Jose Antonio Mayobre of Venezuela, and Felipe Herrera of Chile, who summed up the Latin American view in a trenchant memorandum delivered to Kennedy a few days before the March 13 speech. The Alliance did give a more comprehensive, more evangelical and no doubt more pretentious form to ideas that had already been circulating for a long time in Latin America. As Victor L. Urquidi, a Mexican economist of the ECLA (Economic Commission for Latin America) circle, later wrote, "Although the Alliance for Progress adopted some of the development and financial goals outlined by Operation Pan America, it went far beyond the latter in general concepts" (1964: 149).

The Alliance, as set forth by Kennedy, laid down three goals: economic growth, structural change, political democratization. ("The political problem of mankind," Keynes had written, "is to combine three things: Economic Efficiency, Social Justice, and Individual Liberty" [1931: 344].) These goals were, in theory, mutually dependent. Structural change and political democratization were deemed indispensable in order to assure more equitable distribution of the gains of growth. The implication was that United States economic assistance would be conditioned on, or at least associated with, performance in social and political reform. With the rhetorical bravado of the New Frontier, Kennedy's March 16 speech tied the three goals together in a "vast new Ten Year Plan for the Americas" intended to make every American republic "the master of its own revolution." This "vast cooperative effort, unparalleled in magnitude and nobility of purpose" would "transform the American continent into a vast crucible of revolutionary ideas and effort" and "demonstrate to the entire world that man's unsatisfied aspiration for economic progress and social justice can best be achieved within a framework of democratic institutions" (1962: 171, 172, 175).

In retrospect this language, like the language of the inaugural address before it, seems extravagant. It is plainly open to the charge of creating undue expectations. A dozen years later, revisionists wrote that the hopes excited by Kennedy's rhetoric could not possibly have been realized. The inevitable result was disillusion. Instead of trumpeting forth bold new policies and promising to get all Latin America moving within a decade, said the revisionists, the United States should have worked without fanfare for modest and attainable ends.

There is undoubtedly something in this. In our public utterance we were an over-rhetorical administration. The low profile has increasing charm in a world fatigued with slogans. Yet there are moments when there is no substitute for eloquence. Rhetoric, it might be added, was the coin of political discourse in Latin America. What the hemisphere desperately needed in 1961 was a new political consciousness and purpose. Conceptions as well as acts were necessary to create new moods, to signal breaks with the past, to inspire fresh initiatives; in this sense, words became acts.

There is a reasoned case, set forth by A. O. Hirschman and Leszek Kolakowski, for the underestimation of difficulties and the exaggeration of prospective benefits in the initiation of social change. Men, Hirschman writes, "take up problems *they think* they can solve, find them more difficult than expected, but then, being stuck with them, attack willy-nilly the unsuspected difficulties—and sometimes even succeed." The "principle of the Hiding Hand" is a means not only of bringing repressed creativity into play but also of achieving partial but essential gains. In Kolakowski's metaphor, a mirage may lead a caravan to struggle on through a sandstorm and find, not the lush oasis they thought they saw, but the tiny waterhole that would save them (Hirschman, 1967: 13, 22-23).

Would there ever have been a New Deal, for example, without "over-promising" and "overselling" by Franklin Roosevelt? "Nothing great," as Emerson said, "was ever achieved without enthusiasm." The ten Latin American economists themselves had insisted to Kennedy that the new program must above all "capture the imagination of the masses" (Levinson and de Onis, 1970: 57). As William D. Rogers, a later Alliance chief, put it, "Had the new Alliance not been launched so spectacularly, it might have become, in the eyes of most Latin Americans, merely another U.S. aid program" (1967: 271).

The Kennedy speech was followed by the meeting of the American republics at Punta del Este in August 1961. Here there were danger signals. Some Latin American delegations, distraught at the talk of redistribution, tried to water down the "Declaration to the Peoples of America" in order to muffle the call for structural reform. We have the testimony of Eduardo Frei of Chile that "the decisiveness and skill with which Richard Goodwin of the United States delegation acted at the time secured a final text which, though weakened in some respects [in comparison to Kennedy's March speech], was sufficiently clear to be considered a true interpretation of the real situation in Latin America."

Nor were Kennedy's words and the Punta del Este Charter of August 1961 entirely unavailing. By defining new issues and setting new objectives, the Alliance did begin to alter both the political consciousness and the social agenda of Latin America. Progressive democratic leaders in Latin America embraced the Alliance as an undertaking, in Frei's words, "committed to the achievement of a revolution" and designed to produce "a substantial change in the political, social, and economic structures of the region." Frei enumerated the objectives of "the Latin American revolution." They were destruction of the oligarchies, ending the semi-feudal estates on the countryside and redistributing the land, assuring equal access to education and political power, sharing the gains of economic development, utilizing international capital for the benefit of the national economy. "These," he said, "are precisely the same objectives as those of the Alliance" (1967: 442, 437-438).

IV

The proclamation of the Alliance had a second purpose: to alter the political consciousness of the United States government and to persuade the executive and legislative branches to support the new policies. The Alliance speech was written by Richard Goodwin in the White House. It could never have come out of the State Department that Kennedy inherited from Eisenhower. The Old Latin American Hands mostly disdained the Alliance as a fantasy dreamed up by amateurs. Conventional Foreign Service officers, like the peppery Ellis Briggs, who had served in his day as director of the Office of American Republics Affairs and as ambassador to Uruguay, Peru, and Brazil, denounced it as a "blueprint for upheaval throughout Latin America" and expressed sympathy for those "hard-pressed" Latin chiefs of state to whom Kennedy's exhortation "sounded suspiciously like the Communist Manifesto in reverse." If there were going to be a social revolution anyway, Briggs said, most chiefs of state saw little difference "whether the boot that propelled them toward the political dump-heap was made in Washington, D.C., or manufactured in Moscow, U.S.S.R. . . . If there is a more pernicious doctrine than one which impels the sponsor of an economic and social program to throw lighted gasoline into his neighbor's woodshed, it has yet to come to the attention of history" (Rogers, 1967: 218-219). Briggs by this time was a cranky old man in retirement, but cranky old men in retirement often ventilated the suppressed resentments of officers on duty. One of the prime functions of presidential speeches is to overcome the instinctive bureaucratic resistance to new directions.

The reception was better on Capitol Hill, where the few senators who knew and cared about Latin America (especially Ernest Gruening and Wayne Morse) rallied round the Alliance with enthusiasm. It was worst of all among those who saw themselves most directly threatened by the new departure— North Americans doing business in Latin America and rich Latin Americans.

It is worth emphasizing this point in view of the latter-day theory that the Alliance was cunningly devised by United States capitalists to protect their investments and enlarge their markets south of the border. I cannot recall that businessmen played any role in the formulation of the Alliance, though Peter Nehemkis of the Whirlpool Corporation was an ardent publicist for the new approach and other intelligent businessmen, such as Charles Meyer of Sears, Roebuck and George P. Gardner of the somewhat chastened and reformed United Fruit Company, expressed sympathy for the objectives. A. F. Lowenthal's conclusion on this point seems accurate: "Far from reflecting big business domination of United States foreign policy, the Alliance for Progress commitment emerged in part because of the unusual (and temporary) reduction of corporate influence in the foreign policy-making process" (1973: 17). Why indeed, if the secret purpose of the Alliance was to integrate Latin America more firmly than ever into the capitalist master plan, would the government in Washington have conceivably indulged in revolutionary rhetoric whose only effect was to stimulate and legitimize Latin American desires for economic independence and structural change?

It did not occur to us, for example, to invite United States businessmen to Punta del Este in August 1961 till the week before the meeting. Then they came as observers, not as members of the delegation. Nor did we follow up on their recommendation that a permanent private enterprise committee be established to promote foreign investment (Levinson and de Onis, 1970: 71). No doubt this was a mistake. But it further verified the point that the

Alliance, whatever it was, was not a capitalist plot. Indeed, during the Kennedy years United States private investment in Latin America actually declined. The attitude of the administration provoked Harold Geneen of International Telephone and Telegraph, making one of his early forays into foreign policy, into the agitation that ended in the passage in 1962 of the notorious Hickenlooper Amendment. This amendment, which the Kennedy Administration opposed, required the suspension of United States economic assistance when Latin American governments took strong measures—nationalization or even discriminatory taxation—against United States corporations.

The Latin American oligarchs, with a few distinguished exceptions, resented and detested the Alliance. They felt that Kennedy had wantonly lined up the United States with the radicals who wanted to dispossess them in their own countries. The greatest capitalist nation in the world, as they saw it, had inexplicably become a traitor to its class. Max Freedman, a columnist close to Lyndon Johnson, wrote as late as 1965, the "favored few who now hold the levers of power . . . rightly or wrongly, feel that the Alliance for Progress is an agency for class war financed by the United States and supported by its noble but dangerous idealism" (Rogers, 1967: 94).

For their part, many ordinary Latin Americans, rightly or wrongly, accepted this view and saw Kennedy, if not quite the Alliance, as a force for change. After the United States President received his astonishing welcome in the crowded streets of Bogotá in 1963, Lleras Camargo said to him, "Do you know why these people were cheering you? It's because they think you're on their side against the oligarchs" (Goodwin, 1967: 83). The oligarchs agreed, which is why they tried, with the generally zealous assistance of local North American businessmen, to make life miserable for United States ambassadors who methodically pursued the objectives of the Alliance. A few of these persevering ambassadors were Allan Stewart in Venezuela, James Loeb in Peru, Ben Stephansky in Bolivia, Ralph Dungan in Chile, Murat Williams in El Salvador, John Bartlow Martin in the Dominican Republic, Lincoln Gordon (during the Kennedy years) in Brazil, Edwin Martin in Argentina, Fulton Freeman in Colombia and Mexico.

As for Latin American radicals, they called the Alliance a sham, but some, at least, feared it as a threat. Castro told Jean Daniel, the French journalist, a little patronizingly in 1963, that the Alliance

> In a way . . . was a good idea, it marked progress of a sort. Even if it can be said that it was overdue, timid, conceived on the spur of the moment, under constraint . . . despite all that I am willing to agree that the idea in itself constituted an effort to adapt to the extraordinarily rapid course of events in Latin America.

V

The Alliance, I have noted, had three objectives: economic growth, structural change, political democratization. We understood that in the short run there might well be conflict among these objectives. We also supposed, or hoped, that in the long run they were mutually reinforcing. This was evidently, in the middle run at least, an illusion.

The Alliance was not entirely ineffective as a stimulus to economic growth. In addition to fostering a development consciousness and to redefining the issues of Latin American politics, the Alliance could claim some impact on the physical situation. One original objective, as laid down at Punta del Este in 1961, was a growth rate of 2.5 percent per capita per year. From 1961 through 1967 Latin America grew at the average annual rate of 4.5 percent of the total gross national product; but, because population increased even faster, per capita growth rate was under 2 percent. In 1968 the gross rate was 5.5 percent and the per capita rate 2.5 percent. It is impossible to determine how much of this achievement was due to the Alliance, but a good part of it certainly was. Over the decade this was not a contemptible record; and it brought with it gains in social development—the building of schools, hospitals, low-cost housing, roads, advance in sewage disposal, irrigation and electric power, and so on.

For all this, the Alliance accomplished far less than its founders had hoped. A great deal of the new capital brought into Latin America was offset by an outflow of capital to service and repay past loans and to remit profits to foreign investors. The Alliance did not lighten the weight of Latin America's external debt, nor did it improve Latin America's share in world trade. It reduced neither unemployment nor the inequality of income distribution. It did not significantly increase adult literacy. It did not come close to bringing about the structural changes deemed essential to economic growth as well as to political democratization.

What went wrong? It is tempting to look at the problem in bureaucratic terms—to wonder what would have happened if, for example, the Alliance had been established as a separate organization, like the Peace Corps and Food for Peace, instead of being submerged in the Agency for International Development; if it had been able to get itself into administrative business at once without months of delay; if it had not had to endure the annual auto-da-fé organized by Otto Passman in the House of Representatives; if AID regulations had not required that every project be almost a guaranteed success before it could be attempted; if the Treasury and the Export-Import Bank had not tried to apply bankers' tests to a social revolution; if . . . if. These were, however, superficial considerations. The trouble lay deeper.

Part of the trouble may well have been seeing the undertaking in precisely these terms—as, that is, a United States bureaucratic operation. We all knew it could not be that alone, or even mainly that. Yet the combination of New Frontier activism with the weight of the foreign aid bureaucracy tended to overwhelm our understanding that the Alliance could succeed only as a Latin American effort. "Was there not a paradox, right from the beginning," as McGeorge Bundy reflected in later years, "in announcing an Alliance, whose mainspring must be in South America, in a White House speech?" (Bundy, 1974).

VI

It is hard to know, even in retrospect, how we could have pursued a policy of stimulus without creating the impression in Latin America that the United States could do more by itself than it could possibly do. In our more sober moments we knew that it could not do so much. An impression that it could may have persuaded Latin American governments that they would not have to apply themselves to the task with full rigor. Latin America, heaven knows, had its own problems. The decline in world commodity prices since the bonanza days of the Korean War had sadly depleted its foreign exchange reserves and worsened its terms of trade. The Alliance called for national plans, but there was a shortage both in Washington and in Latin America of people capable of drawing up realistic and workable plans. Statistics in Latin America, in the phrase of the day, were poetry; and, though Latin America had its share of first-class theoretical economists, a gap remained between theory and plan.

At the same time, the remorseless multiplication of people was devouring the gains of production. With an annual population increase of more than 3 percent, Latin America was the fastest growing region in the world. We were well aware of this problem too. Kennedy mentioned it when he unveiled the Alliance and returned to it on other occasions. But what could one do about the birth rate in a Catholic continent? Population control was not mentioned in the Punta del Este Charter and stayed a forbidden subject till late in the decade. When the Catholics were finally prepared to talk about it (as in Frei's Chile), the Marxists condemned it, seeing population control, in the words of Eduardo Galeano, as a sinister plot to "kill guerrilleros in the womb" rather than in the mountains (Times of the Americas, 1974). It was not a policy a rich state could urge on poor states without raising the suspicion that it was trying to keep the poor states weak or was seeking pretexts for the reduction of aid.

There were deeper problems still. It is clear in retrospect that, in supposing

Latin America ripe for revolution, we overrated the demand for change. Cuba, it now seems evident, was an exception rather than an early manifestation of a mighty tide, as both Castro and Kennedy had believed. "Those who make peaceful revolution impossible," Kennedy said on the first anniversary of the Alliance, "will make violent revolution inevitable" (1963: 223). This was superbly true in the long run, but in the short run Washington as well as Havana underestimated the power not only of structural barriers to change but of sheer inertia. In many respects, as John Mander later argued in *The Unrevolutionary Society*, South America was an exceedingly conservative region. The oligarchs of course opposed everything that would diminish their own wealth and influence, and until very recently they had commanded the support of the army and the church. Those in the middle sectors were often too ambitious as individuals to unite in coherent movements for reform. The victims at the bottom of society were often too mired in traditional ways, too underfed and apathetic, or too brutalized to act against the existing order.

As for institutional obstacles to redistributive change, we underestimated the rigidity of the existing agrarian and business structures. These structures defined the effective political and economic community in most countries and controlled the access to education, power, and wealth. The problems of stagnation, rural and urban, unemployment and poverty, could not be tackled, for example, without revising the land-holding system that reserved good lands for a few and sent an endless flow of campesinos to the stinking slums of the cities. Yet, as J. K. Galbraith pointed out, it was an illusion to suppose that land reform was "something that a government proclaims on any fine morning—that it gives land to the tenants as it might give pensions to old soldiers. . . . In fact, land reform is a revolutionary step; it passes power, property, and status from one group in the community to another" (1951: 695).

As we underestimated the strength of inertia and rigidity, we also overestimated the capacity of Latin American progressive democracy to overcome these barriers and bring about a peaceful revolution. The progressive democratic impulse had true roots in the wars of liberation and the nineteenth-century constitutions of the Latin American past. It also had a contemporary base in the rising middle sectors, in the trade unions and for a season, in the universities. Nevertheless, it operated from an exposed position. Not only was it savagely opposed by oligarchs on the right, determined to hold on to their privileges, but it was the primary target of the communist left, who knew that, if the democratic revolution succeeded, theirs would fail.

Moreover, many progressive democratic leaders had the disadvantages of the classical liberal tradition with its elitist and paternalistic overtones. For them the Alliance came a decade too late. By the 1960s they were increasingly out of touch with the younger generation. They remained the best people in Latin America and the most deserving of United States support. But many activist Latin Americans, including some of the most courageous and idealistic among the intellectuals, among the military, among the students, even among the priesthood, were coming to the conclusion that the progressive democratic way was too slow, too reasonable, too much the faith of an older generation, too weak in its political base, too deficient in the ruthlessness necessary to overthrow oppressive and archaic structures and lay the foundations for a just society. Whether violent means could create a just society was another question. But progressive democracy plainly failed to inspire the drive, mystique, and élan "which alone," as Paul Rosenstein-Rodan of the OAS's expert Committee of Nine observed, "could overcome the normal inertia and resistance to change. . . . To create a heroic spirit of mission, an enthusiasm for a peaceful revolution is the main task confronting Latin American leadership." Except for Christian Democratic Chile (Rosenstein-Rodan was writing in 1967), this spirit, as it had shown itself in the New Deal, the Marshall Plan, the development mystique of Nehru's India, was "conspicuously missing in Latin America today" (1967: 34).

One had the sense at times that the great evangelist for the Alliance was not a South American at all but rather Teodoro Moscoso, the eloquent Puerto Rican who headed the Alliance in Washington and tirelessly toured the hemisphere propagating the gospel. Yet, as Kennedy had pointed out, the Latin American nations "and they alone" could do the job. In spite of Rosenstein-Rodan, a "spirit of mission" did exist in Latin America, but it expressed itself in nationalism. This, as Arturo Morales-Carrion, the perceptive Puerto Rican historian whom Kennedy had brought in as a Deputy Assistant Secretary of State—observed, was "the single most powerful psychological force now operating in Latin America. . . . Unless the Alliance is able to ally itself with nationalism, to influence it in a constructive direction, to translate its abstract terminology into familiar concepts related to nation-building, the Alliance will be pouring money into a psychological void" (Schlesinger, 1965: 791-792). This was an alliance that the United States did not make—that perhaps in the nature of things was unmakable; for how was Latin American nationalism to define itself except by defiance of the United States?

VII

Let us assume, as I continue to assume, that the original formula of the Alliance represented the best policy the United States could pursue toward Latin America. There remained the question whether there was not a gap between the will in Washington and the harsh requirements of social change in the hemisphere. Some of us had pondered Louis Hartz's mordant concluding question in *The Liberal Tradition in America:* "Can a people 'born equal' ever understand peoples elsewhere that have become so?" (Hartz, 1955: 309). This was why I wrote in *A Thousand Days* that the approach of the Kennedy Administration "represented a very American effort to persuade the developing countries to base their revolutions on Locke rather than on Marx," and wondered whether such moderation did not fall short of the ferocities of the situation (Schlesinger, 1965: 589). The existence of this gap was not, it may perhaps be said, a revelation reserved for R. A. Packenham a decade later (Packenham, 1973).

"Do we fully understand," Ambassador James Loeb wrote in a memorandum to the White House after fifteen months in Peru,

> the implications of what we like to call the "democratic revolution"? . . . I have sometimes had the impression that we are seeking a nice, neat, tidy, packaged revolution which will harm no one and benefit everyone. This would be fine if we could get it but, however sound the economic premises may be, this conception flies in the face of all we know about the political dynamics of social change [Loeb, 1963].

Chester Bowles had pressed the same point publicly in his Mexico City speech in 1961, though he exaggerated the affinity between the American Revolution and the revolutions of the Third World. Privileged societies, he then observed, had occasionally shown the capacity to adjust to revolutionary change beyond their borders. "But I can remember no instance of a nation so favored as my own becoming a vigorous and effective *participant* in the process of such change. The challenge to the people and the government of the United States is clear. Can we become history's first great exception?" (Bowles, 1961).

Even if the U.S. government tried to become history's great exception, hard political questions remained. Could the Kennedy Administration resolutely hold to the Alliance goals in face of the backlash that would inevitably be generated by the determined pursuit of those goals? Could the administration stay the course when the price would be manifold?—violent opposition from those in Latin America whose privileges were threatened, social turbulence that drove away foreign capital and could be plausibly claimed to "play into the hands" of the communists in a tense period in the cold war, and bitter criticism from the North American business community with no countervailing domestic constituency to support the policy. Could Washington stay the course, above all, when the support for the Alliance goals in Latin America itself was so intermittent, wary, and faltering?

The answer was that even the Kennedy Administration could not altogether stick to the course. Castro himself, in explaining to Jean Daniel why he thought Kennedy's "good ideas aren't going to yield any results," analyzed Kennedy's dilemma with discernment:

> The trusts see that their interests are being a little compromised (just barely, but still compromised); the Pentagon thinks the strategic bases are in danger; the powerful oligarchies in all the Latin American countries alert their American friends; they sabotage the new policy; and in short, Kennedy has everyone against him [Daniel, 1963: 19].

So the Latin American oligarchs simply denied Kennedy's thesis that the choice was between peaceful and violent revolution; they were well accustomed to calling out the armed forces in order to prevent both. "The Alliance for Progress itself," Moscoso said in 1968, "has stimulated or contributed to several of these military interventions since in the view of the Latin armed forces any United States support for social change and material development tends to encourage political instability and social disintegration" (Moscoso, 1968: S 6307). As for United States officials, they hastily pulled back when pressure for structural change threatened to produce civil conflict. This was partly because they were not intellectually prepared for social turbulence; many had been lulled by Walt Rostow's model of the "stages of economic growth" into seeing development as a bland and evolutionary process. Their retreat was even more due to the fact that violence made North Americans personally uncomfortable and unhappy. Perhaps most of all they feared that turbulence would play into the hands of the Marxist revolutionaries. Che Guevara had warned Richard Goodwin in 1961 that there was "an intrinsic contradiction in the Alliance. By encouraging the forces of change and the desires of the masses, you might set loose forces beyond your control, ending in a revolution which would be your enemy" (Goodwin, 1967: 83).

Certainly no one could doubt an intrinsic contradiction between the Alliance and the rest of the United States government. When the Pentagon, the CIA, and, to a degree, the State Department thought about Latin America, the first problem they saw was "hemisphere security." In the atmosphere of the late cold war, this preoccupation seemed more virile and patriotic than the Alliance's interest in development, democracy, and reform. Though the security concern was far from pointless, as the Cuban missile crisis showed, it was quickly reduced by the Pentagon to a simple-minded reading of every decision in terms of a wildly exaggerated communist threat. Simple-minded or not, the unrelenting pressure of the national-security bureaucracy led to a perversion of Alliance programs; the Joint Chiefs of Staff carried more guns than Ted Moscoso. AID administrators were encouraged to seek short-term political results at the expense of long-term development policies, as in the decision to back away from Celso Furtado and SUDENE (Superintendency for the Development of the Northeast) in northeast Brazil. Administrators put aside programs that might unduly upset existing power arrangements and thereby weaken a country's capacity to resist the presumably omnipresent revolutionaries. The security preoccupation led the United States government into a series of programs plausibly designed to protect the development process from disruption and sabotage, but soon to acquire a life, momentum, and horrid impact of their own.

The Bay of Pigs was only the first and most spectacular manifestation of this contradiction. It was Eisenhower's initiative, and Eisenhower's last word to Kennedy before the inauguration in 1961 was that this "effort be continued and accelerated" (Schlesinger, 1965: 164). For various reasons and with considerable internal dubiety, Kennedy let the expedition go ahead. One reason probably was that he knew that Castro would do all he could to wreck the Alliance for Progress. It was a measure both of the early appeal of the Alliance and of the Latin American hope for Kennedy (as well perhaps of ultimate Latin American skepticism about Castro, who after all was only a Cuban) that this abysmal fiasco did not get us into deeper trouble in the hemisphere.

Kennedy had wanted to keep the Bay of Pigs and the Alliance for Progress as far away from each other as possible, but he was wobbled for a moment by his Cuban miscalculation. In his attempt to recover, he headed into the worst folly of his administration: the infatuation with counterinsurgency. It is true that he saw counterinsurgency in political terms, on the Magsaysay model—not strangling people in the dark but promoting civil action and reform in the countryside. However, the kind of people temperamentally attracted to the Special Forces often saw it less benignly. The State Department, to its credit, regarded the counterinsurgency enthusiasm with weary distaste.

Nonetheless General Maxwell Taylor, vigorously seconded by Attorney General Robert Kennedy, succeeded for a season in forcing counterinsurgency on the rest of the government. In a move ideologically related, though administratively distinct, the government set out to guard the flanks of the Alliance by teaching Latin American democracies how to cope with internal terrorism. In practice this came down to equipping and training the Latin American police. In what was seen at the time as a "progressive" decision, police training was taken out of the cover of CIA and made open in AID. AID set up a public safety program, which dispensed gas guns and grenades, riot and shotgun shields, small arms and helicopters to Latin American internal security forces. The State Department set up an International Police Academy to provide individual instruction in modern police methods. No doubt there was a minimal point in all this. David Bell, a humane man, once testified as head of AID that "the publicly assisted police forces have done and can do much to prevent conspiracy and the development of disruptive situations, and to insure an environment of law and order which supports the orderly social, economic and political development of emerging nations" (*Congressional Record*, 1973: S 18239). In Venezuela and Colombia from 1961 to 1963 democratic societies were faced with authentic internal threats. There the counterinsurgency program probably played an indispensable and beneficial role.

But it was certainly abused elsewhere. Though the Costa Gavras film *State of Siege* can hardly be taken as fact, it is not possible to doubt that, on balance, the United States contribution to police training in Latin America gave the status quo a mean and nasty weapon employed promiscuously against all forms of dissent. I must confess that I was not aware of this at the time. But one should have known that police training tempts men of a particular cast of mind. For example, instruction in methods of interrogation can easily lead enthusiasts beyond the curriculum at the Police Academy and end in the justification of torture.

VIII

The counterinsurgency business was a great blind spot on the New Frontier. In our concern with protecting the external processes of democracy, we were too far removed from what the thugs were doing behind the screen. Our concern remained essential, but we discovered that it led us into difficulties even in its own terms. The question soon arose, for example, what United States policy should be when a *golpe* (coup) turned out a constitutional regime. Most of us believed as a general principle in the automatic recognition of all governments that could maintain internal order and meet international commitments; in this light, recognition did not imply approval or disapproval of the regime's character and policy. On the other hand, there seemed cogent reasons to depart from such agnosticism when it came to Latin America. For in Latin America, United States recognition often had a make-or-break effect. How could we be faithful to the democratic principle of the Alliance, how could we offer "constant and unequivocal support to democracy," if we promptly recognized every military regime that overthrew a democratically elected government? One could argue that automatic recognition applied to the rest of the world, but that in the western hemisphere the United States had undertaken special obligations to "the consolidation on this continent, within the framework of democratic institutions, of a system of individual liberty and social justice based on respect for the essential rights of man" (Preamble to the Charter of the Organization of American States).

In any case, Kennedy was conscious of the perplexities involved. When a coup forced out Frondizi in Argentina in 1962, he accepted the recommendation of our Buenos Aires embassy that we regard the new regime as the constitutional continuation of the Frondizi government. But when Haya de la Torre won the presidential election in Peru later that year, and the military seized control to prevent his assuming office, Kennedy at once suspended diplomatic relations and economic assistance. He explained at a press conference, "We feel that this hemisphere can only be secure and free with democratic governments" (1963: 572). In response to United States pressure, the military junta soon restored freedom to the press and political opposition and promised free elections; the United States thereupon resumed relations. When military coups overthrew democratic regimes in the Dominican Republic and Honduras a year later, Kennedy suspended relations as he had in Peru. This time, however, United States pressure did not achieve the same happy results. Kennedy, discouraged by the fact that the suspension policy had so little support in Latin America, rather gloomily decided in the weeks before his death to send his ambassadors back to Santo Domingo and Tegucigalpa. The decision reflected his own doubts about recognition as a weapon of intervention on behalf of democracy.

At the same time, he was privately reappraising the problem of diplomatic relations with Cuba. William W. Attwood, the United States ambassador to Guinea, had returned to the United States to recover from an attack of polio and was sent on special assignment to the U.S. mission at the United Nations. There in the autumn of 1963 he began a series of talks with the Cuban delegate to the United Nations; and soon arrangements were under way for a secret meeting between Attwood and Castro near Havana.

In the meantime, Jean Daniel of L'Express came to Washington on his way to Cuba. He had a talk with Kennedy, who discussed Cuba with some frankness. According to notes dictated by Daniel immediately after the meeting, Kennedy said that through its exploitation and humiliation of Cuba the United States had "created, built and manufactured the Castro regime out of whole cloth and without realizing it." As for the future, Castro had now made Cuba an international—that is to say, a Soviet—problem; and "the continuation of the blockade," Kennedy said, "depends on the continuation of subversive activities" organized by Castro against Latin America. Kennedy asked Daniel to come again on his return; "Castro's reactions interest me." When Daniel reached Havana, Castro, as he told Frank Mankiewicz in 1974, took him to be a special emissary from Kennedy. After hearing his recital, he told Daniel, "Since you are going to see Kennedy again, be a messenger of peace. I want nothing, I expect nothing. But in what you have reported to me there are positive elements" (Daniel, 1963: 16-17; 1973: 151-152, 161).

(Later Castro told Mankiewicz, "Kennedy was the only president with the courage to change his mind" about Cuba [Mankiewicz, 1964; New York *Times*, August 3, 1974].) Two days after Daniel conveyed Kennedy's views to Castro, Kennedy went on to Dallas. Attwood was thereafter informed "that the Cuban exercise would probably be put on ice for a while—which it was and where it has been ever since" (Attwood, 1967: 146).

IX

The experience of the first two years of the Alliance dissipated any illusions we may have had about the ease or speed of Latin American development. Nor did Kennedy make any attempt to conceal the difficulties: quite the contrary—a point that bears on the allegation of overpromising and supports the Hirschman principle of the Hiding Hand. "The problem of the Marshall Plan," Kennedy said in March 1962, "was rebuilding; here it's a case of building. . . . There are a good many local pressures which make the fight harder." Every reform "hurts some group in that country . . . with Communist minorities who are exploiting every discontent. I do think we should have some understanding of how complicated this task is and give this child some strength before we psychoanalyze him." In June he warned against the expectation "that suddenly the problems of Latin America, which have been with us and with them for so many years, can suddenly be solved overnight. . . . It's going to take a long time, but at least in some countries they are making progress." "We do not have the technical skills," he said in September. "We do not have the planning staffs. We have, in a sense, neglected Latin America, so that we are engaged in a tremendous operation with insufficient resources. . . . The assistance we have given has not been enough to keep Latin America even, and particularly when its population increase amounts to almost 3 percent." "We face extremely serious problems in implementing the principles of the Alliance for Progress," he told the Economic Club of New York in December. "It's trying to accomplish a social revolution under freedom under the greatest obstacles. . . . It's probably the most difficult assignment the United States has ever taken on." "There are greater limitations upon our ability to bring about a favorable result than I had imagined," he said a few days later (1963: 231, 495, 676, 883, 889). In April 1963 he enumerated the sources of instability: part "comes from maldistribution of wealth, part of it comes from inadequate wealth, part of it comes from . . . a drop in commodity prices . . . part of it comes from illiteracy" (1964: 308).

Despite the difficulties, despite the possibility that, as Castro was to say, he had "everyone against him," Kennedy saw no alternative but to press forward. In a speech before the Inter-American Press Association at Miami on November 18, 1963, he repeated that "the task we have set ourselves and the Alliance for Progress, the development of an entire continent, is a far greater task than any we have ever undertaken in our history." The task, he said, rested essentially on the shoulders of the people of Latin America. It was they who must undergo "the agonizing process of reshaping institutions," who must "bear the shock wave of rapid change and progress," who must "modify the traditions of centuries." The Alliance was "not an external aid program." It had to fight on the front of social justice. "Privilege is not easily yielded up. But until the interests of the few yield to the needs of the Nation, the promise and modernization of our society will remain a mockery." It had to fight on the economic front. "In pursuit of economic welfare the *Alianza* does not dictate to any nation how to organize its economic life. [This was, of course, a signal to Castro.] Every nation is free to shape its own economic institutions in accordance with its own national needs and will." But in the end the Alliance had to stand on the front of democracy.

> This is at the core of our hopes for the future. There can be no progress and stability if people do not have hope for a better life tomorrow. . . . Whatever may be the case in other parts of the world, this is a hemisphere of free men capable of self-government. It is in accordance with this belief that the United States will continue to support the efforts of those seeking to establish and maintain constitutional democracy. . . . The United States is committed to this proposition.

He concluded: "I support and believe in the Alliance for Progress more strongly than ever before" (1964: 873-875). Four days later he was dead. The Alliance, as he had conceived it and sought to carry it out, died with him.

X

"Let us continue," Johnson said after Kennedy's death; and continue in the main he did, for a while at least. But the one area in which he made a quick and sharp break with the Kennedy policies was Latin America. A few weeks after Dallas he appointed Thomas Mann as his "one voice" on Latin American affairs, replacing both Moscoso as coordinator of the Alliance and Edwin Martin, an able Foreign Service officer and strong Alliance man, as Assistant Secretary for Inter-American Affairs. As William D. Rogers later wrote, "A more dramatic shift in tone and style of U.S. Alliance leadership would have been difficult to imagine" (1967: 226).

Mann's appointment came at a propitious time for slowing the political and social drive of the Alliance. The fear of Castro had given urgency and legitimacy to pressure for structural reform. When this fear diminished—as it had after the missile crisis and after the success of counterinsurgency in Venezuela and Colombia the pressure diminished too. It was also evident that the Soviet Union was not prepared to make a major investment in Latin American revolution. Why, as one Latin American diplomat put it, would Moscow wish to feed a lamb in the mouth of a lion? All this permitted Mann to indulge his natural inclination and liquidate two of the three original goals of the Alliance—structural change and political democratization. Economic development remained a central objective, but even this was often subordinated to the use of the Alliance as a political arm of United States foreign policy and as an economic accessory of the United States business community. "Let's hope Washington will understand that the Alliance is a cause, a crusade—by Latin Americans for Latin Americans," Moscoso wrote me in the spring of 1964, but such a conception could not have been further (as Moscoso perfectly understood) from Tom Mann's mind. Moscoso added presciently: "Making it an instrument of our foreign policy to be used primarily in solving our short-run problems will ultimately destroy it."

In the Kennedy years United States business had had little influence on United States policy in Latin America. Revisionist historians claim that a capitalistic United States opposed Castro and organized the Bay of Pigs on behalf of North American sugar planters. This is demonstrable nonsense. Suppose that the United States had not been a capitalist country at all. Would a communist United States have acquiesced in the takeover of Cuba by a regime ready to offer its country as a base for its major extracontinental rival, any more than the Soviet Union acquiesced in regimes that it considered threatening in Hungary and Czechoslovakia? This is said not to justify American policy toward Cuba but to suggest that it can be better understood in the context of military security than in that of dollar diplomacy. It is a mistake to ascribe to economic ambitions what should more fundamentally be ascribed to political and strategic anxieties. Obviously the United States had not opposed communism in Latin America just because it wished to protect the interests of North American business. It had done so because a communist state in Latin America might become a base for a nuclear threat against the United States. As we learned in October 1962, this was hardly a whimsical fear. Any administration in Washington, whatever its system of ideology or ownership, would have been obligated to take prudent steps to protect the safety of the country.

Business, if excluded from the councils in the Kennedy years, had been waiting in the wings. Its great advantage was the permanence of its interest in Latin America. Politicians and intellectuals concerned themselves with Latin American policy only as opportunity permitted; businessmen with Latin

American interests worked at it in season and out. Moreover, they formed the only strong domestic constituency with demands about Latin American policy. Their demands could always be overridden by strategic considerations; they could be subordinated for a season by the political convictions of a Roosevelt or a Kennedy White House; but the businessmen were still around when everyone else had gone away. Once the Kennedy people were removed, corporations began to find sympathetic ears in Foggy Bottom. As Alphonse de Rosso of Standard Oil of New Jersey later put it, "Not until Tom Mann came back in 1964 did the business community feel that it was 'in' again with the United States government" (Levinson and de Onis, 1970: 72-73).

Early in 1964 Mann set forth the new line before a closed meeting of all U.S. ambassadors and AID mission chiefs assigned to Latin America. The Kennedy idea of favoring democratic regimes was now to be supplanted by a "pragmatic" policy of favoring all regimes that opposed communism and welcomed U.S. corporations. This included military juntas that had over-thrown democratic governments. The protection of United States private investment would have a top priority. Alliance aid would be given in response to presumed economic effectiveness without regard to progress toward structural reform or political democracy. Despite the valiant personal commitment of some of its coordinators, the Alliance, now deprived of its political and social components, became in 1964 and after just another United States aid program, with aid increasingly taking the form of loans, often at high interest rates, repayable in dollars and tied to purchases within the United States.

On the political side the Johnson Administration applauded the military coup that established authoritarian government in Brazil in 1964. In the Dominican Republic, the United States revived the policy of direct armed intervention, and elsewhere it developed ties to conservatism and dictatorship. In Peru the Johnson Administration stopped aid to the democratic, pro-Alliance Belaúnde government in the hope of coercing Lima into making a favorable settlement with the International Petroleum Company, a Standard Oil of New Jersey subsidiary. In 1965, Senator Robert Kennedy, about to leave on a trip to Latin America, asked a State Department official to explain the point of ending aid to a government dedicated to the goals of the Alliance and at the same time increasing aid to the dictatorship in Brazil (which, in these years, received more U.S. aid than any other Latin American country). After listening to the usual cant, Kennedy finally said, "What the Alliance for Progress has come down to then is that you can close down newspapers, abolish congress, jail religious opposition, and deport your political enemies, and you'll get lots of help, but if you fool around with a U.S. oil company, we'll cut you off without a penny. Is that right?" The official replied, "That's about the size of it" (Schlesinger, 1970: 81).

XI

That was about the size of it. "The Alliance for Progress is dead," the Mexican Victor Alba wrote in 1964. "What is left is a bureaucratic structure, mountains of mimeographed paper, a sarcastic smile on the lips of the oligarchs, and pangs of guilt on the part of the politicians of the left who did not take advantage of the Alliance and make it theirs" (Goodwin, 1967: 70-72). As Moscoso saw it in 1965, the Johnson Administration had forgotten the political meaning of the Alliance.

> John F. Kennedy made the right diagnosis three and a half years ago. He saw a revolution in the making and he sought to come to terms with it. Money, skills and bureaucrats were part of his arsenal. But even more important was that he took a political and ideological stand. He stood for change—revolutionary change—and he said so in exalted places. Today we are still using money, more than before. But do we remember that there is a revolution going on? [New York *Times,* February 18, 1965]

Two contrasting articles in *Foreign Affairs* emphasized the difference. In 1966 David Rockefeller, condemning "the policy which prevailed in the early years of the Alliance of placing too much emphasis on rapid and revolutionary social change," praised the Johnson Administration for its appreciation of "the vital role of private enterprise" and its promotion "of a more favorable business climate" (Rockefeller, 1966: 408). What delighted New York bankers depressed Latin American democrats. A few months later, Frei of Chile wrote gloomily in the same magazine about "the alliance that lost its way." The oligarchs and the Marxists had cooperated to destroy "the true meaning of the national effort to accomplish the tasks of the Alliance" and to transform it into a U.S. external aid program, "a creation of the United States exclusively." No doubt the flow of dollars was continuing;

> but there was no equivalent effort on the part of Latin Americans to reform and become more democratic. Hence the Alliance has not reached the people of Latin America for whom it was created. . . . The problem is that what was fundamental to the Alliance for Progress—a revolutionary approach to the need for reform—has not been achieved. . . . There has been no strengthening of the political and social foundations for economic progress. . . . What has been lacking is a clear ideological direction and determination on the part of the political leaders to bring about change.

The Alliance could be saved only by the restoration of its original character "as a common enterprise" and by its becoming openly "identified ideologically with the more progressive groups in Latin America," especially through giving "a decided impulse to the really important transformations such as agrarian reform" (Frei, 1967: 443, 446, 447). To expect such things in 1967 was to imply an obituary.

The most comprehensive attempt to render a judgment on what had happened to the Alliance was made by Robert F. Kennedy after his return from a prolonged Latin American tour. In a powerful speech delivered in the Senate on May 9 and 10, 1966, Kennedy sought to recall the Alliance to its original purposes. The Alliance, he said,

> was not and could not be a program of U.S. assistance, but a coopera-
> tive effort among all the nations of the Americas. It embraced not
> simply economic progress, but social justice, political freedom, and
> democratic government.

It was "a pledge of revolutionary change," for there could be "no preserva-tion of the status quo in Latin America." It meant an end to the "closed society, a society which reserves all wealth and power and privilege for the same classes, the same families, which have held that wealth and power for the last 300 years." The revolution was coming, "whether we will it or not. We can affect its character; we cannot alter its inevitability."

"At the heart of the revolution," Kennedy said, were two great and resistant problems—land reform and education. He saw land reform as, at the root, a political question, necessarily implying major changes in the internal political balance of many countries. The United States, he urged, should clearly associate itself with the cause of land reform. "If we concentrate only on economic progress, there will be no lasting benefit, and it will not work. . . . It is a fraud to give assistance or funds when the money is going . . . to a few wealthy and powerful individuals in the country." He condemned the Hickenlooper approach: "Aid should not be withheld to force special advantages for U.S. business." He called for special support to the govern-ments and forces of reform; reform performance must be "a condition of full participation in the Alliance." He called also for U.S. assistance to any nation that decided that family planning and population control were in its own national interest. As for the threat of communism, he said, "Batista, not Castro, was the major cause of communism in Latin America." He summed up his appeal: "There is a revolution now going on down there, and we must identify ourselves with that revolution."

As Kennedy was well aware, his remarks could hardly have been less relevant to the mood in Washington in the late sixties, with a Latin American policy responsive to the pressures of North American business and a president obsessed with Vietnam. Lyndon Johnson, in any case, thought that Latin

America ended with Mexico. His successor never knew where it began, and the Nixon policy toward Latin America was aptly characterized by Richard Goodwin as one of "malign neglect" (though Allende of Chile would certainly have disputed the word "neglect").

XII

Was the Alliance for Progress a failure? To this question, one can legitimately, I believe, return the answer, Who knows? The Alliance was never really tried. It lasted about a thousand days, not a sufficient test, and thereafter only the name remained. Even that disappeared finally in the Nixon years.

The harder question is: Could the Alliance have succeeded? Its original sponsors badly underestimated the difficulties in its path. What can be said in retrospect? Some of its early sympathizers have sadly concluded that the whole idea was fallacious. Senator Frank Church in 1971 called the Alliance "the high water mark of our innocence in supposing that we could liberate traditional societies from their centuries-long legacy of tyranny and stagnation with a little bit of seed capital and some stirring rhetoric." In practice, he contended, American aid promoted development a good deal less than it strengthened a corrupt and repressive status quo and ministered to the self-esteem of the aid bureaucracies. The fact was, as Church now saw it, that "thoroughgoing social revolution is the necessary prerequisite for the development of much of the third world," and the United States inherently lacked the capacity to foster social revolution in alien societies. The Kennedy Administration had done its best in Latin America, but the effort was foredoomed to failure.

> We failed because we had neither the ability to impose reform from outside nor the will to pursue it from within. The one was simply impossible; the other went against the priority of our own interests as we conceived them. However much we may have wanted reform and development, we wanted "stability," anticommunism and a favorable climate for investment more.

Even with our enormous power and the best of intentions, "there are some things we cannot do, things which are beyond our moral and intellectual resources." Church added: "There is nothing the United States can do or should do to promote revolution—to do so indeed would violate the United Nations Charter and sound traditional standards of diplomacy. What we can and should do is to stop promoting counterrevolution." One effective way to do that would be to end, apart from technical assistance, all bilateral economic aid (1971, S 17182, S 17184-5, S 17186). As for Latin America,

Our national interests can best be served . . . by loosening our embrace. We should keep a decent distance away from their internal affairs, from their military apparatus and their revolving-door governments. This would be best for us and best for them [1970, S 5542].

This catastrophism about development in the Third World was hardly new. In the past, however, it had been largely the self-serving argument of the revolutionary left, which had always denied any community of interest between the United States and Latin America and portrayed a zero-sum conflict between the North American drive for empire and the Latin American struggle for independence. In Latin America this feeling flowered in the 1960s in the "dependencia" analysis, which explained underdevelopment as the functional consequence of the role assigned to Latin America in the structure of world capitalism. The productive systems of Latin American countries were held to be determined by the needs, not of internal development, but of the international division of labor; and the conclusion, in the words of Theotonio Dos Santos, was that "the most powerful obstacles to their full development come from the way in which they are joined to this international system" (Dos Santos, 1971: 235).

The dependency system was thus believed to condemn Latin American countries to a deformed and marginal existence until they were prepared to recapture control over their national economies—which meant dealing severely with foreign corporations and governments as well as with the locals who lived off the dependency process. If development required the end of dependency, this could not be accomplished, it was generally supposed, without expropriation, violence and revolution. Academic economists like Robert Heilbroner (*The Great Ascent,* 1963) had also argued that breakthroughs to economic development were unlikely except through left-revolutionary regimes that preferred social discipline to political democracy and personal freedom. Senator Church's attack on foreign aid was especially significant as evidence of the extent to which development pessimism was penetrating the liberal establishment. By 1974 Church reached the dismal conclusion that without revolution, foreign aid was harmful and with revolution, it was unnecessary (1974, S 18098).

XIII

Is such pessimism justified? There remain humdrum facts of political experience. As J. K. Galbraith reminds us, "Countries have managed to accomplish revolutionary change without great violence in the past. It would be unduly pessimistic to imagine that it cannot happen again" (1971: 249). History shows that modernization has been brought about by a wide diversity of regimes—conservative, liberal, communist, military-nationalist. Even violence, in A. O. Hirschman's witty revision of Marx (1963: 260), may as often be the midwife to reform as to revolution. Every nation has its own balance of traditions, rigidities, resources, skills, leadership, and luck tilts the scales toward development or toward stagnation.

My own impression can be summarily put as follows. The formula of the Alliance for Progress still seems right to me. I was reassured, if a little saddened, to read the other day in an article by the president of the Overseas Development Council that a "major rethinking of development concepts is taking place" and that the rethinkers had reached the astonishing conclusion "that we need development policies which benefit all strata of the population and not just a favored minority" (Grant, 1973: 43). This is what the Alliance for Progress was all about an eon ago. The problem—not, alas, solved by Mr. Grant—is how to do it.

I think there are conditions under which it might be done. The Alliance could have succeeded—could still succeed—if we had the following conjunction of circumstances: (1) a strong progressive democratic revival in Latin America, (2) a strong liberal administration in Washington, (3) North American business divestment in Latin America, and (4) detente with Russia and China. Let me explain briefly.

(1) *A strong progressive democratic revival in Latin America?* I have observed earlier that the progressive democrats faded out in the 1960s partly because they seemed a party of an older generation, and partly because they were not delivering the goods fast enough. Yet which among their competitors in the years since has delivered the goods in any really satisfactory way? Castro? Allende? Perón? Brazil has achieved economic growth; Peru structural change. But economic growth accompanied by repression and torture does not offer a stirring model, nor does structural change which brings with it the closing down of politics and a free press. I may be wrong, but I retain the conviction that the passion for human freedom and public choice is strong and real in Latin America. As Octavio Paz has written, "Socialism without democracy is not socialism." In the light of the terrible experience of the twentieth century, programs of change "will have to be democratic—although they do not have to be imitations of Western bourgeois democracies. They will have to contain the seed of a socialism to come and, above all, they will have to propose models of economic development and of social organization that would be less inhuman and less unjust than those of both the capitalist regimes and of 'bureaucratic socialism' " (1974: 355-356).

If Octavio Paz is right, the democratic left will have a new chance. As Betancourt said, "It is impossible to carry out long-term development programs unless they are conducted by democratic, freely elected governments which are subject to free analysis and criticism by public opinion." Authoritarian regimes may order people about for a time; but every such regime in Latin America, once removed from the national scene, "has left a heritage of fiscal disequilibrium, economic disorder, and deep-seated social rancor" (Moscoso, 1968: S 6307). No one believes any longer, if anyone ever did, that Latin America can be transformed in a decade. It is evident that both the Marxist and the democratic left (and the New Frontier in Washington) overrated the speed and irresistibility of revolution in Latin America. When it is better understood that transformation under any auspices will take a couple of generations, the gradualism, pluralism, tolerance, and reason of the progressive democrats may well come into their own. Somewhere, I am sure, there are young Betancourts, Freis, and Llerases awaiting their opportunity.

(2) *A strong liberal administration in Washington?* This seems inevitable in due course; perhaps very soon. It is, however, less important than the progressive democratic revival, which it must cultivate and embrace. For in the end, as Kennedy suggested so long ago, only Latin Americans can revolutionize their social structures, control their inflation, make adminis- tration and taxation honest and effective, teach their people to read, slow down their population growth. What is a liberal administration to do if there is no progressive democratic revival to embrace? In the interim I incline to the proposal of Y. H. Ferguson (1972: 385) that Washington should prize *both* fundamental economic and social change *and* democracy in Latin America; that, forced to choose, we should regard structural change as the more important; and that we should be cool toward regimes which honor neither goal.

(3) *North American business divestment in Latin America?* With all the talk about economic imperialism, it is sometimes forgotten that the United States economic interest in Latin America is of comparatively recent origin. In 1900, for example, U.S. exports to Latin America amounted to $132 million, less than 10 percent of our total exports; imports from Latin America came to $185 million, less than a quarter of the total (U.S. Bureau of the Census, 1960: 550, 552). As late as 1916, U.S. capital represented less than a fifth of all foreign private investment in Latin America (Galeano, 1971: 209). When U.S. private capital went into the Caribbean before the First World War, it did not do so on its own initiative but at the behest of the U.S. government, which wanted to keep British and German influence at the minimum.

The situation began to change only after the First World War; and the steady growth of U.S. private investment since then has meant that the most sustained pressure on Latin American policy in recent times has come from businessmen with interests south of the border. Nothing has done more to prevent the development of a sensible United States policy toward Latin America. For, though the business community has found it hard to believe, the interests of United States business are by no means the same as the national interest. What is good for Anaconda or United Fruit is not necessarily good for the United States. As Secretary of State Henry L. Stimson, who had seen U.S. intervention at first hand in Nicaragua, observed in 1931, it was "a matter of discretion with a government how far it will protect property of its citizens in another country." If such protection clashed "with broader international or governmental policies, it may perfectly well refuse to interpose." President Eduardo Santos of Colombia soon praised Franklin Delano Roosevelt's Good Neighbor policy on the ground "that where previously American companies were accustomed to threaten the government [of Colombia] by saying an appeal would be made to Washington, the picture was reversed, and it now was the government who made or threatened to make the appeals to Washington." In 1939 a State Department memorandum, commenting on the demands made by American oil corporations in Venezuela, declared: "It must not be permitted them (as occurred in the case of the Mexican dispute) to jeopardize our entire Good Neighbor policy through obstinacy and shortsightedness. Our national interests as a whole far outweigh those of the petroleum companies" (Wood, 1961: 42, 300, 265). These elementary principles were forgotten in the Eisenhower years, largely overridden in the Johnson years, and rejected in the Nixon years. Because a more enlightened policy lacks a strong constituency of its own, even a progressive administration in Washington would be under constant harassment so long as any important share of United States business hopes to make itself rich in Latin America.

Despite all its disadvantages, the injection of U.S. private capital no doubt initially had a stimulative effect in Latin America by bringing in factors of production not available locally. This situation may be changing, however. As Hirschman points out in his classic essay "How to Divest in Latin America, and Why," there is good reason to believe that, at a later stage of development, private foreign investment may become a "retarding influence," stunting the local entrepreneurial, managerial, technological, and capital formation possibilities. This is in addition to the politically disruptive consequences of attempts to protect foreign investors in an age when developing nations are determined to gain control over their economies. There is therefore, Hirschman argues, an inherent conflict between the development of Latin America and the maintenance of the present position of private investors from the United States; and he concludes plausibly that "a policy of selective liquidation and withdrawal of foreign private investment is in the best mutual interests of Latin America and the United States" (1971: 229, 232). Such a policy would safeguard a renewed Alliance against deformation by the business interests that (contrary to the New Left) were not its architects but rather its most powerful foes. Even if Washington does not organize a divestment policy, it seems inevitable that Latin American governments will move rapidly in coming years to control foreign private investment, to Latin Americanize foreign enterprises, and to restrict the repatriation of profits. If private investment has a future in Latin America, it will have to swim with the tide.

(4) *Detente.* As divestment would strengthen the Alliance against deformation by United States business interests, so detente would strengthen it against deformation by the Pentagon and the CIA. There would be no need to calculate every program under the Alliance in terms of its short-term political impact, nor to fear that the destabilizing effects of structural change would "play into the hands of the communists."

These four conditions may not emerge; but it is not entirely inconceivable that they may. The first of these conditions is decisive. "Latin America," Octavio Paz writes, "is a continent full of rhetoric and violence—two forms of pride, two ways of ignoring reality" (1974: 356). The future of Latin America depends only marginally on the United States. It depends essentially on the capacity of the Latin Americans themselves to confront and change their own reality. As they do this, I believe they will find themselves reclaiming the ideas of the Alliance—ideas Latin in their origin and early formulation—and at last making them truly their own.

NOTE

1. Such sentiment has latterly been vigorously repudiated, as, for example, by Lawrence Harrison: "The differences between North America and Latin America are enormous, covering virtually all aspects of human life. . . . It can be argued that there are some Asian societies (Japan is an obvious candidate) which have more in common with the societies of North America than do most of the societies of Latin America." Yet, for all this bravado, even Mr. Harrison concluded by calling on the hemisphere "to stand more firmly on the Charter of Punta del Este" (Harrison, 1971-1972: 181).

REFERENCES

ATTWOOD, W. (1967) *The Reds and the Blacks.* New York: Harper & Row.
BODENHEIMER, S. (1971) "Dependency and imperialism: the roots of Latin American underdevelopment," pp. 155-181 in K. T. Fann and D. C. Hodges [eds.] *Readings in U.S. Imperialism.* Boston: Porter Sargent.

BOWLES, C. (1961) Speech before Mexican North American Cultural Institute, Mexico City, October 19.

BUNDY, McG. (1974) Letter to Arthur Schlesinger, Jr., September 5, 1974.

CHURCH, F. (1974) "Foreign aid program no longer serves American interests." Congressional Record (October 2): S 18097-S 18100.

––– (1971) "Farewell to foreign aid: a liberal takes leave." Congressional Record (October 29) S 17179-S 17188.

––– (1970) "Toward a new policy for Latin America." Congressional Record (April 10): S 5538-S 5544.

DANIEL, J. (1973) Le Temps Qui Reste. Paris: Stock.

––– (1963) "Unofficial envoy: an historic report from two capitals." New Republic (December 14): 15-20.

DOS SANTOS, T. (1971) "The structure of dependence," pp. 225-236 in K. T. Fann and D. C. Hodges (eds.) Readings in U.S. Imperialism. Boston: Porter Sargent.

FAIRLIE, H. (1973) The Kennedy Promise: The Politics of Expectation. New York: Doubleday.

FERGUSON, Y. H. (1972) "The United States and political development in Latin America: a retrospect and a prescription," pp. 348-391 in Y. H. Ferguson (ed.) Contemporary Inter-American Relations. Englewood Cliffs: Prentice-Hall.

FIGUERES, J. (1955) "The problems of democracy in Latin America." Journal of International Affairs 9, 1: 11-23.

FREI, E. (1967) "Urgencies in Latin America: the alliance that lost its way." Foreign Affairs (April): 437-448.

GALBRAITH, J. K. (1971) Economics, Peace and Laughter. Boston: Houghton Mifflin.

––– (1951) "Conditions for economic change in underdeveloped countries." Journal of Farm Economics (November).

GALEANO, E. (1971) "Latin America and the theory of imperialism," pp. 205-223 in K. T. Fann and D. C. Hodges (eds.) Readings in U.S. Imperialism. Boston: Porter Sargent.

GOODWIN, R. (1967) "Our stake in a big awakening." Life (April 14): 66-84.

GRANT, J. P. (1973) "Development: the end of trickle down?" Foreign Policy (Fall): 43-65.

HARRISON, L. (1971-1972) "Waking from the Pan American dream." Foreign Policy (Winter): 163-181.

HARTZ, L. (1955) The Liberal Tradition in America. New York: Harcourt, Brace.

HIRSCHMAN, A. O. (1971) A Bias for Hope: Essays on Development and Latin America. New Haven: Yale University Press.

––– (1967) Journeys Toward Progress: Studies of Economic Policy-Making in Latin America. New York: Twentieth Century Fund.

––– (1963) "The principle of the hiding hand." Public Interest (Winter): 10-23.

KENNEDY, J. F. (1964) Public Papers of the Presidents of the United States: John F. Kennedy . . . 1963. Washington: Government Printing Office.

––– (1963) Public Papers of the Presidents of the United States: John F. Kennedy . . . 1962. Washington: Government Printing Office.

––– (1962) Public Papers of the Presidents of the United States: John F. Kennedy . . . 1961. Washington: Government Printing Office.

––– (1961) Speeches, Remarks, Press Conferences and Statements of Senator John F. Kennedy, August 1 through November 7. Washington: Senate Commerce Committee.

KENNEDY, R. F. (1966) "The Alliance for Progress: symbol and substance." Congressional Record (May 9, 10): 9609-9625, 9705-9716.

KEYNES, J. M. (1931) *Essays in Persuasion.* London; reissued (1963) New York: W. W. Norton.

LEVINSON, J. and J. DE ONIS (1970) *The Alliance That Lost Its Way.* Chicago: Quadrangle.

LOEB, J. (1963) "Some observations on the Alliance for Progress," memorandum to Ralph Dungan, March 7, Schlesinger Papers, Kennedy Library.

LOWENTHAL, A. F. (1973) "United States policy toward Latin America: 'liberal,' 'radical,' and 'bureaucratic' perspectives." Latin American Research Review (Fall): 3-25.

MANKIEWICZ, F. (1974) Telephone interview (September 23).

MOSCOSO, T. (1968) "On Latin America and revolution." Congressional Record (May 23): S 6307-S 6310.

— — — (1964) Letter to Arthur Schlesinger, Jr., May 27, Schlesinger Papers, Kennedy Library.

MUNOZ, L. M. (1956) *An America to Serve the World.* San Juan: Department of Education Press.

PACKENHAM, R. A. (1973) *Liberal America and the Third World.* Princeton: Princeton University Press.

PAZ, O. (1974) "The centurions of Santiago." Dissent (Spring): 354-356.

ROCKEFELLER, D. (1966) "What private enterprise means to Latin America." Foreign Affairs (April): 403-416.

ROGERS, W. D. (1967) *The Twilight Struggle: The Alliance for Progress and the Politics of Development in Latin America.* New York: Random House.

ROSENSTEIN-RODAN, P. N. (1967) "Latin America." Challenge (May-June): 10-11.

SCHLESINGER, A. Jr. (1970) "The lowering hemisphere." Atlantic Monthly (January): 79-88.

— — — (1965) *A Thousand Days: John F. Kennedy in the White House.* Boston: Houghton Mifflin.

Times of the Americas (1974) C.E.L.'s review of Eduardo Galeano's *Open Veins in Latin America* (October 2).

U.S. Bureau of the Census (1960) Historical Statistics of the United States, Colonial Times to 1957. Washington: Government Printing Office.

URQUIDI, V. L. (1964) *The Challenge of Development in Latin America.* New York: Frederick A. Praeger.

WOOD, B. (1961) *The Making of the Good Neighbor Policy.* New York: Columbia University Press.

APPENDIX

As revisionist historians have contended that the Hoover Administration really originated the Good Neighbor policy, so some now contend that the Eisenhower Administration really originated the Alliance for Progress. The following document is of historical interest in suggesting how, in the view of the Kennedy Administration, the Kennedy Latin American policy differed from the Eisenhower Latin American policy.

March 14, 1962

MEMORANDUM TO THE PRESIDENT

SUBJECT: HISTORICAL GENESIS OF THE ALLIANCE FOR PROGRESS

The statement of the N.Y. Times that the Eisenhower Administration thought of the Alliance for Progress and you merely named it is wholly inaccurate and will certainly come as a surprise to those Latin American leaders—such as Kubitschek—who desperately tried to get previous administrations to adopt some such policy without success.

1. For the first seven years of the previous administration there was no policy toward Latin America—merely a continuation of old practices, policies and attitudes.

2. In 1960—alarmed by the growing deterioration of the situation in Latin America and under the prodding of Doug Dillon—we supported the Act of Bogota and asked Congress for $500,000,000 to implement it. This Act was a step forward, but a limited step. It was restricted to U.S. assistance in the field of social progress—the construction of schools, homes, waterworks, public health facilities, etc., and it said that Latin American nations must help themselves in these fields. It was a program of social development, and social development only, on a limited scale with the $500 million to be spent over a period of two years and the fund to be mostly administered ($400 million worth) by the Inter-American Bank.

3. The Alliance for Progress, it is true, incorporated the principles of the Act of Bogota, but went far beyond this Act to a new concept of Inter-American cooperation. A few specifics will serve to illustrate this.

a. The Alianza was based on a long-term program of economic development, a program to increase productive capacity, accelerate rates of growth and make a permanent increase in standards of living. It envisaged a decade-long plan of hemispheric development leading to the stage of self-sufficient growth. The entire program of long-term economic development—the keystone of the Alianza—was new to this Administration.

b. The Alianza introduced the concept of long-term planning and programming. This was absent from previous U.S. policies and yet must be considered the basis for today's development efforts.

c. The entire institutional structure, including the OAS Experts, the Planning Institute, etc.—with the exception of the Inter-American Bank—has been newly created by the Alianza.

d. The stress on social reform as a condition of development aid—though first intimated in the Act of Bogota—has become a matter of central emphasis under the Alianza. It was impossible to demand social reform as a condition of long-term development financing before this, because long-term development financing was not available.

e. The entire program of commodity stabilization is new since our previous policy actually opposed the idea of stabilizing commodity prices.

f. The Alianza was the first to put U.S. support behind programs of economic integration in Latin America.

g. The magnitude of the plans is incomparable—this year we spent approximately three times as much as previous administrations ever spent in any one year.

h. Almost all the political components of the Alianza represent new thought, including our current stress on political democracy (and coldness toward dictatorial governments) and, more important, our basic decision to identify the United States with the progressive democratic forces in Latin American countries.

If the Alliance for Progress had a predecessor it was Brazil's Operation Pan-America and not the policies of the previous administrations. The bitterness of the Brazilian government at our failure to seriously consider Operation Pan-America is the surest evidence of how much things have changed in the last year.

In addition to the specifics of your policies the entire atmosphere of our relations to Latin America, our attitudes, our progressiveness, our receptivity to Latin needs, has shifted dramatically since last January. No one would be more suprised to hear that we were simply following past policies than the democratic leaders of Latin America who have viewed the Alliance—in both public and private statements—as a new breakthrough in Inter-American relations, and the last, best hope of democracy in this hemisphere.

Richard N. Goodwin

PART II

INTRA-LATIN AMERICAN RELATIONS

Chapter 5

PROBLEMS, PERSPECTIVES, AND MODES OF ANALYSIS:

UNDERSTANDING LATIN AMERICAN APPROACHES ⅂

TO WORLD AFFAIRS

EDWARD S. MILENKY

Until recently scholars and policy-makers built models of international politics or made interpretations of state behavior according to the perspectives of the superpowers. It is incomplete at best and misleading at worst to continue this attitude in a multipolar world in which the importance and freedom of smaller countries seem to be increasing. This article is a survey of how a cross-section of Latin American policy-makers and scholars interpret international politics in general and the place of their respective nations in world affairs in particular. Its objectives are first, to examine these various Latin American world views and second, to suggest which conceptual approaches to international politics best seem to explain them.

A cross-section of approaches was constructed around the following criteria: conceptual approaches as distinct from discussion of specific issues; approaches which attempt to build on indigenous experience as distinct from unqualified borrowing of imported social science and .ideologies; a sample as representative as possible of large and small country outlooks—a geographic and political spectrum as wide as possible. Because they have the longest traditions of international activity and superior resources for research, Argentina, Brazil, Chile, and Mexico are most heavily represented. On a strict numerical basis, but probably not in terms of regional influence, Cuba excepted, smaller countries are less represented.

Latin American perspectives on world affairs fall into two general categories. National approaches are concerned with one country's unique position. Regional approaches understand the situations of individual countries as examples of the problems and forces confronting Latin America as a whole.

These differences in approach seem to depend on the career backgrounds of individual analysts. Most of the regionalists are economists and sociologists disposed by training to ground their analyses in basic social forces operating independently of particular national settings. Moreover, most have had experience either in regional international organizations or in university faculties with a close relationship to such organizations. The exclusively Latin American character and mission of the agencies with which the regionalists have been associated dispose them toward a broad cross-national perspective. Included are the Economic Commission for Latin America (ECLA), the Latin American Faculty of Social Sciences (FLACSO), the Latin American Institute for Economic and Social Planning (ILPES), and the Institute for the Integration of Latin America (INTAL).

As a group the regionalists have been heavily influenced by ECLA. Because ECLA undertook the first postwar sustained study of the Latin American condition and was, for a time, the only regional organization with a predominantly intra-Latin American character, it set the pattern for subsequent efforts. Elements of Marxism, particularly Lenin's theory of imperialism, influenced the Commission's approach to relations between developed and underdeveloped countries. This approach, combined with the appeal that Marxism has for many Latin Americans, was another factor influencing many of the regionalists toward a cross-national outlook.

Two other connections make the regionalists a group. Four of the institutions with which the majority of regionalists have been affiliated—ECLA, FLACSO, ILPES, and the University of Chile—are located in Santiago, Chile. Thus there is an opportunity for interchange. Until the final days of the Allende government and the 1973 coup, Santiago also provided a relatively free intellectual environment. Most regionalists are also affiliated with one or more of the fifty institutional members of the Latin American Social Science Council (CLACSO), a transnational service organization for the promotion of research. CLACSO has served as a conduit for research funds and has held several regional social science meetings.[1]

By contrast, most of the nationalists are military men, professional politicians, or diplomats with little or no experience in regional, international, or transnational organizations. Hence their concerns are more focused. Table 1 summarizes the occupations and affiliations of the regionalists and nationalists and identifies them by category.

Both regionalists and nationalists approach Latin America's role in world affairs through the national situations of particular countries or of all countries considered collectively. They analyze the structure of the international

TABLE 1
LATIN AMERICAN FOREIGN AFFAIRS WRITERS

Regionalists

Affiliations:

ECLA	ILPES	Univ. of Chile	FLACSO	Auton Univ. of Mexico	National[a]	Other
Sunkel (C)	Sunkel	Sunkel	Godoy (A)	Gonzalez Casanova (M)	Jaguaribe (B)	Gonzalez Casanova (M)
Furtado (B)	Cardoso (B)	Pinto		dos Santos (B)	Furtado	Trias (U)
Pinto (C)		Cardoso		Frank	Krieger Vasena (A)	
		Kaplan (A)			Kaplan (A)	
INTAL-IDB		dos Santos (B)			Ferrer (A)	
Herrera (C)		Frank (Amer)			Silva Michelena (V)	
Lagos (C)						

Nationalists

Affiliations:

Armed forces	Diplomatic corps	Political office[b]
Villegas (A)	Arujo Castro (B)	Perón (A)
Mercado Jarrin (P)	Alsogaray (A)	Allende (C)
Guglialmelli (A)	Camilion (A)	Velasco (P)
ESG (B)	Castenada (M)	Krieger Vasena (A)
CAEM (P)		Ferrer (A)

NOTES: Past and present affiliations listed. A = Argentina; B = Brazilian; C = Chilean; G = Guatemalan; A = American; P = Peruvian; V = Venezuelan; U = Uruguay. A listing under both categories indicates that the individual has written from both perspectives, most notably Aldo Ferrer, an economist, and Gonzalez Casanova, a political scientist. Jaguaribe's early work is in the nationalist category. The table is limited to the sample discussed or referred to in the body of the article.

a. Other national institution. Furtado was a minister in the Goulart government, Ferrer in the Levingston government, and Krieger Vasena under Ongania. All others are or were in universities.

b. Political office includes the presidency and ministerial positions.

system as it impinges on Latin American interests, define the goals which should be pursued in the international realm, and search for the appropriate means to achieve these goals. These categories will be used to present the views of both groups.

THE LATIN AMERICAN NATIONAL SITUATION

Stanley Hoffman (1968: 183) defined the national situation as the combination of a state's internal features and international position, its complete location in time and space. In this sense the national situation is the first concern of regionalists and nationalists.

Some nationalists stress the potential power of particular countries. Brazilian General Golbery do Couto e Silva (1967: 29-39, 54-57) uses geopolitics to explain the potential of his country. He defines geopolitics as (1) a doctrine of defense constructed around a particular set of national interests and (2) recognition of the state as the essential reality in world politics. Secondarily, geopolitics is the relationship between politics and physical features. Applying his theories, Golbery finds that in South America only Brazil has great power potential by virtue of its location, population, and resources. Although Brazil is remote from the world island of Eurasia, it is the key to the South Atlantic and an essential alliance partner for the United States. Except for its frontiers with Argentina and the latter's unstable dependencies, Paraguay and Bolivia, Brazil is isolated from its neighbors, according to Golbery. The Argentine frontier, Bolivia, and Paraguay are zones of tension because two large powers confront each other. Problems of security and defense also arise because of Brazil's dependence on imported petroleum and because of the location of its major population and industrial centers close to the Atlantic Ocean and the Parana River, which gives access to the interior. In general Golbery stresses the ease with which Brazil will become a great power.

In the minds of many Argentines, Argentina has failed to reach its true power potential. The memory of predepression optimism and importance colors much Argentine thinking about world affairs. Alvaro Alsogary (1969: 49, 72-73), a conservative nationalist and the Ongania government's ambassador to the United States, describes Argentina as a nation whose resources and achievements make it an example of the Latin American potential. He says that if Argentina did not suffer from underdevelopment, inflation, and political instability, it could achieve a standard of living equal to many European countries. Above all, Alsogary emphasizes that Argentina suffers from a gap between its aspirations and accomplishments, a spiritual crisis which can be overcome.

Juan Domingo Perón (1971: 11-14) was still more explicit. He said that Argentina had a mission in world history as a cultural and ideological presence under the banner of Justicialism, which he described as a third position between capitalism and communism. Perón felt that Argentina had accepted the colonial position of supplier of raw materials in place of his program of industrialization during the years between his fall in 1955 and his return to power in 1973. Nevertheless, national liberation under Perónist auspices would restore Argentina to the proper road to fulfillment. (See also Alsogary, 1969: 49, 72-73 and Lagos, 1963: 153-157.)

A regional version of the failed potential thesis emerges from the work of Adalberto Krieger Vasena (1973: 24-36, 148), a conservative and Argentina's Minister of Economy under Ongania. By virtue of its higher caloric intake and income levels, internal unity, ethnic makeup, and western cultural patterns, Latin America is distinct from and ahead of the Third World according to Krieger Vasena. In 1910 many Latin American countries were as developed as much of Europe and were ahead of the British dominions; their loss of status since then is due to their failure to give priority to industrialization. He finds that Latin America could reverse its decline through autonomous action.

More typically Latin Americans describe their nations as the victims of powerful external forces. Peru's Center for Higher Military Studies (CAEM), a war college which prepares officers for higher command, bases its analysis of the Peruvian situation on the military's humiliating dependence on foreign powers and influences for support in fighting a guerrilla war in the 1960s. Its major equipment came from the United States, its jet fighters from France, and its napalm from the International Petroleum Corporation, a local subsidiary of a U.S. firm. The nation's weakness and vulnerability stemmed from its reliance on primary products exports, which were controlled by foreign monopoly capitalism, and from the large and highly visible foreign presence in the country's internal economy. As a part of the U.S. sphere of influence, Peru was a dependent, externally penetrated society serving a foreign power as a source of raw materials, a market, and a location for investment. Furthermore, a history of dependence going back to colonial times had kept Peru out of world decision-making centers (see Villanueva, 1972: 23-59, 63).

Similar views are common in Argentina. Shortly before the ouster of the Ongania government in 1970, a group of military men and civilian technocrats in the National Security Council (CONASE), a high-level government planning agency, produced the National Plan for Security and Development, which described Argentina as a relatively isolated country culturally and economically dependent on outside powers. Its role in world trade, a measure of national importance as well as the major source of income, was declining. The country had failed to achieve mutually beneficial international relationships. To overcome this situation Argentina would have to find a formula for national development that did not depend on international generosity. Aldo Ferrer, an economist and a member of General Levingston's cabinet, has written that Argentina's continuous linkage to the world economy and its lack of internal integration have prevented it from achieving a national economy. In his public statements Argentina's current Minister of Economy, Jose Ber Gelbard, has indicated implicit support for this interpretation of Argentina's national situation.

Two analysts in the nationalist category have also developed the theme of Latin America as victim. Vivian Trias of Uruguay blames the United States for balkanizing and dominating Latin America in a continuation of the old British divide-and-rule policy which created his own country (see Ferrer, 1967). He sees Uruguay menaced by Brazil, which he considers an instrument of subimperialism, serving U.S. interests and in turn receiving U.S. aid and support for its national development. Edelberto Torres Rivas (1970: 491-497, 508-509), Guatemalan lawyer and sociologist with ILPES, describes Central America as a collection of dependent states within the international capitalist system. He feels that the region's external economic links, operating historically through coffee production for export, support internal oligarchical domination. According to Torres Rivas, Central America is now undergoing "subordinate industrialization," an externally induced process which is adapting local economies to complement the metropolitan economy of the United States. As foreigners acquire control of this new industry, Central America is denationalized economically and external domination is strengthened. Torres Rivas' analysis of the Central American condition is an explicit application of elements drawn from three groups of regionalists—the ECLA school, the Marxists, and the dependency theorists. Because it forms a foundation to the others, ECLA's position will be discussed first.

According to ECLA, Latin America's failure to create the conditions for sustained economic growth is its major problem. Internally, people in the rising middle social strata find that foreigners have preempted the most dynamic areas of their national economies. Externally, Latin American countries find themselves excluded from centers of international economic decision-making and locked into a pattern of trade in which they form a primary-products-producing periphery exchanging raw materials for the manufactured goods of an industrial center at declining terms of trade. As a result ECLA and Raul Prebisch, its first Executive Secretary, find that the structure of the world economy is sealing an international division of labor between developed and underdeveloped, rich and poor. In a 1970 report to the Inter-American Development Bank, Prebisch (1970) described Latin America as increasingly self-conscious and upwardly mobile, interested in cooperation with the industrialized nations, but determined to reject all forms of subordination and continuation of the status quo.

The Marxists make explicit use of the concepts underlying the ECLA approach. Fidel Castro and Che Guevara describe Latin America as a semi-colonial, dependent group of nations whose economies have been distorted by imperialism. Beginning with the colonial period, a succession of dominant powers have drawn Latin America into a global capitalist economy in which cheap raw materials are exchanged for expensive manufactured goods. However, in recent times imperialism is in crisis, and the distortions it has imposed on Latin American economies are ripening the objective conditions for revolution. Cuba is put forward as an example of how United States imperialism, based on the control of natural resources, can be broken.

Another Marxist model with some influence in Latin American intellectual circles comes from Andre Gunder Frank, a Berlin-born, United States-educated professor of economic development at the University of Chile. Through class relationships between the respective bourgeoisies, Latin America has been denationalized and relegated to the periphery of a world capitalist economy centered on the United States. Latin America's reliance on exports of primary products forms a relationship which transfers the region's economic surplus to the metropole. This is imperialism within Lenin's definition. Frank claims that only when two world wars and the great depression temporarily weakened ties to the metropole was Latin America able to industrialize, relying during those years on the local bourgeoisie's internal colonial exploitation of the masses. Frank's total world view posits levels of colonial relationships stretching from the Latin American peasant through the local capitalist class to the bourgeoisie of the United States, with global capitalism as Latin America's problem. (For a similar approach by a Brazilian sociologist, see Ianni, 1970.)

Many of the concepts of dependency theorists are the same as those of Marxists and the ECLA school, but dependency theorists attach more importance to international as distinct from transnational class relationships. They also distinguish among economic interests such as industrialists and export entrepreneurs rather than lumping them together as classes.[2] Since they are subject to the technological, commercial, and sociopolitical control of the industrialized countries, Latin American economies are dependent economies in this perspective. Helio Jaguaribe, a Brazilian political scientist, believes that the region's dependence on the advanced countries for science and technology is causing cultural denationalization, while alliances between the dominant groups in Latin America and the United States are producing political denationalization—the disappearance of indigenous political systems with real control over their internal affairs. As multinational corporations begin producing locally in Latin America, a new form of technological dependence is becoming more important than export-related dependence. In contrast to Frank's unified chain of relationships, dependency theorists see an increasingly marginalized mass bringing about revolution in response to the increasing transnational integration of an elite benefiting from a capital and technology intensive manufacturing sector.

With his concept of national viability—the minimum human and material resources required for autonomous development at a given level of societal organization and technology—Jaguaribe (1973: 399-402) introduces a refinement to dependency analysis. Under current global conditions he finds that only Argentina, Brazil, and Mexico are relatively capable of escaping from dependence through autonomous development. Collectively, through integration the Andean Group, Uruguay, and Paraguay could be viable, but all other countries would not. Hence, the continued or prospective existence of Latin American countries as national states is in doubt.

The degree of international power belonging to Latin America is the first concern of foreign affairs analysts. Its membership in wider families of nations is their second concern. Conservatives, such as Alsogary and Krieger Vasena, favor a western orientation. However, claims to membership in the Third World are becoming more common as a support for reactive nationalism and because of visions of Latin America as a victim of western imperialism. Perónists stress that Argentina's experience with imperialism and under-development make it a part of the Third World, a concept attributed to Perón's Third Position. Salvador Allende and the Popular Unity of Chile frequently denounced the industrialized countries and identified with under-developed Africa and Asia against foreign hegemony. Under the Quadros and Goulart governments Brazil flirted with African racial and cultural affinities and was said to serve as an example to the Third World of a nation conquering the tropics. However, economic and cultural links with the West are strong, and pursuit of Third World links has meant the danger of involvement in extra-hemispheric disputes, such as the Middle East crisis, which offer few political dividends.

In order to avoid the pitfall of bloc alignments, while retaining nonalignment as a symbol of nationalism and independence, some Latin Americans prefer to stress the unique qualities of a particular country as an element in the national situation. Mexico's ideology of the 1910 Revolution is the oldest version of nonaligned uniqueness. Official rhetoric rejects all foreign influences and alignments in favor of the indigenous, particularly Indian, elements in national life, and stresses the neutrality of international law and organization as a guide to international behavior. Mexico's internal political consolidation allegedly also enables it to modify pressures toward external dependence. However, Daniel Cosio Villegas, Mexican essayist, and Pablo Gonzales Casanova, a Mexican political scientist whose work spans the regionalist and nationalist categories, believe that the Revolution is spiritually exhausted and has lost its moral authority. (See for example Casanova, 1970; Comercio Exterior, 1973; Jarrin, 1969; Meyer, 1972.)

Peru presents the most contemporary and influential version of nonaligned uniqueness. President Velasco's speeches stress repeatedly that through a unique revolutionary humanism Peru is creating a society based on its own reality and is rejecting as false the conflict between capitalism and communism. For both Peruvians and Mexicans, nonaligned uniqueness is an attempt to assert the reality of a national existence against the feelings of powerlessness and penetration which color other interpretations of the Latin American condition. However, Villegas and Casanova seem to suggest that revolutionary enthusiasm is a perishable commodity (see Velasco Alvarado, 1970).

Taken together, both nationalists and regionalists have a gloomy picture of the Latin American national situation. Most of the attributes of nationstatehood—sovereignty, impermeability to outside forces, and a capacity for independent action—are missing. Some Brazilians, Argentinians, and Peruvians are optimistic. However, these countries have assets of territorial base or revolutionary reconstruction; the optimistic visions of Latin American objectives in the international realm, the means for their realization, and the structure of international power grow out of these assets.

VISIONS OF THE INTERNATIONAL SYSTEM

Bipolar visions tend to stress the existence of a fairly static division of international power, centering on the United States and the Soviet Union. Jaguaribe describes an inter-imperial system in which United States and Soviet empires are in equilibrium. Latin America and Eastern Europe are secure core areas for each power, while Western Europe is partly in contention. The superpowers compete actively in Southeast Asia. Jose Silva Michelena, a Venezuelan sociologist, sees a socialist camp whose objective is expansion under Soviet hegemony and a capitalist camp engaged in imperialism to assure markets and supplies of raw materials. In contrast to Jaguaribe, Silva Michelena (1973) places Latin America in the peripheral zone of the capitalist camp, which the nuclear stalemate has made the main arena of world politics. A former Brazilian ambassador to the United States, João Augusto de Arujo Castro (1971), and Juan Domingo Perón (1971: 11) are the least optimistic, claiming that the United States and the Soviet Union have agreed to freeze the world power structure. For Arujo Castro, this agreement took place in the aftermath of the Cuban Missile Crisis; according to Perón, it happened at Yalta.

Multipolarity may exist, but it may not be important for Latin America. Marcos Kaplan (1972: 1140-1141), an Argentine political scientist and a regionalist, sees the rise of China and moves toward independence in Eastern and Western Europe as evidence of a drift toward a multipolar system. Declining ideological conflict is weakening both blocs and allowing smaller states more freedom, but Oscar Camilion (1969), an Argentine diplomat, cautions that the continuing importance of subversive penetration, conventional warfare, and the global drive toward industrialization still threaten underdeveloped countries with technological dependence and permanent low status positions. Krieger Vasena (1973: 17-21) sees a fluid international situation in which an economically competitive Latin America might attempt to renegotiate its trade and financial arrangements. However, he also notes that the power realignment currently under way is subjecting the developed countries to serious internal problems which will probably make them less willing to allow Latin America to take an active role.

A hierarchical international system in which the gap between developed and underdeveloped countries is most significant to Latin America is another interpretation. Regionalist Felipe Herrera (1969: 103-108), formerly President of the Inter-American Development Bank, notes that only a small group of industrialized countries are engaged in scientific research. Writing before the oil crisis, Horacio Godoy, also a regionalist and associated with FLACSO, emphasizes the concentration of nuclear weapons, gold holdings, and Western Europe. ECLA's division of the world into an industrial center and a raw-materials-producing periphery also suggests a hierarchical international system. Celso Furtado, former Minister of Planning in the Goulart government of Brazil and chief of the Planning Division of ECLA, writes that what matters for Latin America is the hegemony of the United States. Having successfully contained the Soviet Union and reached a spheres-of-influence agreement with it, the United States is now using aid and economic penetration through multinational corporations to assure stability in Latin America, according to Furtado. Furthermore, he sees the multinational corporations integrating with each other and in turn integrating their Latin American subsidiaries into the U.S. economy. All advocates of a hierarchical system agree that the concentration of wealth and power appears to be growing. It will be interesting to see if their analyses change in the aftermath of the Arab world's unprecedented grab for financial power.

Marxists and many dependency theorists go beyond Furtado's indication of a trend toward a transnational world centered around the United States and see a network of alliances among privileged sectors as the critical factor in international relations. Frank's class-based analysis of the Latin American condition leads to such a conclusion. Osvaldo Sunkel, a Chilean economist and a regionalist, claims that a common world culture is emerging under the impact of communications media. Fernando Cardoso (1971: 54), a Brazilian regionalist and dependency theorist, foresees the integration of Latin America into a world economy, but also holds out the hope that emerging indigenous industrial entrepreneurs in Latin America will establish truly national societies.

All visions of the international system—bipolar, multipolar, hierarchical, or transnational—seem to offer Latin America limited options for action. The countries of the region are seen as closed out of the upper rungs of the international power structure and under United States hegemony or substantial influence. The nuclear stalemate has neutralized the potential balancing force of the Soviet Union in most models. However, the frustrations growing out of the unacceptable national situations of Latin American nations, tempered by their evaluations of the international environment, have generated a set of objectives and associated modes of action.

LATIN AMERICAN ENDS AND MEANS

Latin American students of international affairs would have their nations seek a familiar catalogue of objectives: sovereignty and autonomy; national development and, if possible, national power; and a respected position as actors, not objects, in world politics. All of these objectives are interconnected and in practice are pursued as a unit. However, the overriding national priority and key to all others is development.

Development is linked to national power and the achievement of meaningful national sovereignty and autonomy. Military leaders associated with the war schools of Argentina, Brazil, and Peru agree that industrialization is the key to development. Peru's General Edgardo Mercado Jarrin, who served as foreign minister until recently, and Argentina's General Juan E. Gugliamelli, former head of CONASE, stress that underdevelopment increases the risk of subversion and insurgency, and moreover that development is national security. Castro, Guevara, Sunkel, and Jaguaribe stress that industrialization is both an affirmation of national existence and the means of escape from external dependence imposed through international economic relationships. For all four, development will lead to sovereignty if it is autonomous; all key economic decisions must be made within the state by nationals responding solely to their own interests and points of view. Overall, development as an objective is an inward-looking, nation-building process. Even states with strong senses of powerlessness and subordination, such as Peru, view development as a critical, if minimal, objective on the international level as well as on the domestic level.[3]

Beyond the constellation of state-building objectives—development, security, and autonomy—the importance of moving to an active role in world affairs is recognized, even if it falls within the category of wishful thinking. Ferrer, Osvaldo Sunkel, and Raul Prebisch concur in their belief that Latin America must export manufactured products to world markets and must attempt to restructure its international financial and trading relationship in order to assure its continued economic growth and to secure its autonomy. In many cases they note that the import-substitution industrialization program implied by autonomous development has reached its limits. In short, inward-looking nation-building can be only a phase for Latin America.

The first frontier for pursuing all of these objectives is the internal one. In order to build strong nation-states, most analysts agree that Latin America must confront foreign influences at home. Jaguaribe gives Latin America thirty years to begin autonomous development before the pattern of dependence becomes fixed irrevocably. Either revolutionary socialism or independent capitalism based on nationally oriented entrepreneurs is necessary; the latter requires first deposing externally supported oligarchies which depend on the export of primary products. Prebisch has called for recognition of Latin America's determination to assume responsibility for its national economies at all levels. He also asserted that international trade and national development could have contradictory interests and requirements. Therefore, the roles of multinational corporations and foreign technology in Latin American economies must be reduced. Second, in accordance with the development-as-security perspective of Brazilian, Argentine, and Peruvian military men, Latin American countries are called upon to complete a heavy industrial base to to promote indigenous technology.

An independent foreign policy free of permanent alignments and entanglements is proposed as a second means for realizing Latin American international objectives. Mexican diplomat Jorge Castenada (1969: 138-141) describes his country's basic attitude toward world affairs as reserved, a product of its experience with uncontrolled foreign investment under Porfirio Diaz and with foreign intervention. General Velasco's intentions for Peru are similar. Most Argentine students of international affairs agree on the need for an independent foreign policy as well. In all countries a sense of national autonomy is being promoted. More specifically for Peruvians and Mexicans, the theme of nonaligned uniqueness is given practical expression.

Bloc action with other Latin American countries is an extension of an independent international position. Felipe Herrera sees regional integration as an expanded form of self-help designed to strengthen the national state by creating basic industries under multilateral but exclusively Latin American control. For Horacio Godoy and Jorge Castenada integration is a response to a global trend toward regionalism, a way to preserve Latin American values and identities against powerful foreign influences, and an economic necessity imposed by the large scale required for advanced technology. As an aid to industrialization, integration also helps to overcome external dependence in Jaguaribe's view.

Overall, Latin Americans see integration as an adjunct to state-building and not as the route to regional or supranational institutions. General Osiris Villegas of Argentina, who advocated creation of a domestic arms industry and independent industrialization in the 1960s, writes most recently of the need for regional economic cooperation (1973: 29-38). Without regionalism Argentina would have no assurance that its exports would be accepted by more advanced countries, and it would find development in isolation impossible. While Perón condemned the existing integration movement, he pointed to the European Economic Community as an example of national liberation (1971: 17). To sustain industrialization and to support Latin American unity, both Velasco and Allende supported the Andean Pact.

A unified Latin American position before outside countries also finds support. Castenada and Krieger Vasena see the need for joint Latin American negotiations with the United States on economic matters. Gabriel Valdes, Chile's foreign minister under Frei, called upon the United States to accept the emergence of a continental nationalism when he presented the Consensus of Vina del Mar to President Nixon in 1969. However, in practice most supporters of bloc action stop short of overt confrontation with the industrial nations and are not prepared to replace bilateral efforts completely.[4]

Ultimately the limits of self-help are recognized. ECLA has called for a revision of international economic arrangements to reverse Latin America's declining terms of trade and to enhance its opportunities to export manufactured products. Prebisch and others do find a role for foreign investment in partnership with local entrepreneurs. Above all they recognize the need to manage their bilateral relations with the great powers.

In Octavio Ianni's phrase, the United States is the inevitable variable in the Latin American future. Ianni, a Brazilian sociologist and regionalist, concentrates on Latin America's ability to resist U.S. influence and control as an important factor in national self-realization. Jaguaribe sees three alternatives. The United States could continue its present policies until it reaches the limits of its resources and revolution follows in Latin America. By moving to more direct forms of economic and political control, the United States could stabilize the region's satellite status. Or the United States could promote true international community in the hemisphere, Jaguaribe's preferred option. To achieve this end, the United States would have to promote autonomous development in the key countries of Argentina, Brazil, and Mexico, and allow the nationalization and regionalization of the technology required for national development in return for indemnification out of the resulting return to its users.

Despite the recognized importance of the United States, none of the analysts surveyed here, aside from Jaguaribe, offers any program for sweeping changes in relations aside from continued efforts to renegotiate economic and financial ties. They do foresee conflicts over the prices and ownership of raw materials, the transfer of technology, foreign investment, trade, and international financing. None favors a return to the Alliance for Progress era or a renewed emphasis on Pan Americanism. Taken collectively, Latin American world affairs analysts seem to suggest that policy concentrate on the domestic impact of United States influence and on long-term pursuit of economic issues. The absence of sweeping visions suggest Latin American passivity and lack of optimism.

In order to obtain maximum freedom of action, most analysts favor a diversification of Latin America's aid, trade, and financial relations with the world. In particular they look to Western Europe and Japan for expanded relations. Trade with the Soviet bloc and China offers some possibilities, but both are under suspicion as great powers. While some Latin Americans, such as Perón, see a community of interest with the Third World, they look elsewhere for the pursuit of substantive economic gains.

A growing skepticism and impatience characterize Latin American attitudes toward international organizations, most of which Latin Americans regard as creatures of the advanced countries. However, many are prepared to use existing organizations to pursue relations with the industrialized world. Valdes and Sunkel criticize the Organization of American States as primarily benefiting the United States, but they do recognize an inter-American system as a historic and geographical reality. Sunkel notes that international agencies consisting only of developing nations are too weak to be effective. In short, international agencies can be settings for continuing bilateral diplomacy with major powers, but institutionalized international cooperation is regarded as a myth.

All of Latin America's international options as presented by a cross-section of its foreign affairs analysts, lead to the following conclusions. Regionalists and nationalists accept the status of Latin American nations as regional powers at best, as local powers if possible, and minimally as states capable of mastering their internal affairs. Perón, Castro, and Brazil's Superior War School with their dreams of global importance are the exceptions, and even for them the absence of concrete programs of ends and means suggests a definite hollowness in the dream. Therefore, defensive measures at home combined with intra-Latin American cooperation offer the best prospects. Relations with outside powers will be pursued unoptimistically as a matter of necessity. Given prevailing visions of the international system, most of which see either a United States-Soviet spheres-of-influence arrangement or U.S. neutralization of Soviet influence in the hemisphere, major changes are distant.

LATIN AMERICANS ON LATIN AMERICA'S ROLE IN WORLD AFFAIRS

Within the limits of this survey it is possible to conclude that some consensus exists in Latin America on the future of the region and its individual nations in world affairs. Generally, Latin Americans see themselves as members of weak, externally penetrated societies in which great powers, multinational corporations, and international economic relationships play important roles. As a result nation-states in the classic sense of impervious units with a political supremacy over a defined territorial sphere do not exist. Latin American governments are seen as mediators between indigenous and nonindigenous actors and forces. These conditions are the product of under-development and the low power position of Latin American nations in the world. This assessment of the Latin American national condition also explains the preoccupation of scholars and policy-makers with economic forces.

For all analysts, national development is the prime task in foreign affairs. Domestically, development is the most critical issue, and the internal role of external forces makes it a foreign policy issue. Development is also seen as the means for creating sovereign states in the classic mold. Given present international conditions, most theorists and political leaders would probably settle for what they can perceive as balanced interdependence, possibly taking the form of regional cooperation within Latin America. With the exception of some Brazilians and Argentines, most Latin Americans would accept regional international roles, or minimally, a sense of national autonomy. Collective bargaining may produce some limited improvements, but most expect to stay under substantial United States influence. This situation has a high potential for frustration.

Given all of the foregoing factors, most Latin American interpretations of world affairs blur the distinctions between foreign and domestic policy. As a result theories of imperialism and victimization, combined with a tendency toward reactive nationalism, are important in the Latin American world view.

LATIN AMERICAN WORLD VIEWS AND
U.S. FOREIGN POLICY

Although not all of the theorists of international relations cited here are policy-makers, elements of their perspectives are visible in the international behavior of Latin American countries. Dependency theory is echoed in the various manifestoes in which the Special Latin American Coordinating Committee (CECLA) has called for revisions in United States-Latin American economic relations. ECLA's position on world trade is visible in recent statements by President Perez of Venezuela defending higher oil prices and attributing world economic disorder to the traditional disparity between the prices for raw materials and the prices for manufactured products. The Andean Group's restrictions on foreign investment and Argentina's sporadic attempts to build an arms industry are reflections of the autonomous development strategy.

As Prebisch noted in his report to the Inter-American Development Bank, Latin America is increasingly self-conscious and upwardly mobile. This search for self will surely take the form of a quest for foreign policies grounded in indigenous scholarship and indigenously developed world views. Therefore, the implications of emerging Latin American interpretation for United States foreign policy are important.

A blurring of the distinction between foreign and domestic affairs in Latin America combined with a focus on national weakness will make U.S. attempts to move toward noninvolvement and a low profile more difficult. Latin Americans will continue to press for concessions on the transfer of technology, the regulation of multinational corporations, and the rules for international trade and investment. U.S. protestations of disinterest or attempts to separate an official U.S. government interest from the interests of private U.S. corporations and citizens will not suffice. All foreign presences, overt and covert, actual or potential, deliberate and inadvertent, will cause friction.

Sensing that the international system at large is implacable and not subject to manipulation, Latin American governments will be tempted to turn toward internal affairs as much as possible and toward bloc actions as a second choice. As a result, the United States may find that Latin American countries are less amenable to global cooperation, particularly in the management of ecological and economic interdependencies. Attempts to build up the stature and influence of global and hemispheric organizations will fail unless the Latin Americans are convinced that they are equal partners. Reform of the international monetary system, changes in the Organization of American

States, and energy management come immediately to mind. From the U.S. perspective, bilateral rather than multilateral relations may be more successful because the recognized need to treat with the United States may override temptations to engage in intransigence or confrontation in this setting.

LATIN AMERICAN LESSONS FOR ACADEMICIANS

In a preliminary fashion Latin American approaches to world affairs support certain models of the international system and certain approaches to the links between political development and international relations. W. W. Rostow's observation (1971: 23) that external intrusion transmits modernization and evokes reactive nationalism in return seems to explain some of the premises of dependency theory and the linkage of development and national security. Reactive nationalism seems to play a role in the rhetoric of nonaligned uniqueness as practiced in Peru, or the flirtations with the Third World of a Perón or an Allende. Brazilian and Argentine dreams of world power seem to suggest Rostow's conclusion that early modernizers are tempted to engage in regional expansion.

In international politics several models are suggested. Robert C. Good's observations (1962: 7-9) about the role of foreign policy in state-building seem to be confirmed. The military leaders of Argentina, Brazil, and Peru appreciate the role of international activity in confirming national existence, asserting legitimacy, and promoting national unity. Mexicans, Peruvians, and Chileans have resorted to nonalignment to promote a sense of uniqueness. Argentines look to external affairs for a demonstration of the leadership's capacity to act. Models of the international system which stress the role of transnational relations or which characterize states as clusters of global system linked functionally by geographically confined administrative systems provide analytical insight into Latin American perspectives on their various national situations. (See, for example, Burton, 1968; Keohane and Nye, 1972.)

Scholars, diplomats, and idealists have been announcing the emergence of entities beyond the nation-state, visions of spaceship earth, and a world economy and society. Tottering national economies and governments in the developed and underdeveloped worlds and the global impact of famines, crop failures, terrorism, and power plays over scarce natural resources suggest that they may be right. However, in Latin America at least, the overriding goal is still the classical concept of the impermeable, sovereign territorial state. Scholars and policy-makers will have to take notice of such efforts, even if the objective is a phantom.

NOTES

1. Countries represented in FLACSO by public and private delegates: Argentina, Bolivia, Brazil, Chile, Colombia, Cuba, the Dominican Republic, Guatemala, Jamaica, Nicaragua, Mexico, Panama, Peru, Venezuela. Countries with member institutions of CLACSO: Argentina, Bolivia, Brazil, Colombia, Costa Rica, Chile, Mexico, Paraguay, Peru, Venezuela; additional institutional members of CLACSO: ILPES, the Latin American Center for Social Science Research of Rio de Janeiro, the Latin American Demography Center of Santiago.

2. Francisco C. Weffort (1970) criticizes the dependency theorists for confusing nation and class. Weffort, a Brazilian, teaches at the University of Sao Paulo. The range of emphasis between class or group and nation extends from Marcos Kaplan (1969: 141-142), for a class-oriented view, to Osvaldo Sunkel and Pedro Paz (1970: 158-165), for a group- and nation-oriented study. See David Ray (1973) for a critique.

3. On autonomous industrialization see Peruvian career diplomat Canepo Sardon, 1971; Bonachea and Valdes, 1969; Sunkel, 1967; Jaguaribe, 1969; Sunkel and Paz, 1970. For a Marxist interpretation see Frank, 1969a: 18-21; on autonomy see Velasco, 1970: 366; Meirelles Padilha, 1971: 36. Meirelles is Secretary of the Alumni Association of ESG. See also ADESG; "Informe del Presidente de la Republica" (Mexico), p. 407; and Cardona, 1962: 28.

4. The Viña del Mar Consensus was a Latin American position paper produced by the Special Latin American Coordinating Committee, CECLA, representing all of the region except Cuba. On bloc action see Krieger Vasena, 1973: 165-166; and Castenada, 1958: 9-11.

REFERENCES

ALLENDE, S. (1971) "La politica exterior de Chile." Presidential message to Congress, May 21. Reprinted in Revista Latinoamericana de Geopolitica (September).

ALSOGARY, A. (1969) Politica y economia en Latinoamerica. Buenos Aires: Editorial Atlantida.

Andean Commission (1970) "Decision concerning treatment of foreign capital." Decision 24 (December 31) in International Legal Materials 1, 1.

Argentine Republic (1970) Plan Nacional de desarrollo y seguridad 1971-1975. Buenos Aires: Presidencia de la Nacion.

ARUJO CASTRO, J. A. de (1971) "Congelamento de Poder Mundial." Segurança e Desenvolvimento. Rio de Janeiro: ADESG.

BONACHEA, R. E. and N. P. VALDES [eds.] (1969) Che, The Selected Works of Ernesto Guevara. Cambridge: MIT Press.

BURTON, J. W. (1968) Systems, States, Diplomacy and Rules. Cambridge, Eng.: Cambridge University Press.

Cambio social (1970) Santiago: Centro de Estudios Economicos, Universidad de Chile.

CAMILION, O. (1969) "Notas para una estrategia internacional argentina." Estrategia 1, 1 (June).

CANEPO SARDON, A. (1971) La revolucion peruana, ensayo polemico. Buenos Aires: Editorial Paracas.

CARDONA, S. (1962) "La politica exterior de Mexico y el derecho internacional." Ciencia Politicas y Sociales 8, 27 (January-March).

CARDOSO, F. H. and E. FALLETO (1971) Dependencia y desarrollo en América Latina. Mexico: Siglo Veintiuno Editores.

CASANOVA, P. G. (1970) Democracy in Mexico. New York: Oxford University Press.

CASTENADA, J. (1969) "Revolution and foreign policy: Mexico's experience," in C. Astiz (ed.) Latin American International Politics. South Bend: University of Notre Dame Press.

――― (1958) "Pan Americanismo: Posição do Mexico." Revista Brasileira de Política Internacional 1, 3 (September).

Comercio Exterior (1973) "Informe del Presidente de la Republica (Mexico) sobre su viaje por tres continentes." (May).

DO COUTO E SILVA, G. (1967) Geopolitica do Brasil. Rio de Janeiro: Olympia.

Economic Commission for Latin America (1964) El Comercio Internacional y el desarrollo de America Latina. Mexico, D.F.: Fondo Cultura Economica.

――― (1950) The Economic Development of Latin America and Its Principal Problems. United Nations Document E/CN. 12/89/Rev. 1.

FERRER, A. (1973) "Argentina: alternatives economicas del nuevo gobierno." Comercio Exterior 23, 5 (May).

――― (1969) "Industrias basicas, integración, y corporaciones internacionales," in Jaguaribe and others (eds.) La dependencia politica-económica de América Latina. Mexico: Siglo Veintiuno Editores.

――― (1967) The Argentine Economy. Berkeley: University of California.

Fidel in Chile, A Symbolic Meeting Between Two Historical Processes (1972). New York: International Publishers.

FRANK, A. G. (1969a) Capitalism and Underdevelopment in Latin America, Historical Studies of Chile and Brazil. New York: Monthly Review Press.

――― (1969b) Latin America, Underdevelopment or Revolution: Essays on the Development and Underdevelopment and the Immediate Enemy. New York: Monthly Review Press.

GELBARD, J. (1973) Politica económica y social: ruptura de la dependencia, unidad y reconstrucción nacional con la justicia social para la liberación; mensaje del señor Ministro de Hacienda y Finanzas Don Jose B. Gelbard con motivo de celebrarse la 2 Reunion de Gobernadores del Gobierno del Pueblo. Buenos Aires: Presidencia de la Nacion.

GERASSI, J. [ed.] Venceremos: The Speeches and Writings of Ernesto Che Guevara. New York: Macmillan.

GODOY, H. (1968) "La integración de America Latina y el proceso del poder mundial." Estudiós Internacionales 2, 3 (October-December).

GOOD, R. C. (1962) "State building as a determinant of foreign policy in the new states," in L. W. Martin (ed.) Neutralism and Non-Alignment. New York: Frederick A. Praeger.

HERRERA, F. (1969) Chile en América Latina. Santiago: Editorial Zig-Zag.

HOFFMAN, S. (1968) "Obstinate or obsolete? the fate of the nation-state and the case of Western Europe," in J. L. Nye (ed.) International Regionalism. Boston: Little, Brown.

HOWE, M. (1974) "Prices defended by Venezuelans." New York Times (October 7): 57.

IANNI, O. (1970) Imperialismo y cultura de violencia en América Latina. Mexico: Siglo Veintiuno Editores.

――― (1968) "Os Estados Unidos a Situacão Latino-Americana." Revista Civilização Brasileira (September-December).

JAGUARIBE, H. (1973) *Political Development, a general theory and a Latin American Case Study.* New York: Harper and Row.
——— (1969) "Dependencia y autonomia en América Latina," in H. Jaguaribe and others (eds.) *La dependencia politica-económica de América Latina.* Mexico: Siglo Veintiuno Editores.
JARRIN, E. M. (1969) "Insurgency in Latin America: its impact on political and military strategy." B. Pallo (trans.) Military Review 49, 6 (March).
JOHNSON, D. L. [ed.] (1973) *The Chilean Road to Socialism.* New York: Doubleday-Anchor.
KAPLAN, M. (1972) "La politica exterior de América Latina y de Estados Unidos en una situación de cambio." Comercia Exterior 22, 12 (December).
——— (1969) *Formación del estado nacional en América Latina.* Santiago: Editorial Universitaria.
KENNER, M. [ed.] (1969) *Fidel Castro Speaks.* New York: Grove Press.
KEOHANE, R. O. and J. S. NYE [eds.] (1972) *Transnational Relations and World Politics.* Cambridge: Harvard University Press.
KRIEGER VASENA, A. and J. PAZOS (1973) *Latin America, A Broader World Pole.* London: Ernest Benn Ltd.
LAGOS, G. (1963) *International Stratification and Underdeveloped Countries.* Chapel Hill: University of North Carolina.
MEIRELLES PADILHA, T. (1971) "Segurança Nacional." Segurança e Desenvolvimento 20, 147.
MEYER, L. (1972) "Cambio político y dependencia: Mexico en el siglo xx." Foro Internacional 13, 1 (July-September).
PASTORE, J. M. D. (1971) *Politica economica Argentina 1969-1970.* Buenos Aires: Marcos Victor Durrutz.
PERÓN, J. D. (1971) "El problema de la liberación." Revista Latinoamericana de Geopolitica (September) Buenos Aires: Centro de Estudios e Investigaciones Sociales.
PREBISCH, R. (1970) "Change and Development: Latin America's Great Task." Report Submitted to the Inter-American Development Bank. Washington, D.C.: The Inter-American Development Bank.
QUADROS, J. (1969) "Brazil's new foreign policy," in C. Astiz (ed.) *Latin American International Politics.* South Bend: University of Notre Dame Press.
RAY, D. (1973) "The dependency model of Latin American development: three basic fallacies." Journal of Inter-American Development Studies and World Affairs 15, 1 (February).
ROSTOW, W. W. (1971) *Politics and the Stages of Growth.* Cambridge, Eng.: Cambridge University Press.
SILVA MICHELENA, J. (1973) "Tendencias recientes en la política mundial." Estudios Internacionales 6, 23: 10-20.
SUNKEL, O. (1971) "Capitalismo transnacional y disintegración nacional en América Latina." Estudios Internacionales (January-March).
——— (1967) "Politica nacional de desarrollo y dependencia externa." Estudios Internacionales (April).
——— and P. PAZ (1970) *El Subdesarrollo latinoamericano y la teoria del desarrollo.* Mexico: Siglo Veintiuno Editores.
TORRES RIVAS, E. (1970) "Desarrollo, integración, y dependencia en Centroamérica." Estudios Internacionales 4, 12 (January-March).

URIBURU, E. J. (1970) *El Plan Europa un intento de liberación nacional.* Buenos Aires: Cruz de Fierro Editores.

VALDES, G. (1970) *Conciencia latinoamericana y realidad internacional.* Santiago: Editorial de Pacifico.

VELASCO ALVARADO, J. (1970) *La Voz de revolución, discursos 1968-1970.* Lima: Ediciones Peisa.

VILLANUEVA, V. (1972) *El CAEM y la revolución de la Fuerza Armada.* Lima: Instituto de Estudios Peruanos, Campodonico.

VILLEGAS, O. G. (1973) "Estrategia para un futuro." Revista de la Escuela Superior de Guerra 60, 409.

––– (1967) "La industria y la seguridad nacional." Revista de la Escuela Superior de Guerra 45, 374.

WEFFORT, F. C. (1970) "Notas sobre la teoria de la dependencia: ¿iteoria de clase o ideologia nacional?" Revista Latinoamericana de Ciencia Politica 1, 3 (December). Santiago: FLACSO.

Chapter 6

PERU'S DIPLOMATIC OFFENSIVE:

SOLIDARITY FOR LATIN AMERICAN INDEPENDENCE

ROBERT H. SWANSBROUGH

After seizing power in 1968, the Peruvian Revolutionary Junta mounted a diplomatic campaign on behalf of Latin American solidarity. The Peruvian generals advocate Latin American solidarity as the only viable means to achieve political and economic independence and end the hemisphere domination by the industrialized great powers. Solidarity often appears, however, as simply a catchword for joint action against the United States' political hegemony and economic preeminence in the region. Nevertheless, the Junta's campaign for hemispheric unity represents a significant development in the inter-American system.

The Revolutionary Junta deems fragmentation among the developing nations a primary cause of their dependence and underdevelopment, and believes that only solidarity can overcome their powerlessness and poverty. Peruvian leaders assert that disunity among the hemispheric republics—often fomented by the great powers—condemns the region to impotence, frustration, and subordination. The hope for solidarity lies in the growing sense of Latin American nationalism, founded upon a common history and shared economic conditions. These men see the future of the Peruvian Revolution as "indissoluably united" with the destiny of Latin America; similarly, they link the prospect of hemispheric security to the success of the Peruvian Revolution. Therefore, the Peruvian military regime views Latin American solidarity as more than simply a theoretical concept or rallying cry. Solidarity serves as a basic technique to ensure the Peruvian Revolution's autonomy and to fulfill Latin America's political and economic aspirations.

The idea of Latin American solidarity arises from the assumption that shared Latin American values and interests form a basis for coordinated regional policy. Solidarity thus reflects the ideal of hemispheric unity that many Latin Americans have voiced since independence was achieved in the nineteenth century. In Peru this ideal was part of the anti-imperialist program of Haya de la Torre, foe of the Peruvian military in the 1920s. The Revolutionary Junta vigorously promotes the cause of Latin American solidarity as a cornerstone of its foreign policy. Peruvian military leaders believe the growing mineral shortage provides the hemisphere's producer nations with the bargaining power to alter the subordinate relations of the past; they consider the restiveness and aspirations of Latin America the motor force for joint action. Peru's diplomatic offensive thus seems well-timed for maximum impact on a changing hemisphere.

The Revolutionary Junta justifies its October 1968 takeover in terms of the dependency thesis expounded for many years by the United Nations' Economic Commission for Latin America (ECLA). President Juan Velasco Alvarado (1972: vol. 1, 63) declares: "To cancel the traditional dependence of our country is the fundamental object of the nationalist revolution and the central goal of full development of Peru." The proposed settlement between the International Petroleum Company (IPC) and the civilian government of President Fernando Belaúnde Terry had precipitated the military coup in 1968; the Junta then expropriated IPC's interests in Peru. It views the IPC expropriation as only the first battle in a long war to achieve independence from the developed countries.

The military regime considers Peru's dependency the result of a global power structure in which the industrialized nations keep the less developed countries in subordinate positions through their political, economic, and cultural domination. In the post-World-War-II years, according to Peruvian spokesmen, a bipolar international system developed around the United States and the Soviet Union. The two superpowers agreed to transfer the tensions of the ideological conflict to the countries of Asia, Africa, and Latin America because of the dangers inherent in a direct cold war confrontation. Peruvian officials are aware of the disintegration of the bipolar world and the emergence of a multipolar power configuration. The Junta describes Peru's "anti-imperialist" revolution as an integral part of the insurgence of the poor nations of the world against foreign domination. Therefore, Peru must defend its sovereignty and natural riches against the encroachments of the great powers through solidarity with other Third World nations.

This study examines the Peruvian campaign for Latin American solidarity. It discusses Peru's support of other hemispheric nations in confrontations with the United States. The chapter appraises Peru's new leadership role in hemispheric affairs, an outgrowth of its vigorous promotion of unity, and considers Peru's rivals in its bid for regional leadership. It then evaluates the impact of Peru's diplomatic offensive on the United States and questions whether Peru's new international status and activity foster greater domestic support for the Revolutionary Junta.

SOLIDARITY AGAINST U.S. HEGEMONY

Peru demonstrates solidarity with its Latin American neighbors by taking their side in controversies with the United States. Ecuador's historic hostility toward neighboring Peru, a product of wars and border disputes, abated through Peru's policy of hemispheric solidarity. The Revolutionary Government of the Armed Forces protested in 1971 when the United States curtailed military assistance to Ecuador after that country's seizure of American fishing boats. Peru condemned this sanction as neither admissible in law nor tolerable in action, since Ecuador had only exercised sovereign control over its territorial waters. The joint Peruvian-Ecuadorian defense of the 200-mile territorial waters claim and their close economic cooperation within the Andean Common Market helped heal earlier scars and tensions between them. The two nations agreed to develop joint projects in their Amazon border zones and to permit the transit of persons and vehicles in these areas. Peru's solidarity policy, bolstered by political fence-mending, thus contributed toward changing a former enemy into a diplomatic ally (Slaght, 1973).

When Chile's President Salvador Allende visited Peru, President Velasco (1972: vol. II, 171) declared that the 1971 meeting "fortified the sentiment of solidarity between two autonomous and different revolutionary processes." Peru backed the Allende Administration in 1972 when Kennecott Copper Corporation sought a French court order to freeze payment on a shipment of Chilean copper; Kennecott wanted to recover part of the losses from the expropriation of its Chilean properties. Peru and seven other Latin American nations promptly affirmed Chile's right to freely dispose of its natural resources. Several months later Peru voted with the other members of the Council of Copper Exporting Countries (CIPEC) to suspend dealings with Kennecott until the legal maneuvers halted. The members agreed not to take advantage of any vacuum caused by Chile's temporary exclusion from the world copper market. The Peruvian government also supported the attack that Allende made in the United Nations against the economic pressures exerted by the United States on behalf of American firms; the Chilean protest touched sensitive Peruvian memories of their IPC dispute with the United States.

Peru manifested solidarity with Cuba by calling for normalization of relations with Cuba in its June 1972 Organization of American States (OAS) resolution. The resolution's provisions would grant nations the freedom to establish relations with Cuba on the level most convenient to each. Spokesmen point out that the prolonged isolation of Cuba sharply contrasts with the thaw in the cold war, a thaw reflected in the United States' cordial relations with China and the admission of the People's Republic of China to the United Nations. Peru bases its diplomatic stance on the belief that Cuba no longer constitutes a danger to the peace and security of the continent. Peruvian officials argue that even though the vote was 13 to 7 against the resolution, the vote and abstention of Venezuela, the 1964 sponsor of the motion to exclude Cuba, represent the growing opposition to the United States' Cuban policy. Peru reestablished relations with Fidel Castro's regime in July 1972. An agreement on fishing for human consumption cements the restored relations. Cuba sent three vessels to help the joint endeavor in Peruvian waters. Peruvian shipyards also received a $30 million contract to build 98 shrimp boats and 12 tuna boats for Cuba.

The Revolutionary Government endorsed Panama's United Nations effort to remove the Canal Zone from United States jurisdiction; Peru and Panama co-sponsored the Security Council resolution calling for a new treaty and neutralization of the Panama Canal. Peruvian diplomats labeled the Canal Zone a "colonial enclave" at the March 1973 meeting. (See the remarks of Foreign Minister General Miguel Angel de la Flor Valle in *El Peruano*, March 16, 1973.) Peru's Foreign Minister stated that Panama had the sovereign right to freely enjoy the benefits of its natural resources—an argument which echoes Peruvian claims of jurisdiction over its offshore resources. Thirteen nations supported the Security Council motion, compelling the United States to use its veto. During the January 1974 visit of Panamanian General Omar Torrijos to Peru, a joint declaration issued by President Velasco and General Torrijos reiterated support for Panamanian jurisdiction over the Canal Zone and the 200-mile maritime limit and emphasized the continuing solidarity between Peru and Panama.

Peruvians proudly recognize their nation's leadership in international forums on the issue of extending territorial waters to 200 miles. Asserting that sovereign nations have the inalienable right to protect their natural resources, the Revolutionary Junta defends the Peruvian 200-mile thesis on the Law of the Sea, which has been advanced since 1947. Peruvian spokesmen deem the offshore riches of many Third World nations vital for their development, and cite in evidence the rise of Peru's fishmeal industry into a key factor in the nation's economic growth. The opposition of the United States and the Soviet Union to the Peruvian doctrine is held up as evidence that the highly industrialized nations will not allow the developing countries to break their bonds of dependency and underdevelopment: "The controversy over the limits of maritime sovereignty is the conflict of interests between the great powers and the less developed countries." (See, for example, the speech made by Peruvian Foreign Minister General Edgardo Mercado Jarrin to the Latin American Meeting on the Problems of the Law of the Sea: August 4, 1970.)

As proof of its commitment to this doctrine, the military regime headlines Peru's seizures of U.S. fishing vessels and its support for other coastal nations in maritime disputes with the United States. In early 1973 the Peruvian navy captured 23 American fishing vessels in less than a month and fined them $742,860 (see the Washington Post, April 12, 1973). This compares with a total of only 37 seizures and $191,500 in fines and charges during the previous twelve years.[1] The dramatic escalation of the conflict over fishing rights came in response to the United States' 1972 passage of the Pelly Amendment to the Fishing Protection Act. The new provision required the Secretary of State to withhold aid to a country equal to any fines and charges levied against American fishing vessels.

It appears to this observer that Peru's entry into the group of nonaligned nations in June 1973 represented a major diplomatic move to gain Third World support. The Revolutionary Junta's spokesmen at the September 1973 Kabul meeting of nonaligned countries expounded Peru's position on the Rights of the Sea issue. Peruvian officials subsequently heralded the fact that Peru's Resolution of the Law of the Sea was endorsed by over 80 percent of the nations attending the Algerian conference as the "most visible success" in Peru's fight for adoption of this principle (see El Peruano, December 26, 1973). Solidarity thus bolsters the Peruvian initiative to foster the Third World's development and independence.

The Revolutionary Junta also applies the formula of solidarity for independence in its campaign to revamp the Organization of American States. The member states unanimously approved Peru's April 1973 resolution to create a special commission to study the inter-American system. When Peru hosted the first meeting of the Reorganization Commission, Foreign Minister Miguel Angel de la Flor Valle charged that "the so-called inter-American system represents the consolidation of the hegemonic policies of one power within a system based on extracontinental interference and intracontinental tutelage." Peru seeks to revise the Treaty of Reciprocal Assistance in order to free Latin American nations of the risks associated with supporting the global policies of the United States in its cold war struggle with the Soviet Union.

Peru urged the OAS to adopt the principle of ideological pluralism, defined as "the respect for self-determination, non-intervention and the formulation by each society of its own political organization" (1973, OAS

Special Committee to Study the Inter-American System: 27). Peruvians argue that the hemispheric ideal of representative democracy often leads to external intervention by a "Holy Alliance of liberal leanings," which imposes a particular understanding of democracy. When Venezuela threatened to leave the OAS if the goal of fostering democratic governments was altered in any way, Peruvian diplomats responded that ideological pluralism embraced representative governments as well as other types of democratic regimes—such as Peru's Social Democracy with Full Participation. The OAS eventually approved a modified concept calling for a "plurality of ideologies."

The Peruvian Junta spurns the interpretation of continental security that the OAS has followed in recent years. It feels that the United States perverted the idea of regional security from its purpose of preventing extrahemispheric aggression to a pretext for obstructing internal structural changes. Peruvian diplomats promote their concept of security by accenting the importance of development to overcome the internal conditions which breed unrest and poverty in the region. They also seek greater protection against any form of financial or economic coercion by advancing the notion of economic collective security.

The Revolutionary Government incorporated these ideas into its proposal to establish within the inter-American system a Permanent Council for Political and Juridical Affairs and a Permanent Council for Development. Both councils would have their headquarters in Latin America, and each would be authorized to investigate charges of intrahemispheric economic and military aggression. It was hoped that these new mechanisms for regional cooperation would eliminate paternalism, tutelage, discrimination, or intervention. Peru issued an imperative regarding the lack of balance in the relationship between Latin America and the United States:

> Should this effort to create a truly free and constructive inter-Americanism for today and tomorrow fail now, we feel it would be much better for us to go our separate ways; Latin America on one side, the United States on the other, and stop this tiresome game of recrimination and frustration.

The Peruvian ultimatum expressed a question that was being raised in many Latin American capitals: Would a solid hemispheric front outside of the OAS offer the republics better leverage in negotiations with the United States?

UNITY FOR ECONOMIC INDEPENDENCE

The Peruvian Government advances solidary action as the only means of ensuring participation of Third World nations in international economic affairs. The demand for participation rejects paternalistic or authoritarian behavior by the great powers. "The underdeveloped countries cannot continue being objects of policies in whose formulation they have not participated, being assigned the role of mute spectators" (see United Nations General Assembly notes for September 30, 1973). Peruvian officials advise developing nations that their power of negotiation corresponds directly to their unity.

As models for united hemispheric action vis-a-vis the highly industrialized nations, the Revolutionary Junta cites the success of the Special Commission for Latin American Coordination (CECLA), an exclusively Latin American entity, and of the Andean Common Market. Peruvian spokesmen laud CECLA's 1969 adoption of the Consensus of Vina del Mar as proof that Latin American unity can be achieved on economic matters; the document followed the Peruvian Doctrine on International Cooperation formulated by the Peruvian Foreign Ministry (Llosa, 1972: 121). CECLA is considered a possible avenue for regional protests against United States policies, such as the "unfair" dumping of U.S. mineral reserves on the world market, which adversely affect the hemisphere's economies.

Peru's leaders point to the Andean Group's Code on Foreign Investment as an illustration of how collective action allows Latin American nations to defend their economies against the power of multinational firms. The restrictive Code on Foreign Investment, partly patterned after Peru's General Law of Industries, prohibits new foreign investment in sensitive economic sectors and requires fade-out formulas and joint ventures to ensure local ownership and control over key resources and industries. Peruvian diplomats also urge the member nations to establish joint policies on trade and unified positions on commerical relations with the Common Market, Japan, and the East European Council for Mutual Economic Assistance (COMECON).

The Revolutionary Junta emphasizes that the formation of producer cartels permits developing nations to negotiate the best prices for their natural resources. President Velasco bluntly declares: "Union has force" (January 10, 1974, *La Prensa*). In 1969 he told CIPEC that since Peru, Chile, Zaire, and the Congo control 80 percent of the world's exportable copper, they have in their hands the power to attain just and balanced copper prices. Velasco's 1971 address to the Group of 77 called for a realistic and effective union of Third World nations through the creation of permanent organizations to deal with common problems. In 1973 a Peruvian spokesman supported the formation of the Latin American Organization of Energy (OLADE), arguing that the developing countries' natural resources represent the "Power of the Poor."

Peruvian officials view the effectiveness of the 1973 Arab oil boycott as a lesson to open the eyes of other producer nations. The Organization of Petroleum Exporting Countries (OPEC) demonstrated that control over the production and commercialization of natural resources "is an effective instrument to change the terms of dependency, limit the decapitalization of our economies, and attain a better distribution of the world's income," according to Foreign Minister General De la Flor (for full text see *El Peruano*, April 15, 1974). At the 1974 special UN session on raw materials, Peru's Foreign Minister rejected the United States' proposal for an interdependent world without cartels as a euphemism to hide the reality of domination. Instead, Peru advocated the establishment and strengthening of Third World producer associations and coordination among these associations to gain just prices for raw materials. To this end, Peru participated in the June OPEC meeting in Quito. The Peruvian Minister of Energy actively sought the invitation by visiting Arab oil-producing countries and Venezuela, where he stressed Peru's support of OPEC in international forums and noted that Peru would export petroleum by 1976.

Peruvian leaders also advocate the diversification of Latin American export markets in order to reduce the region's dependence on the United States market. Diversification represents an important aspect of Peru's economic policy, as exemplified in trade agreements with communist countries and warm relations with Japan. Peru signed commercial conventions with Hungary, Czechoslovakia, Poland, and Rumania to diversify and fortify Peru's independence from traditional markets; Peru also obtained additional economic, financial, and technical assistance. When Peru and the Soviet Union signed a 1969 trade pact, Peru's Foreign Minister declared that the new commercial front ended "an era in which our trade was channeled in only one direction." In 1970 the U.S.S.R. granted Peru $30 million in credits to purchase Soviet machinery. Peru ignored U.S. entreaties and voted for the United Nations admission of the People's Republic of China; three months later Peru recognized the government of the People's Republic. Peru's "concrete interest" benefited from this policy shift because the Chinese regime announced its support of the Peruvian doctrine of a 200-mile offshore jurisdiction; China also granted Peru a twenty-year, interest-free $42.5 million loan. Peru's trade with communist countries rose dramatically, with 1968 exports of $21 million climbing in 1972 to $128.6 million (IMF Trade Annual, 1973: 193). Commercial credits played a small role in the increased trade, despite the public fanfare. Peru drew only about $10 to 12 million from the $240 million in credits granted by the socialist nations. High fishmeal and mineral prices allowed Peru to purchase cheaper and better products in the West or Japan.

Peru seeks Japanese investment to replace the prominence of American capital in its economy. The Revolutionary Junta's plans for worker participation in management led Japanese private investors to share the U.S. business community's reluctance to invest in Peru. However, the Japanese show less caution than American firms about entering into joint ventures and dealing with state-owned enterprises; Japan's critical need for imported raw materials encourages greater flexibility. The Japanese requirements for minerals such as petroleum coincide with Peru's quest for diversified sources of financing and investment to develop its resources. The Bank of Tokyo announced in 1974 that a consortium of Japanese and foreign banks had loaned Peru $50 million for economic development. Then, in May 1974 the Japan Petroleum Corporation signed a $330 million agreement with Peru's state-owned petroleum corporation PetroPeru to finance petroleum exploration and development in the northern Amazon region and construction of a pipeline from the oilfields to the coast. Peru will pay off the ten-year loan through contracted sales of crude and refined petroleum to Japan at international market prices. Exports to Japan increased from $128 million in 1968 to $167 million in 1972; imports of Japanese goods doubled to a 1972 level of $78 million, giving Peru a favorable trade balance with Japan (IMF Trade Annual, 1973: 192). Peru thus demonstrates to other Latin American nations that an independent foreign policy can lessen economic dependence on the United States.

Although the Junta's nationalist policies resulted in a diminished flow of private capital into the Peruvian economy in the years immediately following the Revolution, the discovery of oil in Peru's remote jungles overcame the misgivings of many investors.[2] Some Peruvian spokesmen, however, still characterize foreign investment as a "suction mechanism" turning the poor Latin American countries into exporters of capital and financers of the spectacular development of the industrialized countries. One official charges that the large multinational firms are "modern corsairs" who do not acknowledge, respect, or obey the laws of any country. This attitude leads the Peruvian government to seek regional and international curbs on the power of multinational corporations. Yet the Junta wants foreign capital, provided that businessmen accept its new rules of the game. However, they issue a clear warning regarding the investment climate in contemporary Peru: "The days of indiscriminate investments, unlimited profits, utilization of Peruvian wealth for the exclusive benefit of foreign enterprises, are definitely over in Peru." (See Velasco, 1972, vol. II: 81.)

HEMISPHERIC LEADER OR THREAT?

Through its diplomatic offensive, the Revolutionary Government achieved Peru's long-sought position of leadership among the nations of the west coast of Latin America. Peru's traditional rival, Chile, was weakened and separated from other hemispheric countries by internal disorders and the Marxist orientation of its president.[3] However, the toppling of the Allende Administration may negatively affect Peru's preeminent stature in Pacific Coast affairs. Peruvian proposals and policies appeared less threatening to the status quo when flanked by the more radical Allende regime.

The Peruvian Junta undoubtedly feels more isolated since Allende's ouster. The Revolutionary Government saw how the economic and financial pressures of the United States contributed to Chile's internal chaos. It finds itself surrounded by rightist military regimes in Chile, Bolivia, Brazil, and Uruguay. And most ominous from Peru's viewpoint, there now looms the danger of an alliance between the hardline governments of Chile and Brazil. The potential of such a combination stirs painful memories of the War of the Pacific and awakens a fear of future hostilities, with oil rather than nitrates as the winner's prize.

This Peruvian nightmare seemed about to become a reality in March 1974 as rumors spread of an anti-Marxist pact between Brazil, Chile, Uruguay, and Bolivia after a summit meeting of their leaders. Brazil's President Ernesto Geisel proposed that Chile cede Bolivia a narrow corridor to the port of Arica. Peru immediately objected that such a plan violated the 1929 Treaty of Ancon; Chile could not offer Bolivia an exit to the sea through former Peruvian territories without Peru's consent. Peruvian leaders referred to a July 1973 Peru-Bolivia declaration in which Peru acknowledged the aspirations of its old friend, Bolivia, for an end to its landlocked situation—but stipulated that they must be realized within international law. President Velasco's comments in the newspaper *El Peruano* reflect Peru's nationalist sentiments on the issue: "In principle, Peru is not going to cede a single inch of its territory."

The question of a Bolivian exit to the sea arose at a time when tensions were high over an arms race between Chile and Peru. Peruvian officials stated after Allende's ouster that its policy toward Chile was nonintervention; each nation had to resolve problems in its own way. However, subsequent disclosures indicate that the Peruvian military leaders assessed the Chilean coup as a change in Latin America's balance of power. President Velasco asserted only a month after the coup that he had read reports that Chile had purchased $50 million worth of arms; he said this action required Peru to obtain more armaments as a national insurance policy. In December, Velasco shocked the hemisphere by admitting that Peru had bought Soviet tanks.[4] Peruvian leaders explained that they first requested arms from the United States but were refused; they then sought French tanks but found them too expensive. The arrival of six Soviet military advisers to demonstrate the new tanks stirred additional rumors. The Revolutionary Junta criticized these rumors as a campaign to portray Peru as a belligerent and champion of an arms race. In an extraordinary move to end speculation about an imminent war, President Velasco issued a ten-point statement which flatly declared: "Peru, loyal to its pacific policy, rejects all possibilities of a confrontation with the Chilean people."

Ironically, the danger of an intrahemispheric conflict arose after Velasco's speech in January 1974 calling for a ten-year freeze on Latin American arms purchases and allocation of these funds for economic and social development. Colombia responded favorably, mentioning its own 1971 OAS proposal for a similar pact; Panama's Torrijos praised the suggestion. Chile's President Augusto Pinochet lauded Velasco's appeal for an arms limitation as "brilliant and fundamental," but then countered by recommending the creation of a commission to determine the bellicose capacity of each nation in the region. Chile knew that Peru had been reequipping its armed forces since 1967. Peruvian diplomats placed the arms freeze idea before the Andean Group but did not present the plan to the OAS. Despite the president's proposal, Peru's Minister of Aeronautics announced in June 1974 that the Air Force would purchase 40 Mirage (French) and Canberra (British) aircraft to replace obsolete units. The Mirage jets are being bought despite Peru's severed diplomatic relations with France in protest over the 1973 French atomic tests in the Pacific; the acquisition shows little confidence in Velasco's arms limitation proposal.

Tensions with other Latin American nations also undercut Peru's solidarity policy. Brazil's suggestion of a Bolivian exit to the sea aroused Peruvian fears about Brazil's expansionist plans, despite Brazil's apparent lack of interest in an anti-Marxist alliance with Chile. Yet bilateral relations benefited from Brazil's desire to purchase Peru's petroleum and minerals, and from interest in a joint development of the Amazon, and completion of the Trans-Amazon highway. Peruvian leaders sharply reacted, though, against President Richard Nixon's praise of Brazil as the future leader of Latin America. Venezuela challenged Peru's hemispheric leadership when President Carlos Andres Perez pledged to use Venezuela's oil wealth to force trade concessions for Latin America from the United States. Peru's resentment was demonstrated in Velasco's criticism of Venezuela's President for wanting to enlarge the anniversary celebration in Peru of the Battle of Ayacucho to include all Latin American presidents.

Mexico is Peru's most active rival for leadership of Spanish-speaking Latin America and recognition as the hemisphere's Third World spokesman. Mexico opposed Peru's call for a world monetary conference in which developing nations and industrialized countries would each have one vote. Mexico stated that there was no need for new mechanisms while the International Monetary Fund (IMF) was considering the global monetary crisis and President Nixon's New Economic Policy. Peru partially won the struggle in 1972 by gaining acceptance of the need to reform the mechanisms of the monetary system and to add representatives of the developing nations to such councils. However, Mexico, not Peru, became a Third World member on the IMF's Committee of 20. Mexico's President Luis Echeverria also sought Third World recognition in 1972 when he proposed that the United Nations adopt a Charter of Economic Rights and Duties of States. The Charter asserts a developing country's sovereign right to freely dispose of its natural resources. But while the two nations clashed on many issues, each continued to deny any desire to be the leader of Latin America.

The death of Juan Peron further weakened Peru's hemispheric campaign. The friendship with Argentina had counter-balanced Chile's approach to Brazil. Peruvian military leaders lauded Peron's administration for its anti-imperialism and common policies with Peru in the OAS and United Nations; they heralded President Peron as a great hemispheric statesman. Peru affirmed solidarity with Argentina by supporting its claim to the Falkland Islands and calling for Argentina's admission to full membership in the Andean Common Market.

The renewed interest of U.S. policy-makers in Latin American affairs also affected Peru's diplomatic offensive. The personal prestige and charm of Secretary of State Henry Kissinger at the 1974 Mexico City meeting of foreign ministers reduced hostility toward the United States. U.S. agreements with Mexico on salinization, with Peru on settlement of claims for expropriated U.S. property, and with Panama on a renegotiated canal treaty signaled a more attentive and sensitive policy toward the region. Mr. Kissinger's speech invoking the "Spirit of Tlatelolco" symbolized a new era of inter-American understanding and cooperation. Peru's gadfly attacks on U.S. regional dominance met increasing hemispheric resistance, since such stridency appeared to threaten the Spirit of Tlatelolco. Solidarity against the United States proved more attractive when Washington ignored Latin America; CECLA's prodding role seemed unnecessary if the influential Henry Kissinger listened and responded to the region's problems. Peru continued to send its extremely well-prepared diplomatic delegations into the field, but the new dialogue muted their efforts; nationalist resentments against Peru's assertive hemispheric policy became evident in OAS reorganization sessions. In addition, the foreign ministers' decision in Atlanta to reform the OAS through majority votes in committee rather than by consensus politics undermined Peru's diplomatic leverage. The momentum of Peru's foreign policy campaign slowed in the face of these new challenges.

FUTURE PROSPECTS

Peru's independent foreign policy and solidarity offensive aimed at the United States concerns American officials and foreign investors. The IPC dispute, Peruvian seizures of U.S. fishing vessels, and its purchase of expensive Mirage jets generated considerable domestic pressure in the United States for strong action against Peru for the bad example it set for other hemispheric nations. However, the employment of American economic and financial sanctions not only failed to deter the nationalist policies of the Revolutionary Junta, it appeared to backfire and harm the broader political, economic, and strategic interests of the United States (Einaudi, 1970).

The United States used its influence to limit international loans to the Peruvian government after the expropriation of IPC. Washington invoked the Pelly Amendment to reduce economic assistance because of the capture of American fishing vessels. The Pentagon turned down the Peruvian military's request to purchase Northrup F-5 fighters. These retaliatory moves by the United States failed to resolve either the IPC situation or the fishing controversy. The Revolutionary Government responded by buying the more expensive French Mirage jet, snubbing Presidential envoy Governor Nelson Rockefeller, and requesting the withdrawl of the American military mission in Peru. Peruvian spokesmen then attacked the United States before the UN Security Council and other forums for the coercion employed to protect U.S. "illegitimate interests."

The settlement of the question of nationalized American companies marks the hopeful beginning of the much vaunted "mature partnership" between the United States and Peru. American investors in a mineral-scarce world wanted the United States to settle the irritating conflicts which inhibited the exploration and extraction of Peru's natural resources. And the Peruvian government, much more confident in its dealings with foreign firms, recognized the need for external capital and technology to exploit the nation's riches—but under its new investment guidelines. El Peruano headlined the compensation agreement as a true victory for Peru, although misunderstandings about its terms compelled Velasco to emphasize that Peru paid only $76 million for the nationalized properties. American banks join international consortiums to finance the development of Peru's minerals; extractive firms willingly accept Peru's new contract which affirms its sovereign control over subsoil resources.

While both Peru and the United States desire a return to normalcy, the new situation represents a significant change from the old relationship. Peruvian diplomats will certainly continue the campaign to reduce United States hegemony in the OAS. Peru will continue challenging U.S. economic dominance through advocacy of hemispheric solidarity on trade and financial issues. Peru's Foreign Minister told the governors of the Inter-American Development Bank in April 1974 that foreign assistance restrictions enacted by the U.S. Congress (Gonzalez Amendment) convert the Bank from a multilateral institution into a bilateral tool to dictate the rules of the game. Increasingly, the Revolutionary Junta will attack Latin America's military dependence on the United States. At the September 1973 Inter-American Army Conference, Peru's Prime Minister accused the United States of manipulating regional military forces for its own interests; he proposed that the OAS shift the headquarters of the "inoperative" Inter-American Defense Board and Inter-American College of Defense from the United States to a Latin American country.

Although the reduction of American economic assistance, a sharp decrease in foreign investment, and the curtailment of international loans to Chile contributed to the downfall of the Allende government, the Peruvian regime weathered a similar attack and continued on its nationalistic course. The absence of a powerful Peruvian veto group to topple the leftist generals distinguishes the Peruvian experience from that of Chile. The Revolutionary Junta carefully maintains a consensus among its military members on the overall direction of the revolutionary process; this prudent approach to decision-making gives the Peruvian Revolution its pragmatic orientation. The Junta's foreign policy successes also serve to strengthen the unity of the Revolutionary Government of the Armed Forces.

Therefore, divisions within the Revolutionary Junta and foreign policy failures may be the Achilles heels of the Velasco Administration. Peru's hemispheric image as a stable, progressive regime may crumble before news of the outlawing of Accion Popular, nationalization of the press, and resignation of the Junta's admirals over policy differences. If other nations perceive Peru as simply another unstable military dictatorship, some of its status and hemispheric influence will diminish. This could undermine Peru's diplomatic offensive and reduce the opportunities for significant foreign policy victories to bolster the Junta's domestic political support.

Critics argue that ties with the Communist and nonaligned countries bring Peru more difficulties than benefits. Fear of Soviet involvement in Peru almost led to a disastrous hemispheric war in which Peru could have lost its oil deposits; rumors of Soviet missiles compelled the Junta to allow newsmen to tour the port of Paita. In addition, membership in the nonaligned bloc sometimes requires Peru to support embarrassing Third World policies and leaders. But internal problems could force Peru's leftist generals to follow an even more aggressive foreign policy in order to divert attention from controversial domestic programs. The Armed Forces appear to manifest greater consensus on Peru's independent foreign policy than on internal issues like freedom of the press.

Latin American disillusionment stemming from the lack of United States action to match the rhetoric of the Spirit of Tlatelolco affords Peru another opportunity to assert its leadership in hemispheric affairs. President Gerald Ford's preoccupation with the U.S. economy may bolster the Peruvian initiative for Latin American solidarity vis-a-vis the United States. Solidarity among the region's republics thus continues to hold a strong attraction as a means to ensure Peru's and Latin America's political and economic independence.

NOTES

1. In the two and one-half years immediately preceding, the Revolutionary Government had seized only three American vessels: Western King (February 23, 1970); Puritan (March 30, 1971); the the Blue Meridian (December 12, 1972). Many observers interpreted this as a softening of the Peruvian position, despite nationalist rhetoric, in an effort to reach an accommodation with the United States.

2. The following figures from the Central Reserve Bank of Peru (1973: vol. I, 76-87) indicate the flow of direct investment into the Peruvian economy after the Revolution: (1968) $20,442,000; (1969) $6,147,000; (1970) $69,553,000. Foreign investment increased after 1970, especially in the extractive sector.

3. For a fuller discussion of the traditional rivalry between Peru and Chile, see Burr, 1967; Carey, 1964.

4. Reports indicate that Peru purchased approximately 100 medium weight Soviet T-55 tanks.

REFERENCES

Banco Central de Reserva del Peru (1973) Desarrollo de la Balanza de Pagos del Peru. Vol. 1. Lima.

BURR, R. N. (1967) *By Reason or Force: Chile and the Balance of Power in South America, 1830-1905.* Berkeley: University of California Press.

CAREY, J. C. (1964) *Peru and the United States, 1900-1962.* Notre Dame: University of Notre Dame Press.

EINAUDI, L. (1970) *Peruvian Military Relations with the United States.* Santa Monica: RAND.

El Peruano. November 30, 1972; March 16, 1973; December 26, 1973; March 29, 1974; April 15, 1974; May 30, 1974.

International Monetary Fund, International Bank for Reconstruction and Development (1973) Direction of Trade Annual 1968-1972.

La Prensa. January 10, 1974; March 20, 1974.

Latin America. June 2, 1974.

LLOSA, L. E. (1972) in D. A. Sharp (ed.) *United States Foreign Policy and Peru.* Austin: University of Texas Press.

New York Times. February 18, 1969.

SLAGHT, D. V. (1973) "The new realities of Ecuadorian-Peruvian relations: a search for causes." Inter-American Economic Affairs 27 (August): 3-14.

Special Committee to Study the Inter-American System (1973). Organization of American States.

VELASCO ALVARADO, J. (1972) Velasco: La Voz de la Revolucion. Lima.

Washington Post. April 12, 1973.

Chapter 7

THE DIPLOMACY OF NATIONAL SECURITY:

SOUTH AMERICAN INTERNATIONAL RELATIONS

IN A DEFROSTING WORLD

ALEXANDRE S. C. BARROS

INTRODUCTION

The cold war which followed World War II was marked in South America by internal war and political subversion. After the Cuban Missile Crisis of 1962 the cold war showed signs of easing in the United States, where the threat of nuclear holocaust was of paramount importance. In South America, however, perhaps because of a combination of inertia and cultural lag, the cold war continued to preoccupy defense-minded civilian policy-makers and military officers. This inertia and the cultural lag have only recently been overcome, and as a result the cold war has eased in South America. The outcome is a new style of foreign policy: the Diplomacy of National Security.

This chapter is an attempt to analyze some of the relations that South American countries are likely to have with their neighbors during the next decade. The first part of this chapter is a short discussion of diplomatic styles, classified as they best serve the purposes of this work. The second part is an analysis of these styles in the diplomatic history of these countries, as well as the various conditions that have influenced the evolution of National Security Diplomacy. The third part is a longer discussion of this diplomatic style and of some of its operational aspects. The fourth part encompasses possible outcomes of the adoption of this style—and all the information points in this direction during the next ten years—focusing especially on aspects of arms races and potential for armed conflict within the area.

DIPLOMATIC STYLES OF SOUTH AMERICAN COUNTRIES

Countries make foreign policy not necessarily as they want to, but as they can. A combination of internal and external conditions influence the foreign relations of a country, and keep a balance between what a nation desires and what is possible to achieve. Sometimes external conditions are more important, sometimes internal conditions affect policy more.

For the purpose of analysis we shall draw two intersecting axes. The horizontal axis represents the external conditions influencing the foreign policy-making of the country. The vertical axis represents the internal conditions. The external conditions can vary from a rigid alliance system to a flexible one. Internal conditions influencing foreign policy usually depend on the ascendancy of private or public interests. The diplomatic style characterized by the combination of a rigid alliance system with the prevalence of private interests is labeled prebendary. The one resulting from a combination of a rigid alliance system with the prevalence of public interest is called stipendal. A flexible alliance system combined with the prevalence of the public interest is called national security. Before going into the discussion of the three styles, it is important to consider briefly the differences between public and private interests, as well as between rigid and flexible alliance systems.

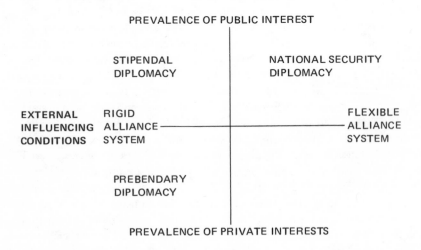

INTERNAL INFLUENCING CONDITIONS

PREVALENCE OF PUBLIC INTEREST

STIPENDAL DIPLOMACY

NATIONAL SECURITY DIPLOMACY

EXTERNAL INFLUENCING CONDITIONS

RIGID ALLIANCE SYSTEM

FLEXIBLE ALLIANCE SYSTEM

PREBENDARY DIPLOMACY

PREVALENCE OF PRIVATE INTERESTS

All modern governments claim that their foreign policy is aimed at fulfilling the national interest (Wolfers, 1952: 481). What is publicly defined as national interest, however, is not always the true national interest. Sometimes it is a mere sum of private interests. Blaisdel (1958: 157) argues that the true national interest is the difference between the product and the sum of private interests. When the foreign policy of any given country is de facto just the sum of private interests, this policy is easily negotiable in all of its points. If, on the other hand, it is the sum of private interests, *plus* something else, then it also concerns the national interest and is not so easily negotiable. Any negotiations within this range have to be the result of private interests *plus* one of the following: a change in cultural values, a shift in ideological postulates, a turn in strategic outlook, or a combination of these.

Because this subject is essentially qualitative and not quantitative, mathematical comparisons are necessarily imperfect. Nevertheless, it is possible to attempt another one: Assuming that there is both a sum and a product of private interests in any society, the difference between the product and the sum could be considered the national interest. This difference could be defined as resources given to, appropriated by, or whose defense has been delegated to the state. In pure mathematical terms the gap between the product and the sum would grow enormously, since the sum grows arithmetically and the product grows geometrically. This gap would then be the non-negotiable part. One flaw of this comparison is that this difference is not so great as the mathematical laws determine because there is, actually, a change in quality as well as in quantity. In the hands of the state, this difference changes more in its quality. It actually means different things than the same resources in the hands of private groups. We thus face now a change both in quality and in quantity (Blaisdel, 1958: 157). According to this argument, the less developed the country, the smaller the sum, the product, and the difference (i.e., the national interest). Consequently, the state is weaker, the area not subject to negotiation is narrower, and it is easier for private interests to control the foreign policy. The converse is also true.

On the external side, the main conditioning factor is the alliance system to which the country belongs. Its degree of flexibility or rigidity is expressed by the degree of freedom enjoyed by the weaker junior countries in any alliance to negotiate their national interest independently from the stronger countries. These considerations having been made, a discussion of the suggested diplomatic styles is appropriate.

Prebendary Diplomacy

Countries practice this style of diplomacy when they are underdeveloped. Limited private interests in a few hands result in a small national interest. In

South America, the practice of prebendary diplomacy characterized the period when countries produced one, or a very small number of raw materials for export. Their foreign policy consisted primarily of the interaction between producer-exporter and the purchasers in the international market. The position of the government was one of mere negotiator for the producer-exporter.

Countries which based their economy on mining had their foreign policy monopolized by one or a very small number of groups which controlled the country's foreign policy. Countries which based their economy on agrarian production had a foreign policy geared toward a less highly concentrated aggregate of private interests. Because production in agrarian countries is more dispersed, more private interests can exist. Consequently, a stronger national interest is represented in the international scenario, at least as far as commercialism is concerned (Cardoso, 1969: 51-82). Both these situations provided ideal conditions for the development of a prebendary diplomatic style, i.e., the foreign policy of these countries was oriented to the satisfaction of the interests of these groups, by means of prebends given to the local elites by international purchasers.

On the chart, the alliance requirements of prebendary diplomacy are located to the left of the vertical axis, but closer to the intersection than they are for stipendal diplomacy. Although prebendary diplomacy exists in a rigid alliance system, it is not as rigid (especially on military terms) as that of stipendal diplomacy. The determinants of prebendary diplomacy are more internal than external and its alliances are more likely to center around economic concerns than military ones. Junior partners in such alliances are then free, as long as they keep in mind the economic interests of the senior partner who has, generally, a monopsony.

Stipendal Diplomacy

Contrary to prebendary diplomacy, the major determinants of stipendal diplomacy are external. It has a rigid alliance system, centered around military interests rather than economic ones. On the chart the location of the internal determinants must be below the intersection on the vertical axis, although they can be quite close to it. The external determinants along the horizontal axis must be to the left of the vertical axis and far from the intersection.

This pattern tends to develop when the weaker country of an alliance is strategically so important for the senior partner that the latter feels justified in investing heavily in order to retain an international image, military bases, or any other type of militarily important monopoly. Whatever the initial intentions of the senior partner, the weaker country gains money or some other "developmental" benefit. In general, the results take the form of economic growth, modernization, etc., which are sustained by the stronger country. In other words, the public interest of the underdeveloped country is fulfilled as a result of an external decision, without an internal demand. Stipend diplomacies did not develop in either Central or South America before the cold war period because they were not necessary. They did develop in Taiwan (until Richard Nixon's trip to China) and in Cuba, which had become strategically necessary to the United States and to the Soviet Union. Two other diplomatic endeavors might have, theoretically at least, ended in somewhat imperfect stipendal diplomacies. They failed for different reasons which are worth discussing here.

Postwar Europe saw the development of the Marshall Plan. Latin America in the 1960s had the Alliance for Progress. It is doubtful that American policy-makers had formulated any plans to develop stipend diplomacies, but some of the conditions were present. Both cases were important enough to justify heavy investment and a rigid alliance. Western European reconstruction, however, gained a *momentum* that allowed those countries to develop economically and launch their own national projects and their own National Security Diplomacy. They soon freed themselves from the strict limitations imposed by the alliance with the United States. In the case of Latin America, the Alliance for Progress failed to produce stipend diplomacies for different reasons. In the first place, the expectations about the rate of growth that the Alliance was to inspire were not fulfilled. Consequently, the needs for investment became too heavy for the United States to bear, without the expected political and economic returns. Moreover, at the time that the failure of the Alliance was acknowledged, the tensions of the cold war had already eased a bit, so the Alliance for Progress lost part of its original political purpose.

National Security Diplomacy

National security diplomacy is characterized by having the internal determinants along the vertical axis, above the intersection. The external determinants on the horizontal axis must be to the right of the intersection. The farther both determinants are from the intersection, the greater the gearing will be toward National Security.

A reasonable degree of economic growth is a sine qua non condition for the practice of this diplomatic style. Underdeveloped countries aspire to practice it. However, they can do so only when they have attained a level of development which allows them to have different interests from their senior partners, and to provide for the implementation and defense of these interests. When the range of policies controlled by the senior partner of an alliance narrows, the alliance system loosens. This shift can happen because junior partners develop fast and are able to implement and defend their interests internationally, or because the senior partner loses either power or interest. In general a combination of these factors accounts for the loosening of alliances.

SOUTH AMERICAN DIPLOMACY: A HISTORICAL VIEW

During the second half of the nineteenth century, the recently independent South American countries practiced national security diplomacy within the continent and prebendary diplomacy with Europe. There were no commercial conflicts with Europe, and the military conflicts in South America were mostly political. South American countries were free to have their skirmishes and redesign their borderlines as long as they continued to supply Europe with raw materials. As improved transportation and communications methods made the world smaller, South America began to assume a greater economic and political importance to the developed countries above the equator, particularly the United States. While Europe concentrated mainly on the newly opened fields in Africa, it gave the United States little competition in South America.

The countries above the equator developed more quickly than did those of Latin America, and as the gap in development grew wider, the type of diplomacy regressed. The Latin American countries were under pressure to accept prebendary diplomacy and to prevent regional wars. The local elite groups interacted less among themselves and concentrated on the interactions along the North-South axis, because these were more capable of satisfying their own aggregate of private commercial interests. From the beginning of this century until World War II, South American diplomacy was mostly prebendary, geared toward the sale of raw products to the United States. The local elite, who profited from these sales, molded their policy so that it satisfied the combination of their interests and those of the only purchaser.

World War II changed this situation. The perception of the world as divided into two irreconcilably antagonistic blocs which permeated the cold war line of thought, considerably tightened the inter-American alliance system which was built under the leadership of the United States (Harrigan, 1970: 3). The Soviet Union on the other side tightened its own pact in Eastern Europe, and the field open for international negotiations narrowed. Before this constriction, most of South America's commerce had been with the United States because it was easier than dealing elsewhere. After 1945, although South American countries might have benefited economically by selling to a more diversified range of markets, political limitations prevented them from commercially crossing a frontier, which was economically and technologically thin but politically very thick. The result was that South American countries made a greater effort to sell less each day to the United States. They also began to limit buying in all fields, especially in arms supplies (Harrigan, 1970: 3; Kemp, 1973: 189; Rouquié, 1973: 23-24).

The effort to sell less to the United States was the result of a practical economic limitation: the United States simply could not absorb all the export production from its allies after they started to increase and diversify their production. South American countries had continued to follow their path toward economic development. Some developed at a faster pace than others, but nearly all were gradually substituting native-made goods for imports and shaping their embryonic industrial profile. Had the situation involved a smaller number of countries, the development of a perfect stipendary relationship might have been possible. As things were, however, the economic costs for the United States were far greater than it was willing to pay. Latin American countries began to look for more diversified markets. Following this movement, the inter-American alliance system loosened. Inertia had allowed it to remain in force even after tensions had eased between the United States and the U.S.S.R.

THE DEFROSTING PROCESS:
MILITARY ASPECTS OF THE QUESTION

The developing South American countries' attempt to widen their markets was considerably restrained by the political, strategic, and military aspects of their relationships with the United States. The fear of a nuclear holocaust which had dominated the foreign policy of the great powers after 1945 was only belatedly and thinly absorbed by South America. In a regional version of the cold war, South Americans felt threatened by political violence and subversion. By means of military training, advisory missions, and arms supply, the United States heavily contributed to the absorption of cold war thought in South America. Inertia, coupled with the insulation of Cuba from the inter-American defense system, helped the fructification of the cold war idea after tensions had eased between the great powers (Rouquié, 1973: 32).

Political peculiarities of South American nations during the 1960s gave way to the rise of the military to a more important role in the policy-making process. This new role of the military appeared in different aspects and produced different political outputs, but it had some important similarities. The delayed perception of the cold war threat in its local version varied in importance in the new policies, but it was never absent (Einaudi and Stepan, 1971). Once the military took this new role in policy-making, they soon noticed that the thin and belated absorption of the cold war threat was somewhat outdated and perhaps did not justify the deployment of huge amounts of resources and energies. The enemy turned out to be militarily irrelevant and easy to fight. It is important to notice that along with these realizations, the military was growing increasingly aware of the dilemmas posed by development (Rouquié, 1973: 9). The members of the South American military elite soon found themselves facing a dilemma. One of their main reasons for taking over the reins of government was to wipe out the threat of subversion which they perceived as a hydra-headed monster. They soon discovered that cutting off each head did not stimulate the growth of others as they had expected it would. Had the military taken over the governments in the old "caudillo" or corrective style, it could have overcome its feeling of purposelessness either by withdrawing or by establishing itself in power as a clique. The recent military seizures of power in South America, however, were aimed at the fulfillment of a more noble mission. The Armed Forces perceive themselves as interpreters of the interests of the collective people.

Lacking the hydra, the military elite suddenly had to redefine their political function. From fighters of internal subversion, they turned into fighters for economic growth and development. The various national formulas for growth which they produced did not change the essential fact that the military elite increasingly considered themselves leaders of their societies, conducting the people to a place of greater national pride, independence, and power. This new role was incompatible with the rigid alliance requirements of the cold war (Kemp, 1970: 29; Rouquié, 1973: 9, 14; Sc).

The shift from warriors in the local cold war to armed sponsors of development took place at different moments in different countries. The Peruvian military were perhaps the first to change; and they shifted their emphasis almost completely to the economic tasks of development (Einaudi and Stepan, 1971: 9-70). Although the Brazilian military are shifting more slowly, their present attitude differs distinctly from that of a few years ago. The Argentinian military were unable to make the shift in their outlook and consequently failed politically. The recall of Perón is nothing more than the de facto acknowledgment of this failure.

Despite the military's change in emphasis, there is no question of abandoning its preoccupation with military security and political control, or its ideological postulates. This assertion is justified by a consideration of some peculiarities of the military profession. Its preoccupation with security matters is an essential value that permeates the military on a world-wide basis. First, regardless of the peculiar function of the military at any particular point, the profession is essentially concerned with the management of violence, be it external war, civil war, internal subversion, or any other form of violence. Second, the military characteristically sees the world as split between friend and foe. With this sort of world view, the friendliness or enmity of another nation is considered a temporary situation (Huntington, 1957: 62-63). Third, preparedness is an essential task of Armed Forces anywhere, irrespective of the weight they may have in the policy-making process (Huntington, 1957: 62-63).

When the military have an important role in policy-making, the situation will undoubtedly be marked by a stronger preoccupation with preparedness and security matters (Wolfers, 1952: 488). Therefore, it is naive to expect the military to abandon their preoccupation with the danger of war, or the imminence of military conflicts. This abandonment would mean losing the essential contents of the military profession; at the extreme, it would mean the extinction of the profession itself (Huntington, 1957: 62-63).

In summary, so far we have seen:

1. The pace of development of South American countries has not been stopped by the cold war. It may, however, have been slowed by the difficulties of finding a market within the commercial frontiers imposed by the cold war.

2. The South American armed forces inherited a cold war doctrine and strategy that was not completely confirmed by reality, i.e., they were unable to participate in the cold war at the level of their professional comrades in the countries that held the nuclear umbrellas. As a result they felt some frustration. Within their own countries, they sooner or later found that the Hydra of subversion which they wanted to fight was far less able to reproduce than they had expected. Moreover, they realized that the revolutionary war doctrines developed for their use were based on the French colonial experience in Algeria and Indochina, and on the American experience in Vietnam. In the French and American cases the total foreign population was equated with the enemy. The South American military found that in their countries, they were not fighting foreigners—the only exception being infiltration of foreign guerrillas into some countries—and they certainly could not equate the entire population of their own countries with the enemy. Yet, they were basing their actions on a doctrine that treated their fellow citizens as enemies. This implied a detachment from compatriots that the military could not accept (Rouquié, 1973: 22-23). Therefore their capacity as warriors of the cold war became seriously impaired and misplaced.

3. The two points above demanded a redefinition of the role of the

military in their societies, particularly because its part in the policy-
making process was growing. Since the military was exercising power
not as a "clique," but as representatives of a corporate nation, the
redefinition would have to take place along the lines of thought and
values of this corporation (Rouquié, 1973: 3). The military's preoccupation with development accorded with the collective desires of
the people. It was, however, insufficient for the armed forces themselves, since such preoccupation left them without an enemy, actual
or potential.

At this point the practical end of the cold war and the loosening of the
Inter-American Defense Pact becomes significant. Like any other tight
alliance system, the Inter-American Defense Pact was characterized by a
multiplicity of aspects which went much further and deeper than the mere
preparation for a forthcoming nuclear war. Its purely military aspects
included a wide array of tasks such as military training, doctrine harmo-
nization, arms supply, replacement and maintenance, joint exercises, etc.
However, the Pact involved political and diplomatic aspects as well.

On the internal political aspect, the cold war centered mainly on the fight
against subversion. On the external diplomatic aspect, the cold war demanded
the construction of a doctrine coherent with both the ideological and the
military aspects of the Alliance for Progress. In order to maintain this
coherence, a forum was established for the discussion and solution of the
common problems posed by this arrangement.

During the peak of the Alliance the predominant slogan was "aid not
trade." With the loosening of the Alliance, trade rather than aid became the
great demand. As we have seen above, the United States was not able, even if
it had been willing, to increase trade substantially with South America.
Unable to compete for the purchases of the United States, South American
countries started to diversify their markets. Since their economies are not
complementary, but competitive, fairly intense disputes over new markets
were generated, and the tendency of this competition is to increase rather
than to decrease.

Any professional military officer knows that in international relations, it is
not sufficient to want something; it is necessary to have the means to
implement and enforce desires. These desires are expressed by means of
military power, actual or potential. The United States was preventing South
American countries from having such power. The U.S. government controlled
its military aid programs and even actual arms purchases in order to avoid the
possibility of any significant military confrontation among South American
countries (Flatley, 1970: 15; Rouquié, 1973: 24). The contradictions of this

situation increasingly sharpened. South American countries could trade and compete commercially on a world-wide basis. Commercially, they were less subject to the restraints of the cold war. Yet, as far as the United States could prevent it, they could not have any military backing for their competitive trade. The United States was claiming the role of inspector of a situation that it no longer controlled.

The commercial balance of these countries allowed them to buy the arms they wanted; the United States simply did not want to sell them. The remnants of the cold war distorted the market situation, i.e., junior partners were allowed to buy only what a presumably monopolistic supplier wanted to sell. As the developing countries grew wealthier, they started to look for alternative suppliers. If they could sell their products, why couldn't they buy the arms they felt they needed? Thus the arms trade is moving from a monopolistic situation to a market situation. The United States' desire to prevent South American countries from arming themselves obviously diminished even more its influence in the region (Kemp, 1973: 207, 230). Moreover, other suppliers began to respond positively to the South American demands for arms. France, England, and the Soviet Union are providing their commercial clients with the arms they demand (Kemp, 1970: 28-29).

The present conditions are ripe for the practice of national security diplomacy. This type of diplomacy does not necessarily mean an arms race or a high likelihood of belligerent actions, although they are possible (Gray, 1971: 65). It simply means that countries have a clearly defined national interest and are capable of enforcing it in the international arena—at least to some degree.

Brazil, Chile, Bolivia, Paraguay, Peru, Ecuador, and Uruguay have governments in which the military has an important role in the policy-making process. This means, by definition, that these countries will be concerned with external security once the internal threats perceived by the military are overcome. In Argentina, Colombia, and Venezuela the military is not so important in policy-making. As has been said above, countries make foreign policy, not necessarily as they want to, but as they can; and if one's neighbors worry about security, it is advisable to have the same worry. Moreover, nonmilitary groups that influence policy-making can be as security minded as the military, and sometimes more so.

Prediction of military behavior of countries presents peculiar problems. Institutions in charge of military policy regard information about their resources and operations as confidential. Therefore, data are either not available or have a limited reliability. Furthermore, data are usually presented at such a high level of aggregation that the lack of specifics makes any analysis difficult. While the amount of available military resources greatly influences the behavior of states, occasionally they engage in military ventures without the military means to sustain them. This occurrence may be a response to someone else's aggressive behavior, or it may be a movement to call attention to a situation perceived as dangerous. Preemptive arms stockpiling, for example, can be used, in a limited way, to round up potential allies (Gray, 1971: 59-60).

DIPLOMATIC-MILITARY PERSPECTIVES
FOR THE NEAR FUTURE

South American countries are not likely to have the resources to get involved in an international war in the next ten years, unless they enter it as allies of more powerful countries, as they did during World War II. Although the United States is increasingly losing the wide control it once had in military matters, it will not abdicate control in Central America because of the proximity to its own territory. South American statesmen and military leaders are aware of this and therefore are not likely to direct any military actions toward Central America. Any possible conflicts will be within the continent and not outside it.

By themselves neither commercial competition nor the traditional rivalries of South American countries would be a sufficient reason for active aggression. A more serious problem may be the ideological differences between governments. Any of these reasons alone is unlikely to generate war, but if these are adequately mixed, the likelihood of war may very well increase. My hypothesis is that ideological differences coupled with traditional rivalries are the ingredients that make war acceptable. If one of these conditions is absent, countries are much more likely to try to solve their problems by nonmilitary methods.

The Stockholm International Peace Research Institute (SIPRI) lists eight boundary disputes in Latin America. Four of them are between South American countries and one is between a South American country and a European country (the Argentine-United Kingdom dispute over the Falkland Islands). Of the four between South American countries, three are active and only one is passive. Kemp (1973: 192-193) lists eleven border and territorial disputes in Latin America; seven of these are in South America.

How are countries likely to react to these disputes? Bolivia for instance has recently claimed its right to an exit to the sea. Although Bolivia is fairly indifferent to whether this territory is at the moment possessed by Chile or by Peru, Chile and Peru find the matter of possession rather more important. Chile called out its reserve army in response to Peru's moving its Armored War College to the border. This is just an example of how small attritions can easily turn into military moves that are preparatory for action.

Wars are less frequent than military moves. However, the latter are essential to classical infantry or armored cavalry war and therefore more likely to be made when countries rely on the classic kind of armed forces. Despite such maneuvers, South American countries are each day relying more on air and sea power for their defense, primarily because of the geographical limitations of land war in the region (Kemp, 1973: 217). Even if South American countries adopt air tactics, they are unlikely to get involved in wars with nonbordering countries. The adoption of this type of war demands logistical support by the army and navy which few of these countries have. Given this setting, it is time to analyze the moves these countries are making in order to increase their military potential. This analysis will be based on Tables 1 and 2, which were computed using the SIPRI data.

South America is sharply divided into three groups of military spenders. The group of the big spenders has two effective members and one contender with very high chances of gaining a place in the group. Brazil and Argentina are the effective members and Venezuela is the contender. Their levels of military expenditure, as well as other factors, such as territorial extension and level of industrial development, make Brazil and Argentina the most likely disputants over leadership in the area.

Argentina has had a relatively stable pattern of military expenditure which has not been increasing at the same rate as that of Brazil. Regression analysis would indicate a downward trend in Argentinian behavior. However, this technique has not always proved to be valid for the prediction of military expenditures of countries, since regression assumes a regularity of behavior which has not always been historically the case in military matters. The Argentinian level of military expenditure has not been highly influenced by internal politico-military problems. Three possible explanations could account for this. First, internal security expenditures may not be computed in the military budget. Second, according to several sources, the Argentinian investments in nuclear power are not computed as military expenditures, but as scientific development. Third, possibly the Argentinian military elite would prefer not to mix external strategy with internal political problems of an episodic nature.

Unlike Argentinian spending, the Brazilian military expenditures have been going up in jumps. Table 1 shows a correlation between political crises and increases in military expenditures. This fact indicates that the level of Brazilian military expenditures has been influenced by the internal political situation. It does not necessarily mean, however, that such expenditures have been made solely because of internal political problems. Some sources explain the great increase in Brazilian military expenditures between 1954 and 1958 by the purchase of an aircraft carrier. However, Argentina also purchased a carrier of comparable size at about the same time, and there is no comparable

TABLE 1

SOUTH AMERICAN COUNTRIES' MILITARY EXPENDITURE: 1948-1971 (in million U.S. dollars at constant prices)

	1948	1949	1950	1951	1952	1953	1954	1955	1956	1957	1958	1959
Argentina	506.3	379.4	268.3	281.5	247.8	270.1	291.7	231.4	292.6	247.0	279.1	253.7
Bolivia	–	–	–	–	–	4.2	–	–	2.4	2.5	2.1	2.8
Brazil	172.3	220.3	219.4	246.2	238.8	241.7	235.3	268.4	323.8	359.1	367.6	288.8
Chile	55.3	68.2	78.1	73.7	–	132.3	84.7	126.3	120.9	129.8	121.0	96.4
Colombia	21.2	24.6	23.2	29.3	40.8	54.4	64.1	63.4	61.7	54.9	50.8	42.2
Ecuador	–	–	–	–	75.2	12.1	–	18.2	20.1	19.3	18.4	16.5
Paraguay	–	–	–	–	–	–	–	–	4.8	4.8	[5.8]	[5.1]
Peru	21.5	28.5	31.3	36.2	35.0	34.2	32.2	34.3	56.5	50.9	57.7	50.8
Uruguay	–	–	–	–	–	–	–	–	–	–	–	[9.4]
Venezuela	42.8	47.6	63.5	63.5	70.5	71.1	69.6	111.4	139.2	117.6	186.2	195.1
Total	829.4	768.6	683.8	730.4	708.1	820.1	777.6	853.4	1,022.0	985.9	1,088.7	960.8

	1960	1961	1962	1963	1964[1]	1965[2]	1966[3]	1967[4]	1968[5]	1969[6]	1970	1971	Total
Argentina	284.9	280.4	269.8	262.6	288.6	276.0	310.7	246.7	260.5	306.5	320.0	–	6,656.6
Bolivia	4.0	4.6	4.7	6.0	12.1	14.3	13.1	12.1	13.0	14.2	15.0	–	127.1
Brazil	267.3	245.1	264.6	259.8	272.8	406.9	340.5	478.9	480.4	529.4	434.6	–	7,162.0
Chile	103.5	105.2	111.6	95.9	94.2	111.5	116.1	127.8	127.1	121.2	(157.1)	–	2,367.9
Colombia	47.3	56.2	88.8	97.1	94.6	101.6	101.6	104.7	137.9	128.3	136.3	(138.0)	1,763.0
Ecuador	22.2	21.1	20.1	17.4	19.8	22.2	24.0	21.9	24.2	24.5	[25.0]	–	422.2
Paraguay	[4.9]	4.2	4.8	5.3	5.5	5.9	7.2	9.2	9.2	10.2	[11.0]	–	121.3
Peru	50.1	[60.0]	[70.0]	80.7	78.7	78.8	78.4	99.6	99.7	94.9	[95.0]	–	1,355.0
Uruguay	[10.8]	14.9	14.9	20.3	19.8	22.4	21.6	24.3	17.9	[18.0]	[18.0]	–	272.3
Venezuela	174.6	151.1	157.8	188.3	197.6	229.1	231.8	259.4	257.4	243.4	247.8	(257.0)	3,778.2
Total	969.6	942.8	1,007.1	1,033.4	1,083.7	1,268.7	1,245.0	1,384.6	1,427.1	1,490.6	1,459.8	395.0	23,940.6

Source and Notes on page 145.

increase in the Argentinian expenses. Therefore, the best explanation lies in internal politics, namely, the fact that the Kubitschek Administration had difficulty in its relations with the Brazilian armed forces and adopted the increase in military expenditures as an internal political strategy. The upward trend in military expenditure from 1964 on is undoubtedly related to the new role that the Armed Forces took in the policy-making process. Although pay raises occurred in this period, they cannot account for the whole increase. A considerable part of this increase can be explained by new purchases and reequipment. Some analysts would also attribute these increases to internal security problems. These three reasons together explain the recent rises in Brazilian military expenditures. It is important to remember that a considerable part of military equipment bought for internal security operations can also be used effectively for external operation.

According to the SIPRI data, there is no pattern of a primitive arms race between Argentina and Brazil. What seems to be clear is that a mutual preoccupation with keeping the balance has combined with cautious moves to avoid such a race. Indications point toward the phenomenon that Gray (1971: 56) calls a sophisticated arms race, i.e., one in which participants, aware that their behavior will determine, at least partially, that of others, may very well choose not to race.

Although Argentina and Brazil are not involved in an arms race, they may be prepared to become so. Both Argentina and Brazil still have a high capacity to expand their investments in military matters, if it is considered necessary by their elites. In such a case, however, Brazil seems to be in a better potential position. The Brazilian level of expenditure per citizen is still far below the Argentinian one. The use of per capita data in this case seems to

SOURCE AND NOTES FOR TABLE 1
SOURCE: SIPRI Yearbook 1968/69 and SIPRI Yearbook 1972, SIPRI, Stockholm, Sweden.
NOTES:
1. 1964: There is a discrepancy between data published in SIPRI Yearbook 1968/69 and SIPRI Yearbook 1972. I have used the 1972 data, on the assumption that they are more accurate, because they are more recent. 1968/69 data are: Bolivia = 5.9.
2. 1965: See note 1 above: Bolivia = 11.8; Peru = 74.6; Uruguay = 18.9.
3. 1966: See note 1 above: Bolivia = 14.3; Ecuador = 24.8; Peru = 77.1; Uruguay = 14.4; Venezuela = 237.9.
4. 1967: See note 1 above: Bolivia = ——; Brazil = 387.5; Ecuador = 19.5; Paraguay = 8.8; Peru = 88.2; Uruguay = 15.0; Venezuela = 265.8.
5. 1968: See note 1 above: Argentina = 246.7; Bolivia = ——; Brazil = ——; Chile = 129.3; Colombia = 106.7; Ecuador = 19.8; Paraguay = 10.0; Peru = 105.7; Uruguay = 16.0; Venezuela = 263.1.
6. 1969: See note 1 above: Argentina = ——; Bolivia = ——; Brazil = ——; Chile = 132.2; Colombia = ——; Ecuador = 19.8; Paraguay = ——; Peru = 93.7; Uruguay = ——.

TABLE 2
MILITARY EXPENDITURES PER CAPITA IN SOUTH AMERICAN COUNTRIES: 1948-1971
(in U.S. dollars at constant prices)

	1948	1949	1950	1951	1952	1953	1954	1955	1956	1957	1958	1959
Argentina	31.04	22.65	15.60	15.95	13.72	14.67	15.56	12.10	15.01	12.43	13.96	12.30
Bolivia	–	–	–	–	–	1.33	–	–	0.74	0.76	0.62	0.81
Brazil	3.56	4.32	4.22	4.62	4.38	4.33	4.12	4.59	5.41	5.86	5.50	4.49
Chile	11.61	11.93	13.44	12.46	–	20.55	13.13	18.68	17.41	18.22	16.53	12.93
Colombia	1.96	2.23	2.06	2.53	3.46	4.49	5.17	5.00	4.76	4.15	3.50	3.05
Ecuador	–	–	–	–	22.44	3.49	–	4.95	5.29	4.96	4.52	3.95
Paraguay	–	–	–	–	–	–	–	–	2.99	2.93	3.43	2.96
Peru	2.66	3.45	3.72	4.16	3.94	3.78	3.49	3.65	5.85	5.12	6.08	4.82
Uruguay	–	–	–	–	–	–	–	–	–	–	–	3.62
Venezuela	9.53	9.45	12.61	12.39	13.35	13.06	12.41	19.29	23.38	19.17	27.26	26.81

	1960	1961	1962	1963	1964	1965	1966	1967	1968	1969	1970	1971
Argentina	14.23	13.31	12.59	12.00	13.10	12.34	13.69	10.60	11.03	12.77	13.69	–
Bolivia	1.15	1.31	1.33	1.45	3.31	3.31	3.86	3.49	3.18	2.95	–	–
Brazil	3.76	3.35	3.51	3.41	3.46	4.94	4.09	5.59	5.44	5.82	4.59	–
Chile	14.03	13.44	13.94	11.55	11.09	13.01	13.26	13.98	13.59	12.65	–	–
Colombia	3.34	3.89	6.01	5.73	5.41	5.62	5.46	5.45	6.95	6.26	–	–
Ecuador	5.14	4.63	4.32	3.61	4.05	4.36	4.50	3.97	4.24	4.15	–	–
Paraguay	2.77	2.31	2.64	2.77	2.79	2.90	3.43	4.25	4.12	4.40	–	–
Peru	4.61	6.05	6.08	7.36	6.96	6.76	6.52	8.04	7.80	7.20	–	–
Uruguay	3.82	–	5.11	7.92	7.38	8.25	7.85	7.79	6.35	6.31	–	–
Venezuela	23.20	20.08	20.04	23.12	23.44	25.12	25.98	27.73	26.55	24.25	–	–

SOURCE: Based on Table 1 and on the United Nations Statistical Yearbook for Population Data.

have a better predictive capacity than any other analysis because military expenditures are always subject to some sort of scrutiny on the part of the population. Since the Argentinian level of military expenditure seems to be quite high already, increasing it without some sort of questioning on the part of the population would be difficult. The interaction between Brazil and Argentina is also influenced by factors other than purely military ones. Their size alone as the biggest countries in South America makes them potential rivals. This potential is aggravated by their geographical location and by the strategic importance of control of the Plata basin. In summary, the situation between Argentina and Brazil is theoretically likely to remain as it is. Despite potential for an arms race, due mainly to competition for leadership in the southern area, several geographical and strategic factors limit the possibility of war. Both countries have large territories. Any war that might involve even partial territorial occupation would be very expensive financially and very difficult politically.

Another point which must not be forgotten is the particular situation of these two countries in the extracontinental scenario. Some sort of extracontinental intervention would soon be made in the event of a war between the two biggest and most developed countries in South America. Since it is highly unlikely that the elite of either country would approve of such intervention in their war, the possibility may prove an effective deterrent. If either Argentina or Brazil decides to go nuclear, the situation would not be changed for long, since both are capable of catching up in a fairly short time. So, in the southern part of the hemisphere, the situation is likely to remain as it is, with both nations involved in a sophisticated arms race, oriented toward maintaining the balance and eventually attempting to solve their problems by political and diplomatic means.

In the northern part of South America, Venezuela is quickly entering the club of the big spenders. Since 1958, when it detached itself from the group of the middle spenders, it has been investing heavily in military materiel. From 1958 to 1961 Venezuela was between the two groups, but since then it has increased its expenditures considerably. With its oil resources and the recent increase in oil prices, it may spend even more. Why has Venezuela been stockpiling? It is not likely that Venezuela has been arming with Argentina in mind. The geographical distance between the two countries would not justify such an investment, even in aircraft. Venezuela is more likely to be taking these steps because of immediate neighbors such as Guyana and Colombia with whom it has border disputes. It is not absurd to think that Venezuela also has Brazil in mind when stockpiling. However, the fact that the Amazon forest lies between any vital centers of the two countries is an indication that Brazil is not the main preoccupation of the Venezuela investments.

What is certain is that most of the Venezuelan arms are oriented toward external rather than internal wars (Flatley, 1970: 12). Colombia and Guyana appear to be the two basic military priorities. As far as Brazil is concerned, Venezuela seems to be stockpiling for self-protection. As Huntington (1957: 62-63) has pointed out, theoretically arms can be used against any enemy, and military men look at other states' capabilities, rather than at their intentions. Whether Venezuela and Colombia will become involved in an arms race remains to be seen. Venezuela's military perspectives look better as far as financial potential and bargaining power with possible arms suppliers go. Nevertheless, Colombia also has its armed forces and equipment oriented to external wars (Flatley, 1970: 12). Moreover, a war in that region is more viable strategically than it is in the southern part of the continent. Given this state of affairs, the relations between Venezuela and Colombia may be more prone than those between Argentina and Brazil to evolve into aggressive behavior.

Two other members of the group of middle spenders are Peru and Colombia. These two countries have no border dispute. Moreover, Peru is preoccupied with Chile, and Colombia is preoccupied with Venezuela. Therefore, a confrontation between Colombia and Peru appears unlikely. The situation between Peru and Chile presents a greater potential for conflict. In addition to being in the same group of spenders, the two countries have border disputes, historical feuds, and, at this point, considerable ideological differences between their governments. The combination of factors makes a conflict between them the most likely one to occur in South America in the next ten years.

The small spenders all seem to be still unable to attempt the practice of national security diplomacy, even on a limited scale. Uruguay's geographical location and its present economic crisis (which has no end in sight) prevent it from enforcing its desires with other nations. Aid from another country could improve its outlook, but the chances of finding a patron other than Argentina or Brazil are not great. Brazil and Argentina are likely to hold back from Uruguay's assistance, since both countries have more important interests which they may not want to jeopardize because of a dispute involving Uruguay. Uruguay will probably continue to play its limited role between two giants.

Ecuador's position is not enviable either, but it seems to be better than Uruguay's. To a degree it can count on the continuation of attrition between Chile and Peru. This has the advantage of keeping Ecuador's southern border relatively free from preoccupations and of preventing Colombia from making any southward move, unless as a response to a move made by Peru.

Bolivia and Paraguay would, theoretically, be in a situation of ideal competition, if it were not for their geographical location. Their situation in the middle of South America limits almost totally their military possibilities. They do, however, have a relatively good bargaining position with their neighbors because the competitive interests of their neighbors give them some leverage.

CONCLUSIONS

The practice of national security diplomacy in South America is becoming a viable option for some of the countries and is still not possible for some of the others. Those countries which can practice national security diplomacy do so in varying degrees. Brazil and Argentina have global strategy in mind. The middle spenders can operate on the basis of this type of diplomacy only with their own immediate neighbors. The small spenders have practically no possibility of practicing this type of diplomacy. Uruguay has a chance of playing off Argentina and Brazil, a role from which it may benefit, but which limits its options. Ecuador is more or less in the same situation as Uruguay, although it is somewhat more comfortable, since the possibility of disputes between Colombia and Peru is somewhat remote. Bolivia and Paraguay do not seem to have too many chances open. Their geographical positions limit their strategic options, and their lack of economic potential for arms prevents them from gaining military support for their interests. Colombia and Venezuela are able to practice this type of diplomacy toward other countries, but they are more likely to concentrate on each other.

It seems to be clear that South American international politics for the next ten years will be decided by the countries in the area, with very little participation by any superpowers. In this sense South America is unlikely to reproduce a situation similar to either Vietnam or the Middle East. Some of the South American countries may be defending ideological postulates similar to those of a superpower, but they will probably defend these ideologies on their own and defend their national interest rather than those of the superpower.

The idea of superpower zones of influence no longer seems to exist in South America, since there are now some countries which are capable of enforcing their own interests. One way or another the area is escaping the influence zone of the United States. This does not mean a shift of alliances, but rather the development of another independent power zone in the world.

REFERENCES

BLAISDEL, D. C. (1958) "Pressure groups, foreign policies, and international politics." The Annals of the American Academy of Political and Social Sciences 319 (December).

CARDOSO, F. H. (1969) *Mudancas Sociais na América Latina.* São Paulo: Difusão Européia.

EINAUDI, L. and A. STEPAN (1971) *Latin American Institutional Development: Changing Military Perspectives in Peru and Brazil.* Santa Monica: Rand.

FLATLEY, T. W. (1970) "Latin American armed forces in the 1960s: a review." Military Review 50 (April): 10-20.

GRAY, C. S. (1971) "The arms race phenomenon." World Politics 24 (October): 39-79.

HARRIGAN, A. (1970) "Inter American defense in the seventies." Military Review 50 (April): 3-10.

HUNTINGTON, S. (1957) *The Soldier and the State.* New York: Vintage.

KEMP, G. (1973) "The prospects for arms control in Latin America: the strategic dimensions," pp. 189-243 in P. C. Schmitter (ed.) *Military Rule in Latin America.* Beverly Hills: Sage.

――― (1970) "Dilemmas of the arms traffic." Military Review 50 (July): 20-32.

LOFTUS, J. E. (1968) *Latin American Defense Expenditures, 1938-1965.* Santa Monica: Rand.

ROUQUIÉ, A. (1973) "Military revolutions and national independence in Latin America: 1968-1971," pp. 2-57 in P. C. Schmitter (ed.) *Military Rule in Latin America.* Beverly Hills: Sage.

SCHMITTER, P. C. [ed.] (1973) *Military Rule in Latin America.* Beverly Hills: Sage.

Stockholm International Peace Research Institute (1973) SIPRI Yearbook 1972. Stockholm: Almqvist & Wiksell.

――― (1971) *The Arms Trade with the Third World.* Stockholm: Almqvist & Wiksell.

――― (1970) SIPRI Yearbook 1968-1969. Stockholm: Almqvist & Wiksell.

WOLFERS, A. (1952) "National security as an ambiguous symbol." Political Science Quarterly 67 (December).

PART III

INTER-AMERICAN RELATIONS

Chapter 8

"NEW DIALOGUE" ON LATIN AMERICA:

THE COST OF POLICY NEGLECT

BEN S. STEPHANSKY

I

For five years the United States government ignored problems in the Western Hemisphere. Then in October 1973 it appeared to recover from its lapse of memory. Secretary of State Henry Kissinger offered the suggestion that a "new dialogue" be opened between the United States and the Latin American and Caribbean countries. Meriting a "new dialogue" constituted an instantaneous vast improvement for Latin America in the United States' scale of international priorities, and Secretary Kissinger's suggestion, therefore, evoked an immediate response. Within a month, Latin American and Caribbean foreign ministers as well as special representatives convened in Bogota, Colombia. They took note of the Secretary's initiative, drew up the "Document of Bogota" as a proposed agenda for the "new dialogue," and thus set the stage for the talks to begin.

Author's Note: *The meeting was cancelled in January, 1975, after this essay was written. The cancellation was a gesture of unanimous protest against certain allegedly "discriminatory" provisions of the Trade Relations Act, dealing with trade preferences for developing countries, adopted by the U.S. Congress and signed by the President in December 1974. In response to the cancellation, it now appears that the United States prefers to retreat from the "regional diplomacy" of the Conference of Foreign Ministers on the ground that Latin America obtained excessive leverage in that arena. Thus having brought the Conference of Foreign Ministers of the Americas into being with the "new dialogue," the United States seems to wish to return to "bilateral diplomacy" where its own leverage is stronger. These developments only serve to illuminate further the growing ideological obstacles to Latin American policy discussed in this essay, reflecting the high cost of neglect of the region by the Nixon administration.*

The first meeting took place in Mexico in February 1974, where the "Spirit of Tlatelolco" was kindled and the Conference of Foreign Ministers of the Americas came into being. The second "dialogue" took place in April 1974 in Washington, followed the same month by what appeared to be a "mini-dialogue" in Atlanta where the Fourth General Assembly meetings of the Organization of American States were held. The next session of the "new dialogue" is scheduled for March 1975 in Buenos Aires, Argentina.

These initial meetings have generated three major policy documents: the aforementioned Document of Bogota, the Declaration of Tlatelolco after the meeting in Mexico, and a Communiqué, following the Washington meeting. The Buenos Aires meeting will undoubtedly produce another document, as will subsequent meetings. Latin America's protracted policy drought thus appears to have passed to a time of policy plenitude. In the United States, the State Department is now "thinking policy" on Latin America; and a variety of private groups, eager to advise the policy-makers, is adding to the luxuriant growth of policy alternatives.

For students of Latin American policy, the outbreak of action at the policy front provides a kind of clinical laboratory for policy analysis. A variety of very lively policy issues can now be examined, and hypotheses can be tested regarding the underlying, as well as the more immediate, policy determinants at play on the action front. For the policy-maker on the Latin American front, the flurry of policy activity poses a different kind of issue. Although it is necessary that he be instructed about the determinants of policy, his role, as a practitioner of the "applied arts" of diplomacy requires him to deal with the visible and manageable attributes of those determinants and the way they interact at the negotiating front. It is particularly at the point of interaction of the determinants that opportunities are created for shaping policy. The diplomatic skill lies in the ability to discover and utilize those opportunities.

It is from the perspective of the practitioner that this piece is written. It focuses, therefore, on the opportunities for success of the "new dialogue," the major policy event in the hemisphere following a prolonged period of non-policy. Stated another way: Against the background of a five-year absence of policy, which translates into missed opportunities that may no longer be retrievable, will the Conference of Foreign Ministers have enough interacting and manageable policy determinants to shape a new policy for the hemisphere? The Conference of Foreign Ministers is barely beyond its inception, and its initial dialogues have been conducted in a spirit of great cordiality—attributable no doubt to the flattery bestowed upon Latin America by Secretary Kissinger's presence. Yet, the evidence is already discernible of profound ideological differences between the United States and Latin America which developed and hardened during the era of non-policy. These have been temporarily laid aside to permit the exploration of an ample agenda of non-ideological issues. Nevertheless, the ideological differences will haunt the "new dialogue" to the end, and will impose upon the non-ideological issues the heavy burden of whatever success the "new dialogue" may achieve.

Thus Latin America becomes part of a world in which negotiations with the United States are conducted in the limiting context of ideological divergence. If the Conference of Foreign Ministers can establish their own "detente" on ideology, a technique in which Secretary Kissinger excels, and if enough non-ideological issues can be agreed upon, the Conference on Foreign Ministers can enjoy a limited success. Indeed, under these conditions, the realistic prospect is that the "new dialogue" will not produce a new policy for the hemisphere, but rather a patchwork of "pragmatic" arrangements with which, if adjusted periodically, the hemisphere can live for the indefinite future. To achieve even this limited success, however, the new administration must avoid a relapse into the habit of amnesia about the hemisphere.

II

At the outset of the "new dialogue," the Conference of Foreign Ministers took two important decisions. The first decision, taken at the Mexican meeting, was to conduct its functions outside the structure of the formally constituted Inter-American System. The second decision, taken at the Washington meeting, was the rejection of Secretary Kissinger's invitation "to build a new Community." (His opening address to the Mexican meeting offered the suggestion on the occasion that he invoked the "Spirit of Tlatelolco.") Both decisions were at bottom ideological in character, and they provide a measure of the ideological distance that now separates the United States from Latin America. For the effect of these decisions is to contain the United States in an unaccustomed role of bystander as Latin America pursues a powerful ideological impulse to redefine and transform its relations with the United States and with nations outside the Western Hemisphere.

Latin America's determination to shape the course of its own world— always a latent force in the region's history—began to gather strength during the 1960s. Exactly when the process decisively took hold would be difficult to identify with precision. There is less difficulty in ascribing its cumulative momentum throughout the decade to a number of diverse factors. One would have to include in a list of those factors the "demonstration effect" of Cuba's slipping away from United States domination, establishing its "Socialist" state, and transferring its vital economic ties to the Soviet Union. These achievements account for the widespread sympathy Cuba currently enjoys among Latin American countries. Most of them dislike and even fear its socialism, but being embarked in a similar liberating enterprise, they accept the Cuban example as a genuine expression of contemporary Latin American history.

Another factor in the 1960s that prepared Latin America for its era of self-assertion was the Alliance for Progress, both in its affirmative and in its negative aspects. Among its positive features, the Alliance nurtured a "development consciousness." It encouraged sophisticated economic planning, demonstrated the possibility of managing domestic and multilateral development institutions, and produced a new "stable" of technically trained development talent. Thus the Alliance contributed to a growing self-confidence in Latin America's ability to manage its own development. Among the Alliance's negative features were the arbitrary prescriptions, the often onerous "conditions," the bias favoring the private sectors, and the "cold war" orientation. On this side the Alliance contributed to a growing restiveness with the externally dictated terms for the region's development. Thus both the positive and negative aspects of the Alliance conspired to exert their influence in creating a significant threshold of regional self-reliance during the decade of the 1960s.

Still another factor operating during the decade was the emergence of the United Nations Economic Commission as an influential instrument for economic development. Several of the achievements of the Economic Commission on Latin America (ECLA) paralleled those of the Alliance, particularly in economic planning and in technical training. Its most important contribution, however, was the design of regional economic integration. Both because it was an instrument operating outside the reach of United States authority, and because it opened the vision of larger and more viable economic units, ECLA served to enforce Latin America's impulse to extend the frontiers of independent action.

Finally, no comment on the 1960s can fail to note the surge of popular nationalism that spread to encompass virtually the entire region. The longer course of its evolution is unpredictable, for it can be courted by widely divergent political philosophies. But it is a factor that henceforth will be reckoned with in the region, either, for example, by forced containment as in Brazil, or by extension of popular institutions and social programs as in Venezuela. The visible effect of popular nationalism in Latin America's internal life was that two institutions, the Church and the Military, were wrested from their traditional support of the remaining oligarchies. As a force that could be directed toward Latin America's external relations, popular nationalism was readily mobilized during the 1960s to support Latin America's challenge for recuperation of its "sovereignty" from the United States.

Whatever additional factors may have been at work, it was clear by the end of the decade that they had converged into an ideology of independence from the long-standing primacy of United States interests in the region. The evidence that a new and powerful determinant was undeniably shaping events in the region during the latter 1960s was the eruption of aggressive challenges by no fewer than eleven Latin American nations in less than half a decade. These countries took issue with the United States on matters that, until then, had been endowed with the status of seemingly unbreakable traditions. The Latin states made new claims on sea boundaries and the limits of fishing territories; new restrictions on foreign investments; new demands for national participation—often for a controlling interest—in foreign-owned enterprises. They insisted on new schedules of taxes and royalties on foreign-owned petroleum and mining companies; nationalization of basic resources or their reservation for national exploitation; or outright expropriation of these basic resource industries.

The Nixon Administration had already assigned a low priority to Latin America at the very outset of its accession to office—the absence of any mention of Latin America in President Nixon's inaugural address was widely noted. So it recoiled from Latin America's pressures into a so-called policy of "low profile." There was a generous flow of rhetoric about a "new partnership" and a "special relationship" borrowed from the report of the turbulent Rockefeller mission in the spring of 1969, but the same year in fact witnessed the onset of the five-year retreat from policy. The Nixon Administration's withdrawal reaction is of more than casual interest, since it set the stage for the surrender of what may well have been the last opportunity for continuity of Latin American policy premised on a community of hemispheric interests between the United States and Latin America.

That opportunity occurred in June 1969, when the Consensus of Viña del Mar (named after the resort city in Chile where it was formulated) was delivered to President Nixon by the then foreign minister of Chile, Gabriel Valdés, on behalf of all the Latin American countries with the exception of Cuba. The Consensus was the work of Latin America's ministers of economy, finance, and foreign affairs, who were convened by a special Latin American coordinating committee (CECLA). Since 1964, CECLA had unsuccessfully sought to acquire official recognition within the Alliance for Progress as the coordinating instrument through which Latin America could assert its own voice in Alliance programs and policies. The committee was largely ignored by the Alliance, despite a brief moment of recognition by the United Nations in 1964 when it coordinated the positions of Latin American countries at the United Nations Conference on Trade and Development. CECLA came to the fore in April of 1969, when President Nixon announced the Rockefeller mission as his earpiece to "listen to the leaders" of Latin America, "and to consult with them concerning the development of common goals and joint programs of action." Refusing, however, to invest the Rockefeller mission with credibility, CECLA convened the ministers' meeting to formulate by "its own definition" Latin America's proposals for hemispheric policy. As it turned out, the Nixon Administration confirmed its retreat from Latin American policy by ignoring both Governor Rockefeller's recommendations and those presented in the Consensus of Viña del Mar.

The Rockefeller report stands as an anachronistic museum piece in its misinterpretation of recent Latin American history, a misreading that helps to illuminate by way of contrast the affirmative thrust of the Consensus of Viña del Mar. The central premise of the Rockefeller report was that the Alliance for Progress had failed. The thread of logic thereafter was spun as follows: Latin America was experiencing a "general frustration over the failure to achieve a more rapid improvement in standards of living. The United States, because of its identification with the failure of the Alliance for Progress . . . is blamed." This general feeling has "led increasing numbers of people to pick the United States as a scapegoat and to seek out Marxist solutions to their socioeconomic problems." The "rising frustrations" of the people "with the failure of their own governments to meet their needs" also make all of the Latin American nations "a tempting target for Communist subversion. In fact it is plainly evident that such subversion is a reality today with alarming potential." The crescendo of the argument placed Latin America at a "crossroads."

> The question of whether systems of freedom with order and justice will survive is no longer rhetorical. . . . At the moment, there is one Castro. . . . There can well be more in the future. And a Castro on the mainland, supported militarily and economically by the Communist world, would present the gravest kind of threat to the security of the Western Hemisphere.

The measure recommended in the Rockefeller report to curb the "forces of subversion that operate throughout the Western Hemisphere" was the establishment of a "civilian-directed Western Hemisphere Security Council" administering an enlarged program of United States grants to Latin American countries for military equipment, and training Latin American military and police personnel in the United States and Panama.

The Rockefeller report thus reached back into the 1950s for its rhetoric to interpret the region's recent history in the context of an outdated cold war strategy. Latin America's efforts to terminate the United States role as mentor of Latin America's development were misread as a "subversive" threat. This misinterpretation, and indeed the proposal for a new security structure to contain the political consequences of that "subversive" threat, richly merited the almost universal critical reaction it provoked in Latin America.

Drowned in the wave of Latin America's hostility to the "Western Hemisphere Security Council" were some eighty meritorious recommendations for economic and social cooperation advanced in the Rockefeller report. Standing alone, these recommendations could conceivably have engaged the proposals of the Consensus of Viña del Mar—that is, if the Nixon Administration had assigned a higher priority to Latin America. Since, instead the administration's interest in the region was tepid, Latin America's hostile rejection of the Rockefeller report—and the hostile and often violent reception accorded the Rockefeller mission in most of the twenty countries visited—was enough to persuade the Nixon Administration to set the Rockefeller report aside.

Had Latin America enjoyed even a modest priority rating with the Nixon Administration, the Consensus of Vinà del Mar would have been eagerly welcomed. The Viña del Mar meetings took place during an "eyeball to eyeball" confrontation between the United States and Peru over the expropriation of the International Petroleum Company and the tribulations of the Rockefeller mission. Considering these events and the general ferment of the times that imparted a militant flavor to the meetings, the Consensus that emerged was remarkably moderate. Moreover, it offered a policy prescription far more realistic than either the passivity of the Nixon Administration or the security structure proposed in the Rockefeller report. To be sure, the Consensus demanded a necessary change in United States outlook, but in return it offered continuity in mutual policy determination for the hemisphere. Upon receiving the Consensus proposals, President Nixon was asked to recognize that the Consensus had "far-reaching importance for the United States, because never before has your country encountered a Latin America united on its own definition." That its "own definition" still preserved hemispheric unity was clearly stated in the purpose of the Consensus: "To propose new approaches . . . for establishing jointly with the United States . . . new bases for inter-American economic and social cooperation."

It is of historical interest that contrary to the Rockefeller report's view of the Alliance for Progress, the Consensus of Viña del Mar did not pronounce the Alliance a failure. Its vision of policy was premised on the continuity of hemispheric interests between the United States and Latin America that were embodied in the Alliance. What the Consensus contemplated and urged was a renegotiation of the Alliance to accommodate an equal role for Latin America in Alliance policy and decisions. To this end the Consensus proposed that a reconstituted CECLA be recognized as the permanent Latin American negotiating body. Supported by various technical subcommittees, it would assure Latin America's equal voice in the Alliance. The United States and Latin America would have an equal voice in a readjusted inter-American system. Together, the Consensus proposed, they could work more directly and more effectively on the ample agenda of issues that were impeding Latin America's growth and development.

The Nixon Administration wholly ignored the Consensus of Viña del Mar. It thus permitted to pass into oblivion the last occasion on which Latin America visualized that it could achieve its historic purpose to shape its own world within a hemispheric community of compatible interests with the United States. It was an event of spectacular irony, therefore, when, at the opening of the "new dialogue" in 1974, Secretary of State Kissinger delivered what could have been the response to the Consensus of 1969: "We meet here as equals," he stated,

> representatives of our individual modes of life but united by one aspiration, to build a new community. We have an historic foundation on which to build. . . . On behalf of President Nixon, I commit the United States to undertake this venture with dedication and energy. . . . Today—together—we can begin giving expression to our common aspirations and start shaping our common future.

These remarks would have been received with strong enthusiasm by a Latin America in the mood of the Consensus. But much had happened during the interval between the Consensus and the "new dialogue" which Mr. Kissinger's statement ignored. The changes of five years were reflected in the address of Mexico's President, Luis Echeverria Alvarez. "Latin America," he stated, "forms part of the Third World. Its struggles are coincident with and parallel to those being made by other nations against colonialism, modern attempts at subjugation, injustice in international transactions." Other spokesmen also dwelt on the theme of Latin America as a "separate identity" linked to the Third World. Latin America, it was made plain, did form part of a "new community," but that "new community" was not the one offered by Secretary Kissinger.

Had Secretary Kissinger been less innocent of recent Latin American history, he would have known that when the United States turned away from Latin America in 1969, Latin America turned away from the United States. The evidence was abundant that by the time the "new dialogue" was proposed, Latin America had consolidated its control over its basic resource industries—mainly through the route of expropriation. The Andean Pact countries had pioneered in developing more rigorous terms for the regulation of foreign investment. Other nations had followed and had reserved new lines of activity for exclusive national exploitation. Latin America had established a vast, new network of diplomatic and commercial relations with countries around the world. It had significantly opened the continent to investment activity for Japan, Western Europe, the Soviet Union, Canada; activities reflected in a declining share of United States investment in the region. The Latin American nations had begun to concert their efforts to bring the transnational corporations under control. In short, Latin America had broken out from under the preponderant United States influence and had, with great vitality, charted a course that now linked the region to the world outside the Western Hemisphere. Latin America's disposition to join world-wide "clubs" to demand better terms for increasingly scarce primary products, plus mounting worldwide inflation and the energy crisis, may well have caused the United States to belatedly recognize the full impact of Latin America's new orientation and call for the "new dialogue."

What needs to be understood at this juncture of the "new dialogue" is that the changes that have occurred since the United States and Latin America turned away from each other, were not adjustments of convenience. On Latin America's part, these were expressions of a profound change in ideological orientation. The ideological impulse that underlies the changes were evident in the reactions of the foreign ministers rejecting the "new community." Even before the "new dialogue" opened, Latin America had informed the United States in thirteen concise paragraphs of the Document of Bogota that (to adopt a familiar analogy) it had a new "game plan" for its part of the Western Hemisphere. The Document is well worth pondering, for it definitively separates and distinguishes Latin America's own interests in the hemisphere from those of the United States. In summary, the Document stated:

Latin America's growing and positive nationalism constitutes a vigorous force for Latin American unity. It implies a common will to define Latin America's own personality as a community of sovereign states with its own historical, cultural, and social character.

Internally, Latin America is determined to extend its regional integration—indeed, in order to achieve its own development, the duty of each country is to cooperate integrally, sharingly, and solidaristically. With this cooperation the subregional organizations of integration can be consolidated continentally.

Externally, the community to which Latin America belongs is the community of the Third World, the world of the developing countries. It is through joint cooperation with the developing countries that Latin America can command the following: just and equitable terms for its basic products, favorable trade terms, the elimination of trade barriers, access to technology, and proper conditions for loans from international agencies. Thus together with the developing world it can emerge from the condition of dependency.

The organizational mechanism for both continental and external coordination is a further strengthened CECLA, Latin America's instrument for joint Latin American action.

At no point in the Document, prepared for the "new dialogue," did any indication appear of the issues that Latin America might wish to place on the negotiating agenda. What the Document presented was the one non-negotiable agenda item: its ideological position, stated by Latin America, about Latin America. On this matter, the United States was a bystander. The inference to be drawn was also very plain. The issues to be negotiated in the course of the "new dialogue" could not be considered in the context of mutual hemispheric interests; rather they were to be considered in the context of separate interests, separately defined. For Latin America, the United States is another country of the world, albeit a very important one, that stands outside the Latin American part of the hemisphere.

At the first meeting of the Conference of Foreign Ministers the "new community" was rejected, and action was taken to operate outside the formal Inter-American System. In view of the ideological distance that now separates Latin America from the United States, the reason should be self-evident. The reason is that the Inter-American System—the Organization of American States and its related treaties and organisms—is no longer acceptable. Structured during the long era of the United States' unchallenged power in the hemisphere, many of the System's institutions incorporated that reality. The System has long symbolized, therefore, the domination of Latin America by the United States. It contains an abundance of institutions and functions created by the now outdated Alliance for Progress. Furthermore, it is encrusted with a coating of cold war resolutions and actions that are repugnant to Latin America.

The degree of incompatibility between contemporary Latin America's ideological stance and the ideology once represented by the Inter-American System is denoted by the difference in the roles played by the OAS. The Economic and Social Council of the OAS was the negotiating center for the Alliance for Progress, but, except for very minor documenting functions, the OAS will play no role in the work of the Conference of Foreign Ministers. CECLA, not the OAS, will perform the staff and coordinating functions for the Conference of Foreign Ministers. The Inter-American Development Bank has considered withdrawing its charter from the OAS, where it is deposited, and transferring it to the United Nations. One of the OAS Councils, that on Education, Science and Culture, has considered technology to lie in its domain; and the OAS Economic and Social Council would normally have been assigned the subject of transnational enterprises. Nevertheless, the Conference of Foreign Ministers has created two important committees, one on technology and another on multinational corporations. It is an open secret that Cuba will be invited to attend the next meeting of the Conference of Foreign Ministers in Buenos Aires, and in all likelihood will attend. Thus the Conference of Foreign Ministers, not the OAS (which Cuba would never join in its present form), will be the agent for "normalizing" Cuba's relations with Latin America.

That the Inter-American System is "in crisis" is generally recognized. For more than a year a special OAS commission has been wrestling with the gigantic task of its reorganization. In line with its outlook, the Document of Bogota emphasized, in its seventh point, that the System must be restructured to take account of "the new political, economic, social, and cultural conditions of the American States," as well as of the new "Hemisphere and World circumstances." What the exact shape of the new System will be is not yet foreseeable. It can, however, be safely predicted that a sturdier and more complete Latin American organization will emerge, and that any new "Inter-American" relationship will be adjusted to represent an equal status between the two parts of the hemisphere.

III

To prevent the ideological distance between the United States and Latin America from becoming an ideological chasm, the success of the Conference of Foreign Ministers will rest heavily on the more pragmatic, non-ideological issues to be negotiated. These are, of course, the economic issues. In broad terms the case can readily be made that in the economic realm, the United States and Latin America continue to "need each other." Latin America requires external resources and markets particularly to sustain its diversifying economies. The United States requires basic materials, including petroleum and minerals, and can well benefit from capital exports, a declining share of the Latin American market could still mean a higher export trade in absolute terms. Along with this general equation of needs, however, some warnings should also be raised.

In an ideological mood, Latin America may well infuse seemingly pragmatic issues with ideological content. This could happen, for example, in the case of investment regulations for transnational enterprises, in the matter of trade preferences, on the question of transfer of technology, on the issue of limiting foreign investment in Latin American common market industries, and on matters of aid and the operation of international agencies. It is difficult to see how many of these and perhaps other issues can be readily separated from their ideological content. In particular, two complex issues, transnational enterprises and technology transfer, have been placed on the top of the agenda for consideration at the next meeting of the Conference of Foreign Ministers, and will test the depth of Latin America's ideological disposition. Trade preferences are sure to follow soon, although apparently a provisional agreement under the forthcoming United States trade legislation permits Latin America a period of appeal and possible negotiation in cases where either tariff or non-tariff regulations are considered excessively disadvantageous for Latin American products. In this case the OAS Economic and Social Council, temporarily at least, may be the agency to alert Latin America to possible disadvantages and to provide the setting for negotiation.

Whether a climate of "detente" on ideology can be created to permit negotiations to proceed successfully, will test the skill of the Conference of Foreign Ministers. Unfortunately, as is often the case, political issues can arise to agitate negotiations on issues otherwise open to pragmatic solution. If, for example, the Panama Canal question is not settled—and it has been referred to in the communiqués following the first two meetings—it could go hard with the "new dialogue's" negotiations.

There are some other areas of danger, external to the Conference of Foreign Ministers, that could derail negotiations. Although Latin America has united on its ideological posture, and can unite readily on its common economic front vis-a-vis the United States, its internal unity displays some tensions. There is, for example, the matter of Brazil's expansion of economic influence. Argentina, because it feels challenged in its leadership role in South America, and smaller countries, because they feel "penetrated," can become very restive about this expansion. President Nixon commented in 1972 that "as Brazil goes, so goes the rest of the Latin American continent." It is to be hoped that the United States is no longer guided by such a sentiment. If the United States is tempted to play on the tensions attending Latin America's internal adjustments to the emerging strength of any country or subregional bloc, it can reap a whirlwind. The United States must assume that no part of Latin America will return to the fold of a hemispheric community, and that special favors bestowed on any nation or any bloc will not gain any bargaining advantage. Although Latin America may well enjoy important bargaining advantages at this time, its external long-term needs should move it toward new accommodations with the United States on pragmatic issues. The United States should accept Latin America's solidarity on a common economic front as a major premise in its approach to the "new dialogue."

One of the vexatious problems that lie ahead for the Conference of Foreign Ministers is the question of the future of the smaller countries in the Caribbean and in Central America. They will require special treatment for a long time, which Latin America may be less able to afford than can the United States. Here again may lie a source of temptation; but if the United States acts wisely, it will encourage the Inter-American Development Bank, the World Bank, and the subregional Caribbean and Central American development banks to balance any special role it may play in these smaller-state subregions. In fact, it may be advantageous to have the Conference of Foreign Ministers design and act as broker for any special United States attention to these areas.

Finally, one must take account of the possible erosion of Secretary Kissinger's "credibility" with the Latin American foreign ministers following the September 1974 revelations of the CIA's "destabilization" operation in Chile during the Allende regime, and in view of the role of the so-called 40 Committee over which Secretary Kissinger presided in sanctioning the CIA operation. Supreme confidence in Secretary Kissinger was a psychological ingredient of no small importance in the adoption of his suggestion to initiate the "new dialogue"; and whether its effective continuity has been seriously damaged is surely a question that will confront the next meeting of the Conference of Foreign Ministers. But even if the Conference can survive a diminished Secretary Kissinger, will the mounting number and complexity of international issues require more of his time and attention than he can possibly be expected to manage, particularly if new emergencies erupt in the Near East or elsewhere?

If the success of the Conference of Foreign Ministers hangs on these threads, it would be prudent, well before the March 1975 meeting in Buenos Aires, to "institutionalize" its continuity. The Conference is potentially too valuable for both Latin America and the United States to be permitted to falter, let alone be discontinued. Now that the "new community" is disposed of, the foreseeable success of the Conference lies in its important pragmatic piecemeal achievements. While less ambitious, these will constitute the basic texture of United States-Latin American relations for the indefinite future. It follows, then, that the Conference of Foreign Ministers may very soon find it advantageous to create a larger number of working committees than the two it created at the last meeting. Provided with sufficient staff and resources, those working committees could continue in the event of any major interruption in the work of the Conference itself.

IV

The prospects for success, failure, or partial success that lie ahead for the Conference of Foreign Ministers cannot be considered without reference to one other ideological factor—the United States' own ideological climate. Ideologically, the United States can contemplate with equanimity a separate Latin American identity in the Western Hemisphere, oriented toward the Third World. It does, however, have some difficulty with individual countries. The collective ideology with which Latin America confronts the United States implies no internal consensus for political uniformity among the Latin American nations. There is, in short, ideological solidarity for dealing with the United States; but internally, political ideology is greatly diversified. It is on this threshold, involving the bilateral relations between the United States and individual Latin American countries, where the United States' ideological climate comes into play, and can clash with the individual political ideologies of Latin American countries.

Several countries in Latin America are governed by cruel and oppressive political regimes, which have virtually enshrined the erosion of human rights as a matter of ideological principle. Brazil considers the violation of human rights a necessary condition for economic development; Chile conceives it as a "state of war" to extirpate a socialist ideology; Bolivia regards it as principle of political stability, as do other military regimes. The United States should feel an obligation to respect the collective will of Latin America to define its identity and its orientation. On the other hand, the United States owes no automatic obligation to deal intimately with any nation whose violations of human rights clash with its own commitment to human values.

This does not suggest or imply for the United States any policing role of another nation's behavior. It does imply an option to withdraw to a limited, and formally correct relationship where the United States judges that violations of human rights have reached an intolerable level, or even worse, where the violations have been accorded an ideological justification.

In the new configuration which Latin America presents to the United States, confusion can well be born that each individual country automatically embodies the high ideals and values of the region taken together. That does not follow. If it did, the United States would need to feel compelled in a number of cases to enter into intimate relations with a brutal military regime, offer it generous assistance and cooperation, and forgo the human contact with its people and its human, social, and intellectual institutions. That cannot be an acceptable obligation for the United States.

It would be well for this question to be raised at the next session of the "new dialogue." The new relationships of the hemisphere are being designed to adjust to Latin America's determination to shape its own world. The recognition of that legitimate, and, at bottom, human impulse, cannot be regarded as compatible with the destruction of human rights. The Document of Bogota overlooked the Universal Declaration of Human Rights adopted by the United Nations in 1948. If, as part of the agenda of the next meeting of the Conference of Foreign Ministers, there cannot be a meaningful reaffirmation of the Declaration, then the United States can at least define where it stands and what options it reserves for itself.

Chapter 9

THE UNITED STATES AND PUERTO RICO:

A CRITIQUE

ROBERT W. ANDERSON

Puerto Rico is of no little symbolic importance in the inter-American community. It is the only Latin American country never to have achieved even nominal independence and the only one to have come under the direct imperial control of the United States. For many, it remains a living symbol of United States imperialism in the Caribbean. On the other hand, it is often cited as a model for democratic development in Latin America and the Third World. Though still perhaps a "remnant" of the United States maritime empire, it can take its place in lists of countries that have attained relatively high gross national products per capita—indeed, as of 1969, it had a higher rate than that of Italy, the U.S.S.R., or Ireland (see Cohen, 1973: 87, 146). Over the last two decades Puerto Rico has often been referred to as a showcase for democratic economic development, a model of democratic stability and maturity, and a land well on the way toward "takeoff" and true development (see Friedrich, 1959; Denny, 1968; Wells, 1969).

So Puerto Rico represents two conflicting symbols in Latin America. One is that of the last vestiges of American imperialism in the hemisphere; and the other that of benign American tutelage in the ways of democratic develop- ment and economic progress. Both ingredients must be considered in any attempt to understand the situation of Puerto Rico and its comparative significance in inter-American affairs.

In the United States much discussion of Puerto Rico and both official and popular opinion regarding the island are based solidly on the notion of the "uniqueness" of the Puerto Rican experience: Puerto Rico's present com- monwealth status reflects a special relationship with the United States, often described as creative, unusual, original, which is comparable neither to the juridical sovereignty of her Latin American neighbors, nor yet to the federated states of the North American Union. Puerto Ricans are U.S. citizens. The functional attributes of this citizenship, however, differ from those of other citizens residing in the fifty federal states. They are a collectivity which in English is called a "Commonwealth" and in Spanish a "Free Associated State"—two terms which do not mean the same thing at all, but which, when used in contradictory juxtaposition, add a further dimension to the "uniqueness" of Puerto Rico's status. The terms and concepts which attest to the island's alleged political uniqueness can be seen at best as expressions of confusion over the ambiguities and contradictions in present-day legal and political relations between the United States and Puerto Rico, and at worst as attempts to hide the realities of colonial dependency and political inferiority.

The theory of Puerto Rico's uniqueness, then, is a cloak for disguising or rationalizing the underlying ambiguities and uncertainties of a still-unsuccessful attempt to cope with a fundamentally colonial situation. In this world imperial domination and colonial dependency are hardly unique. The problem of United States-Puerto Rico relations can most readily be understood, in my view, within the context of the wider problem of colonialism and the challenge of decolonization. This article will attempt to deal with the current manifestations of this problem.

At this writing, the problem of Puerto Rico's status vis-a-vis the United States and the rest of the world has taken on renewed salience. The status debate has been formalized in recent months in Puerto Rico and Washington by the creation of a joint United States-Puerto Rico "Ad Hoc Advisory Group." It is the latest in a brief historical series of similar groups charged specifically with looking into the problems of United States-Puerto Rican relations within the context of the presumably developing commonwealth arrangement. As a result of its deliberations, some specific recommendations may be made to Congress and to the federal Executive Branch for modifications or improvements in the commonwealth status. Presumably, such modifications will be in the direction of greater autonomy for Puerto Rico and a consequent lessening of colonial vestiges.

In the United Nations, the non-aligned and socialist-bloc countries have kept the case of Puerto Rico alive in the Committee on Decolonization, where they are numerically powerful. In 1953 the General Assembly decided that Puerto Rico had achieved full self-government the year before with the advent of the Commonwealth and that the United States was therefore relieved from submitting annual reports on its stewardship as demanded by Article 73 of the United Nations Charter. Nevertheless, the case of Puerto Rico is not closed as far as the international community is concerned. This is perhaps a small problem for such a powerful and self-sufficient nation as the United States, but it is one which can become increasingly bothersome in a world officially committed to decolonization. Whatever their ideological or political motivations may be, there are countries which will consistently keep the issue alive in the United Nations as long as there is reasonable doubt about the purity and completeness of the decolonization process in Puerto Rico.

Finally, the status debate on the island itself has intensified in recent years. This is saying a good deal, since the status issue in Puerto Rico has always been the ultimate center of political issues on the island (see Anderson, 1965). Political issues in Puerto Rico are forged into ideological stands and emotive commitments as they are transmuted into alternative preferences regarding national identity and the desired (final) relationship with the United States. In other words, the colonial problem in Puerto Rico defines the heart and soul of its people's political attitudes and behavior. The intensification of the status issue in Puerto Rican politics during the past six years or so is reflected in the fact that a statehood-oriented party has emerged as the most powerful formally organized electoral opposition to the majority party, which is pledged to a continuation of the commonwealth status. Owing to a split in the majority party (*Partido Popular Democrático*, PPD) in 1968, this statehood-oriented party (*Partido Nuevo Progresista*, PNP) won control of the governorship and of the lower house of the legislature and governed, albeit precariously, for the next four years. Although it lost again in 1972, it is clearly a force to be reckoned with, and an alternating two-party system for the foreseeable future is quite conceivable.

The fact that one side of this two-party alignment is committed to the idea of federal statehood in a future which is not seen as unreasonably distant brings the status issue to the fore in a peculiarly poignant fashion. The local opposition which the commonwealth defenders have to face on the electoral front sees commonwealth as at best a transitory status on the way to full assimilation in the American union. The defenders of commonwealth must advocate increasing measures of autonomy for Puerto Rico in order to justify the decolonizing nature of their preferred status. At the same time, they face a powerful local opposition which emphasizes growing participation in the American federal system with an eye on full membership as a federated state. The internal dynamics of the Puerto Rican party system make it exceedingly difficult for the commonwealth defenders to press forward on their own initiative for significantly broader areas of local autonomy. Yet a number of large difficulties stand in the way of formal assimilation. The constraints of the U.S. federal system and the conservatism of Congress when considering the problems of overseas territories, would erect enormous political obstacles to statehood for Puerto Rico if it were ever to be proposed seriously to Congress. Moreover, the international community is sensitive to any changes in status away from self-determination and independence.

A complete rethinking of the perspectives from which to view the problems of Puerto Rico's decolonization is necessary. Before turning to an outline of this perspective, I will deal with the nature of the status debate as it has emerged in the last few years, and discuss the reasons why the debate in its present guise seems to me to be earmarked for sterility. The status problem should be restated in a way which can be conducive to substantive rather than euphemistic solutions.

THE STATE OF THE STATUS: 1974

The Ad Hoc Advisory Group which is presently studying possible modifications in the commonwealth arrangement is the second such group to be convened. The United States-Puerto Rico Status Commission, in its report of 1966, suggested that if the Puerto Ricans chose commonwealth status, these committees should be set up as mechanisms for studying and recommending ways of developing, improving, or "culminating" the commonwealth (United States-Puerto Rico Status Commission, 1966a: 8-9). The Status Commission, holding that commonwealth, statehood, and independence were equally worthy solutions to the status question, stated that it was up to the Puerto Rican people to decide; and on July 23, 1967, the plebiscite was held. With some two-thirds of the registered voters participating, a little over 60 percent of the ballots cast were for commonwealth status, and 39 percent were for statehood. The vote for independence was negligible, since most of its supporters boycotted the referendum.

A severe internal conflict in the PPD prevented the government from immediately establishing the ad hoc committee, and the victory of the statehood-oriented PNP in 1968 threw the popular-commonwealth strategy into temporary disarray. Much to the chagrin of the PPD leadership, which still controlled the Senate, the new administration under Governor Luis A. Ferré did proceed to create an ad hoc committee in conjunction with the Nixon Administration. However, it was done in a manner which joined the issue again along strict partisan lines.

This ad hoc committee was created solely to study the possibility of the presidential vote for the people of Puerto Rico. Its members were appointed in April 1970, and its formal title was the "Ad Hoc Advisory Group on the Presidential Vote for Puerto Rico." It submitted its report on August 18, 1971. The PPD, through its new leader, then president of the Senate, Rafael Hernández Colón (he was to be elected governor in 1972), bitterly criticized the Ferré Administration for establishing a committee to deal with one isolated aspect of possible modifications in the commonwealth arrangements. Moreover, the aspect was one which would lead to greater identification with the federal system rather than to enhance autonomy for Puerto Rico. In November 1970, the Central Council of the PPD, meeting in the town of Aguas Buenas, passed a lengthy declaration categorically rejecting assimilation (statehood) and calling for "fundamental changes" in the relations between Puerto Rico and the United States within the commonwealth framework. The declaration questioned the adequacy of the ad hoc committees in dealing with these problems (the committees are composed of equal representation of Puerto Ricans and North Americans) and called for a new Constituent Assembly to be convoked once the party was again in power. The purpose of this assembly would be to hammer out the necessary modifications in the commonwealth arrangement for presentation to the U.S. Congress and other pertinent federal authorities.

Hernández Colón testified before the ad hoc committee on the presidential vote on March 3, 1971. Quoting from the 1962 Joint Resolution 1 of the Legislative Assembly of Puerto Rico, he insisted that improvements in the commonwealth must be carried out as an "integral and organic develop-ment," rather than in the piecemeal fashion indicated by exclusive consid-eration of the presidential vote. He reiterated his party's commitment to a constituent assembly were it to win the elections of 1972. Such an assembly, after the interval of PNP domination on the island, would give the U.S. Congress a necessary reaffirmation and revalidation of the commonwealth mandate of 1967.

As expected, the Ad Hoc Advisory Group failed to heed the admonitions of the Senate president and of others who testified in similar vein. Its report recommended the presidential vote for Puerto Rico and suggested that a plebiscite be held to ratify the people's will on the matter. The committee rejected the claim that commonwealth should be dealt with exclusively from an "integral approach," pointing out that attempts to deal with the problem in a comprehensive manner, such as through the aborted Fernós-Murray Bill of 1959, had failed.[1] It found the presidential vote for Puerto Rico to be "feasible and just," and the "moment opportune for action by Puerto Rico and the United States" (Ad Hoc Advisory Group, 1971: 7, 12). After Hernández Colón became governor, the presidential vote idea was virtually dropped, and the agenda of the present ad hoc committee does not mention it.

The idea of a Constituent Assembly has also been dropped. It was hardly mentioned by the *populares* during the 1972 campaign, and, contrary to the Aguas Buenas declaration, the ad hoc committee mechanism was revived as the method of initiating recommendations for change in United States-Puerto Rico relations. The present Ad Hoc Advisory Group is composed of seven Puerto Rican members, named by the governor, and seven U.S. representatives appointed by the president. Ex-Governor Luis Muñoz Marín and Senator Marlow Cook of Kentucky are co-chairmen.[2]

In December 1973, the Puerto Rican members of this committee drew up a document consisting of "guidelines, proposals, and background data" for the consideration of the committee as a whole. It consists of fifteen areas in which, from the Puerto Rican point of view, improvements in the commonwealth arrangement are possible and desirable. The governing principle for the overall review of the Federal Relations Act should be, according to this declaration, "maximum self-government or maximum participation within the framework of the free associated state concept." The Federal Relations Act consists of the substantial parts of the Organic Acts for Puerto Rico (the Foraker Act of 1900 and the Jones Act of 1917) which were unaffected by Law 600 of 1950 authorizing the steps leading to the Constitution of Puerto Rico. It continues to refer to Puerto Rico as a "possession" of the United States and extends to Puerto Rico federal laws "not locally inapplicable"—an area which, excluding federal tax laws, is exceedingly vast and patently expanding. (See Section 9 of the Federal Relations Act, 64 Stat. 314.)

Other points for discussion for the Ad Hoc Advisory Group include such things as Puerto Rican participation in immigration policy, possible exemption from the coastwise shipping laws, widening Puerto Rican participation in regional trade agreements, greater local control over financial and investment regulations, reduction of federal intervention in environmental protection, possible Puerto Rican control of communications, and ways in which Puerto Rico may participate in federal decisions and legislation affecting the island. The approach from the Puerto Rican side is wide-ranging and "integral" and hinges on the still rather abstract concept of commonwealth/free associated state.[3]

The official position of the government of Puerto Rico was formally presented to the committee by Governor Hernández Colón on April 27, 1974. He reiterated the familiar theme of originality and creativity of the commonwealth situation as a special way of emerging from the evils of colonialism. He stated that the people of Puerto Rico wished neither independence nor statehood, but rather "maximum self-government" while being "permanently associated with the United States"; but that the "flower of self-government" was not yet in "full bloom." He suggested that the terms of the Federal Relations Act should be modified in order to prevent the automatic application to the island of congressional laws which are "inadvertently detrimental to the best interests of the people of Puerto Rico." He mentioned as examples the federal environmental laws, the Federal Communications Commission's jurisdiction in Puerto Rico, federal plant and animal protection safety laws, federal labor laws such as the Taft-Hartley Act and the Fair Labor Standards Act, the Immigration and Nationality Act, various federal shipping laws, and the federal trade and tariff enactments. These refer to areas which should be under the jurisdiction of the commonwealth. He suggested that Section 9 of the Federal Relations Act be amended so that unless Congress specifically extends the application of a law to Puerto Rico, it would not apply to the island. In addition, Puerto Rico should have the right to object formally, through a plebiscite, to a bill passed by Congress and extended to Puerto Rico without the latter's participation or consent.

These demands for improving commonwealth are most significant. On the one hand, they state clearly that the acquisition of self-government in 1952 was at best a partial attainment. Federal control continues to cover vast areas of fundamental economic and social import on the island. On the other hand, an assumption is made that Puerto Rico is a functioning, albeit special, collectivity within the American federal system, and that its peculiarities and special national interests can best be preserved within the framework of that system. As Governor Hernández Colón put it in his testimony before the ad hoc committee: "[Al] though citizens of the United States, the Puerto Ricans collectively are a people recognized as such by the United States," and "the Commonwealth relationship is a fresh and creative concept within American constitutional law and there are few constitutional limitations on its development to maximum self-government." These two assumptions are basic moral and legal props for the commonwealth faith. They are essentially unprovable and are hardly adequate bases for arguing that colonialism has come to an end in United States-Puerto Rican relations.

The problem of the proper relation between Puerto Rico and the United States is normally transmuted into a debate on *status*. That is, it becomes a controversy about legal definitions and constitutional categories and constructions. In order for commonwealth not to be *called* a colony, for example, it is necessary to prove that Puerto Rico stopped being a "territory" of the United States the moment the Constitution of 1952 went into formal effect, and that Congress no longer holds ultimate plenary authority over the island in accordance with the territorial clause of the U.S. Constitution. In a closely reasoned, highly legalistic article published in 1959, the future governor, Hernández Colón, argued that Puerto Rico became a "state" in 1952 as a consequence of Law 600 and the ensuing constituent act which produced the commonwealth constitution. He pointed out that a territory is legally a creation of Congress, whereas a state predates Congress and is the creation of its people. Puerto Rico, he argued, was turned into a sovereign state by Law 600, in the same manner as formally admitted states. Congress by that act indicated its intention of abdicating its territorial powers over Puerto Rico. Thus, by a wave of the wand of judicial exegesis, the people of Puerto Rico achieved their "sovereignty"–a limited sovereignty, to be sure, but legally and morally valid all the same. It remains for the Supreme Court to validate such a determination and to confirm thereby the solution to Puerto Rico's status problem.

Several years later a careful observer of Puerto Rican constitutional developments stated that "if the courts should hold that the federal government no longer operates within Puerto Rico on the basis of the territorial clause, it gives the Puerto Rican people the desired limitation on the rights of federal government activity in Puerto Rico–some area of sovereignty–and at the same time continues the federal government's necessary role in the area of foreign and national security" (Leibowitz, 1968: 632). After 22 years of judicial silence on the issue, the U.S. Supreme Court has finally indicated that it might be moving in that direction. In a recent decision (Calero-Toledo vs. Pearson Yacht Leasing Co., No. 73-157), the Court held that Puerto Rico ceased to be a "territory" in 1952 and has become a state "within a common and accepted meaning of the word." It deemed Puerto Rico to be "sovereign over matters not ruled by the Constitution of the United States and thus a 'State' " within the policy of the federal statute creating three-judge federal district courts.

If this decision caused satisfaction among the defenders of commonwealth, it was also greeted with enthusiasm by statehood adherents. It certified Puerto Rico as a "state" and was silent about any special characteristics which would juridically distinguish Puerto Rico from any of the other fifty states. Understandably, adherents of statehood interpreted the decision as another stroke sealing Puerto Rico into the irreversible box of outright assimilation into the U.S. system.

The attempts to define and to solve the question of United States-Puerto Rico relations in purely legal and constitutional terms do little to dispel the confusions and aggravations of the problem. To define the status problem in purely legal and constitutional terms is to stand the problem on its head. The problem is not simply one of defining an acceptable legal solution. It is not a matter of solving the problem of "sovereignty" in a way which will satisfy the lawyers and the constitutionalists.

When the United States invaded Puerto Rico in 1898 and then took it over as a prize of war, it did not simply change a superficial constitutional "status." (A common Puerto Rican euphemism is to refer to what happened in that year as merely a "change in sovereignty.") It went systematically and openly about the tasks of colonizing the newly acquired territory and its population, through political domination, economic penetration, and cultural Americanization (for the educational process of the last, see, for example, Negrón de Montilla, 1971). If we are to persist in speaking of the "status problem" of Puerto Rico, it should be with as clear an understanding as possible of the social and political dimensions of the problem. These are rooted in more than 400 years of colonialism, the last 75 of which have been under the overpowering aegis of the North American brand of imperialism. To tinker with the constitutional subtleties of commonwealth in the hope of dissolving the traumas of colonialism and its heritage is, truly, to plow in the seas.

DIMENSIONS OF THE STATUS ISSUE

International Relations

The United Nations' attention to the Puerto Rican case has already been mentioned. The case would be of legitimate interest in the international community even if there were no Cubans in the United Nations to raise the defensive hackles of the U.S. delegates; and it would be so as well even if the commonwealth were less ambiguous than it is or were headed inexorably toward federal statehood. The case cannot be discussed exclusively as a domestic problem of the United States, to be worked out in splendid isolation in conjunction with the island and within the hermetic confines of the North American constitutional system.

In the first place, there is the simple fact that the United Nations does have the case of Puerto Rico under advisement. In 1973 the General Assembly accepted a resolution which had been adopted the previous year by the "Special Committee on the Situation with Regard to the Interpretation of the Declaration on the Granting of Independence to Colonial Countries and Peoples." In this resolution the Committee:

1. *reaffirms* the inalienable right of the people of Puerto Rico to self-determination and independence in accordance with General Assembly resolution 1514(XV) of December 1960.

2. *requests* the government of the United States of America to refrain from taking any measures which might obstruct the full and free exercise by the people of their inalienable right to self-determination and independence, as well as of their economic, social, and other rights, and in particular to prevent any violation of these rights by bodies corporate under its jurisdiction . . .

3. *decides* to keep the question under continuous review [U.N. General Assembly A/9023 Part I 6 Nov., 1973: 34-35].

The U.S. delegation scorned the resolution as an unwarranted intervention in the internal affairs of the United States and Puerto Rico. Similarly, Puerto Rican government spokesmen ridiculed it, especially since the Cuban delegation had been the ones to press the matter and the principal testimony before the committee had been provided by Puerto Rican independence leaders whose electoral successes had been minimal. As a resolution, it is perhaps no more than a minor irritant to the United States. Yet international pressures such as these may have had something to do with the reopening of status conversations through the ad hoc committee arrangements, however modest they may be.

Other aspects of international pressures on the Puerto Rican situation bear more closely upon the immediate dilemmas of the commonwealth. The above-quoted resolution implies an identification of self-determination with independence which can be questioned in the light of other United Nations statements on the matter. Resolution 1514 (XV) of 1960 states that an acceptable solution to the problem of colonialism is that of "free association" with another country. Principle 7 of that resolution states that for such an association to be valid, it must be "the result of a free and voluntary choice" expressed through "democratic processes." The "freedom to modify the status" of association in the future must be retained, and the "associated territory should have the right to determine its internal constitution without outside interference." Puerto Rico's status as an "associated state" within the meaning of these dicta from the United Nations is questionable at best. There is doubt about the degree of "integration" of the commonwealth/free associated state into the federal constitution, and thus about the revocability of the steps taken in 1952 and afterward; there is doubt as to the inviolability of the Puerto Rican constitution from federal intervention; and, above all, there is more than a little doubt regarding the international juridical personality of Puerto Rico (see Friedrich, 1968: 98-99; Cabranes, 1974).

There is a long and difficult road to traverse before these doubts can be effectively dispelled. Governor Hernández Colón has indicated to the current Ad Hoc Advisory Group that ways must be explored to gain Puerto Rico a wider and more autonomous role in international affairs. Some observers have pointed out that Puerto Rico could easily participate in a number of international organizations, including the United Nations, as either full or associate member or observer, without changing the present constitutional status of the island.[4] Such participation could help to buttress internal autonomy and to establish the international standing of the island as a free associated state. All that would be necessary from the Puerto Rican side would be the commitment to pay the pertinent quota for membership, the will to play an autonomous role in international affairs, and the approval and good offices of the United States.

Individual Puerto Ricans have held important diplomatic posts for the United States in the inter-American area, especially during the Kennedy-Johnson administrations and the optimistic heyday of the Alliance for Progress. To date, however, Puerto Rico's role on the international scene has been mainly that of passive agent rather than active principal. It could not play an active and autonomous role in the Caribbean area through such organizations as the Caribbean Commission and its successor, the Caribbean Organization, between 1946 and 1964, because they were both dominated by the metropolitan colonial powers. After withdrawing from the moribund Caribbean Organization in 1965, the commonwealth government created the Caribbean Development Corporation (CODECA) in an attempt to stimulate economic cooperation in the Caribbean through individual projects of a concrete and pragmatic nature, without the formal trappings of an international organization (Corkran, 1970). This experiment was stifled by the statehood-oriented Ferré Administration, but that of Governor Hernández Colón is presumably committed to widening Puerto Rico's role as an autonomous entity on the international scene.

How this might be done is one of the matters on the agenda of the present ad hoc committee. The approach of the commonwealth defenders must be cautious, because the principal domestic opposition on the island is hostile to an autonomous international posture and the American politicians and policy-makers are predictably reluctant to concede anything other than a symbolic role in this regard to a commonwealth within the U.S. federal system.

The exigencies of anticolonialism in the world environment, the inherent ambiguities in Puerto Rico's international status, and local and stateside constraints, all contribute to the complex international dimension of the Puerto Rico status problem.

The Economics of "Development"

The evolution of commonwealth status paralleled and complemented the commitment to industrialization through private investment from the mainland. Indeed, one can hardly be conceived without the other. In economic terms, commonwealth means exemption from federal taxes, fiscal autonomy to grant exemptions from local taxes, tariff-free access to the stateside market, ultimate protection by the American constitution, and free movement of peoples between the island and the continental United States. In other words, it continues the basic conditions governing the relations between the island and the mainland since the earlier, openly colonial, Foraker and Jones Acts. Tax exemption for new industries, extensive services to mainland foreign investors—including worker training programs, industrial research facilities, and government-owned and -leased physical plants, an ample and relatively low-wage labor supply with an "escape valve" via unrestricted immigration to the United States to relieve the pressures of excess population—were and are the principal mainstays of Puerto Rico's economic development. A continuation of the basic conditions of Puerto Rico's relations with the United States was considered essential for the success of this development. Puerto Rico's political evolution could not be at the expense of its economic progress, and economic progress depended on not changing in any fundamental way the basic conditions of United States-Puerto Rico relations. The commonwealth is the result of this attempt to square the circle. Political considerations were to be subordinated at every turn to the strategies of economic developmentalism. Given the quantitative growth of the Puerto Rican economy over the last 25 years and its heralded claims of success, the consequence has been to make the political status problem a functional appendage of economic policy.

The commitment to maintain a wide-open-door policy for the attraction of foreign (mainly but not exclusively North American) investment is demonstrated in the suggestions for changes in the commonwealth status currently emanating from the sectors of the Puerto Rican government principally concerned with economic development, labor relations, and matters of trade and employment. The administrator of the Puerto Rico Industrial Development Company and others desire greater autonomy for the island in order to maintain its exemption from federal minimum wage legislation and from federal legislation on environmental quality. The Taft-Hartley Act and the Occupational Safety and Health Act are cited as examples of federal legislation which should not apply to Puerto Rico. The Secretary of Agriculture mentions a number of federal statutes from which Puerto Rico would be exempted if commonwealth autonomy were to expand in the desired direction.[5] It is in the name of wider freedom from federal restrictions and regulations over commerce and industry that greater autonomy is solicited. As phrased in terms of freedom and autonomy these claims have an admirable ring; but local regulations in these areas would not equal the restrictions of existing federal rules. In the area of environmental protection, for example, *Fomento* administrator Moscoso recently told the Ad Hoc Advisory Group that after all "a rich nation like the United States can afford methods of pollution control that are too costly for Puerto Rico."

The strides in economic growth, which have resulted in a per capita GNP of $1,410 per year (in 1969), the steady decline of agriculture and the rise of manufacturing, dramatic increases in the construction industry, a hyperactive rate of urbanization, and the recent establishment of capital-intensive petrochemical industries on the island, have been paced off to the rhythm of a steady and seemingly irreversible integration of the island economy with that of the mainland United States. To speak of "autonomy" in such a context of economic intertwining and dependency is to speak of mere toenail-clipping on the body politic of Puerto Rico. The autonomy which is being sought in the name of commonwealth seems at most to be an autonomy of convenience which would give added measures of competitive advantage to Puerto Rico over the states of the Union, to be justified because of its colonial roots and still "developing" nature. Whether Congress will grant the kind of autonomy in which these advantages would accrue to Puerto Rico and not to any of the federated states is questionable, to say the least.

The economic dimensions of the status question imply a series of powerful restraints on any effective expansion of autonomy for the commonwealth. Paradoxically, wider political autonomy could mean ever closer economic dependency; in consequence the distinction between commonwealth and federated statehood becomes normatively unimportant.

Social Change and Cultural Identity

The decline of agriculture and the rise of manufacturing and service industries as principal sources of wealth, the rapid rate of urbanization and suburbanization and a burgeoning middle class, and high levels of consumption patterns and mobility are all positive indications of Puerto Rico's "modernization." What bearing do these quantitative transformations have upon the future of United States-Puerto Rico relations? Are "modernization" and "Americanization" equivalent terms? Does the development of a consumer-oriented dynamic society increasingly integrated with (dependent upon) the United States economy make the consciousness of cultural distinctness politically irrelevant? Has the policy of economic development with its social consequences already "solved" the status problem? Is it not true that at this stage no more can be done except to iron out some of the ragged edges and resolve the legal and terminological contradictions of the formal existing status?

The basic rationale of the defense of commonwealth status requires an affirmative answer to these questions. Before such a rationale can be accepted, however, certain facts must be explained and accounted for. In the process, it will be seen that the social and cultural dimensions of the status problem are, if anything, more relevant and central now than ever.

Along with the favorable indices of economic growth persists a steady unemployment rate of between 12 and 13 percent. These are official figures, which probably underestimate the real extent of unemployment and underemployment on the island. Along with a pattern of massive immigration to the United States, which has resulted in over one-third of the total Puerto Rican population living in the continental United States, there exists a pattern of foreign immigration to Puerto Rico which has been a source of concern in recent years. It is a main reason for proposals that Puerto Rico be allowed to participate in the formulation of immigration policy in order to protect Puerto Ricans from competition for scarce jobs, principally of the skilled variety and in the professions.[6] (This suggestion is clearly aimed at the influx of Cuban immigrants which began in the sixties.) A recent study made under the auspices of the federal Equal Employment and Opportunity Commission has concluded that there is a pattern of discrimination against Puerto Ricans in the employment practices of important sectors of the local economy, and a clear preference for "continentals" (a euphemism for North Americans) and Cubans.[7] From the other side, the Puerto Rican proposals for control over immigration of aliens to the island prompted the U.S. members of the present Ad Hoc Advisory Group to bring up the question of how such local authority could be justified to American officials in whose jurisdiction are found large numbers of "aliens" and "large minority groups," such as Puerto Ricans! [8]

These are only examples of the issues which must be raised in the discussion of United States-Puerto Rico relations. Economic development and social transformation have not flattened the cleavages pertinent to the status question; on the contrary, they may have aggravated them. It is a truism that "values" are changing rapidly. Of course Puerto Ricans have a vastly different set of behaviors and attitudes from those of 25 years ago. But these changes do not mean "Americanization" in the sense that culturally or politically relevant differences between the United States and Puerto Rico are dwindling. It is possible that the opposite is true.

The feeling of nationhood in Puerto Rico (as distinct from nationalism as a political force) is pervasive, and there is no reason to believe it has diminished significantly in recent years. The problem in the current debate over status is that the emphasis on the degree of integration with the United States ("association" or "union," commonwealth or statehood) assumes that the basic problems of national identity and cultural integrity are not central issues but peripheral matters which will fall into place no matter which constitutional choice is made in the future. This relegates the status debate to the plane of constitutional phrase-making and immediate economic convenience.

The Politics of Colonialism

The issue of United States-Puerto Rico relations is perceived and carried forth within the context of political institutions forged from three-quarters of a century of North American colonial domination. The American arrival at the turn of the century came at a time when domestic political alignments on the island had resulted in the victory of those who had sought a degree of self-governing autonomy under Spain, as against the Spanish assimilationists. With the American takeover, assimilation with Spain disappeared as an alternative, and political cleavages in Puerto Rico began to revolve around alternative methods of acquiring the long-sought-after autonomy, from the Americans instead of from the Spaniards. The Liberal-Autonomist political elite in 1898 and the years immediately afterward saw that the North American constitutional structure provided a natural framework for redeveloping autonomy and self-government in the new imperial orbit. An offshoot of that same elite saw in the concept of federated statehood the most promising solution to Puerto Rico's problem of autonomy. These two strains, autonomy versus statehood, have dominated the ideological cleavage between Puerto Rican political parties from 1900 to the present (Anderson, 1965; Pagán, 1959). Both represented similar responses to the immediate fact of North American hegemony; they were both attempts to accommodate the desire of Puerto Rican self-expression and autonomy to the realities of that hegemony.

As differences of emphasis on the way to adjust Puerto Rican aspirations to the American federal structure, these two approaches were easily channeled into political party organizations. The Foraker Act established an electoral system which was subsequently expanded. In the early 1900s adult manhood suffrage was established for the election of the lower House of the insular legislature. (By 1936 women had received the right to vote.) In 1917 the Senate was added as a popularly elected body; and in 1947 the Puerto Rican electorate was given the authority to elect the governor. (Mayors and municipal assemblymen gained office by popular election throughout the entire period.) The electoral system has institutionalized the framework of the autonomy-statehood controversy. In a political party and electoral system rooted historically in the limited search for acceptable accommodation to the constitutional realities of American political superiority and committed accordingly to the rules laid down by the existing political system, pro-independence forces have been inevitably unsuccessful (see Anderson, 1965: 117). The electoral system, as the normative capstone of the political process on the island, has been the principal means for legitimizing dependency and for producing a status issue which limits the effective choice to the alternatives of full or partial assimilation.

In the analysis of United States-Puerto Rico relations the nature of the political institutions called upon in Puerto Rico to deal with those relations should be considered as well. Rooted as they are in a long history of colonial domination, they are a part of the problem, not its exclusive means to solution.

THE NEED FOR RESTATEMENT

The cutting edge of the problem of United States-Puerto Rico relations is political, not legal, and it cannot be reduced to a simple matter of rational choice among three free-and-equal alternative "statuses." It is a problem of the growth of political institutions in Puerto Rican society and of attitudes of acceptance of and subordination to the United States and the resistances offered to that process. When the last resistances are broken down, the result—the obvious "solution"—will be full federated statehood; the process of colonialization will have been completed. In fact, such a knowledgeable and experienced observer of the Puerto Rican scene as Professor C. J. Friedrich (1968) has suggested that statehood seems to be the logical outcome for Puerto Rico before the century is ended.

The commonwealth, as an operative legal status and as an abstract idea, is an attempt to organize and to channel the resistances to this ultimate formal assimilation. Yet at the same time it accepts the attachment to the American federal system. The ideological "anticolonialist" defense of commonwealth emphasizes the unique and special interests of Puerto Rico and presumes that these interests can be protected and furthered only within the "associated state" framework. The more realistic rationale for commonwealth status is the pragmatic notion that this middle-of-the-way autonomy is the only feasible way of maintaining order and a reasonable facade of functional consensus in a society profoundly divided between the desire for independence and the wish to be full-fledged Americans within the federal system. The incompatibilities of the two "final" solutions to Puerto Rico's political identity problem are infused into the pragmatic ambiguities of commonwealth. The commonwealth solution is unassailable as a political enterprise, since it functions within the world of real institutions rather than that of abstract and unattained goals.[9] Ideally, it is the Puerto Rican version of the "end of ideology."

The argument for the commonwealth and the confidence in its future development rest upon certain presumptions and beliefs, whose validity must underlie that of the commonwealth itself. At the least these are unsettled and open to question.

First is the faith in the flexibility of the political and constitutional system of the United States and its ability to accommodate new forms within its federal structure. Closely related to this is the assumption that the United States system is not imperialistic; that Puerto Rico, in spite of its original colonial ties with the United States, has passed into the American federal system as a functioning unit, equal in dignity and moral worth, though unique in operation. These assumptions are essentially definitional and unprovable. Any functioning political system must be flexible enough to allow for changing conditions if it is to survive, and the North American system has high marks in this regard. But flexibility is not unlimited, and the constitutional experimentation implied by the commonwealth will require constant probing and challenging in an unending chain of uncertainty. And the effectiveness of making the present status seem different by giving it an adjective other than colonial depends largely on credulity.

The commonwealth idea hinges also on the confidence that confrontation politics will be avoided on the island. This assumes that the commonwealth/autonomy middle ground, represented at present by the Popular Democratic Party, will continue to act as a buffer against the ideological-status extremes of statehood and independence. In order for this political strategy to be effective, however, popular support for these "minority" positions should keep a balance. At least in electoral terms, this balance does not exist. As measured in voting returns, parties identified with the statehood cause have increased their proportion of the total vote from 25 percent in 1956 to over 43 percent in the elections of 1968 and 1972; whereas the Independence Party (PIP) was in 1972 barely able to muster the minimum percentage of total votes to continue to qualify as a legal party, and, incidentally, fell into organizational disarray after the elections. The governing party cannot claim to be mediating between two roughly equal popular forces legitimately pressuring for their respective but incompatible status choices. In effect it has to discard independence sentiment as a "bargaining" counter in its negotiations for wider autonomy; the electorate has rendered independence an "illegitimate" alternative. Instead of a confrontation between "independence" and "statehood" in which commonwealth emerges the continuing mediator, the struggle becomes one between "commonwealth" and "statehood" over degrees of assimilation. Under these conditions the tendency over time would most probably be toward statehood.

Another implication in the theory of commonwealth is the strategic assumption that whatever might be the case in other dependent areas, Puerto Rico is faced with a real problem of conflict between the feeling of nationhood and the exigencies of economic security and progress. Ideally, one would like to balance the two—and that is what the rhetoric of commonwealth tries to do—but in the ultimate analysis, economic considerations take precedence. Thus the links with the United States must continue ("common defense," "common citizenship," "common market," and "common currency"), and again the tilt toward federated statehood is evident.

The crowning assumption of commonwealth is that it is possible to institutionalize ambiguity. Ambiguity and uncertainty are, of course, integral parts of human behavior, especially in politics. The toleration of ambiguity is a mark of maturity and a principle of behavior to which every practical politician must be sensitive. However, to erect ambiguity into a constitutional principle and the hallmark of a people's identity is something else again. The inherent instability of such an arrangement could conceivably be disguised by massive self-delusion, continual isolation from the rest of the world, or systematic repression, but these are hardly ingredients of a genuinely decolonized relationship.

After 22 years of formal existence, the commonwealth has not developed along the lines of autonomous evolution suggested by its proponents (see, for example, Friedrich, 1959, 1968). It is possible that the present discussions in the Ad Hoc Advisory Group will eventually result in some modifications. Yet the essence of the commonwealth arrangement is that there can be no guarantees of modification and no way of knowing in what direction, how extensive, nor how lasting such modifications may be. Furthermore, even if no significant changes whatever are forthcoming—not an unreasonable possibility considering the history of previous attempts—the commonwealth theory provides absolutely no moral or legal basis for redress or complaint by Puerto Rico. The assumption of unlimited patience is inherent in the commonwealth status.

If no significant breakthrough is made soon toward more autonomy for the commonwealth, the line of demarcation between commonwealth and statehood will be increasingly difficult to maintain. Aggressive reaffirmation of cultural distinctions and dramatic policy decisions in the collective name of Puerto Rico (such as the government's recent decision to purchase the Puerto Rico Telephone Company from International Telephone and Telegraph and its present negotiations to buy and operate the shipping facilities to and from the island) can be invoked to underscore Puerto Rico's "real" and effective autonomy, irrespective of formal constitutional maneuverings. Such dramatic policy decisions are limited in scope and politically risky however. As for cultural distinctiveness, it is a thin reed upon which to base political autonomy, since contacts between Puerto Rico and the mainland are constantly increasing owing to the movement of people back and forth. Commonwealth is based on the possibility of maintaining a separate national identity while remaining a part of the U.S. federal system. The political structure of that identity must be separate, as well; hence, "commonwealth" is preferred to statehood, and a distinction is made between being a functioning part of the American union and being an "integral" part. Independence is discarded, because it implies rejection of the United States and the presumed benefits of American citizenship. Thus the burden of defending Puerto Rican nationhood shifts to those who officially share with statehooders the commitment to permanent union with the United States. If the pressure from the independence movement is politically ineffective while the statehood movement gains adherents, the ability of the popular defenders of commonwealth to hold fast to their middle line cannot help but be threatened.

It is fair to question at this point whether the myth of Puerto Rico's "uniqueness" can be maintained indefinitely. In a letter to his co-chairman of the Ad Hoc Advisory Group, ex-Governor Muñoz Marín refers to the "unique political experiment in our constitutional system" and to "the unique historical record of Commonwealth status." The Puerto Rican members of the committee feel that this insistence is necessary because of the American members' presumption that "statehood is the proper measurement of the Commonwealth status," an assumption which is "respectfully" rejected by the Puerto Rican members.[10] If the federal system of the fifty states is taken as the model, then the "essence" of commonwealth is ignored and statehood is the yardstick for comparison and evaluation. Statehood becomes the goal, even though it may be politically impossible. After 22 years of commonwealth, this is hardly encouraging testimony to the process of decolonization.

If the defense of commonwealth requires a rejection of federated statehood as the point of reference, the search for other models is equally problematical. Some suggest that the island be called officially in English a "Free Associated State," and that it would then take its place among other "associated states" in the world community.[11] That such an international status has not existed up to now is recognized, but the argument is that there are no juridical obstacles to such a role. Yet unless the model for analyzing Puerto Rico is to be akin to that of Byelo-Russia or the Ukraine, it is difficult to conceive of a genuine "associated state" with a strongly organized internal movement pledged to assimilation and with ready lobbying contacts and allies in the metropolitan power. Aside from moves toward commercial arrangements in the Caribbean, Puerto Rican leaders have made no concerted attempts to prepare local opinion for a possible systematic autonomous role in international organizations. They are clearly restrained by Puerto Rico's subordination to the federal power in foreign affairs and common defense, as well as being sensitive to the political opposition which would presumably arise to such a visible slackening of the ties to the United States.

How long can Puerto Rico continue to steer its precarious course between federated statehood and associated autonomy? Perhaps in another 22 years these same questions will be posed again by a different set of actors. Or perhaps the political alignment over the last quarter-century has weighted the die to the advantage of statehood and ultimate assimilation, and common-wealth will be reduced to a kind of holding operation against statehood. If so, then new perspectives must be joined and new strategies devised if colonial-ism is ever to be eradicated from United States-Puerto Rico relations.

RENEWED PERSPECTIVES: A CASE FOR INDEPENDENCE

It might appear astounding, if not downright heretical, to suggest that independence is the most fruitful perspective from which to view the problem of United States-Puerto Rico relations. After all, there is no denying the electoral facts of life on the island: the Independence Party barely achieved 5 percent of the total vote in 1972; in the three previous elections it failed even to maintain its legal status as a party; independence polled a negligible return in the plebiscite of 1967; and statehood sentiment seems to be on the upswing. These facts are enlisted constantly to attest to what is presumably an incontrovertible truth: Puerto Ricans do not wish to be independent.

This article is not an essay into prophecy; nor does it offer a blueprint for political strategy. Enough has already been said to show how inordinately difficult, perhaps impossible, the acquisition of independence for Puerto Rico would be. Nevertheless, assuming the desire to maintain Puerto Rico's cul-tural and political identity in spite of its dependency on the United States, a commitment to independence seems the only viable normative stance.

Elections in Puerto Rico are relatively free of fraud and irregularities. Yet, as was pointed out above, no matter how honest it is, the electoral process is an integral part of the "status problem" itself. The political party system in Puerto Rico developed at a time and in a context in which independence was out of the question; until at least the 1930s there was never the slightest official glimmer in Washington of possible support for island indepen-dence.[12] The parties and electoral system have developed as part of the political adjustment to the structure of North American dominance, and at best, it ameliorated this dominance. Independence as an operative ideal cannot fit comfortably into such a context; and the assumption that the desire for independence can be shown by the electoral system is a chimera.

The popular vote at any given time should not be taken as the true measure of status sentiment on the island. To do so turns the status problem into a triviality and, like the excessively legalistic approaches mentioned earlier, ignores its profounder dimensions. The feeling of distinctness, the clinging to the native language, the vital assumption that North Americans are "foreigners" withal—in short the consciousness of nationhood—permeates Puerto Rican public opinion far beyond what shows in the electoral statistics (see, for example, Nieves Falcón, 1970: 234-262). The sentiment for indepen-dence, active or latent, is undoubtedly more extensive than the simple electoral returns would indicate.

How can one speak seriously of independence in the face of the obvious increase in organized statehood sentiment? Have we not already seen this phenomenon effectively limit the ability of the commonwealth defenders to exact larger spheres of autonomy? Is not the trend toward statehood inexorable and irreversible? These trends are, indeed, portentous. Nevertheless, the statehood "solution" is far from inevitable. In the first place, and in strictly electoral terms, it is possible that statehood sentiment has peaked; between the elections of 1968 and 1972 the statehood-oriented party's proportion of the total vote actually decreased from 43.5 percent to 43.3 percent. In the second place, status sentiment is only very tenuously manifested in party voting; voting for a statehood party may be essentially a protest vote or the effect of other issues in the campaign. (Actually, although the status issue always looms in the background, there is usually an effort not to make it a direct central issue in the campaigns.)

In addition, there is no justification in assuming that the voter who openly identifies with statehood has no feeling of nationhood. The willingness to vote for or identify with one party or the other does not necessarily indicate the degree of one's cultural or national identity. Finally, and most important of all, were Puerto Rican statehood ever to be formally proposed to the Congress, the procedural and political obstacles to statehood emanating from the United States could so traumatize Puerto Rico-United States relations as to exacerbate rather than solve the status problem. Controversial and emotional problems concerning language, culture, racial attitudes, and national pride would surely be invoked and could easily rekindle the problem into dangerous dimensions.

Such an eventuality is unlikely, however. In order for statehood to be seriously entertained by Congress, a clear and consistent majority in its favor must be registered on the island, and as has been implied above, the chances are that the dynamics of the party and electoral system will probably prevent this occurrence. The problem is more likely to be one of a gradually increasing tendency toward statehood, as reforms for greater commonwealth autonomy are blunted or frustrated by Congressional resistance and continuing statehood-oriented ideological opposition on the island. The result may well be stagnation and impasse. Statehood will become no more viable than before; yet the politically inspired illusion of its imminence would preclude any genuine breakthrough toward autonomy and "improvement" of commonwealth.

If this is an accurate appraisal of the present situation, then the commitment to independence is the only feasible alternative. Anything less simply prolongs and institutionalizes the "status issue" as a permanent dilemma in a never-to-be-resolved colonial situation. Only from the perspective of independence can the deeper dimensions of the status problem be appreciated and confronted. Only from this perspective can the course of real decolonization be effectively undertaken, including, even, the viable development of the idea of associated statehood.

The conversion of this perspective into political reality may seem nearly impossible. In 1953 Ambassador Henry Cabot Lodge made an innocuous and safe declaration to the United Nations stating that the President of the United States would recommend the granting of independence to Puerto Rico were the insular legislature so to request. For true Puerto Rican independence the United States would have to go further and admit that the electoral process is not the end-all and be-all of a political system, particularly since the system was born in colonialism and nurtured in dependency. From the Puerto Rican side independence would require major acts of political will in reaffirming the non-negotiable aspect of nationhood and ultimate autonomy. It would require the subordination of perceived economic interest to political freedom and the realization that economic well-being is not necessarily inexorably tied to the American connection or to American citizenship.

Perhaps this is all utterly impossible; but if so, the unsettled problem of United States-Puerto Rico relations will continue to be a source of increasing domestic and international vexation well into the twenty-first century. Kalman Silvert (1971: 200) has observed that Puerto Rico seems to be a case in which the problems are political "in the grand sense." It is a society pervaded by politics at virtually every turn; the normative politics of "status" and the problems of identity and purpose permeate public life in a variety of dimensions. As such it is a fascinating challenge for the political scientist; but more importantly, it represents the ultimate challenge to the formidable tasks of decolonization in the western hemisphere.

NOTES

1. The Fernós-Murray Bill (H.R. 5926) would have significantly broadened the areas of Puerto Rican autonomy along lines similar to those being discussed today. The bill was never reported out of committee.

2. The other members for the United States are Senators James L. Buckley of New York and J. Bennett Johnson, Jr., of Louisiana; Representatives Don H. Clausen of California and Tom Foley of Washington; Richard Ogilvie, former Governor of Illinois; and Paul Howell, President of the Howell Corporation of Houston, Texas. For Puerto Rico the members are Resident Commissioner Jaime Benítez; Senate President Juan Cancel Ríos; Speaker of the House Ernesto Ramos Yordán; Secretary of State Víctor Pons; Senator Justo Méndez (Independent, formerly of the PNP); and Angel Rivera, a banker and former Secretary of the Treasury in the Ferré Administration.

3. The citations in the text are from the public documents relative to the current Ad Hoc Advisory Group and are taken from typescript copies on file at the committee's offices in San Juan and at the Library of the Department of State of Puerto Rico.

4. This was the position of the former head of the Caribbean Development Corporation (CODECA), Luis A. Passalacqua, in his testimony before the Ad Hoc Advisory Group on December 7, 1973. Governor Hernández Colón submitted as an appendix to his testimony an as yet unpublished study by Professor W. M. Reisman of the Yale Law School which elaborates this theme in detail.

5. These positions were submitted to the Ad Hoc Advisory Group in public testimony on April 27, 1974, by *Fomento* administrator Teodoro Moscoso and Secretary of Labor Luis Silva Recio.

6. Specific suggestions in this regard were made before the Ad Hoc Committee in Labor Secretary Silva Recio's testimony.

7. This "Study to Determine the Extent and Ramifications of Color, Sex, and National Origin Discrimination in Private Employment in Puerto Rico," dated February 1974, was prepared by the San Juan-based Center for Environmental and Consumer Justice. The reference in the text is from the "Conclusions and Recommendations" in a typescript copy of the study.

8. This question was among several others formally raised by the American side in a letter from co-chairman Cook to co-chairman Muñoz Marín. They were reproduced in the San Juan *Star* of April 18, 1974.

9. A clear and unambiguous presentation of this basic rationale was given by Jaime Benítez, now Resident Commissioner in Washington and at that time Chancellor of the University of Puerto Rico, in testimony before the Status Commission in 1965 (United States-Puerto Rico Status Commission, 1966b: 353-360).

10. This letter is reproduced in the San Juan *Star* of June 8, 1974.

11. This suggestion is made in the report by Dr. Reisman, mentioned in note 4.

12. An independence bill was introduced in the Senate by Senator Tydings in 1936. It was opposed by many Puerto Ricans because of its economically punitive nature. The same senator introduced similar bills in 1943 and 1945. They were never seriously considered (see Anderson, 1965: 50-58, 96-100).

REFERENCES

Ad Hoc Advisory Group on the Presidential Vote for Puerto Rico (1971) "Presidential Vote for Puerto Rico." Washington, D.C.: Government Printing Office.
ANDERSON, R. W. (1970) *Gobierno y partidos políticos in Puerto Rico.* Madrid: Editorial Tecnos.
––– (1965) *Party Politics in Puerto Rico.* Stanford: Stanford University Press.
CABRANES, J. (1974) "The evolution of the 'American empire': Puerto Rico and the Trust Territory of the Pacific Islands." Reprinted in the Congressional Record 119 (April 12).
COHEN, J. (1973) *The Question of Imperialism.* New York: Basic Books.
CORKRAN, H. (1970) *Patterns of International Cooperation in the Caribbean 1942-1969.* Dallas: Southern Methodist University Press.
DENNY, B. (1968) "The United States and Puerto Rico: a century of success 1898-2000." Howard Law Journal 15 (Fall): 70-87.
FRIEDRICH, C. J. (1968) "Puerto Rico, the next state of the Union." Howard Law Journal 15 (Fall): 88-100.
––– (1959) *Puerto Rico: Middle Road to Freedom.* New York: Rinehart.

HERNÁNDEZ COLÓN, R. (1959) "The Commonwealth of Puerto Rico: territory or state?" Revista del Colegio de Abogados de Puerto Rico 29 (May): 207-258.

LEIBOWITZ, A. H. (1968) "The applicability of federal law to the Commonwealth of Puerto Rico." Revista Jurídica de la Universidad de Puerto Rico 37, 4: 615-675.

NEGRON de MONTILLA, A. (1971) *Americanization in Puerto Rico and the Public-School System 1900-1930.* Río Piedras, Puerto Rico: Ediciones Edil.

NIEVES FALCON, L. (1970) "La opinión pública y las aspiraciones de los puertor-riqueños." Río Piedras, Puerto Rico: Centro de Investigaciones Sociales, Universidad de Puerto Rico.

PAGAN, B. (1959) *Historia de los partidos políticos puertorriqueños 1898-1956.* San Juan: Librería Campos.

SILVERT, K. (1971) "The Caribbean and North America," pp. 193-210 in T. Szulc (ed.) *The United States and the Caribbean.* Englewood Cliffs, N.J.: Prentice-Hall.

United States-Puerto Rico Commission on the Status of Puerto Rico (1966a) "Status of Puerto Rico." Washington, D.C.: Government Printing Office.

――― (1966b) "Status of Puerto Rico." Hearings, Vol. 2. Washington, D.C.: Government Printing Office.

WELLS, H. (1969) *The Modernization of Puerto Rico.* Cambridge: Harvard University Press.

Chapter 10

UNITED STATES POLICY TOWARD BRAZIL:

ASSUMPTIONS AND OPTIONS

THOMAS E. SKIDMORE

BACKGROUND: RECENT U.S. POLICY TOWARD LATIN AMERICA

Since 1945 U.S. interest in Latin America has been a function of perceived "threats" to our national security, both geopolitical and ideological. In the late 1930s U.S. policy-makers grew concerned over Axis penetration of Latin America. The possible rise of German, Italian, and Japanese influence had grave strategic implications. We badly needed war materials (quartz, natural rubber, etc.) which, if shipping lines across the Atlantic and Pacific were cut off, only Latin America could supply. Equally important, the Atlantic coast of South America had vital strategic value in case of all-out anti-submarine warfare.

The war came and the United States needed both raw materials and bases. We paid Brazil's price, in part by agreeing to finance her fledgling steel industry, which President Vargas and his military leaders wanted badly. We worked closely with the Brazilians in their war mobilization effort, supplying both technology and financing. We furnished transport and assistance for the

SOURCE NOTE: This paper was prepared at the request of the Commission on United States-Latin American Relations sponsored by the Center for Inter-American Relations in July 1974. It is primarily a description of the historical trends and operative assumptions in United States-Brazilian relations and therefore contains relatively little discussion of specific issues, such as the 200-mile limit, trade in soluble coffee, and the Nuclear Non-Proliferation Treaty. For better or worse, the Brazilians are following their own model of development. To understand what they believe they are doing is essential if we are to understand how U.S. relations with Brazil might develop over the next five years.

Brazilian Expeditionary Force to the European theater. This combat effort by Brazil probably cost the United States more than it was worth (the training and equipment of the Brazilians was disconcertingly poor), but it had great symbolic importance for Brazil.[1]

U.S. interest in Brazil waned after the war, as it did in all of Latin America. The United States showed a modest concern for Brazil's economic development (to which our first commitment had been the Export-Import Bank loan for the steel industry in 1942). During the Truman Administration a joint United States-Brazil Economic Commission produced a broad study documenting the bottlenecks obstructing economic development (especially in power and transportation) and suggesting how foreign (particularly U.S.) assistance might aid in their removal. But the advent of the Eisenhower Administration in Washington (with fiscally conservative George Humphrey as Secretary of the Treasury) dashed Brazilian hopes. Instead of implementing the study, the United States urged Brazil (and all other "developing countries") to create a "favorable atmosphere" for private investment.

Between 1945 and 1959 the U.S. government saw no threat serious enough to demand fundamental changes in its Latin American policy. Concern over the cold war did stimulate the creation of a network of military assistance agreements, which Brazil joined in 1952. From the U.S. viewpoint, events in Latin America were under control. The political radicalization in Guatemala, for example, which the U.S. government branded as a stalking horse for Soviet penetration, could be easily eliminated in 1954 by an inexpensive CIA-engineered coup.

The scene changed in 1959. The Cuban Revolution loomed as a dangerous threat to American policy-makers. By the end of 1960 another CIA-sponsored intervention was in preparation. The disaster at the Bay of Pigs in 1961, and Fidel's unmistakable turn toward Soviet protection, accelerated a fundamental rethinking of the U.S. Latin American policy which had begun in the final months of Eisenhower's presidency (Milton Eisenhower's report on his Latin American fact-finding journey had given the first impetus).[2]

The principal result was the Alliance for Progress, launched with great ceremony in early 1961. Through it the United States was making a large-scale commitment to join Latin Americans in an integrated, multilateral approach to demonstrate how elected governments could achieve both economic growth and social reform. It would therefore prove the superiority of the democratic-reformist path to development, thus furnishing an answer for those, on the right and left, who preached the need for authoritarian methods. For the United States the Alliance had a vital corollary. Latin American governments had to be able to protect themselves against violent dissenters. Insurgency required counterinsurgency. The mystique of the

Green Berets was as significant an element in the Kennedy foreign policy as the lofty commitments of the Alliance for Progress.

What is the balance sheet on the years since the Alliance began?[3] The record makes melancholy reading for those who found in the Alliance a realistic set of goals and a viable path of action. Popularly elected governments are now rarer than at any time in the last thirty years. Colombia and Venezuela are the only major polities we might safely call competitive. As for setbacks to the Alliance, no case is more dramatic than Chile. It was often said to have a deeper and stronger democratic tradition than any other country in Latin America. Under President Frei (1965-1971) it received the second highest per capita assistance of any Alliance member. Yet the polarization grew. In September 1973 the Allende regime was toppled by a military coup entitled to join ranks with the most brutally repressive known to South America in this century.

The Alliance's second goal—rapid economic growth, has proved equally elusive, especially in per capita terms. Growth has been most rapid in Brazil, where an authoritarian regime has largely ignored the third goal—social reform. For large-scale evidence of reform, one must turn to Cuba, another authoritarian regime, albeit of a very different kind. Yet Cuba has had little economic growth, despite large-scale assistance from the socialist bloc. Nowhere do we find the combination of democracy, growth, and reform envisioned by the planners of the Alliance.

The counterinsurgency corollary of the Alliance, on the other hand, has been applied with great success. Thanks to extensive U.S. assistance through Public Safety programs and military training agreements, Latin governments have shown themselves more than equal to armed opposition from within. Che Guevara's plan for a continental revolution to begin in Bolivia did not survive the guns of United States-trained Bolivian Rangers. His failure, one among many less-publicized guerrilla adventures throughout Latin America, demoralized the continent's revolutionary left and confirmed the effectiveness of U.S. counterinsurgency doctrines. The urban guerrillas, swimming in the sea of big-city anonymity, later enjoyed a brief, if brilliant, moment of glory in Uruguay and Brazil. Just after it had seemed the Tupamaros might force great change in Uruguay, they collapsed under brutal police measures of the kind which Brazil has used so successfully. By the beginning of the 1970s the violent path to power seemed to have closed. At least one element in Kennedy's Latin American policy worked.

That success does much to explain why the United States has been relatively uninterested in Latin America in recent years. If it takes a threat to get our attention, the absence of any threat frees U.S. policy-makers to concentrate elsewhere. Merely wishing for a re-think of our Latin American policy will not make it happen. There has to be genuine interest on the highest levels of U.S. government. For the sake of argument, let us assume that a careful reexamination of U.S. Latin American policy may be undertaken. What trends within Latin America ought to be taken into account?

TRENDS IN LATIN AMERICA:
EMPTY STOMACHS AND POLITICAL RADICALS?

Spreading authoritarianism

The end of the 1950s had seen the passing of dictatorial regimes in Latin America—the "twilight of the tyrants," as Tad Szulc termed it in 1959. The emergence of new regimes in Argentina, Cuba, Venezuela, and Peru was an important factor for the architects of the Alliance for Progress. They wanted to show that representative governments could achieve economic growth and fundamental social reforms, and thereby make democracy seem legitimate to the forgotten masses. Unfortunately, history did not cooperate. The 1960s and early 1970s dealt harshly with democracy in Latin America.

What has been the U.S. reaction? One early setback—in Peru—provoked strong U.S. disapproval. A military coup occurred in July 1962, just before a run-off presidential election in the Peruvian Congress (no candidate had received the constitutionally required plurality in the popular election). To show its disapproval of the coup, the U.S. government refused to recognize the new military regime and suspended all aid. Relations were soon restored when the junta promised elections. Fernando Belaúnde, a prime example of the democratic reformers the Kennedy Administration wanted to help, was elected President but left office in 1968 in the wake of another coup. Ironically, however, this military regime held on to power and launched the most extensive reform program in Latin America outside of Cuba and Allende's Chile.

Throughout the 1960s Americans debated what kind of political regime our policy *should* attempt to encourage. On one hand the public is often caught up by the "Wilsonian urge," the idea that the United States is fundamentally a beacon in the world for free, representative government. It then follows that we should use our influence to promote democracy for other peoples, as Woodrow Wilson believed he was doing for Mexico in the early years of its revolution. The "Wilsonian urge" has been strongest among U.S. liberals, who yearn for a more "moral" foreign policy.

In the end, however, our government has found little difficulty in quickly recognizing and supporting right-wing authoritarian regimes which have seized power by military coup. Brazil in 1964 and Chile in 1973 are prime examples. If we assume that this "realistic" bias will continue, what costs will be involved? What price does the United States pay for close identification with authoritarian regimes? What of the alienation created among the suppressed sectors—labor, dissenting intellectuals, opposition clergy? What will happen if and when these groups come to power?

Growth without welfare

In the late 1950s most economists in the United States and other developed countries assumed that steady economic growth could be achieved in "underdeveloped" countries if their governments followed sensible policies. Admittedly there were problems, for which outside assistance was essential. Frequently mentioned was the need for international agreements to stabilize prices of primary products, so that producing nations could be reasonably certain about their future foreign exchange earnings. And outside capital was needed, from both private and public creditors abroad. A network of international commodity agreements was negotiated and additional foreign capital was channeled to Latin America. Looking back, we see how inadequate (and sometimes counterproductive) these measures were, as well as the naiveté about the problems bedeviling poor countries trying to grow rapidly.

Sustained growth in per capita terms has proved very difficult to achieve. Most alarming, the capital flows for many countries have become negative, reflecting repayment of earlier loans and remission by private investors, both foreign and domestic. The increasing foreign debt burden in many cases threatens to swallow up a dangerously large fraction of foreign exchange earnings needed for vital imports. The widening technology gap is another current worry. There are also disturbing trends within Latin American economies. Where sustained high growth has occurred, as in Brazil and Mexico, income distribution has worsened. In major countries with lower growth, such as Argentina and Chile, inflation has badly distorted the decision-making process. Rapid growth with increasingly egalitarian distribution of the benefits has not occurred in any major Latin American country.

What is the U.S. stake in these economic troubles? One response is the "humanitarian" reaction, analogous to the "Wilsonian urge." Many Americans want to see other peoples gain a decent existence. This impulse is obvious in the attitude which leads an impressive number of Americans to make themselves part of such overseas philanthropy as the Peace Corps or Project Hope. But such sentiments are hardly the basis on which to make foreign policy, and they seldom prevail against baser interpretations of national interest when the chips are down.

Another rationale often advanced for U.S. interest in economic growth in LDC's is the "empty stomach theory of revolution." According to this view, only an increase in the size of the economic pie can help societies withstand pressures for political radicalization. This argument was used freely in the early days of the Alliance. The miserable living standards of northeast Brazil, for example, were dramatically publicized in an effort to mobilize U.S. opinion into supporting economic and financial assistance for the area. The regional office set up by USAID in Recife, nerve center of the northeast, commanded funds greater than USAID missions in the capital of any Latin American country, except Brazil. The "empty stomach theory" was often coupled with the humanitarian argument, thereby justifying heavy U.S. involvement on the grounds that it would help the impoverished while also making them less susceptible to radical organizers, whose success might later threaten U.S. national security.[4] To state the "empty stomach theory" is to expose its errant logic. History reveals no simple correlation between misery and revolution, in Latin America or elsewhere. Starving citizens rarely seize political power.

A third justification for U.S. interest in Latin America's economic problems is more selfish. Don't we need LDC's to absorb our overseas investments, buy our exports, and furnish our raw materials? Establishment academics dismiss this explanation far too handily. What elements of truth does the "anti-imperialist" theory contain? During the recent years of rising deficits in the U.S. balance of payments, Latin America has furnished a surplus for the United States (Griffin, 1971).[5] Had it not been for the purchases and capital flows from Latin America, our overall deficit would have been even greater.

As for needing to place U.S. overseas investment, Latin America has become less important than fifteen years ago. Since then the most rapid increases in U.S. investment abroad have occurred in Canada, Japan, and West Europe. Yet the overall yield from exports to and investments in Latin America offers a convenient plus on our international account. What about raw materials? Would the loss of Latin American sources of supply cripple the U.S. economy? The answer is probably no, although it could cause serious dislocation. Venezuelan oil is the most important raw material, with others, such as manganese, uranium, and bauxite, also important.

In sum, the radical (or anti-imperialist) argument does not furnish a convincing overall explanation for U.S. involvement, although, to be fully understood, that argument requires a global analysis of the course of capitalist development. In particular cases, however, threats to U.S. investments have often triggered a sharp reaction by the U.S. government. The Hickenlooper amendment was an attempt to guarantee U.S. governmental protection. But the ongoing debate in the United States indicates there is no longer consensus on the once-strong assumption that the U.S. national interest is synonymous with the fate of private U.S. investors.

The Missing Reforms

Few of the ambitious targets for social reform stipulated in the Charter of Punta del Este have been approached. Bringing a larger fraction of Latin Americans up to the minimum standard in nutrition, literacy, and public health has only begun. Rapid growth of population makes the task even harder. Most discouraging, income distribution—the best single measure of changes in social welfare—became more unequal in most LDC's around the world between 1957 and 1968. A recent study has shown that during this period only five noncommunist LDC's combined economic growth with increasing equity, and none were in Latin America.[6] The real beneficiaries of growth have been the middle and upper sectors, who have increased their ability to enjoy standards of living achieved by their counterparts in north Atlantic industrial societies.

The U.S. response has followed several lines. The humanitarian impulse leads North Americans to think that social reform ought to be occurring in Latin America—especially in the areas we regard as important instruments of mobility, such as access to land ownership and free public education. An equally important argument for most Americans stems from the "empty stomach theory." Since the poor cannot forever be denied their fair share of income, it is argued, they will become impatient for structural changes in their society. Reforms must come soon—because they are just but also because they are needed to rob revolutionaries of their best issue.

The resulting rationale is "reformist-preemptive," a view which heavily influenced the architects of the Alliance. Economic assistance was supposed to go only to governments which had demonstrated their commitment to rational economic planning *and* basic social reforms. But how much is social reform worth? Profoundly egalitarian measures are most often promoted by political radicals who are economic nationalists striving to reduce, if not liquidate, foreign economic interests. What should happen when our sympathy for reform conflicts with our support for endangered economic interests of Americans? Most articulate Latin Americans have few doubts that the latter will prevail.

WHY SINGLE OUT BRAZIL?

Brazilians have few doubts that they are worth singling out, not only for U.S. attention, but for world attention. Theirs is the largest country in Latin America, both in area and in population. In the last several years they have posted the highest economic growth rate of any major nation in the world. They make no secret of their belief that by the end of this century, if not sooner, they will be a major world power.

Brazilian-United States Relations: Background

From the U.S. standpoint, Brazil has great economic importance in Latin America. We are Brazil's largest single trading partner and the leading source of private investment capital (the United States has provided about 40 percent of Brazil's present total foreign investment of $4.2 billion; U.S. Foreign Policy, 1972 [1973: 437-438]). Brazil's relative importance was underlined recently when the managers of the Overseas Private Investment Corporation (OPIC) found themselves forced to institute a rule that no more than 10 percent of OPIC's coverage shall be in one country, because the applications for Brazil loomed so large.

In politico-military terms, Brazil has long enjoyed special status in U.S. policy toward Latin America. Baron Rio Branco, Brazil's Foreign Minister from 1902 to 1912, guided Brazil into a policy of close diplomatic alignment with the United States, in contrast to Argentina's ambition to become a hemispheric counterweight to the United States. Brazil was the only major Latin American country to enter World War I. By World War II, Brazil's cooperation was even more vital to the United States, which placed a high priority on Brazil's raw materials and her strategically important Atlantic coastline.

After 1945, the relationship was reaffirmed in a series of United States-Brazilian agreements by which, for example, the U.S. military have been able to maintain a liaison officer in the Brazilian Higher War College.[7] These and other military links were to prove especially important as the Brazilian military assumed a growing political role. In the early 1960s, however, Brazil's generally pro-United States foreign policy began to change. President Jânio Quadros, elected in 1960, launched an "independent foreign policy" with overtures to Fidel's Cuba and gestures toward Third World nations in Africa and Asia.[8] Quadros' sudden resignation cut short that venture. His successor, Goulart, continued, if more cautiously, the attempt at an independent line. During Goulart's presidency (1961-1964) emphasis was given to making Brazil a leader within the "developing" world by attacking the operation of the international economy which was allegedly discriminating against poorer nations.

In 1964 Brazil swung back sharply to a pro-United States policy. The same anti-communism which impelled the military to overthrow Goulart made them natural allies of the long-time anticommunist power, the United States. In 1965 Brazil sent troops to join the United States (under OAS auspices) in the "peace-keeping" operation required by U.S. intervention in the Dominican Republic. Brazil also strongly supported the U.S. policy of keeping Cuba isolated. In short, under military leadership, Brazil became the most markedly pro-American major nation in Latin America. The reasons were partly ideological and partly economic. Even if the generals believed their own rhetoric about the dangers of subversion in the western hemisphere, they knew they could gain greatly increased economic assistance from the United States and the multilateral agencies if they restored a "respectable" economic policy which would welcome, rather than menace, foreign investment.

The Brazilian Model

Since 1964 the military-dominated governments have produced a new model of development—one which is arousing increasing interest abroad. What were its origins? [9]

Through the 1950s Brazil had successfully combined high growth rates, rapid inflation, and electoral government. Brazilians facetiously explained their success as due to a peculiar gift that allowed Brazilians to break the rules of respectable economic policy-making and still achieve growth. Whatever the explanation, the boom began to falter in the 1960s. By 1962 Brazil faced low growth and increasing social and regional inequalities, problems for which the Alliance for Progress supposedly offered a strategy. In 1962-1964 the economic crisis became steadily worse, as Brazil's foreign creditors demanded fundamental policy changes which would have meant political suicide for Goulart's increasingly populist government. The immediate symptoms were a runaway inflation and a debt repayment schedule Brazil could not possibly meet. The time for procrastination was over. When the coup came in April 1964, it was the right, rather than the left, which proved stronger. The military conspirators and their civilian collaborators who seized power were spurred by the fear of a widespread mobilization, led by a coalition of rural workers, big-city university students, urban workers, and noncommissioned military officers.

From 1964 to 1969 Brazil experienced a steady move toward authoritarianism. The strength of the regime—ostensibly justified on grounds of national security—was also a great aid to technocratic policy-makers, who were much freer to make decisions without the need for the frequent public accountability demanded in an open political system. [10]

The Brazilian model has achieved remarkable success in its economic growth rate. GDP (Gross Domestic Product) has grown at the rate of 10 percent annually for the years 1967 to 1973 (data from Vilar de Queiroz, 1974). Continuing inflation has been neutralized by price and wage controls, by an ingenious system of "indexation" for domestic financial obligations and contracts, and by "mini-devaluations" in the foreign exchange market. The troublesome constraint on the balance of payments has been eased by a highly successful export drive, with the value of exports rising 18.4 percent annually for the period 1967-1973. There is, however, a dark side to the

Brazilian "miracle." The distribution of income worsened (at least between 1960 and 1970) and little was done in the way of social reform, especially for rural dwellers.

Politically Brazil has remained under military control. The resulting stability was produced by crushing any armed or militant opposition through surveillance and police brutality. Continued military rule has been possible only because the higher officers have remained united vis-a-vis the civilian sector. Dissenters among the military either remain silent or go into retirement, where their voices carry little weight among the uniformed. Brazil is thus governed by a military-technocratic alliance proud of its recent record of economic growth which its members believe is rapidly carrying the country toward the status of a world power.

How long is the Brazilian model likely to last? Long-term predictions would be foolhardy. For proof, one need only look at the recent events in Portugal. Bad economic weather for Brazil might arouse wider opposition and erode the legitimacy of the regime. The stunning defeat suffered by the government party (ARENA) candidates at the hands of the opposition (MDB) in the November 1974 Congressional elections would appear to confirm this prognosis. It would seem prudent to ask whether the extraordinarily high growth rates in GDP and exports can be sustained indefinitely. In the short run, however, only a division among the military officers could open up ("decompress" is the current phrase in Brazil) the political scene so that civilian political sectors could compete freely. That seems unlikely for the next three to five years. For that period a military-dominated authoritarian government will probably remain in power. Before we can consider U.S. policy toward that Brazil, however, we must first ask how its leaders conceive of their country's international role.

BRAZIL'S INTERNATIONAL ROLE: A CHANGING SELF-IMAGE

Since the beginning of the century the Brazilian elite has aspired to world power status for their country. Before World War I the ambition was expressed in a boastful manner, known as *ufanismo* (from *ufanar,* the Portuguese verb "to be proud of," but best translated as chauvinism).[11] This confidence was dealt a rude blow soon after the war, when the League of Nations failed to award Brazil a permanent seat on the Council. Brazil responded by resigning from the League in 1926. World War II gave Brazil a new opportunity to exercise her international ambitions. Her leaders bargained with the United States for economic and military help in return for their bases and raw material. At the war's end they felt that their close association with U.S. forces in European combat had given them a major boost toward becoming a credible international power.

Between 1945 and 1964 Brazil's international self-image was tied to her economic ambitions. President Kubitschek's drive for "fifty years' development in five" thrilled many Brazilians, as did the construction of the futuristic new capital of Brasilia. But the economic crisis of the early 1960s sapped much of that self-confidence. The coup of 1964 occurred in an atmosphere of national self-doubt.

The doubts of 1964 gave way to disillusion among Brazilians in the political center and left. By early 1967 Brazil had gone through the wringer of economic stabilization for three years, yet it was still losing ground in per capita economic growth terms. Only after 1967 did growth resume, raising Brazil's international ambitions along with it.

The Brazilian government sought to exploit this elán by arousing a new spirit of ufanismo. Slogans appeared everywhere (showing them was compulsory): *Ninguém segura mais êste pais!* (Nobody can hold this country back!) When Brazil retired the world soccer cup by winning it for an unprecedented third time in 1970, even opponents of President Garrastazú Médici thought he gained enough reflected glory to qualify as a genuinely popular President. Brazilians disgusted by authoritarian government drew pride from the evidence that Brazil was on the move. Whatever its political imperfections, Brazil was approaching international status at a faster pace than most Brazilians had dared hope in the early 1960s. The signs were reassuring. By 1974 Brazil's foreign exchange reserves exceeded those of Britain (IMF, 1974:19), while the profit-troubled German headquarters of Volkswagen were congratulating themselves for their booming subsidiary in Brazil.

As for the Latin American context, Brazilians make no secret of seeing themselves as a leader. This self-image has a long history, evident especially in Brazil's role in the two world wars. A more recent precedent was President Kubitschek's proposal for "Operation Pan America" in 1959, which Brazilians regard as the authentic birth of the idea of the Alliance for Progress. Brazil's traditional rival has been Argentina, but that country's chronic political instability and sluggish economic growth has left it on a far less dynamic path than Brazil, as General Perón was well aware during his brief return to the presidency.[12]

Brazil's size and ambitions have led her government to disdain acting primarily within any Latin American multilateral structure, such as the OAS. Under the Alliance for Progress, for example, Brazil refused to send her economic projects and programs through the multilateral machinery. Her leaders believed that Brazil deserved to deal directly with the United States. That presumption has grown stronger during the recent years of rapid growth.

Meanwhile Brazil has been very active in relations with the Spanish American nations on her borders. Paraguay has agreed to a massive hydroelectric project at Itaipu which will supply power to Brazil.[13] That move sent shock waves through the Argentine foreign ministry, which saw Paraguay slipping ever farther into the Brazilian sphere of economic domination. Energy needs also prompted agreements with Bolivia. Brazil is anxious to ensure a ready supply of oil and natural gas from the fields of eastern Bolivia. Here again, Argentina looked on with grave concern. Uruguay, another neighbor, has interested Brazil not as a source of energy, but as a possible source of political radicalization. It is widely believed that the Brazilian police showed the Uruguayans how to liquidate the Tupamaros. However true, the Brazilian government was greatly pleased that the new military regime, installed in Montevideo in February 1973 (thinly disguised by Bordaberry's continuing as President), eliminated their urban guerrillas, who were a source of support—psychological and probably material—for their counterparts in Brazil.

The Brazilian government's current drive to strengthen relations with her neighbors is also geopolitical. The Plata basin, for example, has often been a theater of combat for the last three centuries. The Amazon basin is another area which Brazilians have traditionally considered as vulnerable to foreign penetration. Thus the Trans-Amazonian Highway is justified on the grounds not only that it will open up vast areas for settlement, but also that it will facilitate Brazilian political and military sovereignty in an area previously under only tenuous Brazilian control.[14]

Do Brazil's current international ambitions extend to claiming leadership in the Third World? President Jânis Quadros' "independent foreign policy" was based on the hope that Brazil would gain new leverage by breaking away from her historically close association with the United States. The new president's round-the-world trip between his election in 1960 and his inauguration in 1961 symbolized this search for a Third World role. On the day that Quadros resigned in 1961, Vice President Goulart was visiting Red China, an indication of his attempt to lead a break-out from the cold war terms in which Brazil had conceived its role. His delegation's championing of LDC's economic rights against the industrial powers (including Russia and East Europe) at the UNCTAD (United Nations Commission for Trade and Development) conference in early 1964 was tangible evidence of that desire to lead the Third World.

Since 1964 the military-dominated governments have been less interested in a Third World role for Brazil.[15] Why? First, because Quadros' "independent foreign policy" had become identified with the radical nationalist left. The military saw it as further evidence of a dangerous diversion from Brazil's authentic role within the Christian Free World, led by the United States. For them, anti-Americanism was a natural concomitant to rising threats against property and discipline at home. Insofar as identifying with the Third World might mean neutrality in the contest between the United States and the U.S.S.R. (the original meaning of the term "Third World"), the post-1964 leadership has shunned it.

In economic terms Brazil's relationship with the Third World is more complex. Since 1964 Brazil has toned down the rhetorical appeal for better trading terms in the world economy. Instead, she has worked to diversify and increase her exports, and to attract capital by the prospect of high profits, high interest rates, and the assurance of political stability. Having greatly bettered the terms on which she deals with richer nations, Brazil has shunned identification with the continuing weakness of most LDC's. That stance also makes sense as Brazil finds herself competing with other LDC's to market key exports, such as coffee and sugar. There is also a readiness to seek economic contacts with the socialist bloc. The clearest case is trade with the Soviet Union, which Brazil's military governments have promoted more successfully than any of their populist predecessors.

Finally, we should note that the term "Third World" is now largely outmoded. Polycentrism has rendered obsolete the idea of a homogeneous, united world Communist camp. The old cold war lines have shifted and blurred in the process of detente. Even if Brazil wanted to lead the Third World, it is not clear how she could do so.

Brazil's first priority in charting her international role, aside from support for the United States on basic East-West issues, is her economic self-interest. Well aware of the vulnerability which results from reliance on only a few sources of capital and technology, Brazil is diversifying her dependence by increasing exports and locating new markets. Agreements with Japan for gaining capital and technology in return for iron ore and foodstuffs are typical of Brazil's attempt to maximize her possibilities for growth through the widest possible range of foreign economic relations.

THE COMPONENTS OF U.S. POLICY TOWARD BRAZIL

Direct U.S. assistance

Brazil has ranked very high among the postwar recipients of U.S. government assistance. The total of loans and grants for economic and military programs from 1946 through 1973 was $2.8 billion. (Export-Import Bank loans are excluded from these and subsequent figures.) The heaviest assistance came in the years following the coup of 1964, when Brazil underwent an extensive stabilization program (see Figure 1).[16] Bilateral assistance has dropped sharply since 1969. This decline began as a U.S. response to Brazil's sharp authoritarian turn in 1968-1969. It also coincided with the incoming Nixon Administration's decision to reexamine U.S. policy toward Brazil.

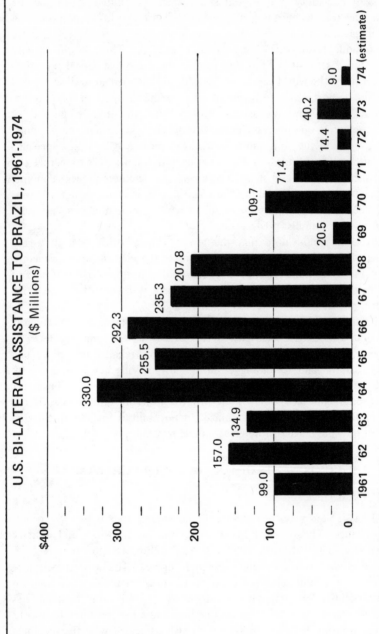

U.S. BI-LATERAL ASSISTANCE TO BRAZIL, 1961-1974
($ Millions)

Source: Dept. of State, Policy, Planning & Coordination: Statistics and Reports Division

Figure 1.

Subsequent U.S. economic assistance has been granted primarily in education and health, areas said to help people while not directly aiding a government which has become harder and harder to defend. Small-scale military assistance has continued in the range of $10 million to $20 million annually.

Ironically, the United States started reducing economic assistance just as it was becoming less important to Brazil. By 1969 Finance Minister Delfim Neto's boom had been under way for almost two years, and was rapidly attracting foreign capital and credits. Whatever leverage the United States might hope to wield over Brazilian policy was greatly reduced. As one State Department Brazil hand put it, "We figured we couldn't demand political liberalization when the military government began, in case they defied us and became even more arbitrary. And when they went more authoritarian, we were powerless because they no longer needed our aid."

The options in the area of direct U.S. assistance are three: to phase it out completely, to maintain the present low level, or to attempt an increase. The first two are almost synonymous. Any significant increase seems unfeasible, both because Brazil does not need it—in terms relative to other LDC's—and because the U.S. Congress, with its growing animosity to foreign aid, would hardly approve it.

U.S. government-financed links with Brazilian sectors

Although they do not appear in the figures on U.S. direct assistance, there are many other activities financed by the U.S. government. The exchange of military officers is one of the most important. Officers from each country are sent to the other for participation in advanced training programs, such as the general staff course. The United States also maintains a sizable military mission in Brazil, including representatives of all three services. The extent to which these military contacts have influenced Brazilian policy-making is a moot point. The U.S. military feel that the arrangements serve the U.S. interest because they help keep our government well informed about attitudes, practices, and ideas among a Brazilian sector which over the last decades has amply demonstrated its importance. It may also be that U.S. military have aided and abetted the growing authoritarian Brazilian mentality as part of their goal of maintaining a network of reliable anticommunist allies around the globe.

The U.S. government subsidizes contacts in other areas as well. Academics are exchanged under the Fulbright program and USAID contracts, in order to help develop teaching and research programs in Brazil. The objectives range from improving in Brazil the knowledge and study of U.S. civilization (Fulbright) to the strengthening of agronomical research in the interior of Minas Gerais (USAID contracts). It is assumed that the U.S. interest will be served by this greater exposure of Brazilians to American civilization and technology. Other such programs, sponsored by private U.S. institutions (Ford Foundation, Rockefeller Foundation, American Field Service), are subsidized by the American public in the sense that the funds in question accrued partially from the U.S. taxes their donors were permitted to waive by endowing foundations.

Labor leadership is another area identified by the U.S. government as important for exposure to U.S. influence. The American Institute of Free Labor Development (AIFLD) finances visits by U.S. labor leaders to Brazil and trips by Brazilians to the United States. It is assumed that Brazilian labor leaders will observe (and emulate) the American-style bread-and-butter strategies, thus checking the domination of labor unions by radical nationalist or Communist elements. Finally, the United States finances trips to the United States by leaders from many walks of Brazilian life (theater, education, library science, business, and literature). These "leader grants" have undoubtedly played a role in maintaining a cadre of voices sympathetic to the United States among opinion-makers in Brazil.

United States-Brazilian economic relations

Most United States-Brazilian economic relations are not under the direct control of the U.S. government, but are nonetheless subject to its influence. Many Brazilians, like many Latin Americans, believe that these private economic ties are the central question in relations between North America and Latin America. What *ought* to be the U.S. government's attitude toward U.S. investment in Brazil? Is our national interest to be forever equated with the fortunes of private U.S. investors in Brazil? If not, how does it differ? This problem cries out for attention and yet receives little systematic analysis in the United States.

Our government presently does much to encourage private U.S. investment abroad. For Brazil, as for other LDC's, OPIC (Overseas Private Investment Corporation) offers to insure investors against such risks as war and uncompensated expropriation. The U.S. government (whose public monies are the ultimate guarantee of OPIC) thereby reduces the risk which might otherwise dissuade investors from making further commitments in Brazil. But does it serve our national interest to encourage more U.S. investors into a country when their ordinary risk calculations might otherwise keep them away?

The Hickenlooper amendment explicitly identifies U.S. public interest with the fate of private investors. That law prohibits our government from extending economic assistance to any country which expropriates property of U.S. citizens without arranging prompt compensation. Although the State Department has managed to apply the law with remarkable restraint, its spirit was explicitly reaffirmed in President Nixon's important statement on "Economic Assistance and Investment Security" on January 19, 1972.

We need a much clearer understanding of the role of private foreign investment in Brazil, as in all of Latin America. Virtually everyone agrees that economic nationalism is a force which will remain strong in the future. One of its prime targets will be foreign investment. Is it not time for the U.S. government to look to an era when private *dis*investment may be the order of the day? The reasons for Brazilian (and Latin American) suspicion of U.S. investment are not far to seek. Official U.S. data (U.S. Policies in Brazil: Hearings, 1971:215) show that between 1960 and 1969 profit remittances exceeded new net direct investment by $57 million, with remittances from Brazil to the United States exceeding net capital from the United States every year but three.[17] The steadily rising accumulation of U.S. investment there suggests that before long the remissions and repatriation (if past experience is any guide) will outweigh any level of new investments which might reasonably be expected, thus creating a strain on the balance of payments. It is true that Brazil's past deficits would have been greater if the new investment had not occurred. But if present rates of remission and repatriation are projected into the future, then the long-run cost of that new investment may lead Brazilians to want to change the rules governing such investment.

As economic historians have often pointed out, over the long haul Brazil will have to depend primarily on its own internal savings to finance growth. Capital inflows since 1945 have too often been allowed to substitute for domestic savings, rather than merely bridging a temporary domestic savings "gap." Brazilians have probably saved less than they would have if the foreign capital had not been available to finance growth. The question which should be posed is: Who benefits from private U.S. investment in Brazil? Since the answer is complex, it is all the more important to ask it now. Is the U.S. national interest likely to diverge significantly from the interests of private investors in the future—when the Brazilian government may wish to establish national control over her many economic sectors controlled by foreigners?

ALTERNATIVE APPROACHES TO U.S. POLICY TOWARD BRAZIL

There are three different policy approaches which the United States might adopt toward Brazil over the next three to five years. Although they cannot always be clearly differentiated in practice, for purposes of analysis it is useful to sketch them in simple terms.

Minimal intervention

Under this policy the U.S. government would end economic assistance and stop trying to shape Brazil's future. Since 1964, it could be argued, our aid has strengthened an increasingly repressive regime. That contradicts America's oft-repeated commitment to support freedom around the world. The minimum interventionists go even further. They argue that *any* significant U.S. government involvement is likely to become destructive. Whatever ostensibly noble purposes our assistance may have served at the outset, it inevitably draws U.S. power into historical processes over which we cannot and should not have control. The psychological, material, and physical blood-letting in Indochina should be sufficient lesson.

In Brazil the minimum interventionists would eliminate the elaborate military ties, and would stop using U.S. public resources to encourage our citizens to invest in Brazil, leaving them to take their own risks. Meanwhile the U.S. government would help prepare for the divestiture which is very likely to come. This policy approach has been best spelled out by Senator Frank Church (especially in his conduct of the 1971 hearings on U.S. Brazilian policy and in his Senate speech in the 1972 Senate defeat of the foreign aid bill).

Anti-authoritarian, reformist

This policy would call for the United States to intervene discreetly in favor of political liberalization and social reform, while maintaining formally correct diplomatic relations with the government. At its extreme, this policy would call for direct support for the opposition, like the U.S. efforts in October 1945 against the governments of Vargas and Perón. It worked in Brazil, as the military deposed Vargas and ended the authoritarian Estado Nôvo. In Argentina it backfired, as U.S. Ambassador Braden inadvertently furnished the winning slogan: "Braden o Perón!" It goes without saying that clandestine U.S. intervention has been common in Latin America. The CIA activities to "destabilize" the Allende regime in Chile are the most recent to be publicized, but such tactics have also been used against the right, as in the support for the opponents of Trujillo's dictatorship in the Dominican Republic.

For present-day Brazil, this policy might specify that any U.S. assistance (admittedly now at a very low level) be conditional on the government's ceasing police repression and opening up the political system. In part the United States attempted this policy in 1969, when the newly arrived Nixon Administration decided to freeze commitments to Brazil pending a study of the regime's more authoritarian trend, evident since late 1968.

Pro-government

Like the last alternative, and in contrast to the minimal intervention policy, a pro-government policy would call for an ambitious U.S. role in Brazil. The assumption would be that the American policy can make a significant difference in Brazil's development. Just as in the 1964-1968 period, when U.S. assistance, especially economic, helped the Brazilian regime gain confidence and international respectability, so now the United States should wholeheartedly endorse a government which has created a new model of rapid economic development among LDC's. That would mean praising the Brazilian regime as worthy of imitation elsewhere in Latin America. There have already been military coups in Argentina (Ongania: 1966-1970), Uruguay (military regime: 1973-), and Chile (September 1973-), which show the influence of the Brazilian model.

Furthermore, the United States would recognize that Brazil has become a very useful "subimperialist" client-state in Latin America. It is a reliable vote on security issues within the OAS. With her newfound economic power Brazil can be a U.S. surrogate in extending aid to the rightist governments in Bolivia and Uruguay. Since the United States can now afford to sleep more soundly as far as South America is concerned, it behooves us to reward Brazil in every appropriate way. President Nixon's effusive tribute to General Médici ("as Brazil goes, so goes Latin America") when the Brazilian President visited Washington in December 1971, epitomizes such recognition.

This pro-government position would favor continuing vital links between the United States and the Brazilian military. It would also suggest that we discourage the regime's militant opponents by restricting their activities in the United States (through visa decisions, harassment when in the United States, etc.). The U.S. government would also encourage U.S. private investment in Brazil, on the assumption that the capitalist, pro-American type of government is likely to continue indefinitely, especially if given our enthusiastic support.

CONFLICTING PRIORITIES

Just to outline these (oversimplified) policy alternatives is to remind ourselves how narrow is the range for probable change. U.S. policy toward Brazil, as toward Latin America and the LDC's, depends upon our ranking of priorities. Although they have been left implicit thus far, they are now worth discussing directly.

(1) *Prevent anti-American radicalization:* Traditionally anti-American radicalization has meant preventing any swing toward political leaders who would threaten U.S. private investment. Until 1959, there seemed little likelihood that any such leaders would gravitate into the political and military camp of the Soviet Union, even though the network of security pacts and OAS agreements were posited on the existence of an external threat to the Americas. In the Guatemalan case of 1954, the United States sponsored a coup against a regime supposedly heading for the Soviet orbit. In fact it was

unlikely that the Soviets would have attempted a bridgehead in Central America, perilously far from the origins of their supply lines. The Soviets lacked even a diplomatic mission in Guatemala.

After 1959, however, the scene changed. Cuba joined the Soviet camp in the most fundamental sense—as a military base. That ominously altered the superpower balance, which was only partially restored by the deal following the missile crisis of October 1972. The United States forced the Soviets to dismantle the base's offensive capacity in return for a commitment to attempt no further military intervention in Cuba. Since then the Soviet Union has tacitly honored our right to help prevent what we see as serious radicalization elsewhere in the hemisphere, as in Brazil in 1964, the Dominican Republic in 1965, and Chile in 1973.

(2) *Protect U.S. economic interests:* By this priority the U.S. government ought to place first the protection of our economic interests whether in the form of private U.S. investment, or in the form of supplies of vital raw materials (oil, etc.). The need for a tough policy toward the confiscators is seen as great because latent nationalist sentiments all over Latin America could be kindled by a few challenges to U.S. investments. If we maintain an unflinching stand, it is argued, nationalists will know that attacks on our property are bound to provoke firm action, including possible intervention (perhaps through support for conspiratorial opposition) or retaliation in the international economy.

This priority rests on the assumption that the United States cannot afford to see any of its economic interests jeopardized in Latin America. Economic nationalists are usually also political radicals. Chile under Allende illustrated well the combination of economic nationalism (seizing extensive U.S. properties with no realistic prospect of compensation) and political radicalization. Because the Russians have little desire to recruit further satellites in Latin America (which they would find unduly costly and dangerous to protect), the United States did not have to worry about dealing with the Soviets when the time came for "containing" the radicalization in Chile. The Chilean left knew that little help could come from outside. The opposition, on the other hand, could count on foreign support (U.S. government, international agencies, etc.) once they gained power and launched an orthodox economic policy including: (1) commitment to restore to their former owners most of the foreign properties expropriated, confiscated, or seized by nationalizers; and (2) a tough stabilization program. Peru must be seen here as an exception. Peruvian nationalization of United States-owned investments was not accompanied by any major challenge to the United States-dominated security system.

(3) *Promote social reform:* This priority would call for us to support

thoroughgoing social change wherever it occurs, even at the cost of possible anti-American radicalization. Obviously this would require the U.S. government to place the welfare of the majority of Latin American populations ahead of the interests of U.S. investors. Supporting arguments would include the belief that U.S. national interest *ought* to imply favoring broad social welfare above all, both because it is the just goal, and because in the long run it will benefit the United States. Our security, it would be argued, will flow neither from the military reliability of supposedly pro-American regimes, nor from strengthening Latin American sectors which promote gross inequalities within their countries, but from the growing well-being of entire Latin American peoples.

Does our discussion matter? Or will U.S. policy even be a major variable in Brazil's development over the next three to five years? Because our present level of economic assistance is so low, and the probability of its being increased so slim, what leverage could the U.S. government possibly have?

The question should be phrased in different terms. The real choice is about the kind of future that Americans will be symbolically endorsing. The legacy of our recent policy is unmistakable. Despite subsequent doubts, our government has strongly supported the "Revolution of 1964" as a victory for the free world and a model of economic development. Does this Brazilian regime represent the shape of the future that we want to promote? Recently we have learned to our sorrow how foreign commitments can grow. This ought to be a time for the application of a long-neglected quality in U.S. foreign policy— humility. For myself, I think we should move to a policy of minimum intervention. Which is perhaps only another way of recognizing that the future of Brazil lies in the hands of Brazilians.

NOTES

1. The most detailed scholarly account of Brazil's wartime relationship with the United States is McCann (1973). An interpretation much more critical of U.S. motives, also documented from unpublished Brazilian sources, may be found in Bandeira (1973).

2. Milton Eisenhower has discussed his role in helping shape United States-Latin American policy in Eisenhower (1963).

3. A very useful survey of the record for the 1960s is Levinson and de Onis (1970).

4. A wealth of information on U.S. activities in the Northeast may be found in Roett (1972) and Page (1972).

5. In 1972 the United States had a surplus on current account of $821 million in transactions with Latin America. (U.S. Dept. of Commerce, 1973: 52).

6. Adelman (1974), which summarizes some of the more important findings in Morris (1973).

7. A valuable source of documents and information on post-1945 U.S. policy toward Brazil, with emphasis on the period since the 1964 coup, is U.S. Senate, Subcommittee on Western Hemisphere Affairs of the Committee on Foreign Relations (1971: May 4, 5, and 11), hereafter referred to as *U.S. Policies in Brazil: Hearings.*

8. For a detailed study, see Storrs (1973). For the more recent period, see Rosenbaum (1972).

9. For greater detail on the coup of 1964 and its origins, see Skidmore (1967). For a critical analysis of the U.S. role in Brazil's development during the 1960s, see Martins (1974).

10. I have analyzed the role of the technocrats in Skidmore (1973).

11. For an analysis of pre-World War I ufanismo which attempts to put it into historical context, see Skidmore (1974: 99-102).

12. Nonetheless, Argentina is still a much more developed economy, when measured in per capita terms. Brazil's per capita GDP in 1971 was estimated by the United Nations to be U.S. $449, whereas Argentina's was U.S. $1,261. *U.N. Department of National Accounts Statistics, 1972,* Vol. III (1974: 4). For an example of the Argentine elite's deep worry over Brazil's rapid growth, see Sigaut (1972).

13. Extensive information on this project is given in Pereira (1974).

14. The thinking of the Brazilian military on the strategic importance of the Amazon valley is well documented in Tambs (1973). A collection of commentary on the highway project is given in Pereira (1971).

15. The relationship between post-1964 domestic policy and Brazil's potential in foreign relations is discussed in Gordon (1972).

16. By mid-1966 the American mission had grown to 920 U.S. citizens, plus a thousand Brazilian employees. The new Ambassador, John Tuthill, was appalled at these numbers, and launched "Operation Topsy," which resulted in a 32 percent reduction. He was worried especially about the American image (Tuthill, 1972: 62-85).

17. During these hearings before the Church subcommittee, William Ellis, USAID Director for Brazil, stressed the "positive effect on our balance of payments" resulting from the profit remissions of U.S. investors (Hearings, p. 244).

REFERENCES

ADELMAN, I. (1974) "Strategies for equitable growth." Challenge (May-June): 37-44.
––– and MORRIS, C. T. (1973) *Economic Growth and Social Equity in Developing Countries.* Stanford: Stanford University Press.
BANDEIRA, M. (1973) *Presenca dos Estados Unidos no Brasil.* Rio de Janeiro.
EISENHOWER, M. (1963) *The Wine Is Bitter: The United States and Latin America.* New York.
GORDON, L. (1972) "Brazil's future world role." Orbis 16, 3 (Fall): 621-631.
GRIFFIN, K. (1971) "The role of foreign capital," pp. 225-244 in K. Griffin (ed.) *Financing Development in Latin America.* London.
International Monetary Fund (1974) International Financial Statistics 27, 5 (May).
LEVINSON, J. and J. DE ONIS (1970) *The Alliance That Lost Its Way.* New York.
McCANN, F. D., Jr. (1973) *The Brazilian-American Alliance, 1937-1945.* Princeton: Princeton University Press.
MARTINS, C. E. (1974) "Brazil and the United States from the 1960's to the 1970's," pp. 269-301 in J. Cotler and R. R. Fagen (eds.) *The United States and Latin America: The Changing Political Realities.* Stanford: Stanford University Press.

– – – (1972) "Brasil-Estados Unidos dos 60 aos 70." Cadernos Cebrap 9. Sao Paulo.
PAGE, J. A. (1972) *The Revolution That Never Was: Northeast Brazil, 1955-1964.* New York: Grossman.
PEREIRA, O. D. (1974) *Itaipu: Prós e Contras.* Rio de Janeiro.
– – – (1971) *A Transamazônica: Prós e Contras.* Rio de Janeiro.
ROETT, R. (1972) *The Politics of Foreign Aid in the Brazilian Northeast.* Nashville: Vanderbilt University Press.
ROSENBAUM, H. J. (1972) "Brazil's foreign policy: developmentalism and beyond." Orbis 16, 1 (Spring): 58-84.
SIGAUT, L. J. (1972) *Argentina-Brasil: Prejuicios y Realidad.* Buenos Aires.
SKIDMORE, T. E. (1974) *Black into White: Race and Nationality in Brazilian Thought.* New York: Oxford University Press.
– – – (1973) "Politics and economic policy making in authoritarian Brazil, 1937-1971," in A. Stepan (ed.) *Authoritarian Brazil: Origins, Policies and Future.* New Haven, Conn.: Yale University Press.
– – – (1967) *Politics in Brazil, 1930-1964: An Experiment in Democracy.* New York: Oxford University Press.
STORRS, K. L. (1973) "Brazil's independent foreign policy, 1961-1964: background, tenets, linkage to domestic politics and aftermaths." Ph.D. dissertation. Cornell University.
TAMBS, L. A. (1973) "Geopolitics of the Amazon." Presented at the Twenty-Third Annual Latin American Conference. University of Florida, Gainesville (January).
TUTHILL, J. N. (1972) "Operation Topsy." Foreign Policy 8 (Fall): 62-85.
U.N. Department of National Accounts Statistics, 1972 (1974). New York.
U.S. Department of Commerce (1973) Survey of Current Business 53, 12 (December). Washington, D.C.: Government Printing Office.
United States foreign policy, 1972 (1973). A Report of the Secretary of State. Washington.
U.S. Senate, Subcommittee on Western Hemisphere Affairs of the Committee on Foreign Relations (1971) United States Policies and Programs in Brazil, Hearings 92nd Congress. 1st Session. Washington, D.C.
VILAR DE QUEIROZ, J. M. (1974) "The economic miracle: the next phase." Presented at a Conference on Politics and the Brazilian Economy (sponsored by the Johnson Foundation), Racine, Wisconsin (April 17-18).

PART IV

LATIN AMERICA AND THE WORLD

Chapter 11

PRINCIPLED PRAGMATISM IN THE FACE OF

EXTERNAL PRESSURE: THE FOREIGN POLICY

OF THE ALLENDE GOVERNMENT

CARLOS FORTIN

INTRODUCTION: SOURCES AND INITIAL
FORMULATION OF ALLENDE'S FOREIGN POLICY

Foreign relations is the one area in which the performance of the government of President Salvador Allende in Chile was praised by both its supporters and its opponents.[1] Polarization of political opinion was intense in Chile, and this unanimity over foreign policy is a measure of the success Allende and his Foreign Minister Clodomiro Almeyda achieved in devising and implementing a policy that combined strict adherence to certain fundamental positions with flexibility. To be sure, the acid test of the policy, i.e., the finding of a tolerable modus vivendi with the United States, was interrupted by the coup of September 1973, which occurred shortly after the Chilean and the American governments had agreed to resume discussions. These discussions were making some progress toward solving the outstanding differences. However, the view cannot be completely dismissed that by the time the talks were resumed the differences had reached a point of no return—except through a more or less unconditional surrender of the Chilean stand on questions as sensitive as the compensation to the American copper companies and the treatment of the International Telephone and Telegraph Company (ITT).

Even if this were so, it would not necessarily reflect badly on Allende's foreign policy, as it is obvious that the relations with the United States were a function of a complex set of factors, among which the attitude of the American government toward Chile was paramount. Indeed, it has been suggested that this attitude was always one of total rejection of the Allende experiment, and that consequently there never was a real chance of accommodation (Petras and Morley, 1974). This point will be dealt with below.

On the other side, it can be argued that if a compromise was at all possible, the Allende government's global foreign policy had placed Chile in a good bargaining position to arrive at it.

The purpose of this article is to identify the main features of the foreign policy of the Allende government and to explore the factors that shaped its formulation and its implementation in the context of the international situation surrounding Chile. Within this framework special attention will be paid to the relations with the United States.

Principles, Practicalities, and External Constraints: The Sources of Allende's Foreign Policy

The foreign policy of the Allende government was the result of the interplay of three different factors: the general theoretical position of the government toward the world economic and power structure; the experience of the country in the conduct of its foreign relations; and the external constraints imposed on Chile as a result of the socioeconomic policies of the government. The word "interplay" is not meant here to have any mechanical connotations; the resulting policy was clearly not due to the sheer operation of those three factors, but rather to the way in which they were perceived and incorporated in the policy process by the decision-makers involved.

According to the theoretical outlook of the Allende government, the existence of underdevelopment in the world is linked to the process of expansion of world capitalism and international exploitation. This goes beyond the "center-periphery" types of models proposed by the Economic Commission for Latin America in the 1950s and the 1960s, and comes closer to Marxist theories of imperialism and the so-called dependence theory of underdevelopment as elaborated in recent Latin American social science writing. (See among many others Cardoso and Faletto, 1969; Dos Santos, 1970, 1973.)[2]

One of the most explicit presentations of this view of contemporary world problems was given by Allende himself in his opening speech at the United Nations Conference on Trade and Development (UNCTAD III) that met in Santiago in April 1972:

> The first point to be recalled is that our community is not homogeneous, but divided into peoples that have grown rich and peoples that are still poor. . . . Secondly, the toil and the resources of the poorer

nations subsidize the prosperity of the affluent peoples. . . . Over the last twenty years, the ebb and flow of foreign capital into and out of the Third World has meant a net loss for us of many hundreds of millions of dollars, besides leaving us in debt to the tune of nearly 70 thousand million. . . . Thirdly, this economic, financial and trade order, so prejudicial to the Third World precisely because it is so advantageous to the affluent countries, is defended by most of these with bulldog tenacity, through their economic might, through their cultural influence, and, on some occasions, and by some powers, through almost irresistible forms of pressure, through armed interventions which violate all the commitments assumed in the Charter of the United Nations [Allende, 1973: 175, 176].

This adherence to a broad view of the world's political and economic problems was, as will be seen below, very much present in the formulation of the general foreign policy aims of the *Unidad Popular* coalition program, under which the 1970 presidential campaign was fought. In the design of more specific policies and their implementation in office, however, those broad principles were combined with the other factors mentioned above.

To begin with, the Chilean tradition of conduct of foreign relations contained an element of pragmatic appraisal of the relevant international power realities. This did not preclude a certain amount of international activism, particularly in the Latin American arena, where after World War II Chileans had been among the leaders in the creation of such influential regional organizations as the Economic Commission for Latin America of the United Nations and the Inter-American Development Bank. In the period immediately preceding the Allende government, Chilean foreign policy also played a significant role in the articulation of a more self-assertive attitude in Latin America. This attitude was expressed in a growing sense of identity and differentiation from the United States, in an awareness of the need for international control of the penetration of foreign capital, and in the encouragement of regional and subregional integration. Chile's participation was instrumental in bringing about the Consensus of Viña del Mar and in redefining a new continental role for the Special Coordinating Commission for Latin America (CECLA); it was also substantial in the establishment of the Andean Pact, whose common regime for the treatment of foreign capital represented a first step toward controlling the activities of multinational corporations on the continent.

Thus, the Allende government could benefit from an experience that lately had been largely convergent with its own basic approach, and which could also help to identify realistic goals for foreign policy.

This identification was particularly relevant because of the external context of Chile's foreign policy, which posed some important problems and constraints. It was clearly to be expected that both the domestic policies and the international outlook of the government would create difficulties with the United States. Depending on the magnitude of those difficulties, the conflict could extend to other Western powers and to the Latin American countries most amenable to United States pressure. In addition, the Latin American context generally was not particularly favorable, with right-wing, anti-Communist governments in Argentina, Brazil, Paraguay, Uruguay, and, after the coup of August 1971, Bolivia. The risk of growing international isolation was one that the new foreign policy had to deal with most carefully. On the other side, the incipient process of détente inaugurated by Nixon's "era of negotiation" address of 1969 opened up possibilities of increasing relations with the socialist world without aggravating likely difficulties with the United States.

International Policy in the Program of Unidad Popular

The interaction of the preceding factors was already noticeable in the formulation of aims of foreign policy contained in the campaign manifesto of Unidad Popular, the coalition of parties that backed Allende in 1970. The general ideological commitment was forcefully expressed at the outset:

> The aim of the government of Unidad Popular in its international policy is to affirm the complete political and economic independence of Chile. . . . A firm sense of identity of Latin American interests and resistance to imperialism will be fostered by means of a foreign policy which relates to people rather than to Foreign Ministries [Allende, 1973: 49].

Imperialism was moreover openly identified with the United States, Pan-Americanism in any form was rejected, and the Organization of American States was denounced as a tool of the United States government. At the same time, however, the program stated that "relations will be maintained with all other countries regardless of their ideological or political position" as long as the principle of self-determination was respected. This meant "a vigilant and active defence of the principle of non-intervention and the rejection of all forms of discrimination, pressure, invasion or blockade proposed by imperialist countries" (Allende, 1973: 49).

Thus, the 1970 program already contained two of the elements that were to become cornerstones of Allende's foreign policy: the principle of ideological pluralism in international relations and the exclusion of intervention in the internal affairs of other countries. It is apparent that both ideas—in addition to falling in line with general attitudes long held by the Chilean left—were very much geared toward improving the external position of the government in the face of the context briefly described above. The conception of "ideological frontiers" could only act against the Allende government by isolating it; any concessions to the possibility of external intervention, whether military or not, was also a major potential danger.

The other major component of the foreign policy formulation of the program was the insertion of Chile into the broader context of Latin America and the Third World as a whole. In addition to the affirmation of Latin American identity vis-a-vis the rest of the world, the program endorsed the idea of Latin American integration, provided it took place "on an economic base which has been liberated from the imperialist patterns of dependence and exploitation" (Allende, 1973: 51). Solidarity and support were pledged with all dependent and colonized countries, particularly with those developing struggles for liberation and independence.

Friendly relations were anticipated with socialist countries, and Cuba was mentioned in the context of a promise of solidarity "expressed in practical terms" (Allende, 1973: 50).

ALLENDE IN OFFICE: CHALLENGE AND RESPONSE IN FOREIGN POLICY

The ideas just examined constitute, of course, only the broadest outline of an approach to international relations. After its inauguration at the beginning of November 1970, the Allende government had to address the task of translating the ideas into a workable foreign policy. This was done with one basic principle in mind. This was to minimize international conflict in nonessential areas in order to be able to concentrate on facing the inevitable conflicts in essential areas, in particular in the relations with the United States. The new government was aware that the level of potential external conflict was high owing basically to its general orientation in the internal arena.

To be sure, the Allende government moved swiftly to put into practice some of the most controversial elements in the campaign plank. Relations with Cuba were reestablished on November 11, 1970. Moreover, the resumption of relations was presented as an act of explicit rejection of the sanctions imposed by the OAS in 1964, which were still formally in force. The announcement by President Allende stated that the sanctions violated the right of self-determination and were therefore a transgression of the Charter of the United Nations (Allende, 1973: 67-68). Later, diplomatic relations were established with the People's Republic of China and the German Democratic Republic, as well as with Nigeria; and commercial relations were opened with North Korea and North Vietnam.

From then on, the policy pursued could be thought of as composed of three closely connected and partially overlapping elements:

a. an effort to consolidate a system of international contacts and relations to prevent the possibility of isolation;
b. the display of a substantial amount of activism and initiative especially in the area of international economic relations with a view both toward achieving concrete results and toward broadening contacts and potential support;
c. a preoccupation with the maintenance of the basic areas of external conflict within manageable terms without renouncing fundamental aspects of the government's internal or international policy.

These elements reinforced each other in some cases. In other cases they conflicted, and it was then a matter of judgment to establish priorities and decide in favor of one over the other. They will be examined in turn.

Consolidation of International Links

The efforts in this area were basically directed toward the Latin American countries and the socialist world. Increased links were also introduced with the developing countries of Asia and Africa, and they will be discussed in the following section. Attention was paid, too, to the need not to upset traditional relations with Western Europe, Canada and the other developed Commonwealth countries, and Japan.

In the case of Latin America, the pursuit of the policy was closely allied to the principle of ideological pluralism in international relations. A first and major element was the improvement in the level of relations with Argentina. This was no doubt aided by the fact that the government of President Lanusse, although politically conservative, was also announcing the end of the "ideological frontiers" thesis. Moreover, it was attempting to reach an agreement with the Peronist movement that could make possible a devolution of power to a civilian government, and, possibly most important of all, it was increasingly concerned with Brazilian influence—backed by the United States—in Latin America as a whole and in the Rio de la Plata basin in particular.

The rapprochement started early in Allende's term and progressed quickly to culminate in the signing in July 1971 of an agreement that ended a procedural impasse in the solution of the old border dispute in the Beagle Channel; immediately afterward Allende made his first trip abroad to meet Lanusse in Salta, Argentina. A joint communiqué was issued that reaffirmed the principle of ideological pluralism in Latin American relations and touched on a number of concrete issues of common interest.

A short time later, the Allende government started a diplomatic campaign oriented toward the Andean Pact countries. Chile reasserted its total support for the Pact and emphasized the principles of economic nationalism embodied in agreements such as Decision 24 on common treatment for foreign capital. In August 1971, President Allende made state visits to Peru, Colombia, and Ecuador. He was enthusiastically received, and signed declarations that affirmed the right of Latin American nations to restore relations with Cuba, rejected economic pressure as a tool of foreign policy in the continent, and stated the need to reinforce the joint action of Latin American countries and of developing countries generally.

This display of support-winning diplomacy turned out to be particularly well timed. Shortly before the visit started, the left-wing regime of President Torres in Bolivia was overthrown by a right-wing military coup, thus increasing the danger of isolation for Chile in the continent. Chile did not have diplomatic relations with Bolivia because of border disputes, and the Allende government had also been active in trying to reopen discussions with the Bolivian government with a view to restoring normal relationships.

The diplomatic effort in Latin America was accompanied by a significant increase in economic and commercial relations. Imports from Latin American countries, which in 1970 represented 20.6 percent of total Chilean imports, rose to 34.6 percent in 1971 and to 38.7 percent in 1972 (Instituto de Economía, 1973: 410). The most marked increase was with Argentina, which at the end of 1971 represented a larger share of Chile's total imports than the United States. Other substantial increases took place in the trade with Mexico, with which diplomatic relations were also extremely cordial, and of course Cuba, whose Prime Minister Castro visited Chile in November 1971.

Not surprisingly, the policy did not go so far as significantly improving relations with Brazil. These remained coolly normal at the diplomatic level, although at the beginning commercial and financial links were also intensified. As the internal policies of the Allende government became more radical, and as the conflict with the United States escalated in 1972, relations with Brazil deteriorated even further. The accusation has even been made that at least some private Brazilian business concerns helped finance opposition groups in Chile (Szulc, 1973; Simons, 1974).

On the whole, the Latin American strategy of the Allende government proved highly successful. Coinciding as it did with a mood of self-assertiveness and independence in Latin America (CECLA, for instance, publicly and rather harshly criticized the United States' protectionist measures adopted by the Nixon Administration in August 1971), it emphasized the point that Chile's socialist government, although committed to introducing revolutionary changes in the country's socioeconomic structure, was also prepared to work within the Latin American family to bring about a more just international order and to increase the influence of the region in the inter-American and world contexts. In so doing, it expressed tendencies that were already apparent but had not openly surfaced, such as the need to revise the position of Cuba in the Latin American context.

The other element in the consolidation effort had to do with the relations with the socialist countries. Again a number of diplomatic moves were combined with a substantial increase in commercial and financial relations. Imports from the Soviet Union and Eastern Europe grew from 0.5 percent of total imports in 1970 to 7.0 percent in 1972 (Instituto de Economía, 1973: 410). Exports, particularly of copper, also increased to socialist countries. Loans, short-term lines of credit and supplier credits, as well as long-term finance for investment projects, were agreed upon. Technical assistance was also provided by the Soviet Union, the German Democratic Republic, and other socialist countries.

As all this was accomplished, however, care was taken not to upset traditional relations with Western Europe. Thus, for instance, Western Europe remained the largest market for Chilean copper, and buyers in Great Britain, Italy, and West Germany—the three largest European consumers of Chilean copper—were given assurances that the opening of new markets would not be at the expense of the traditional markets of friendly European nations.

Activism in the World Arena

At the same time that the strategy of consolidation was under way, the Allende government started to take an increasingly active part in certain areas of inter-American and world relations. This role both reflected its general political orientations and served to expand contacts and support. In taking this line, the Allende Administration was doubtlessly moving into conflictive areas; however, the support-mobilizing potentiality of the issues involved was sufficiently important to outweigh the drawbacks of possible conflict. In some cases, moreover, initiatives responded to external pressures generated by other elements in the government's policies.

The activist role of the Allende government in international affairs concentrated in three areas: firstly, the restructuring of the inter-American system; secondly, the full integration of Chile in the activities of Third World countries as a whole; and thirdly—closely linked with the previous areas—the taking of initiatives in the sphere of international economic relations.

Allende's Government and the Organization of American States. As was mentioned before, the program of Unidad Popular already contained a strong rejection of Pan-Americanism and a denunciation of the OAS as a tool of the United States; it also announced a proposal to create a purely Latin American organization. Shortly after taking office, Allende elaborated on these themes in a major foreign policy speech in which he responded to remarks by President Nixon in his State of the World message of 1971. The ideas presented by Allende summarized the attitude of his government toward the OAS and the inter-American system generally.

The fundamental premise was that two misconceptions of the inter-American philosophy and its institutional embodiment, the OAS, made the system unacceptable and had led to its present state of crisis. These were, on the one side, the notion that the system was composed of a number of equal partners, and that in the OAS every country's voice counted as much as every other's; and on the other side, the notion that there was a community of interests between the United States and Latin America. The reality, Allende said, was quite different. The United States was unmeasurably more powerful economically and politically than all Latin American countries, whose economies, furthermore, were dominated by American capital, trade, and finance. Therefore, there was no community of interests. Latin America's interest lay in limiting the outflow of capital as profits to the American companies, while the interests of both those companies and the American economy as a whole lay in maximizing those profits. This led to an even deeper difference. The best way to ensure the continuation of a position of hegemony for the United States was to maintain the status quo in Latin America, in terms of both international inequalities and internal domination; on the contrary, the aspiration of the Latin American peoples was to end dependence and to introduce basic changes either by reform or by revolution.[3]

In the conflict, the interests that prevailed were those of the strongest. The myth of legal equality among nations in the OAS was then basically an instrument to conceal the domination of the inter-American system by the United States.

This critique, Allende added, did not mean that Chile would withdraw from the OAS. It did mean that Chile would propose some fundamental changes in the philosophy and the structure of the organization (Allende, 1973: 105-107).

The proposed changes were first officially announced at the meeting of the General Assembly of the OAS held in San José, Costa Rica, in April 1971. They suggested the introduction of an institutional set-up whereby the Latin American countries—along the lines of the CECLA experience—would seek common positions to be then discussed and negotiated with the United States. The neatest way of putting this approach into effect would be the creation of another organization composed of all Latin American countries including Cuba, but excluding the United States. The headquarters of the new organization would be in Latin America and not in Washington. Foreign Minister Almeyda made a formal proposal at the meeting of the General Assembly of OAS in Washington in April 1973, and it was supported by Peru and Argentina. After discussions at various levels a Special Committee for the Reorganization of the Inter-American System started deliberations in Lima in June 1973. The proposal, however, ran into opposition from other Latin American governments, and before any compromise could be worked out, the overthrow of Allende deprived the initiative of essential support.

Allende and the Third World. In view of the elements contained in the program and of the general philosophy that oriented the foreign policy of the Allende government, it is not surprising that the policy included a sustained effort to incorporate Chile in the system of Third World nations.

From the beginning, the Allende government attempted a policy of strengthening relations with underdeveloped countries of Asia and Africa. This policy was facilitated by the fact that Chile was successful in securing the seat of UNCTAD III to be held in April 1972, which provided an opportunity for extensive preparatory contacts. Chile took active part in the meeting of ministers of the underdeveloped countries within UNCTAD known as the Group of Seventy-Seven, which met in Lima in preparation for the Santiago Conference, and it helped to draft the final Declaration, Principles, and Program of Action. The Conference itself was also an occasion to reiterate Chile's commitment to a Third World policy. In his opening speech, Allende emphasized the community of interests of all countries of the underdeveloped world and warned about the need to achieve "full unity, unconditionally backed by every single one of our countries" in order to be able to transform the inequitable international structure. Allende also emphasized the necessity for the peoples of the Third World to be aware of the internal implications of dependency. Certain indigenous ruling interests tend to connive with foreign domination. Furthermore, a form of alienation of national consciousness can take place which results in the subconscious acceptance of a "view of the world worked out in the great dominant centres and presented in scientific guise as the explanation of our backward state" (Allende, 1973: 178-179).

A major move in this area was the full incorporation of Chile under Allende in the Group of Non-Aligned Countries. Chile had attended the Third Non-Aligned Conference of Lusaka in 1970 only as an observer. The intention to become a full member was announced by Allende in his first state of the nation message to Congress in May 1971 (Allende, 1973: 168) and was implemented in September that year (Palma, 1972: 142). Chile then attended the meeting of Foreign Ministers of the Non-Aligned Countries held in

Georgetown in August 1972 and later played a very active part in the preparation of the Algiers Conference of Non-Aligned Countries which took place in September 1973. The meeting of experts in preparation for the Algiers Conference was held in Santiago, and Chile's contribution was decisive in the drafting of the resolutions on the treatment of foreign investment.

Chile also intensified its participation in the Inter-Governmental Council of Copper Exporting Countries (CIPEC)—whose other members are Peru, Zaïre, and Zambia—and pressed the need to increase the role of the organization in the world copper market. Although technical and political factors prevented any practical action, CIPEC went a long way in the clarification of common objectives for all member countries and in the identification of appropriate mechanisms for action.

Chile and the Issue of Economic Rights of Underdeveloped Nations. The Allende government's emphasis on the unity of the Third World was closely linked to the question of the economic position of the underdeveloped countries in the international structure and the defense of their economic rights vis-a-vis the developed world. Once again this line was directly related to the basic philosophy referred to before; in addition this issue had a special importance because the internal and external policies of the Allende government made Chile a particularly likely target for certain forms of economic pressure.

As early as his first message to Congress, Allende referred to the need to maintain the apolitical character of multilateral financial organizations:

> The member countries of those institutions cannot be challenged as to their right to choose whatever form of government they wish. And the international institutions of finance cannot be permitted to be the instrument of powerful countries against the weak. To exert direct or indirect pressure in order to create obstacles to the financing of technically suitable projects is to debase the proclaimed purposes of these organisms, and it is an oblique way of interfering in the internal life of those countries and of damaging the interests of their people [Allende, 1973: 169].

This theme was to continue in the forefront of Chile's foreign policy, particularly since after the nationalization of copper, the United States started to oppose any credits to Chile within the World Bank and the Inter-American Development Bank (IDB). Both the Governor of the Chilean Central Bank in the 1972 annual meeting of the Board of Governors of the World Bank and the Chilean Minister of Finance in the 1973 Assembly of Governors of IDB strongly made the point that Chile was being discriminated against for political reasons, and that the procedure was contrary to the charter and the spirit of the institutions involved. The plea could not but strike a responsive note in Third World nations over whose heads always hung the danger of similar discrimination. It also struck a sympathetic chord in Western European countries, some of which were prepared to support the financing of projects for Chile. [4]

In 1972 two events contributed to introduce another main theme in Chile's approach to international economic relations. In March and July that year, American syndicated columnist Jack Anderson revealed evidence to the effect that ITT had been engaged in activities designed to prevent the election of Salvador Allende in 1970 and to bring about the overthrow of his government in 1971. An investigation of the allegations was ordered in September 1972 by the Foreign Relations Committee of the United States Senate, whose Subcommittee on Multinational Corporations conducted hearings on the matter for nine days in March 1973. The investigation and the hearings basically confirmed Anderson's allegations (U.S. Senate, 1973a; U.S. Senate, 1973b). [5]

The feeling of outrage that these revelations produced in Chilean public opinion—which led President Allende to propose the nationalization of a subsidiary of ITT in Chile in May 1972—was compounded in September 1972 by a decision of Kennecott Copper Corporation. Co-owner, through a subsidiary, of the nationalized copper operation of El Teniente, the company decided to contest in European courts the validity of the Chilean nationalization and to attach the proceeds of the sale of Chilean copper in France. [6] Another attachment was obtained in Holland shortly afterward, and in January 1973, a large tonnage was attached in Hamburg. All the attachments were vacated later on, but the ordinary proceedings to contest the validity of nationalization continued; similarly, such proceedings were initiated in Sweden and Italy, where attempts at securing attachments had failed.

For Chile then, the question of transnational corporations directly intervening in the internal affairs of developing countries or challenging the sovereign right of countries to their natural resources, acquired a sudden immediacy and added to the concerns already couched in more general and theoretical terms. Chile's position was that both issues, the activities of transnational corporations and the sovereignty over natural resources, transcended its own particular predicament and became an issue of concern for the whole of the developing world. While requesting support in its fight against the multinationals, Chile suggested that the Third World had also a general interest to defend (Allende, 1972: 14).

In July 1972, as a consequence of Chile's denunciation based on the ITT revelations, the Economic and Social Council of the United Nations passed a unanimous resolution calling for a special study. A group of eminent personalities would be convened to study the function and effects of transnational corporations in the process of development especially in the developing countries. After reviewing the repercussions in international relations of such development, the commission is expected to recommend appropriate international action.

The subject of the control of the activities of multinational corporations in underdeveloped countries was not, of course, introduced by Chile in the world of international organizations.[7] Chile's experience with ITT, however, put it in a different and urgent perspective, and Chile itself became a champion of the need to intensify the control over multinational corporate action. A result of this approach was the document proposed by the Chilean government at the meeting of experts that took place in Santiago in preparation for the Conference of Non-Aligned Countries of September 1973 in Algiers. The document, which was approved by the experts and later submitted to the conference itself, reviews the problems of the activities of multinational corporations in underdeveloped countries and suggests a number of concrete courses of action to increase the control of the host government (Gobierno de Chile, 1973).

In addition to the issues involving multinational corporate action, the Kennecott conflict concerned the question of sovereignty over natural resources, an issue on which most Third World countries are particularly sensitive. Chile had based its decision to nationalize on a number of resolutions of the United Nations—especially Resolution 1803 (XVII) of 1962. These resolutions recognize the right of any state to recover its natural resources. They also establish that litigation in connection with the nationalization process is under the jurisdiction of the nationalizing country, unless that state voluntarily accepts to submit the issue to international arbitration. It was precisely this right of the state to decide on any controversies arising from the nationalization of natural resources that Kennecott was denying when contesting Chile's nationalization in European courts. Chile was therefore able to present the question as a general one concerning the sovereign prerogatives of small nations in a world of economic giants. The response evoked by Chile's position was prompt and categoric. By November 1972, resolutions had been passed in Latin American forums and in the Trade and Development Board of the United Nations, where the spokesman for the African Group expressed their total solidarity with Chile. A similar resolution was passed by the Conference of Ministers of the Non-Aligned Countries that met in Guyana in August 1972. At the end of November, an Extraordinary Meeting of the Ministers of Mines of the CIPEC countries took place in Santiago at the request of the Chilean government. The members unanimously passed resolutions to the effect that any act that impedes or hinders the exercise of the sovereign right of states to dispose freely of their natural resources constitutes economic aggression; and that Kennecott had waged such economic aggression against Chile. The member countries of CIPEC agreed to sever all forms of economic or commercial relations with Kennecott. They further agreed not to replace Chilean copper if the actions of Kennecott succeeded in closing certain markets for Chile. The principle was reaffirmed that any dispute about nationalization of natural resources belongs in the exclusive jurisdiction of the courts of the nationalizing state. Finally, an agreement was reached to create a permanent mechanism of protection and solidarity that could be quickly brought into action in the event of economic aggression against a member country. The front of economic defense was broadened by means of a recommendation to initiate formal contacts with the Organization of Petroleum Exporting Countries (OPEC).

Another area in which Chile placed much emphasis was that of the foreign debt of developing countries. At the time Allende took office, fully one-third of the total revenue of the Chilean economy in hard currency should have been devoted to repaying the foreign debt. In this, Chile was perhaps an extreme case, but by no means atypical. As Allende's speech to UNCTAD III put it:

> We developing countries already owe more than $70,000 million, although we have contributed to the prosperity of the wealthy peoples from time immemorial, and more particularly in recent decades. External debts, largely contracted in order to offset the damage done by an unfair trade system, to defray the costs of the establishment of foreign enterprises in our territory, to cope with the speculative exploitation of our reserves, constitute one of the chief obstacles to the progress of the Third World [Allende, 1973: 190-191].

Chile was also in the forefront of the critique of the existing world trade and monetary arrangements, demanding a voice for the developing world in the negotiations under way to face the obvious crisis of the system and in the subsequent decisions.

The Impact of Activism. The policy of activism of the Allende government was a function of the general orientation of its foreign policy as well as a response to specific challenges to Chile's international position. It was, furthermore, focused on issues that were likely to produce sympathetic responses in developing countries irrespective of internal political orientations. To that extent, it no doubt reflected the mood of the times within the Third World, and that may account for its clear success. Other Latin American and Third World countries were developing aggressive foreign policies as well. Without attempting to attribute to Allende's government what were the results of a complex variety of factors, it is fair to grant Allende a substantial credit for the general spirit of assertiveness and independence of the Third World in the early 1970s. Perhaps a good illustration of this spirit is the change in the inter-American climate exemplified by the meeting of the Economic Commission for Latin America in Quito in March 1973. The final document, approved by all Latin American countries (with the United States abstaining), incorporates the major issues raised above.[8] Finding that the progress of the International Development Strategy of United Nations in Latin America is meager, it criticizes the protectionist policies of the European Economic Community (EEC) and the United States. The document refers to the hostility and economic aggression faced by countries that attempt to introduce structural changes in their societies. It calls for participation of the developing countries in trade and monetary negotiations, and reaffirms the preference of the Latin American countries for multilateral public aid for development over bilateral aid or direct private investment. It also insists on the need for multilateral lending organizations to be free from control by developed countries and asks the United States to grant a relatively long moratorium on the payments that Latin America has to make on its foreign debt. That such a document should have been signed by both Brazil and Cuba is a major event in inter-American history, and one to which—to say the least—the foreign policy of the Allende government was a contributing factor.

Conflict and Conflict Management
in Allende's Foreign Policy:
The Relations with the United States

The third major area of Allende's foreign policy was that of the relations with the United States. This is hardly surprising, as Chile had been firmly within the sphere of economic and political influence of the United States for the preceding decade. This dependence had not been substantially diminished by the more assertive course impressed on to Chilean foreign policy by Frei's Foreign Minister Gabriel Valdés. Between 1961 and 1970 Chile had been the largest per capita recipient of Alliance for Progress loans in Latin America (U.S. Senate, 1973a: 113); at the time of Allende's election over half of Chile's massive foreign debt was with the United States. In addition, the United States provided close to 40 percent of Chile's total imports; the incidence was even higher in imports of capital equipment, machinery, and spare parts, and in the crucial sector of copper mining, over 90 percent of the imported requirements came from the United States. Other areas of high dependency were those of spare parts for the automotive sector, and of oil. Although there were no oil imports from the United States, over 60 percent of the supplies for Chile came from American companies (SEREX, 1972). All this trade was based on a network of financial arrangements whereby American private banks maintained lines of credit in favor of Chile and major suppliers granted credit terms for purchases, often with the guarantee of the Export-Import Bank of the United States. In 1970, short-term lines of credit from American banks amounted to about U.S. $220 million, and loans and credits from the World Bank and the IDB, in which the United States is highly influential, amounted to a yearly average of about U.S. $80 million between 1965 and 1970 (Allende, 1972: 7). Between 1964 and 1969 the direct aid from the American government to Chile was about U.S. $300 million. Finally, two American corporations co-owned and managed three mining operations which accounted for 80 percent of the total production of copper of Chile and about 60 percent of its total foreign exchange revenue.

It was a major objective of the Allende government to reduce this dependence on the United States. Added to that were various other factors unwelcome to the United States such as the composition of the political base of the government, which included the Communist Party; its internal policies, oriented toward radically changing the socioeconomic structure of Chile in a socialist direction, and thus running against the ideological bias of the American government as well as against the interests of traditional U.S. allies in Chile; and the government's international policies, particularly in the inter-American sphere. Thus, it is little wonder that the course of Allende's foreign policy was one of conflict with the United States. The very dependence that was at the core of the conflict would clearly make it both difficult and risky for Chile to pursue a conflict course. As was anticipated above, the way the government of Allende faced this predicament was to minimize the less important elements of conflict with the United States, while taking a firm stand in all matters regarded as essential for the policies of the government. Within those limits, it attempted to work out a livable arrangement with the American government.

The Emergence of Conflict. It is by now fairly well established that the hostility of the United States government toward the prospect of an Allende government in Chile led to early attempts to prevent such an election and inauguration. A policy of frontal opposition was defined before there were any concrete measures of the Allende government vis-a-vis American economic interests in Chile. The hearings of the Foreign Relations Committee of the United States Senate have established that in the period following the September 1970 election, the U.S. Central Intelligence Agency was actively discussing plans to create economic chaos in Chile in order to prevent the confirmation of Allende by Congress (U.S. Senate, 1973b: 9-11, 16, 19). There are indications in the hearings and elsewhere that this might not have been the only such action from American official bodies.[9]

The overt position of the United States government toward the Allende government was presented in February 1971 by President Nixon in his State of the World message to Congress. The message expressed concern for the degree to which the ideology of the newly inaugurated government might influence its actions. Chile's decision to establish relations with Cuba was described as a challenge to the inter-American system and contrary to the collective policy of the OAS, calling for careful watch of the development of Chile's foreign policy by both the United States and its colleagues in the OAS. The policy, however, was to keep open lines of communication and not to be the first to damage the traditional relationship between Chile and the United States. "In short," Nixon said, "we are prepared to have the kind of relationship with the Chilean government that it is prepared to have with us" (Nixon, 1971: 54).

Allende replied to this statement in a speech whose tone was conciliatory, although the contents were uncompromising. He rejected identification of the inter-American system with United States interests, as mentioned above. However, the speech recognized positive aspects in President Nixon's acknowledgment of the legitimacy of the Chilean government, and his state-ment of willingness to cooperate with all Latin American countries regardless of their ideological position and to respect their self-determination. Allende defended the reestablishment of relations with Cuba as an act of moral reparation for an injustice committed in the name of ideologies that were not those of Chile, and one that was decided with the abstention of Chile. Furthermore, Mexico never broke off relations with Cuba and this was not regarded as a threat to the inter-American system. "The government of Chile" the speech went on, "wants amicable relations with the most powerful country in the hemisphere, providing we are allowed the freedom to express differences, to dissent and to negotiate from different points of view" (Allende, 1973: 108). He further announced that the Chilean government had agreed with Admiral Zumwalt for the U.S. carrier *Enterprise* to visit Chile.

An early indication of the difficulties ahead was provided by the sudden decision of President Nixon to cancel the *Enterprise* visit to Chile. This reversal was reportedly due to the advice of Mr. Kissinger and was made in order to avoid giving the impression of support for a Marxist president (Petras and Morley, 1974: 35-36).

At around the same time, an economic mission headed by Pedro Vuskovic, the Chilean Minister of the Economy and a close adviser of Allende, went to Washington to discuss the economic relations between Chile and the United States. It is reported that in the talks U.S. officials raised the issue of the compensation in case of nationalization of United States interests in Chile. The interests were estimated in North American circles at about U.S. $1 billion, the bulk of which was represented by the equity participation of American companies in the copper mining industry in Chile (Petras and Morley, 1974: 35).

The Copper Issue. The activity of American corporations in Chilean copper goes back to the second decade of the century when Kennecott Copper Corporation and The Anaconda Company set up subsidiaries to exploit three large copper mines. Between 1961 and 1970, the production of the three companies accounted for over 80 percent of the total exports of Chilean copper. During this period Chile was the largest exporter of copper in the world and second only to the United States and the U.S.S.R. in total production.

It is estimated that the companies earned about U.S. $1.8 billion in profits, with an estimated total investment of around U.S. $500 million (Nudelman, 1973: 24). In 1964 President Frei proposed a plan to partially nationalize the copper industry. As a result, in 1967 Chile bought 51 percent of the shares of the Kennecott operation (paying for it about U.S. $13 million more than the total book value, since Kennecott demanded a revaluation of assets before the sale could be done). In 1969, Chile bought 51 percent of the Anaconda operations at book value. For all practical purposes the American companies continued managing the mines and remained in charge of sales and purchases of inputs. As a result of tax reductions agreed upon at the same time as the purchase contracts, the companies' profits increased 160 percent on the average between 1967 and 1970 (see generally Moran, 1970; Novoa, 1972; Nudelman, 1973).

In his campaign Salvador Allende had announced the intention of nationalizing the copper industry, thus recuperating for the national economy the full benefit of the exploitation of its main natural resource. This position was also adopted by the Christian Democratic candidate Radomiro Tomic. In December 1971, the Allende government submitted to Congress a constitutional amendment to nationalize the copper companies. The bill included provisions for compensation on the basis of book value (in the case of Kennecott, the book value before the revaluation of 1967) less certain deductions. The most important of these deductions was that of the excess profits the companies had derived from their operations in Chile between 1955 and 1970, over and above what could be regarded as a normal and fair international profit (1955 was the year in which the companies were obliged by Chilean law to keep their accounts in Chile). The president of Chile was empowered to order the deduction of the whole or part of the excess profits.

This formulation was deemed insufficient by the U.S. government, which has long maintained that under international law the appropriate standard for the expropriation of foreign property is that of prompt, adequate, and effective compensation.

The Chilean Congress unanimously approved the constitutional amendment in July 1971, and in September, President Allende issued his decision on the deduction of excess profits: no further compensation was to be paid to Kennecott in addition to the amount paid for the 51 percent of the shares; no further compensation was to be paid to Anaconda in addition to the three installments already paid for the purchase of the 51 percent of the shares. There was the possibility of compensation on book value for a smaller and newer Anaconda mine as well as for a recently opened mine owned by another American company, Cerro Corporation. Chile also took upon itself the payment of the nationalized companies' debt to third parties, estimated at about U.S. $700 million.

On October 13, 1971, Secretary of State Rogers issued a statement expressing the deep disappointment and concern of the U.S. government at what was termed a "serious departure from accepted standards of international law." Application of the deduction for excess profits was criticized as contrary to law and equity. More ominously, the statement read:

> Should Chile fail to meet its international obligations it could jeopardize flows of private funds and erode the base of support for foreign assistance, with possible adverse effects on other developing countries. The course of action which the Chilean government appears to have chosen, therefore, could have an adverse effect on the international development process [Department of State Bulletin, 1971].

The response of the Secretary of State was called "moderate" at the time. Several analyses of U.S. policy-making in this connection have suggested that there were two positions: that of the Treasury which favored a hard line and that of the State Department which favored a policy of negotiation and compromise (Petras and Morley, 1974: 50; Collins, 1973: 71). The public statements of all officials concerned appeared to favor an open-door policy. Yet there is a great deal of evidence that the American government had already embarked on a policy of putting maximum economic pressure on the Allende Administration.

The Fronts of Pressure: International Credit. In his speech to the General

Assembly of the United Nations of December 4, 1972, President Allende denounced the existence of a veritable economic and financial blockade against Chile. Loans from multilateral organizations had dried up; lines of credit from the American private banking system had been drastically reduced; suppliers' credits in the United States had been withdrawn as had Eximbank loans and guarantees; disbursements on loans from U.S. public entities contracted during previous governments had been interrupted; and American multinational corporations had attempted to prevent the Chilean copper trade. Allende did not impute the blockade to the American government, although he also mentioned the interruption of American bilateral aid. However, the implicit message was clear that responsibility for the blockade was laid upon the United States government.

Nine months later, events lent particular poignancy to Allende's words and reopened a debate in academic circles on the whole question of the economic blockade. The debate, however, seems at points to have confused in a single issue what really are separate although related questions. Did the United States government decide on, and implement, a policy of restricting bilateral aid and credits to Chile and influencing international organizations to prevent credits to Chile? Was this policy based on economic considerations concerning the credit-worthiness of Chile or on political considerations concerning the need to protect American private investment in Chile? What was the effect of such policy on the influx of international finance to Chile? Finally, what effect did the changes in the flow of finance have on the Chilean economy and, for that matter, on the survival of the Allende government?

A full discussion of all four questions would far exceed the possibilities of this chapter and indeed its purpose. We can, however, summarize the available evidence in so far as it is relevant to our present survey of the relations between the United States government and the Allende government:

a. It seems reasonably well established that the United States government adopted a formal policy of withholding aid and credits to Chile and of using its influence in the World Bank and the IDB to prevent loans to Chile. The reason given for this policy was not related to Chile's credit-worthiness, but rather to the fact that Chile had nationalized or was in the process of nationalizing American private interests without compensation.

This policy was decided upon and implemented well before the decision on excess profits of the copper companies had been made by Allende—in fact, before the constitutional amendment had been adopted by the Chilean Congress. In a preface to a book on expropriations dated June 1971, Secretary of State William Rogers, after discussing the Chilean copper case, described in the following terms the policy of the U.S. government: "The U.S. government is dragging its feet on fresh unilateral development lending to the offending countries. And it is doing what it can to slow down loans by the World Bank and the Inter-American Development Bank until the valuation questions are settled."[10]

The policy was hardened after the excess profits decision. On January 19, 1972, an official statement delivered by President Nixon made explicit the decision of the United States government to refuse bilateral aid and withhold support in multilateral banks for loans to countries that expropriate a significant American interest without reasonable provision for prompt, adequate, and effective compensation. It appears that precisely that policy had already been followed for some time by the U.S. Treasury (Petras and Morley, 1974: 65).

Finally, in March 1972, with the support of the Nixon Administration, the U.S. Congress passed the Gonzalez Amendment, which requires the president to instruct the U.S. Executive Directors in the World Bank and in the Inter-American Development Bank to vote against loans for countries that have nationalized United States-owned properties unless the president determines that satisfactory compensation has been given, or the dispute has been submitted to arbitration or negotiations in good faith are in progress with a view to providing prompt, adequate, and effective compensation.

b. It is also reasonably well established that the policy of the U.S. government was decisive in denying Chile access to certain sources of foreign finance. Here the argument has been put forward that some of those sources would have been closed irrespective of the U.S. government policy because of Chile's lack of credit-worthiness. A related problem, raised by U.S. government spokesmen when replying to President Allende's speech in the United Nations, is the degree to which the United States could actually influence those sources.

The first and clearest case is that of Eximbank. The ability of the United States to influence Eximbank's decisions is not really an issue, as Eximbank is an agency of the United States government. In June 1971, Eximbank denied Chile a loan for $21 million to finance partially the purchase of three Boeing jets by the Chilean state airline. In August that year Eximbank's president further informed the Chilean ambassador in Washington that Chile could not expect any more loans or guarantees until the question of compensation for American property was settled. In addition, Eximbank suspended the guarantee and insurance program for commercial banks and suppliers of Chilean imports, and as of June 1972 it suspended disbursements on existing loans negotiated under previous governments. It is generally admitted that the decision on the Boeing loan was politically motivated and not related to Chile's credit-worthiness (Collins, 1973: 72; Petras and Morley, 1974: 60). It could be argued that credit-worthiness considerations affected decisions taken after Chile interrupted the payment of its foreign debt in November 1971. However, it should be noted that the June 1972 suspension of disbursements came after Chile had agreed with the Paris Club on general renegotiation terms and bilateral negotiations with the U.S. had already started. Indeed, around the same time an agreement to refinance Chile's private debt was signed with 27 commercial U.S. banks. No doubt, in the second half of 1972, the Chilean economy had begun to deteriorate, but there the relevant question is to what extent that deterioration was also a function of Eximbank policies toward Chile. This will be dealt with briefly below.

Of course, no new bilateral aid was given by the United States government—except for military purposes—and, although modest disbursements on existing loans continued, they were more than counterbalanced by repayments.

The United States government's ability to influence decisions of the Inter-American Development Bank is again not seriously questionable. To begin with, any loans from the Fund for Special Operations are subject to veto by the United States. Such loans require a two-thirds majority of the Board, and the United States controls 40 percent of the votes. As for other loans, opposition from the United States tends to prevent the request from being submitted to the Board at all (Petras and Morley, 1974: 68). During the Allende period, IDB granted only two loans totaling U.S. $11.6 million to Chile. These were approved for university projects early in 1971. Three development projects, in the petro-chemical, electrical, and natural gas areas, were never submitted to the Board, and there is general agreement that this was due to opposition from the United States government. (In fact some other member-nations were annoyed. At the time of the coup they were building pressure for some kind of a loan to Chile.)[11] Again the credit-worthiness argument seems to have been totally absent. In fact, even after the moratorium of November 1971—a normal procedure, when renegotiation is undertaken—Chile continued to pay the debt to both the IDB and the World Bank. IDB continued to disburse money on loans already made, but for the whole period between December 1970 and December 1972, this money was barely $10 million more than Chile's repayments (Sigmund, 1974: 327).

Finally, the World Bank did not approve any loans whatsoever to the Allende government. Although the United States does not have formal veto power in this case, it wields considerable influence, particularly since submission of projects to the Board can be made only by the management. Three projects presented by the Chilean government were never submitted to the Board. The Bank's management raised with Chile the question of compensation to the American copper companies as early as September 1971 when, again, there was no question of credit-worthiness. At that time approval was likely for a loan for a fruit and vineyard project which satisfied all the technical requirements. It seems clear that the indefinite postponement of the loan was due to the compensation problem and not to credit-worthiness considerations. It also appears that, in addition to falling in line with general Bank policy toward nationalizations, the decision was influenced by the position of the United States. Disbursements on existing loans continued. However, repayments by Chile equaled the loan money in 1972, and for 1973 the prospects were that Chile would be a net exporter of capital to the World Bank.

The political character of the behavior of IDB and the World Bank becomes clearer when compared to that of the International Monetary Fund. At the time the IMF was undergoing an internal power struggle, in which European and Latin American governments opposed attempts by the United States to replace IMF president Pierre-Paul Schweitzer. In addition, internal regulations made it more difficult for the United States to prevent loans for balance of payment support to Chile, some of which had an automatic character. The fact is, that for all the doubts about credit-worthiness expressed by the World Bank, IMF lent Chile $187.8 million in 1971-1972 and issued an optimistic report on the prospects of the Chilean economy for 1972. This, in turn, seems to have influenced the level of bilateral credits from Western European and other countries which either maintained or increased somewhat their levels of short-term financing to Chile. This further weakened the credit-worthiness argument.

c. As for the impact of the American policy on the Chilean economy, at the least it considerably aggravated the balance of payments problems created by the drop in copper prices and the pressures on imports that resulted from redistribution of income. The effect of the Eximbank policy should not be underestimated. The withdrawal of guarantees meant that suppliers credits were withdrawn, so that Chile had to start paying for imports in advance. This severely affected its balance on current accounts and its reserve position, which in turn was possibly a factor in the drastic reduction of short-term lines of credit from American private banks. These dropped from about $220 million in 1970 to about $30 million in 1971 and 1972. A self-aggravating process was then triggered. Imports from the United States decreased from approximately $340 million in 1970 to $200 million in 1971 and about $150 million in 1972 (SEREX, 1972). The areas most seriously affected were those such as spare parts for American machinery in the copper mines and in motor vehicles, where alternative sources were impossible to find. It was estimated that by early 1972 about 30 percent of the buses in Chile were immobilized for lack of parts (Collins, 1973: 73).

The Foreign Debt and Attempts at Accommodation. The other major area of pressure—closely linked to that of international credit—was the Chilean foreign debt. In November 1971, the Allende government requested a renegotiation of its debt with foreign public institutions and suspended payment. The renegotiation took place in the so-called Paris Club, which is composed of all fourteen major creditor countries of the Western world. In the negotiations the United States delegation introduced the question of compensation for nationalized foreign property as a prerequisite for an agreement on refinancing. Chile refused to commit itself to any specific agreement on compensation that could interfere with the proceedings under way with the copper companies. Through the mediation of some Western European countries a formula was agreed upon. "The Chilean representatives confirmed their government's policies of recognition and of payment of all foreign debt and its acceptance of the principles of payment of just compensation for all nationalization in accordance with Chilean and international law" (Banco Central, 1972: 4). The formula was ambiguous, because according to Chilean law the companies had no claim, while according to the United States' interpretation of international law they did. On this basis a general agreement was reached in April 1972 to postpone payment of 70 percent of the services due by Chile between November 1971 and December 1972. The general agreement was to be followed by specific negotiations with each creditor country. Chile was subsequently able to reach agreements with all of them except the United States. As a condition of the renegotiation the American government insisted that Chile agree to settle the compensation dispute by means other than the one established in the constitutional amendment. Notes were then exchanged in September and November 1972, and negotiations took place in December 1972 and in March, June, and August 1973. In the negotiations Chile proposed to resort to the Treaty for the Settlement of Controversies signed by both countries in 1914. The treaty calls for the establishment of an Investigating Commission to review the issues and submit a report, upon which the governments are to attempt a direct settlement. If they are unable to do so, the dispute can be submitted to arbitration. According to Chile's proposal, the investigation should deal not only with the compensation issue, but with all of the outstanding problems between the two countries, including U.S. policy in multilateral lending organizations, and trade and financial relations.

The United States objected to the application of the treaty because it did not lead to a compulsory decision. It proposed instead a compulsory international arbitration solely on the question of the compensation to the copper companies. The same procedure could then be followed with respect to ITT.

This solution was not possible according to Chilean law because the copper nationalization had been made through a constitutional amendment. Any decision of an international arbiter which modified the amendment would have to be approved by the Chilean Congress as if it were another constitutional amendment; this the Chilean government was, of course, in no position to guarantee. Furthermore, the American proposal meant to disregard the substantive criteria for compensation adopted by the constitutional amendment, and to introduce new criteria based on purported international standards. Within the framework of the 1914 Treaty, the Chilean government was prepared to discuss the criteria, with a view to arriving at a compromise. It was not, however, prepared to accept the introduction of an altogether new set of criteria, particularly since it rejected the thesis that there are universally accepted criteria to judge the adequacy of compensation (Novoa, 1972: 349-350). [12] Finally, Chile maintained that the activities of ITT to subvert the Chilean internal political process made impossible the inclusion of its case in any general treatment of the question of compensation settlement.

Some new avenues of solution—including the joint application of the 1914 treaty and presentations by the Chilean government to the Special Copper Tribunal set up by the constitutional amendment—were being explored by the two governments when the coup of September 11, 1973, took place.

Concluding Remarks

It seems fair to conclude that the United States government applied as much pressure as was necessary to create effective economic difficulties for Allende without provoking a frontal break that would have stirred opposition in other international quarters. It has been remarked that if the United States had wanted a true blockade, it would have included an embargo on spare parts to Chile and on imports from Chile, as well as cutting off assistance (Sigmund, 1974: 337). Such thoroughness was either not possible or not necessary. An embargo based solely on Chile's dispute with private American interests over her basic natural resource was not a realistic possibility in terms of international politics. Moreover, Allende's global foreign policy certainly increased the political cost of such a course. A cutoff of pipeline assistance was probably difficult in the multilateral institutions. Commitments already existed, and Chile was honoring its own repayment obligations. A cutoff of multilateral institutional assistance was also unnecessary, since, as we saw before, repayments almost equaled the disbursements. The case for disbursements under direct aid was similar. In any case, after June 1972, even disbursements on existing loans by American institutions stopped. All along the American government tied this controlled but effective pressure to a satisfactory solution of the question of compensation for American interests. Since the end of 1971, however, the solution proposed by the United States raised serious constitutional and political problems for Chile and the Allende government. Consequently, it was clear that rigid adherence to that prerequisite would necessarily lead to an impasse. [13]

The Chilean view was that a modus vivendi was possible, despite the major differences in ideological outlook of both governments. Chile believed that the United States government was basically concerned with finding an acceptable solution to the question of American interests in Chile, rather than in using that issue as a pretext to create the conditions for the overthrow of Allende. This perception has been criticized as essentially erroneous by some analysts (Petras and Morley, 1974: 79). In any case, as long as the Allende government refused to surrender to the pretensions of the American companies, the belief also tended to lead to an impasse.

Impasse, however, did not mean immobility of the situation. It weakened the Allende government, while American pressure was on. Nevertheless, had other factors improved the foreign exchange position of Chile, it would have probably been able to withstand the pressure and thus succeed in redefining in different terms the chances of a lasting compromise with the United States. Allende's foreign policy, with its success in strengthening Chile's international position, would no doubt have contributed significantly to that redefinition. The increase in the prices of copper in 1973 brought the possibility nearer. It is not unlikely that the perception of that possibility was one of the determining factors of the timing of the coup.

NOTES

1. The right-wing opposition oriented its critique of Allende's foreign policy toward showing how the internal policies of the government had weakened the possibility of satisfactory international action. Even so, the adequacy of the approach taken by the Foreign Ministry was conceded (Orrego, 1972: 110).

2. This literature was familiar to Clodomiro Almeyda, himself a respected political scientist who has also written on the subject (Almeyda, 1971).

3. Allende emphasized the continuity of this line of thought with the Consensus of Viña del Mar and the work of CECLA and quoted Frei's Minister of Foreign Relations Gabriel Valdés. When communicating the resolutions of the Viña del Mar Conference of 1969 to President Nixon, Valdés said that "the interests of the governments of Latin America and those of the United States are not the same. In fact each tends in many ways to contradict each other" (Allende, 1973: 106).

4. It appears that Western European attitudes were a factor in determining a more open policy within the International Monetary Fund. See below for further reference to this problem.

5. The main facts established in the hearings were:

a. Before the Chilean presidential election of September 1970, the Chairman of the Board and Chief Executive Officer of ITT offered a substantial fund to the CIA to be used to support the conservative candidate, Alessandri, against Allende.

b. After the popular election, but before the election in Congress between the two highest pluralities (Allende and Alessandri), ITT offered Henry Kissinger and the Director of the CIA one million dollars. The fund was to support any plans of the U.S. government to form a coalition in the Chilean Congress to prevent Allende from becoming president. ITT also offered direct support, financial or otherwise, to the key adviser of the Alessandri candidacy.

c. Around the same time, the CIA and ITT, which had kept in close contact and exchanged political intelligence in connection with Chile, considered a plan to create economic chaos in Chile, which was finally rejected by ITT.

d. After Allende was elected and inaugurated, ITT organized in Washington an Ad-Hoc Committee on Chile composed of leading business concerns with interests in Chile. Its purpose was to put pressure on the U.S. government to take a hard line vis-a-vis Allende.

e. In September 1971, ITT proposed to a special assistant to President Nixon an eighteen-point plan designed to ensure that Allende "does not get through the next six months" (U.S. Senate, 1973b: 16-17).

6. The conflict over the nationalization of copper is discussed in more detail below.

7. In fact, in 1970 the Brazilian government requested the Economic Commission for Latin America to prepare a study on the subject.

8. The document was based on a proposal drafted by a group of experts that met in Santiago under the chairmanship of the Chilean delegate (CEPAL, 1973).

9. Assistant Secretary of State Charles Meyer testified that the purported policy of non-interference in the Chilean election had been adopted and pursued until September 4, 1970. In the ITT hearings in the U.S. Senate it was established that the policy was the subject of high-level review within the U.S. government shortly after the election took place. The review was in the form of a special meeting of the so-called Forty Committee, an interdepartmental group, then chaired by Dr. Henry Kissinger. This committee controls the covert operations of the CIA. Mr. Meyer, who attended the meeting, refused to disclose to the Senate the contents of the discussion, or the resulting instructions sent to the American ambassador in Santiago. The hearings also established that shortly afterward, on September 29, 1970, the chief of the CIA's Clandestine Services, acting on instructions of the Director of the CIA, contacted ITT's Vice-President for Corporate Relations to propose a plan to accelerate economic chaos in Chile. The plan would pressure the Chilean Congress to vote against Allende. If he was elected, it would weaken Allende's position. ITT rejected the plan as unworkable (U.S. Senate, 1973b: 9-10). According to an ITT representative in Santiago, the American ambassador had received authority from Washington on September 15 for certain actions to prevent Allende from taking power. The then ambassador to Chile refused to tell the Senate subcommittee what his instructions were, and the State Department refused to provide copies of the cables sent to Santiago (U.S. Senate, 1973b: 6-7). A memorandum from the ITT liaison man with the CIA summarizes a later meeting with the Chief of Clandestine Operations at CIA Headquarters. It states that the CIA was approaching "select members of the armed forces in an attempt to have them lead some sort of uprising—no success to date" (U.S. Senate, 1973a: 622).

10. Around the same time, Treasury Under-Secretary Walker testified before a Congressional subcommittee on what the U.S. position within the World Bank or the IDB would be if the Allende government requested a loan:

I would put it within the context of an expropriation of property in which there has been absolutely no indication up to this time that the compensation will be adequate or timely. On that basis if a loan to Chile were to come up today in the Inter-American Development Bank or the World Bank—the World Bank has a rule and they would not lend to Chile under these circumstances, but the IDB has no such rule—there is no doubt in my mind what Secretary Connally's instructions to Mr. Constanzo (U.S. Executive Director) would be [Petras and Morley, 1974: 62].

11. Professor Sigmund writes: "It appears almost certain that U.S. influence was exercised to delay submission of the Chilean projects to the Bank board." He then goes on to denounce press reports to the effect that the Bank, following the coup, would have approved new loans for Chile, "a move that would have lent weight to the charge of a prompt and decisive U.S. policy reversal . . . at this writing no new IDB loans to the military government have been approved" (Sigmund, 1974: 327). According to various reports in the Chilean pro-junta press, between January and June 1974 the IDB approved a total of $201 million to the Chilean government, thus presumably lending significant weight to the worst suspicions deplored by Professor Sigmund.

12. The United States Supreme Court has also acknowledged that the issue of compensation for nationalized foreign property is basically a clash of interests between capital-exporting and capital-importing countries and that there seem to be no universally accepted standards. This was in the famous Sabbatino decision of 1964.

13. A former NSC staff member with responsibility for Latin America, in an interview with Petras and Morley in August 1973, stated:

> To adopt a policy where virtually every investment dispute escalated into a government to government dispute was wrong. That is pretty much where we are right now. It would be difficult for us to isolate investment-expropriation issues from political issues. . . . I think it is very difficult for Allende to work out a solution which the U.S. government could ever consider a reasonable one [Petras and Morley, 1974: 67].

REFERENCES

ALLENDE, S. (1973) *Chile's Road to Socialism.* London: Penguin Books.
——— (1972) "Exposición del Presidente de la República de Chile ante la Asamblea General de las Naciones Unidas." Santiago.
ALMEYDA, C. (1971) *Sociologismo e Ideologismo en la Teoría Revolucionaria.* Santiago: Editorial Universitaria.
Banco Central de Chile (1972) Economic News 19 (April 30).
CARDOSO, F. H. and E. FALETTO (1969) *Dependencia y Desarrollo en América Latina.* México: Siglo Veintiuno Editores.
CEPAL, Comisión Económica para América Latina (1973) "Primera reunión del Comité de Expertos de Alto Nivel: Informe." Santiago: Naciones Unidas.
COLLINS, J. (1973) "Tightening the financial knot." IDOC 58 (December): 70-74.
Department of State Bulletin (1971) "U.S. responds to Chilean decision on compensation for expropriation." (November 1).
DOS SANTOS, T. (1973) "The crisis of development theory and the problem of dependence in Latin America," pp. 57-80 in H. Bernstein (ed.) *Underdevelopment and Development: The Third World Today.* London: Penguin Books.
——— (1970) "The structure of dependence." American Economic Review 60, 2 (May): 231-236.

Gobierno de Chile (1973) "Reunión a nivel de expertos del comité de paises no-alineados encargado de analizar el problema de las inversiones privadas extranjeras." Santiago: Ministerio de Relaciones Exteriores.

Instituto de Economía (1973) *La Economía Chilena en 1972.* Santiago: Universidad de Chile.

MORAN, T. H. (1970) *El Cobre es Chileno: Dependencia e Independencia en la Economía Política del Cobre Chileno 1946-1970.* Santiago: Universidad de Chile.

NIXON, R. M. (1971) "United States foreign policy in the 1970s: a report to the Congress." Washington, D.C.: Government Printing Office.

NOVOA, E. (1972) *La Batalla por el Cobre: Comentarios y Documentos.* Santiago: Editorial Quimantú.

NUDELMAN, P. (1973) "La compensación a las compañías del cobre nacionalizadas por el gobierno de Chile." Santiago: Corporacion del Cobre.

ORREGO VICUNA, F. (1972) "El sistema de la política internacional de Chile: ¿auge o decadencia?" pp. 95-112 in T. P. MacHale (ed.) *Visión Crítica de Chile.* Santiago: Ediciones Portada.

PALMA, A. (1972) "The Popular Unity government's foreign policy," pp. 140-144 in J. A. Zammit (ed.) *The Chilean Road to Socialism.* Brighton: Institute of Development Studies.

PETRAS, J. F. and M. H. MORLEY (1974) "U.S.-Chilean relations and the overthrow of the Allende government." Binghamton, N.Y.: State University of New York.

SEREX, Secretaría Ejecutiva de Relaciones Económicas Externas (1972) "Análisis de las vinculaciones comerciales con los Estados Unidos." Santiago: Banco Central de Chile.

SIMONS, M. (1974) "The Brazilian connection." The Washington Post (January 6).

SZULC, T. (1973) "The view from Langley." The Washington Post (October 21).

U.S. Senate (1973a) "Multinational corporations and United States foreign policy." Hearings before the Subcommittee on Multinational Corporations of the Committee on Foreign Relations. Washington, D.C.: Government Printing Office.

——— (1973b) "The International Telephone and Telegraph Company and Chile 1970-1971." Report to the Committee on Foreign Relations by the Subcommittee on Multinational Corporations. Washington, D.C.: Government Printing Office.

Chapter 12

LATIN AMERICA AND THE

INTERNATIONAL LAW OF THE SEA

E. D. BROWN

In the post-1945 era, it has become part of the conventional wisdom of observers of international maritime affairs that there exists something which can be called a Latin American view of the law of the sea, though, until recently, the rest of the world has not paid a great deal of attention to it. As a Peruvian writer (de Soto, 1973: 126) has rather bitterly put it,

> The great European scholars of the first half of the century, if and when they did not simply ignore the theses put forward by these three countries [Chile, Ecuador, and Peru], depicted their attitude as that of a lunatic fringe.

As recently as the Second United Nations Conference on the Law of the Sea (UNCLS II) in 1960, acts such as Peru's seizure of the Onassis whaling fleet in 1954 were still almost universally condemned as flagrantly illegal acts contrary to the freedom of fishing on the high seas.[1] More recently, however, the specter of the dread 200-mile maritime zone has gradually lost its terror and it has become fashionable to speak of a Latin American "contribution" to the development of the law of the sea. The purpose of this chapter (completed during the first week of UNCLS III meeting in Caracas) is to identify and assess the value of this Latin American contribution.

For the purpose of this study, Latin America is defined to include the Caribbean island states as well as the South and Central America states. It is necessary to include the Caribbean islands for two reasons. First, the policies and claims of continental states bordering the Gulf of Mexico and the Caribbean are in part molded by the existence of the Caribbean island chain.

Second, some of the Caribbean island states, together with their continental neighbors, have taken part in the preparation of the regional and subregional declarations on the law of the sea which are referred to below.

HISTORICAL PERSPECTIVE

The history of the modern international law of the sea can perhaps best be understood by perceiving it as a continual conflict between two opposing, yet complementary, fundamental principles—territorial sovereignty and the freedom of the high seas. During the development of the modern system, there has usually been a geographical area where the freedom of the high seas was the predominant principle and other areas where the predominant principle was that of sovereignty. The boundary between the two areas has never been stable, however, and its precise position at any one time has been largely determined by the selfish interests of the most powerful maritime states of the day.

With the benefit of hindsight, it is not difficult to identify trends in the law of the sea and recognize the policy interests of the Powers which lie behind them.[2] For example, the extinction of freedom of the seas brought about by the carve-up of the Mediterranean by the Italian states between the eleventh and the sixteenth centuries, and Pope Alexander VI's attempted division of the Atlantic between Spain and Portugal in 1493 both reflect monopolistic trading policies of the leading maritime powers of the day. Similarly, the rejection of the Iberian claims by Elizabethan England and the Dutch United Provinces was based not on any attachment to abstract notions of "freedom" but on commercial self-interest. It was not accidental that the Grotian magnum opus, *Mare Liberum*, was published in 1609 or that Selden's *Mare Clausum* saw the light of day in an England concerned to exclude the Dutch from the North Sea fisheries. In short, the concept of freedom of the seas tends to be used as an ideological tool where the national interest so requires and in any particular historical period the law generally crystallizes in a set of rules reflecting the interests of the predominant Power or Powers. Identification of these Powers has not been difficult in the past because of the relatively small number of states involved, the relatively simple interests they had in the sea, and the relatively straightforward political milieu in which they operated. There is no difficulty, for example, in perceiving that between the beginning of the nineteenth century and the end of the Second World War the freedom of the sea was firmly established as a fundamental principle of international law largely because it reflected the economic and security interests of Britain and subsequently of the United States.

Since the Second World War, however, there has been a radical change in the international political background. Since 1943, 74 countries have achieved independence, making a total of 149 independent nations. Of these 149, about 115 are coastal states, and 58 of these coastal states have achieved independence since 1943.[3] While it is true that a large proportion of these new states are very small, seriously underdeveloped, or both, they neverthe- less share two features which make their views important in this context. They have voting strength in UNCLS III and, in common with the older developing states, especially those of Latin America, they are often conscious of their group solidarity and of the need to review traditional legal doctrines to ensure compatibility with their own interests. The freedom of the seas and the delimitation of maritime zones are high on the list of their priorities for reconsideration.

The basic questions which these states have been asking and are continuing to ask are as follows. Has freedom of the seas become tantamount to a freedom for the developed states to exploit and possibly overexploit the offshore fisheries of the developing states? Has it become a freedom to pollute these waters; a freedom of deployment of nuclear-armed submarines? If so, is the traditional acceptance of the desirability of maximizing the area of the high seas any longer justifiable or has the time come for a swing back to mare clausum?

Paradoxically, it was the leading advocate of the freedom of the high seas, the United States, which, in 1945, set in motion the chain of events which may well end with the acceptance by the international community of a new regime for the oceans based on a 200-mile zone of national jurisdiction. Although state practice was by no means uniform, the great majority of coastal states still claimed at that time only a three-mile territorial sea and did not claim additional resources jurisdiction in areas beyond the territorial sea. In the Truman Proclamation of 1945 (United Nations, 1951: 38), the United States departed from this tradition by laying claim to exclusive jurisdiction and control over the natural resources of the continental shelf. The United States was at pains to stress that the freedom of the seas was preserved in the superjacent waters and claimed jurisdiction only over resources, not over the seabed itself. Viewed in historical perspective, this limitation is less important than the fact that the American initiative, which could have been treated as an illegal appropriation of high seas resources contrary to the principle of the freedom of the high seas, was rapidly accepted as the seed from which a new regime would develop under international customary law.

A few Latin American states, inspired by the Truman Proclamation, adapted the thinking behind it to their own interests and made what were essentially resource-jurisdiction claims to the living resources of similarly extensive maritime zones. Their practice of claiming 200-mile maritime zones, initiated by Chile in 1947 and strenuously opposed by the major maritime Powers from the beginning, has gradually acquired respectability. With this respectability it has become known as the Latin American contribution to the development of the law of the sea. It now has considerable support throughout the developing world and may be regarded as the seed from which the concept of the exclusive economic zone (EEZ) or patrimonial sea has grown. In this latter form, the idea of national jurisdiction over the resources of an extensive (out to 200 miles) maritime zone has attracted growing support not only from the developing world but also from many important developed maritime Powers. Many observers, including this writer, hope that UNCLS III will be able to reach an accommodation between various interest groups on the basis of a regime which will provide for a twelve-mile territorial sea and an EEZ beyond it extending to a maximum of 200 miles. [4]

It may be readily acknowledged that the practice of some Latin American states has given birth and respectability to the general concept of a 200-mile maritime zone. It must also be said, however, that references to "Latin American state practice" or to a Latin American view or approach are misleading generalizations. When the analyst descends from the abstract notion of a 200-mile zone and examines the detailed claims made by Latin American states, he finds that "Latin American state practice" exhibits considerable variety, and in some cases confusion, in the juridical nature of its claims and in its terminology. Latin American governments have clearly been conscious of the need to clarify and unify their policies if they are to have maximum impact in UNCLS III, and this awareness explains the convocation of the three conferences at Montevideo and Lima in 1970 and at Santo Domingo in 1972. As the analysis of the Declarations adopted by these Conferences shows and the multiplicity of proposals submitted to UNCLS III by different factions confirms, they have not been altogether successful in erecting a united front. It is hoped that the following analysis of, first, the three regional Declarations; second, individual state practice; and third, the draft articles submitted to the United Nations by Latin American states, will enable the reader to identify the considerable area of agreement already achieved, while at the same time remaining aware of the continuing diversity of interest and policy.

LATIN AMERICAN DECLARATIONS
ON THE LAW OF THE SEA

Before turning to an analysis of the detailed policies of the individual Latin American states on the question of maritime limits, it may be useful to provide an overview of the main issues involved by undertaking a brief study of the main elements of the general declarations on the law of the sea to which some of them have subscribed in recent years. The signatories of the three Declarations were as follows:

Montevideo 8 May 1970	Lima 8 August 1970	Santo Domingo 9 June 1972
Argentina	Argentina	
Brazil	Brazil	
Chile	Chile	
Ecuador	Ecuador	
El Salvador	El Salvador	
Nicaragua	Nicaragua	Nicaragua
Panama	Panama	
Peru	Peru	
Uruguay	Uruguay	
	Colombia	Colombia
	Dominican Republic	Dominican Republic
	Guatemala	Guatemala
	Honduras	Honduras
	Mexico	Mexico
		Costa Rica
		Haiti
		Trinidad and Tobago
		Venezuela

The first point to note is that whereas all nine of the signatories of the Montevideo Declaration claimed a maritime zone of some kind out to 200 miles, none of the additional five states who joined in the Lima Declaration had made a 200-mile claim. In the Santo Domingo Declaration, the signatories include only one Montevideo signatory, Nicaragua, and one other 200-mile claimant, Costa Rica. In addition, the five non-200-mile Lima signatories were joined by three more non-200-mile states: Haiti, Trinidad and Tobago, and Venezuela.

Montevideo Declaration

In many ways it might have been better if the Declaration of Montevideo on Law of the Sea (International Legal Materials, 1970, IX: 1081) had never seen the light of day. Its preamble states that the intention was "to embody in a joint declaration the principles emanating from the recent movement towards the progressive development of international law." In fact, close study of the "Basic Principles of the Law of the Sea" contained in the Declaration merely serves to reveal the variety of policies still existing even among the nine 200-mile claimants who alone had been invited to the conference. Thus, these "Principles" provide a poor basis for implementation of the signatories intention "to co-ordinate their future action with a view to defending effectively the principles embodied in this Declaration."

It would appear that in order to draft a text acceptable to all the signatories, so many elements had to be avoided that, in the end, there was room for little but the invocation of the vague natural law arguments customarily resorted to in defense of claims for which evidence is lacking in the current law. If the Declaration is studied to determine (a) the criteria by which maritime limits may be established, (b) the types of jurisdictional zones accepted in Latin American practice and the terminology used to refer to such zones, and (c) the degree to which freedom of navigation and overflight is permitted in. such zones, the results are instructive.

As regards criteria for the establishment of maritime limits, Principle 4 embodies the exploitability criterion for determination of the outer limit of the continental shelf. Such a formula would permit the extension of the continental shelf beyond the 200-mile zones claimed by the signatories and was, no doubt, inserted at the behest of Argentina. Apart from Principle 4, the remaining principles are extraordinarily vague about maritime limits. Reference is made to adjacency, to the need to develop economies and raise living standards, to geographical and geological characteristics, and to factors governing the existence of marine resources and the need for their rational utilization. Natural law thinking is, of course, still much favored among Latin American international lawyers. This is hardly surprising when the objective is to encourage the development of new norms of international customary law by the promulgation, constant reiteration, and implementation of doctrines which were originally clearly contrary to the established law. Nevertheless, these principles are stated at such a high level of abstraction that it is difficult to see what limits at all they place on maritime limits.

The same vagueness is apparent over the questions of types of jurisdictional zone and terminology. Reference is made to the continental shelf, but whether the reference is to the geological phenomenon or to the legal concept is not clear. Reference is also made to areas under maritime sovereignty and jurisdiction—a conveniently ambiguous term which would cover any type of claim. No reference, however, is made to the territorial sea, to exclusive fishing zones, or indeed to any other relatively precise functional zone. This again is not surprising because it reflects the fact that, although some of the signatories claim a territorial sea, variously defined, others regard the very term as taboo and as an undesirable remnant of the old regime they are endeavoring to replace.

Perhaps the most surprising principle embodied in the Declaration is Principle 6:

> 6. the right to adopt, for the aforementioned purposes, regulatory measures applicable in areas under their maritime sovereignty and jurisdiction, without prejudice to freedom of navigation by ships and overflying by aircraft of any flag.

The clear implication is that freedom of navigation (not merely innocent passage) and overflight is permitted in the 200-mile zone. In reality, however, as will be seen below, policies on this point differ considerably among the nine signatories, and although the widely publicized text of the Declaration nowhere hints at the fact, a *majority* of the signatories made declarations rejecting this principle (Uruguay, 1971: 152, cited in Hjertonsson, 1973: 70).

Lima Declaration

Viewed in the context of the proceedings of the Lima Conference as a whole, the "Lima Declaration of the Latin American States on the Law of the Sea" (International Legal Materials, 1971, X: 207), though more precise than the Montevideo Declaration, adds little of substance to it and reflects even more the continuing variety of policies espoused by the Latin American states.

The same questions may be asked here as were posed in relation to the Montevideo Declaration.

Concerning the establishment of maritime limits, reference is again made to the "geographical, geological and biological situation" of the coastal state and to its "socio-economic needs and responsibilities." The only significant change is the requirement that "the extent of their maritime sovereignty or jurisdiction" should be established "in accordance with reasonable criteria."

On the question of types of jurisdictional zone and the terminology used to refer to them, it is noticeable that the Lima Declaration favors the phrase "sovereignty *or* jurisdiction" (italics added) rather than "sovereignty *and* jurisdiction" (italics added). The same point is underlined by the preambular statement that the joint declaration "will take into account the plurality of existing legal regimes on maritime sovereignty or jurisdiction in Latin American countries." Although, once again, the continental shelf is the only zone specifically referred to, other than "the maritime zones subject to its sovereignty or jurisdiction," there is an important new emphasis on two of the activities in the zone over which jurisdiction will be claimed. Principle 4 mentions one.

4. The right of the coastal State to prevent contamination of the waters and other dangerous and harmful effects that may result from the use, exploration or exploitation of the area adjacent to its coasts.

The seriousness with which maritime states view the possibility that a coastal state may attempt to impose unacceptable restraints on foreign shipping in the exercise of such anti-pollution jurisdiction hardly needs to be underlined.

Similarly, the potential threat to freedom of scientific investigation implicit in Principle 5 is obvious.

5. The right of the coastal State to authorise, supervise and participate in all scientific research activities which may be carried out in the maritime zones subject to its sovereignty or jurisdiction, and to be informed of the findings and the results of such research.

On the question of freedom of navigation, Principle 3 of the Lima Declaration follows the same lines as Principle 5 of the Montevideo Declaration. The regulatory rights of the coastal state are said to be "without prejudice to freedom of navigation and flight in transit of ships and aircraft, without distinction as to flag." Once again, however, Brazil, Ecuador, Nicaragua, Panama, and Peru were unable to accept this principle as applicable to their own maritime claims (Hjertonsson, 1973: 72).

Dissent was not, however, confined to particular points in the Declaration. More important in any assessment of the significance of the Declaration as representative of Latin American thinking is the fact that six of the states attending the Conference as full members—Barbados, Bolivia, Jamaica, Paraguay, Trinidad and Tobago, and Venezuela—declined to sign the Declaration. A seventh state, Costa Rica, which claims a 200-mile exclusive fishing zone, attended only as an observer. The attitude of Bolivia and Paraguay is, of course, explained by their position as landlocked states and that of Jamaica (and possibly Barbados) by its shelf-locked position. The other dissenters, Costa Rica, Trinidad and Tobago, and Venezuela all subsequently signed the Santo Domingo Declaration.

Santo Domingo Declaration

On Colombia's initiative, the following fifteen Caribbean states attended the Santo Domingo Conference in June 1972: Barbados, Colombia, Costa Rica, the Dominican Republic, El Salvador, Guatemala, Guyana, Haiti, Honduras, Jamaica, Mexico, Nicaragua, Panama, Trinidad and Tobago, and Venezuela. Other Latin American states attended only as observers. The "Declaration of Santo Domingo" (International Legal Materials, 1972, XI: 892) was signed by only ten of the fifteen members of the conference. Barbados, El Salvador, Guyana, Jamaica, and Panama declined to sign the Declaration. Of the ten signatories, only one, Nicaragua, had previously laid claim to an extensive maritime zone—an exclusive fishing zone claimed in 1965. The remainder were in a sense the silent majority of Latin America, none of them having actually claimed a maritime zone beyond twelve miles. If the Declaration which they adopted is subjected to the same tests as the Montevideo and Lima Declarations, it will be seen that it may be distinguished from them on two main counts. First, the emotive language and rhetorical, natural law justifications of the earlier declarations are replaced by statements of principle which clearly recognize the desirability of "international agreement, preferably of a worldwide scope" on the geographical extent of the maritime zones. Second, instead of rejecting traditional categories out of hand, the Declaration builds upon the traditional concepts and terminologies of the territorial sea, continental shelf, and high seas by adding to them the concepts of the patrimonial sea and the international seabed.

Whether the resultant package should properly be described as a Latin American contribution or should be recognized as a development to which the African states, particularly Kenya and Tanzania,[5] had made a major contribution is a matter of little importance. The main point is that, without sacrificing the substance of what the earlier declarations sought to realize, the Santo Domingo Declaration has attained a new level of precision, moderation, and negotiability which was previously lacking. The Declaration is comprised of seven sections, the first three of which will be commented upon here.

The first section is on *the Territorial Sea.* It recognizes the desirability that the breadth of the territorial sea should be the subject of an international agreement, preferably worldwide. It recognizes, however, that in the meantime each state may extend its territorial sea to twelve miles.[6] The traditional character of this zone is further underlined by the declaration that ships of all states should enjoy the right of innocent passage through it.

The second section, which is on *the Patrimonial Sea,* is valuable chiefly because of the precision with which it delimits the geographical and jurisdictional scope of this zone.

The desirability of international agreement on the breadth of this zone too is acknowledged, but a *maximum* of 200 miles is specified for the territorial sea plus the patrimonial sea.

As for the nature of the jurisdiction to be enjoyed by the coastal state in the patrimonial sea, it is made quite clear that what is being sought is a bundle of specified rights, not blanket sovereignty over the zone and everything in it. The rights claimed are:

(1) sovereign rights over renewable and nonrenewable natural resources in the waters, seabed, and subsoil and, as a corollary, the right to adopt the necessary measures to ensure these sovereign rights;
(2) the right to regulate the conduct of scientific research. This is not

described as a sovereign right and its assertion is coupled with the acknowledgment of the corresponding duty to promote such research;

(3) the right to adopt the necessary measures to prevent marine pollution.

It has to be realized, of course, that these provisions are simply in outline form and will require detailed drafting and negotiation before they can hope to secure widespread acceptance. Nevertheless, the approach to the question implicit in this section encourages the belief that the Declaration will provide a basis for successful negotiations. The limited nature of the rights claimed (though of course they are still very extensive in scope), coupled with the clear recognition of freedom of navigation, overflight, and laying of submarine cables and pipelines, makes it clear that the residual principle governing this zone will be that of freedom of the seas rather than sovereignty. Freedom of navigation· will thus continue to be a basic right rather than merely a fragile exception to the principle of sovereignty. It is important for this reason that the scope of the coastal state's anti-pollution jurisdiction and of its jurisdiction over scientific research should be carefully defined.[7]

The third section of the Santo Domingo Declaration, which is on *the Continental Shelf,* contains three elements. First, the 200 meter and exploitability criteria of Article 1 of the 1958 Geneva Convention on the Continental Shelf are adopted.[8] Second, a statement is made of the need to "promote a study concerning the advisability and timing for the establishment of precise outer limits of the continental shelf, taking into account the outer limits of the continental rise."[9] Third, it is made clear that the adoption of the concept of the patrimonial sea will not solve the problem of the outer limit of the continental shelf. Adoption of the outer limit of the continental rise as the outer limit of the legal continental shelf would in itself imply that this would be so, since this geological feature lies well beyond 200 miles in some parts of the world—notably off the Argentinian coast. The matter is placed beyond any doubt by the provision that

> In that part of the continental shelf covered by the patrimonial sea the legal regime provided for this area shall apply. With respect to the part beyond the patrimonial sea, the regime established for the continental shelf by International Law shall apply.

The odd-men-out. Barbados and Jamaica declined to sign this Declaration as they had declined the Lima Declaration. They were joined by El Salvador, which is of course a Pacific state rather than a Caribbean one; Guyana, which was probably worried over its boundary dispute with Venezuela,[10] and Panama, which also has a Pacific coast.

STATE PRACTICE CLASSIFIED

If, in studying the individual practice of each of the 26 states of Latin America,[11] the observer is to perceive patterns, identify trends, and understand alliances, it is essential to attempt to classify the claims made and group together similar classes of claim. It might be expected that the major influence on policy on maritime limits would be the geographical situation of the state and its consequent opportunities and needs. This might suggest a classification based on geographical situation—west coast fishing states, central landlocked states, east coast fishing and broad continental shelf states, shelf-locked northern and Caribbean states. To a limited extent, this classification is employed below. The major criterion of classification is, however, type of jurisdictional claim, and the major heads of division are:

I   Classical Territorial Sea;
II   Modified Territorial Sea;
III   Functional Zones;
IV   A fourth section has been added to cover the views of Landlocked and Other "Geographically Disadvantaged" States.

For the purpose of this analysis, the term "classical territorial sea" will be used where the coastal state claims sovereignty over the territorial sea, irrespective of its breadth, subject only to a right of innocent passage for foreign shipping (but *not* for foreign aircraft in the airspace above the territorial sea).

The term "modified territorial sea" will indicate that the coastal state has accepted further limitations on the exercise of its sovereignty in and over the territorial sea by recognizing the right of foreign shipping to enjoy freedom of navigation (as on the high seas; more extensive than innocent passage) and of foreign aircraft to enjoy freedom of overflight.

One point is worth making here. Traditional and still generally accepted terminology presumes that, where the claim (no matter how modified) is to a territorial sea, the residual principle obtaining in the zone concerned will be that of coastal state sovereignty. Thus, except to the extent that they are expressly limited, the sovereign powers of the coastal state are presumed to prevail. Sovereignty over an area involves not only the negative right to exclude the activities of other states, but also the corresponding positive duty to protect the interests of other states. Thus, it might be expected that where the intention was to secure exclusive rights only over resources, the coastal state would not claim a comprehensive territorial sea, but would be satisfied with a limited claim to an exclusive fishing zone, continental shelf, EEZ or patrimonial sea—claims described in this study as *functional zone* claims. In such cases, the presumption would be in favor of the principle of the freedom of the seas, which would continue to prevail except as limited by the claimed resources jurisdiction. Unfortunately, the formulation of such claims is sometimes affected by national pride, confused thinking, or the tactical calculation that it is better to claim more than you ultimately hope to secure. It is important, therefore, in examining state practice—especially if the object of the study is to reconcile apparently different claims—to concentrate on the substance of what is claimed rather than on nomenclature. It will then be apparent that, in many cases, it appears to be a matter of chance whether a particular state opts for an extended territorial sea or an extended functional zone. Where the former is chosen, it is also a matter of chance whether the state claims a classical territorial sea or a modified territorial sea.

I—Classical Territorial Sea Claims

The practice of the following five states may be considered under this head:

A. Ecuador, Panama, and Peru, which have coordinated their policies by jointly submitting to the United Nations Seabed Committee "Draft articles on fisheries in national and international zones in ocean space."

B. Brazil and El Salvador.

A. Ecuador, Panama, and Peru. All three were signatories to both the Montevideo and Lima Declarations.

Ecuador was also a party, with Chile and Peru, to the Santiago Declaration on the Maritime Zone, 1952. This proclaimed "as a principle of their international maritime policy that each of them possesses sole sovereignty and jurisdiction over the area of sea adjacent to the coast of its own country and extending not less than 200 nautical miles from the said coast" (United Nations, 1957: 723, 724). Since the Declaration was not to "be construed as disregarding the necessary restrictions on the exercise of sovereignty and jurisdiction imposed by international law to permit the innocent and inoffensive passage of vessels of all nations through the zone," it appeared at first sight to be embodying a classical territorial sea claim. In fact, it is not at all clear what the juridical nature of the zone was intended to be. The preamble to the Declaration and subsequent statements by the parties and their domestic legislation confuse the issue, though the better view probably is that the claim was to a functional zone, with freedom of navigation and overflight unaffected.[12]

In any event, it was not until 1966 that Ecuador made a clear claim to a 200-mile classical territorial sea (United Nations, 1970: 78). Even then, it appears to have been prompted less by any need for more extensive sovereign rights than by domestic political needs resulting from the revelation that the previous government's lack of energy in enforcing the 200-mile claim against the United States vessels was the result of a secret agreement with the United States.[13] The escalation of the "tuna war" in the following years may have bolstered the popularity of the Ecuadorean administration, but it also made any future moderation of the Ecuadorean claim much more difficult. United States-Ecuadorean relations reached their lowest point in 1971 with the suspension of military sales to Ecuador and the threat of further financial sanctions in response to a new round in the "tuna war" seizures of United States clippers. This in turn led to charges of "aggression and coercion" in violation of Article 19 of the Charter of the Organization of American States.[14] Fortunately, more moderate counsel seems to have prevailed over an incensed Congress in Washington; the military sales ban has been lifted and, at the end of 1973, President Nixon determined that it was not in the national interest to impose foreign assistance sanctions on Ecuador (cited in International Legal Materials, 1974, XIII: 500). This new attitude can only encourage rational, as opposed to nationalistic, policy-making and may prove to be important in the context of the UNCLS III proceedings. Nevertheless, it might still be wise to bear in mind the observation of a United States analyst that:

> Ecuador's defense of its stand has become an issue of national sovereignty and national dignity. . . . There is no question that Ecuador is receiving a great deal of sympathy and support throughout Latin America, if not for the justice of its claim, then for its tenacity and defiance of U.S. might [Hagen, 1972: 98].

Panama, facing both the Caribbean and the Pacific, declared a 200-mile classical territorial sea in 1967 (United Nations, 1970: 105).

Peru. It is arguable that the Peruvian 200-mile claim should not be classified as a classical territorial sea claim. Peruvians will certainly object to it, since the very term "territorial sea" is abhorrent to them as an obsolete remnant of the old law. Nevertheless, by claiming sovereignty over the airspace above her 200-mile "jurisdictional waters" and permitting only innocent passage through them, Peru would seem to have joined the group of states claiming classical territorial seas (see also Hjertonsson, 1973: 49-50). It must be added, however, that, like Ecuador, Peru is chiefly concerned with securing exclusive rights in the rich off-shore fisheries, and the precise juridical status of the zone claimed was by no means clear prior to 1965, when airspace sovereignty was asserted (Hjertonsson, 1973: 49-50). It is still less than certain.

It hardly needs to be emphasized that the Peruvian Government, like that of Ecuador, has been in the front line throughout the "tuna war" with the United States. As the guardian of national pride, its political freedom of action is thus also considerably circumscribed.

The jointly sponsored draft articles. Limitations of space forbid a detailed analysis of these two complementary drafts, but their most interesting features may be briefly noted. There are six points of interest in the "Draft articles for inclusion in a convention on the law of the sea" (United Nations, Volume III, 1973: 30-35).

1. "Territorial sea," "high seas," and other such traditional terms are superseded by "adjacent sea" and "international seas," though "continental shelf" is retained.
2. "Sovereignty and jurisdiction" extends to an adjacent sea of 200 miles maximum *and to the airspace above.*
3. A regime of free navigation is envisaged for the adjacent sea, but it is subject to "the duties of peaceful coexistence" (a phrase which might be used to justify any attitude to foreign warships and the carriage of goods by, to, or from states regarded as posing threats to peaceful coexistence). Free navigation is also subject to compliance with the provisions laid down by the coastal state regarding inter alia the preservation of the marine environment and scientific research (see working papers 1 and 2 cited in note 7). As far as they are relevant, the same provisions apply to aircraft. Additional provisions may be laid down for passage "within a limit close to" the coast to safeguard national peace, order, and security.
4. It is agreed that arrangements should be made to allow geographically disadvantaged states and land-locked states to enjoy preferential rights in the adjacent seas of their more fortunately situated regional or subregional neighbors.
5. It is envisaged that the continental shelf may extend beyond 200 miles.
6. The coastal state is to have a "special interest" in maintaining the productivity of the renewable resources in any part of the international seas adjoining its "adjacent sea."

Part I of the "Draft articles on fisheries in national and international zones in ocean space" (United Nations, Volume III, 1973: 107) merely spells out in more detail the sovereign rights enjoyed by the coastal state in its "adjacent sea" for the conservation and exploitation of fisheries. More interesting are the provisions of Article I of Part III, under which:

The coastal State shall enjoy preferential rights to exploit living resources in a sector of the sea adjacent to the zone under its sovereignty and jurisdiction, and may reserve to itself or its nationals a part of the permissible catch of such resources.

This latter provision is hardly the stuff of which compromises are made. However, in general the substance of the two drafts seems to have been considerably influenced by the proposals made in Latin America and elsewhere for a patrimonial sea or exclusive economic zone (EEZ). Thus, there is a hint of the acceptability of the EEZ 12 + 188 formula in Article 5 of the general draft articles and the provisions made for pollution control, scientific research, regional arrangements, and land-locked countries follow the same lines as some of the EEZ proposals. The more unacceptable elements (peaceful coexistence in Article 4 of the general draft and preferential fishing rights beyond 200 miles in the fisheries draft) may well prove to be negotiable.

B. *Brazil and El Salvador.* The claims of Brazil and El Salvador differ from those of Ecuador, Panama, and Peru chiefly in that the former divide the 200-mile territorial sea into two zones for fishery purposes. In an inner zone (of 100 miles in Brazil and 12 miles in El Salvador) foreigners are excluded from the fishery altogether, whereas in the outer zone they may be licensed to fish on payment of the prescribed fees.

Brazil, which extended its territorial sea from 12 miles to 200 miles only in 1970 (International Legal Materials, 1971, X: 1224), was the last of the three east coast countries to make a 200-mile claim. The other two, Argentina and Uruguay, had made 200-mile claims in 1969. Unlike her two southern neighbors, however, Brazil asserted a full classical territorial sea claim. According to one report (Calmon Filho, 1970: 7), there were two basic reasons for the Brazilian move. The first was the need to protect marine resources from indiscriminate fishing by foreigners, especially Russians, North Americans, and Japanese. The second was the need to exclude Soviet ships which were thought to be conducting research on ocean currents which would be of military value to them. It may be that this latter fear, real or imagined, explains the exclusion of foreigners from the inner 100-mile zone. Whatever the reason, the new Brazilian policy has made this country one of the most hard-line advocates of the 200-mile policy.

It is clear that neither the United States to the north nor the Argentine to the south can be happy about the restraints on overflight implicit in the Brazilian claims. It has not, however, prevented the United States from concluding in 1972 (International Legal Materials, 1972, XI: 453; and 1974, XIII: 89) and renewing at the end of 1973 (International Legal Materials, 1974, XIII: 496) an Agreement on Shrimp. Though without prejudice to the position of the two states on Brazil's 200-mile claim, the agreement goes a long way toward recognizing Brazil's fishery jurisdiction in the 200-mile zone (see further Brown, 1973: 180).

Perhaps in order to underline its individualist position, Brazil has submitted to the United Nations Seabed Committee "draft articles containing basic provisions on the question of the maximum breadth of the territorial sea and other modalities or combinations of legal regimes of coastal State sovereignty, jurisdiction or specialised competences" (United Nations, Volume III, 1973: 29). They are brief and add little or nothing to the proposals submitted by other delegations but seem designed to emphasize the acceptability of a plurality of regimes, leaving it to the coastal state's discretion how much it wishes to claim within the maximum of a classical territorial sea of 200 miles.

El Salvador. The position of El Salvador, established in its Fishery Act of 1955 and its Constitution of 1962, is midway between that of Brazil on the one hand and Argentina and Uruguay on the other. Like Brazil, it claims sovereignty over the airspace above its 200-mile zone. Like Argentina and Uruguay, however, it permits freedom of navigation through the zone and allows licensed fishing by foreigners in the area between 12 miles and 200 miles from its coast.

II–Modified Territorial Sea Claims

To distinguish the position of Argentina and Uruguay, the two states falling under this head, from that of states claiming functional zones may be considered unnecessary hair-splitting. It is true that, so long as freedom of navigation and overflight is granted, there may be very little practical difference between a modified territorial sea claim and a functional zone claim. Nonetheless, the beneficiaries of free navigation and overflight would certainly feel that their rights were on a much more secure basis if they flowed from the residuary principle of freedom regulating the area rather than existing as an exception to the principle of coastal state sovereignty.

The *Argentinian* law of 1966, which extended Argentinian sovereignty out to 200 miles, specifically provides in its Article 3 that, "the provisions of this law shall not affect freedom of navigation or of air traffic" (United Nations, 1970: 45). It appears that it is only within a three-mile limit that the traditional territorial sea regime applies to navigation and overflight (Hjertonsson, 1973: 57).

Licensed fishing is permitted in the 12 to 200 mile zone under a Decree of 4 January 1967 (United Nations, 1970: 45).

Understandably, in view of its very extensive continental shelf, Argentina has adopted the 1958 Geneva Convention formula (see note 8) on the outer limit of the continental shelf. This allows her to claim exclusive continental shelf jurisdiction beyond the 200-mile limit on the basis of either the 200-meter depth criterion or the exploitability criterion.

Uruguay's 200-mile territorial sea claim dates back only to December 1969

(García-Amador, 1972: 39) and specifically includes the airspace above. Like Argentina, Uruguay has adopted the 1958 Geneva Convention formula for the continental shelf and allows licensed fishing by foreigners in the 12 to 200 mile belt. Freedom of navigation and overflight is also provided for, but in the zone beyond twelve miles rather than three miles as in Argentina.

Like Brazil, Uruguay has also submitted to the United Nations Sea-Bed Committee a set of "draft articles on the territorial sea" (United Nations, Vol. III, 1973: 23) which recognizes a maximum breadth of 200 miles. A perceptive preamble explains that the object of the draft is to establish a new balance in the interplay between the two principles of the freedom of the high seas and sovereignty.

> Through the concept of plurality or duality of regimes of the territorial sea, therefore, this institution is given a new structure which maintains as its essential feature the prevalence of the principle of sovereignty but adapts it to the realities it has to govern and dynamically reconciles the right of the coastal State with those of other States and of the international community.

Lack of space permits only a few comments on some of the key provisions.

In general, the regime envisaged by the draft is very similar to that described by others as a patrimonial sea or exclusive economic zone. The basic pattern is sovereignty over 200 miles, with innocent passage in the first twelve miles and freedom of navigation, overflight, and pipeline and cable laying beyond. The control to be exercised by the coastal state over pollution and scientific research is similar to that envisaged by EEZ advocates. Like the latter, Uruguay also makes special provision for land-locked states, envisaging, among other things, that they should enjoy preferential fishing rights in the zone beyond twelve miles.

The only part of the draft which would seem to present more of a problem to maritime states than do the various EEZ proposals is the provision in Article 16 that freedom of navigation and overflight beyond the twelve-mile line might be subject to regulations "enacted by the coastal State *with regard to its security* [italics added], the preservation of the environment, the exploration, conservation and exploitation of resources, scientific research and the safety of navigation and aviation." Such a formula might permit far-reaching interference with the passage of inter alia warships and military aircraft.

III—Functional Zone Claims

This group includes three states—Chile, Costa Rica, and Nicaragua—which have already made 200-mile functional zone claims; as well as the following eight others which, as signatories of the Santo Domingo Declaration, have indicated their support for this approach to the problem of maritime limits: Colombia, Dominican Republic, Guatemala, Haiti, Honduras, Mexico, Trinidad and Tobago, and Venezuela. Three of the latter—Colombia, Mexico, and Venezuela—have also submitted to the United Nations Sea-Bed Committee "draft articles of treaty," which are based on the Santo Domingo Declaration.

A. *Chile, Costa Rica, and Nicaragua. Chile,* which is not a party to the Santo Domingo Declaration, nevertheless falls into this group because, beyond a three-mile territorial sea and a twelve-mile contiguous zone for matters of state security and fiscal affairs, it claims simply sovereignty and exclusive control over all natural resources in the waters, seabed, and subsoil out to 200 miles.[15] Beyond the three-mile limit, freedom of navigation and overflight are unaffected.

Costa Rica, a signatory of the Santo Domingo Declaration, following a period of considerable confusion since its adherence to the Santiago Declaration of 1952, finally proclaimed jurisdiction over a 200-mile patrimonial sea in 1972.[16]

Nicaragua, also a party to the Santo Domingo Declaration, still appears to maintain a three-mile classical territorial sea, but claims an exclusive 200-mile fishing zone in the waters beyond (United Nations, 1970: 656). The zone is not divided for the purpose of licensing foreign fishing.

B. *Colombia, Dominican Republic, Guatemala, Haiti, Honduras, Mexico, Trinidad and Tobago, and Venezuela.* In the present context it must suffice to say that none of these eight signatories of the Santo Domingo Declaration has claimed extensive maritime limits except in relation to the continental shelf. In some cases, this simply reflects the land- or shelf-locked nature of some of the Caribbean states. In others, such as Colombia and Venezuela, boundary disputes may have further delayed the assertion of extensive claims.

The main features of the Santo Domingo Declaration have already been outlined above. It remains to refer to the "draft articles of treaty" sponsored by Colombia, Mexico, and Venezuela, the three leading Santo Domingo states (United Nations, Volume III, 1973: 19). For the most part, the draft articles follow very closely the provisions of the Santo Domingo Declaration, and it will suffice to draw attention to the points on which they differ significantly:

1. *Territorial Sea.* The breadth of the territorial sea is now firmly fixed by Article 2 and "shall not exceed 12 nautical miles."
2. *Patrimonial Sea.* Here again, a more direct provision requires that the patrimonial sea should not extend more than 200 nautical miles from the baseline of the territorial sea.
3. *Continental Shelf.* Whereas the Santo Domingo Declaration had

adopted the 1958 Geneva Convention formula, the draft articles discard the depth/exploitability criteria and fix as the outer limit of the continental shelf "the outer limits of the continental rise bordering on the ocean basin or abyssal floor." This implies that the continental shelf may extend beyond the patrimonial sea. Accordingly, Article 15 provides that, "with respect to the part beyond the patrimonial sea, the regime established by international law for the continental shelf shall apply."

4. *High Seas.* Perhaps influenced by the similar provisions in the draft articles jointly sponsored by Ecuador, Panama, and Peru, draft Article 17 provides that:

> The coastal State has a special interest in maintaining the productivity of the living resources of the sea in an area adjacent to the patrimonial sea.

If, like the west coast states, the Santo Domingo signatories intend to claim the right to reserve for their nationals "a part of the permissible catch," it will not improve the prospects of the draft articles as a basis for negotiation.

IV—The Landlocked and Other "Geographically Disadvantaged" States

A. Landlocked States. Of the two Latin American landlocked states, only Bolivia has played an active part in promoting the interests of the landlocked group of states. *Paraguay*'s support seems to have been confined to her opposition to the Lima Declaration, which, as was seen above, made no reference to the interests of the landlocked states.

Bolivia's policy is reflected not only in her negative attitude to the Lima Declaration but, more constructively, in the "Draft articles relating to land-locked countries" submitting to the United Nations Sea-Bed Committee in July 1973 (United Nations, Volume II, 1973: 12) and the "Draft articles relating to land-locked States," cosponsored by Afghanistan, Bolivia, Czechoslovakia, Hungary, Mali, Nepal, and Zambia (United Nations, Volume II, 1973: 16).

Bolivia is not only a country which needs a sea outlet for its vast oil and mineral wealth; it is also a country which possessed such an outlet until it lost its coastal territories to Chile in the Pacific war of 1879-1883. It was hardly surprising, therefore, that Bolivia was unable to support the Lima Declaration, in the absence of any reference at all to landlocked states (Hjertonsson, 1973: 72) and that she felt obliged to develop her own set of draft articles.

The main elements in the Bolivian draft articles are as follows: first, while acknowledging that detailed arrangements must be made by treaty with the neighboring state or states, Bolivia seeks to emphasize the objective existence of a right of transit for the landlocked state. This right derives from the principle of freedom of the seas and the recognition of the seabed beyond national jurisdiction as the common heritage of mankind.[17] The far-reaching transit rights which she seeks include the right to improve transit links and equipment at her own expense.

Second, the right is sought to enjoy either national standard treatment in the use of the coastal state's port installations and equipment or to establish her own free zone within the port area.

Third, equality of treatment is sought with coastal developing countries to participate in the exploitation of the living and nonliving resources of the adjacent sea, continental shelf, and EEZ.

The provisions of the jointly sponsored draft articles are broadly similar to the Bolivian proposals.

B. Other "Geographically Disadvantaged" States. Perhaps the most obvious case of a disadvantaged state in the Caribbean is Jamaica, and it has sought to promote the interests of states so placed by preparing a set of "Draft articles on regional facilities for developing geographically disadvantaged coastal States" (United Nations, Volume III, 1973: 110). Though drafted in somewhat broad and imprecise terms, the main thrust is clear. In regions such as the Caribbean, some of the coastal states are "locked" in by the maritime zones of neighboring states. The thrust of the draft is that provisions should be made for the nationals of such disadvantaged states to enjoy preferential and reciprocal rights to exploit the natural resources of the area beyond a twelve-mile limit on the basis of regional or subregional agreements.

The remaining five states still claim only a three-mile territorial sea and, with the exception of Cuba, are all former British dependencies: the Bahamas, Barbados, Grenada, and Guyana. As has been seen, none of these states has supported any of the three Latin American Declarations on the law of the sea. The writer has no information as to whether they will eventually support the Santo Domingo position or throw in their lot with the more limited Jamaican initiative.

Finally, brief mention should be made of one further factor which adds to the complications of securing a unified approach to the law of the sea in Latin America. There are still in the region a large number of what the Jamaican Draft articles refer to as "territories under foreign domination or forming an integral part of metropolitan powers outside the region."[18]

CONCLUSION

The purpose of this chapter was to identify and assess the value of the Latin American contribution to the international law of the sea. In pursuing this objective, attention has been concentrated almost exclusively on the question of maritime limits, on which Latin American practice has been particularly significant. In a more comprehensive study, reference would have to be made also to the views of the Latin American states on the regime to be established for the exploitation of the resources of the seabed beyond the limits of national jurisdiction. Here it must suffice to note that these views are reflected in a "Working paper on the regime for the sea-bed and ocean floor, and the subsoil thereof beyond the limits of national jurisdiction," submitted to the U.N. Sea-Bed Committee in 1971 by thirteen states: Chile, Colombia, Ecuador, El Salvador, Guatemala, Guyana, Jamaica, Mexico, Panama, Peru, Trinidad and Tobago, Uruguay, and Venezuela (UN Document A/AC.138/49). Its main distinguishing feature is its insistence that the international authority to be set up should be "the sole entity, public or private, empowered to carry out exploitation activities in the area of the sea bed beyond the limits of national jurisdiction" (de Soto, 1973: 130).

Returning to the main theme of this chapter, the conclusion to which this study seems to point is that the main contribution of Latin America has been its recognition of the Truman Proclamation for what it really was—the initiation of a new era in the international law of the sea. The characteristic feature of the new era has been the assertion by coastal states of exclusive resource jurisdiction over considerable areas of the waters adjacent to their coasts. In the three decades since 1945, Latin America has provided the crucible in which the new "mix" could be tested and developed. As the above analysis makes clear, the process of development is still far from complete, but the remaining work is being done on a global rather than a regional Latin American level. There seems little doubt, however, that one specifically Latin American contribution will survive: the establishment of the magical figure of 200 miles as the breadth of the zone of national jurisdiction.

NOTES

1. In November 1954, five vessels belonging to the Onassis whaling fleet were seized twelve miles off the Peruvian coast, taken to port, and released about a month later only on payment of a fine of $3 million (Comisión Permanente del Pacífico Sur, 1972: 23).

2. For a more extended treatment of the following historical material, see Brown, 1973: 157-159 and 167-168.

3. Figures based on U.S. Department of State (1969): Appendix II, updated from other sources.

4. For a full account of the origins, scope, and significance of these new doctrines, see Brown, 1973: 167-186.

5. For further on this, see Brown, 1973: 170-176.

6. Compare this with the more definite formula embodied in the "draft articles of treaty" cosponsored by Colombia, Mexico, and Venezuela. See the heading "State Practice Classified, III—Functional Zone Claims," section B.

7. Some of the Latin American views on these questions are reflected in the working papers and draft articles submitted to Sub-Committee III of the U.N. Sea-Bed Committee in 1973:

(1) Working paper on scientific research within the zone subject to the sovereignty and jurisdiction of the coastal state, submitted by Brazil, Ecuador, El Salvador, Panama, Peru, and Uruguay (UN Document A/AC.138/SC.III/L.45).
(2) Working paper on the preservation of the marine environment, submitted by Ecuador, El Salvador, Peru, and Uruguay (UN Document A/AC.138/SC.III/L.47 and Corr. 1).
(3) Draft articles on responsibility and liability, submitted by Trinidad and Tobago (UN Document A/AC.138/SC.III/L.54).
(4) Draft article on consent to conduct marine scientific research, submitted by 21 states including Argentina, Brazil, Ecuador, El Salvador, Mexico, Peru, and Trinidad and Tobago (UN Document A/AC.138/SC.III/L.55).
(5) Working paper on coastal state enforcement of standards for prevention of pollution from vessels: basic zonal approach, submitted by seventeen states, including Colombia, Jamaica, Mexico, and Trinidad and Tobago (UN Document A/AC.138/SC.III/L.56).

8. In terms of the 1958 Convention,

the term "continental shelf" is used as referring (a) to the sea-bed and subsoil of the submarine areas adjacent to the coast but outside the area of the territorial sea, to a depth of 200 metres or, beyond that limit, to where the depth of the superjacent waters admits of the exploitation of the natural resources of the said areas.

9. The same comparison may be made as suggested in note 6.

10. For details, see Hjertonsson, 1973: 63-65.

11. Including Bolivia and Paraguay, which, though landlocked, have clear policies on maritime limits.

12. The juridical nature of the zone claimed in the Santiago Declaration is discussed in Auguste, 1960: 139; Ferron, Volume I, 1958: 170 and Volume II, 1960: 71; García-Amador, 1963: 73; García-Amador, 1974: 36-38; and Hjertonsson, 1973: 24-26.

13. According to a report from Ecuador by Paul L. Montgomery (*New York Times,* April 8, 1968), "In late 1963, after several changes of government there [in Ecuador], the United States reached a secret agreement with the military junta on the problem. The United States, which then recognized only a 3-mile limit, agreed to respect a 12-mile boundary if Ecuador would not insist on the other 188 miles. This worked satisfactorily until 1966 when there was another change of government and the secret agreement was abrogated." See also Hjertonsson, 1973: 35, note 46.

14. A full account of the 1969-1971 phase in the "tuna war" and of the OAS proceedings is given in Hagen 1972.

15. Though a party, with Ecuador and Peru, to the Santiago Declaration (1952), Chile has not enforced its jurisdiction against foreign fishing boats to any significant extent, mainly, it would seem, because foreign vessels confine their activities for the most part to the richer waters of Ecuador and Peru. On this and details of Chilean legislation, see Hjertonsson, 1973: 27-28 and 50-53.

16. The position prior to 1972 is explained in Hjertonsson, 1973: 66-67. The

patrimonial sea claim of 1972 is reported in Food and Agricultural Organization, 1973: 5.

17. The latter principle is recognized in the Declaration of Principles governing the Sea-Bed and the Ocean Floor and the Subsoil thereof beyond the Limits of National Jurisdiction (A/RES/2749 [XXV]), adopted by the United Nations General Assembly on December 17, 1970, by a vote of 100 to 0 with 14 abstentions.

18. They include the following:

France: French Guyana, Guadeloupe, and Martinique.
Netherlands: Netherlands Antilles and Surinam.
United Kingdom: Antigua, British Honduras, British Virgin Islands, Cayman Islands, Dominica, Falkland Islands, Monserrat, St. Christopher (St. Kitts)-Nevis-Anguilla, St. Lucia, St. Vincent, Turks and Caicos Islands.
United States: Canal Zone, Puerto Rico, and Virgin Islands of the United States.

All four of these administering powers claim a three-mile territorial sea and twelve-mile fishery limit for their metropolitan territories. France is reported, however, to have claimed an eighty-mile fishery limit for French Guyana in 1972 (according to Mr. Bakula, Peru, speaking in the Second Sub-Committee of the U.N. Sea-Bed Committee on March 13, 1973 [A/AC.138/SC.II/SR.52: 59].

REFERENCES

AUGUSTE, B. B. L. (1960) *The Continental Shelf: The Practice and Policy of the Latin American States with Special Reference to Chile, Ecuador and Peru.* Geneva: Droz.
BROWN, E. D. (1973) "Maritime zones: a survey of claims," pp. 157-192 in R. Churchill, K. R. Simmonds, and J. Welch (eds.) *New Directions in the Law of the Sea. Collected Papers.* Vol. III. New York: Oceana.
CALMON FILHO, P. (1970) reported in O Estado de Sao Paulo, April 3, p. 7.
Comision Permanente del Pacífico Sur, Chile-Ecuador-Perú (1972) "Infracciones en la zona maritima del Pacífico Sur." Secretaría General, Quito, Enero de 1972.
DE SOTO, A. (1973) "The Latin American view of the law of the sea." India Quarterly XXIX (April-June): 126-137.
FERRON, O. de (Volume I, 1958, Volume II, 1960) *Le Droit international de la mer.* Geneva: Droz.
Food and Agricultural Organization (1973) "Limits and status of the territorial sea, exclusive fishing zones, fishery conservation zones and the continental shelf." FAO Fisheries Circular No. 127, Rev. 1.
GARCIA-AMADOR, F. V. (1974) "The Latin American contribution to the development of the law of the sea." American Journal of International Law 68 (January): 33-50.
——— (1972) "Latin America and the law of the sea." Law of the Sea Institute, University of Rhode Island. Occasional Paper No. 14.
——— (1963) *The Exploration and Conservation of the Resources of the Sea.* Leyden: Sijthoff.
HAGEN, V. M. (1972) "The Latin American-United States fishing rights controversy: dilemma for United States foreign policy (1969-1971)," in Fishing Rights and United States-Latin American Relations. Hearing before Subcommittee on Inter-American Affairs of the Committee on Foreign Affairs. February 3: Appendix 4: 72-128.

HJERTONSSON, K. (1973) *The New Law of the Sea.* Leiden: Sijthoff.
United Nations (1973) "Report of the Committee on the Peaceful Uses of the Sea-Bed and the Ocean Floor beyond the Limits of National Jurisdiction." General Assembly Official Records: 28th Session. Supplement No. 21 (A/9021). Volumes I-VI.
——— (1970) National Legislation and Treaties Relating to the Territorial Sea, the Contiguous Zone, the Continental Shelf, the High Seas and to Fishing and Conservation of the Living Resources of the Sea, United Nations Legislative Series (ST/LEG/SER.B/15).
——— (1957) Laws and Regulations on the Regime of the Territorial Sea, United Nations Legislative Series (ST/LEG/SER.B/6).
——— (1951) Laws and Regulations on the Regime of the High Seas. United Nations Legislative Series (ST/LEG/SER.B/1).
United States Department of State (1969) "Status of the world's nations." Geographical Bulletin No. 2 (August).
Uruguay (1971) Presidencia de la República Oriental de Uruguay, América Latina y la Extensión de Mar Territorial–Régimen Jurídico. Montevideo.

Chapter 13

THE IMPACT OF THE HIGHER

OIL PRICES ON THE LDC'S:

THE CASE OF LATIN AMERICA

PEDRO-PABLO KUCZYNSKI

The sudden sharp rise in international oil prices at the end of 1973 was the most discussed economic subject in 1974. The reactions of consuming countries to the increase in prices by the Organization of Petroleum-Exporting Countries (OPEC) evolved during the year. The year began with an initial flurry of concern, then a period of relative calm (roughly in the second and third quarters of the year), and finally—as a number of special circumstances wore off—serious worry both in the industrialized oil-importing countries and in many of the non-OPEC developing countries. In the United States, Europe, and Japan, the view of the problem had, of course, much to do with changing seasons; nevertheless, developing countries also changed their views on the oil question in much the same way as the industrialized countries.

A number of factors led to the relative optimism of mid-1974. First, oil—like other imports—is paid for with some delay after the order is made. An increase in international oil prices of approximately 125 percent was announced at the end of December 1973, after various increases which took

SOURCE NOTE: *I am indebted to Aliro Parra and his colleagues at Parra, Ramos & Parra of Caracas, for invaluable assistance with some of the statistics in this chapter. The responsibility for the data and content of this chapter, however, is entirely my own. This essay was written in May 1974 and revised in October 1974; because of the rapid changes in the world economy at the time, some of the argumentation in this chapter is illustrative and conjectural in nature.*

[271]

place in the course of 1973,[1] but the first major impact was not reflected in substantially higher payments by buyers until the end of the first quarter of 1974 or later. Second, the impact of the rising oil payments was softened by large-scale borrowing and by high commodity export prices. Some of the industrialized oil-importing countries (mainly the United Kingdom, France, Italy, and, to a lesser extent, Japan through its banking system) borrowed very large sums in the Euromarkets in the first half of the year, partly in anticipation of future import payments, thus partially offsetting the impact of the higher payments upon their international reserves. In the case of the developing economies, the extraordinarily high level of international commodity prices, which prevailed until about mid-1974, tended to relegate to the background possible doubts about the future viability of their balances of payments despite the much higher cost of imports, preeminently, but not exclusively, due to higher oil prices.

The analysis of the impact of higher oil prices on developing countries in 1974 was made difficult because during most of the year the majority of western industrial countries suffered a combination of unusually sharp inflation mixed with some evidence of a recession. For the developing countries, a recession in Japan, the United States, and Western Europe, which absorb about 70 percent of their exports, would greatly compound the difficulties arising from the higher oil prices, since such a recession would, after a lag, inevitably lead to a downturn in commodity prices. By the third quarter of the year, it was fairly clear that the prices of a number of primary commodities were already coming down sharply (for example, coffee, copper, cotton, and wool), thus placing many developing countries in a situation of sharply declining terms of trade.[2]

The analysis of the immediate impact of oil prices on the oil-importing countries of Latin America and the Caribbean is subject to the same uncertainties which affected other developing countries in 1974. For the "short run," let us say for the sake of argument the period 1974-1976, the major question is the effect of the higher oil prices and of concomitant changes in international financial arrangements upon the balance of payments and the rate of economic growth. Significant effects upon employment and ultimately upon income distribution are also likely. Beyond that, even greater uncertainties arise, such as the degree to which countries will be able to become more self-sufficient and to shift to growth patterns which use less energy.

This chapter is divided into two parts, with the first examining the possible financial effect of higher oil prices in the short run, and the second looking at the possible evolution of development patterns further in the future.

THE NEAR TERM

The Effect of Oil Prices:
Latin America vs. Other Developing Countries

As in the case of the rest of the world, the "energy crisis" in Latin America is a matter of oil prices. If the market prices prevailing at the beginning of 1974—i.e., $9.50 to $10 per barrel delivered—had continued throughout the year, the oil imports of developing countries which are net importers would have totaled between U.S. $17 and U.S. $19 billion, depending on whether volume was at the same level as in 1973 or whether it had risen in line with domestic economic activity in the importing countries. Scattered evidence for the first months of 1974 suggests a drop in the rate of increase in consumption to a much slower rate of increase than in 1973.

Table 1 summarizes the relative impact of the higher cost of oil imports for Latin American oil-importing countries compared to other developing countries. Although the projection refers to 1974, the actual payments impact takes place during the year from the date of the first major payments at the higher oil prices, namely the year beginning March-April 1974. The table is based on the price assumption above. As of October 1974 this appears about 10 percent below likely average import prices for 1974. In the table, as in the rest of the chapter, the developing countries are taken to exclude Greece, Portugal, Spain, and Yugoslavia.

Unfortunately, the table is based on tentative estimates and approximations because of the substantial lag in the availability of the relevant information. Moreover, there are obvious dangers in lumping together disparate countries into broad categories such as "Less Developed Countries (LDC's)" or "Latin America." Still, a few qualified generalizations are possible. For Latin America as a whole, the immediate impact of the higher oil prices is more manageable from a balance of payments point of view than it is likely to be for the majority of the other developing countries, largely those of Africa and Asia. There are various reasons for this. Again taken as a whole, Latin America had in 1974 a relatively much higher level of international reserves to draw on than the rest of the developing world. A related phenomenon is that most Latin American countries have had and will probably continue to have better access to the capital markets of the world (in their case, largely the Eurodollar market) than most of the countries of Africa and Asia, if they have to use this route to cover balance-of-payments deficits.[3] Second, even the Latin American countries which are large oil importers, such as Brazil and Chile, do meet some part of their needs from domestic crude output. This is hardly or not at all the case for most of the large oil importers

TABLE 1

OIL IMPORTS: LATIN AMERICA VERSUS THE OTHER LDC's, 1973 ESTIMATES, 1974 PROJECTIONS

		Latin America	Other LDC's	Total
1. Imports of crude and derivatives			1,250	1,750
Volume (million barrels)	1973	500	1,310	1,835
	1974	525		
Value (million U.S. dollars)	1973	2,300	4,675	6,975
	1974	5,300	13,100	18,400
Additional value of imports (million U.S. dollars)	1974/73	3,000	8,425	11,425
2. Gross international reserves at end of 1973 (million U.S. dollars)		11,494	18,233	29,797
3. Grants and net loan inflows from OECD countries to official sector, 1972 (million U.S. dollars)		3,521	7,896	11,417
4. Additional oil imports in 1974 as percentage of 2		26.1%	46.2%	38.3%
percentage of 3		85%	107%	100%

NOTE: Only net oil importers are included. The Arab petroleum exporters plus Ecuador, Indonesia, Iran, Nigeria, and Venezuela are excluded throughout the table.
SOURCES:
    Oil Volume: Author's estimates based on 1971 and 1972 data published in **Ministerio de Minas e Hidrocarburos de Venezuela: Memoria 1972**, and U.S. Department of the Interior, Bureau of Mines, **International Petroleum Annual, 1971.** The 1974 projection is purely illustrative, and assumes a 5 percent increase in consumption in LDC's, compared to about 8 percent in 1973.
    Oil Value: For Latin America, see Table 2; for other countries, an average c.i.f. price of U.S. $3.50 per barrel is assumed for 1973; a c.i.f. price of $10 is assumed for all countries for 1974. In fact, for much of 1974, the price by most importing countries was higher, so that the calculations are purely illustrative.
    International Reserves: International Monetary Fund, **International Financial Statistics,** May 1974.
    Official Capital: Author's estimates based on 1972 data in **World Bank/IDA-Annual Report 1974.**

in Asia and Africa. A number of the larger Latin American economies, such as Argentina, Colombia, and Mexico, are at or near balance in meeting their oil needs from domestic output. While a few of the net importers in Africa and Asia are in a similar position, the proportion of economies with very weak balance of payments in those two regions is much higher than in Latin America. Evidently, the oil price rise affects the weak much more than the strong. If the additional cost of oil imports is in the range of the estimate shown in the table for 1974—and there is no reason to doubt the rough magnitude of the estimates—it would have represented in one year about the same as the annual net inflows of capital (i.e., grants and loans net of principal repayments) which the official sectors of developing countries have been obtaining in recent years. Fortunately for Latin American countries, these inflows have been less important for the health of their balances of payments than they have been for other developing countries, especially for those of the Indian subcontinent. India usually weighs heavily in aggregate statistics on developing countries, and the $1 billion or so of additional annual cost of oil imports, together with the ensuing rise in fertilizer prices and the sharp rise since 1973 in the cost of food imports, presents that country with a massive financial problem, which has been mitigated only by large-scale financing of oil imports by Iran. No Latin American country is likely to be faced with a problem of such magnitude.

The Near-Term Effect of Oil Prices
upon Latin American Countries

The capacity of the various Latin American countries to pay the higher oil import prices varies greatly. Three broad groups can be distinguished among the net oil importers: those with no petroleum production at all, those with some domestic production but with a major reliance on imports, and those with an occasional or minor need to import. Across these categories, however, there is another dividing line of equal importance: the existing financial strength of a particular economy, especially the level of its international reserves, and the prospects for the growth of its foreign exchange earnings.[4] Although each country is evidently its own special case, the very simplified graph (Figure 1) gives a very broad view of the possible groups of net oil importers as of 1974.

The magnitude of the immediate problem for each country depends on the size of the oil import bill and on the strength of its balance of payments. Both parameters are shown in the chart; the ratio of oil imports to international reserves serves as a proxy for the vulnerability of the balance of payments. For the longer run, a better proxy for the underlying strength of the balance of payments would probably be the past growth of the volume of exports. Colombia is still a small net exporter, but it could become a net importer within two or three years unless exploration is greatly intensified. In one breakdown, the three groups of countries mentioned above can be distinguished: those with only a limited reliance on imports of oil (Argentina and Mexico), those which rely entirely on imports (all of the smaller economies of the region), and a few intermediate cases. However, within the last two groups, there are substantial differences between countries in their financial capacity to withstand the higher cost of imports without curtailing economic growth. Most of the smaller economies have low reserves and relatively high oil import bills. They are likely to be seriously affected. For the short run, the seriousness of the financial problem will depend largely on

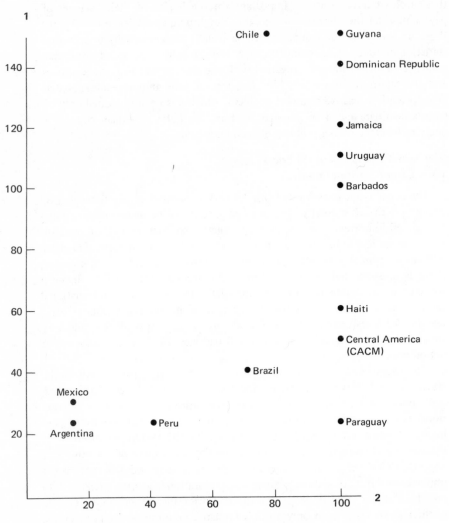

1 = Value of expected 1974 imports of crude and derivatives as a percentage of Dec. 1973 gross international reserves.
2 = Value of expected 1974 imports of crude and derivatives as a percentage of total domestic consumption.

Source: Table 2

FIGURE 1: LATIN AMERICA: NET OIL IMPORTERS — 1974

whether commodity prices for their exports hold up or, which is more likely, on whether the cyclical downswing which became apparent in mid-1974 turns out to be a sharp one.

The cases of Chile and Brazil have special features. For Chile, the additional annual cost of $200 million or so in oil imports hindered its efforts during 1974 to put the balance of payments back on an orderly basis. In the first half of 1974, the effects of the oil price rise on the balance of payments were more than offset by higher export earnings, owing to the extraordinarily high international price for copper. After copper prices began to fall about mid-year, the external constraint upon the economy became once again more visible, although not to the same degree as in 1971-1973. In Brazil, the high level of international reserves at the time that the higher oil prices were announced (gross reserves were over $6 billion at the end of 1973) gives the economy a cushion for some time before a significant curtailment of imports and hence of economic expansion might have to take place. The size of the problem diminished at the end of 1974 with the apparently large, but as yet unquantified oil discoveries at the Campos field, off Rio de Janeiro. In the meantime, the question for Brazil is more one of planning than of immediate financing needs. However, the rise in oil prices has not only contributed to reactivate domestic inflation, but has also shown up the potential vulnerability of the balance of payments. In 1974, domestic crude output (which was virtually stagnant for the previous five years) is estimated to have covered only 21 percent of total petroleum consumption, compared to 30 percent in 1971. As of mid-1974, oil imports were projected to amount to about 25 percent of total merchandise imports in 1974. Until the new oil discoveries can be translated into output, hopefully substantial, the challenge for Brazil is whether in the future exports and capital inflows can continue to grow at a fast enough pace until the pattern of energy production can be shifted in relative terms away from imported crude toward domestic sources, such as hydro-electric power. In 1974, imported crude provided about one-third of total energy consumed in Brazil.[5]

In sum, the magnitude and suddenness of the rise in oil import costs have presented most Latin American countries with a major problem of managing their balance of payments. The eventual magnitude of the problem will depend not only on oil prices themselves but also on trends in commodity export prices and on the availability of compensatory financing. The emergence of the balance of payments problem has coincided with the diminished availability of medium-term commercial lending from the Euro-currency markets to the developing countries which had large-scale access to it in the period 1970-1973 (mostly the resource-rich with a proven record of debt service). This diminished availability was itself the result of competing demands in the market (mainly because of

TABLE 2
SELECTED LATIN AMERICAN COUNTRIES: OUTPUT AND IMPORTS OF CRUDE AND DERIVATIVES

	Output		Gross Imports			Gross International Reserves (million U.S. $ as of end 1973)
	Total 1973 (million barrels)	Growth Rate 1965-1973 (average annual % change)	Volume 1973 (million barrels)	Value (million U.S. $) 1973	1974[1]	
Net Importers—Total=	418.2	...	503.4	2,269.6	5,093	10,839
Argentina	153.7	9.4	38.3	190.8	383	1,318
Mexico	165.0	7.0	43.8	287.8	438	1,356
Peru	25.8	2.2	14.8	67.1	148	551
Brazil	62.1	12.2	270.8	1,152.7	2,708	6,417
Chile	11.6	-1.5	28.1	120.0*	340	200*
CACM[2]	—		24.6	111.9	246	475
Dominican Republic	—		12.5	56.8	125	88
Haiti	—		1.0	4.4	10	17
Jamaica	—		16.4	74.5	164	128
Panama	—		26.2[3]	97.3[3]	262[3]	not applicable
Paraguay	—		1.4	6.8	14	57
Uruguay	—		25.5	99.5	255	232
				Net Exports		
Net Exporters—Total=	1,453.1	...	1,445.0	5,155.0	12,695	3,316
Bolivia	17.3	38.5	21.0	70.0*	190	72
Colombia	72.7	-0.1	37.1	74.7	40*	534
Ecuador	74.6	91.2	68.1	271.3	615	241
Venezuela	1,228.6	-0.6	1,167.3	4,214.0	10,500	2,420
Trinidad and Tobago	59.9	4.1	151.5	525.0*	1,350*	49

Notes and Sources on page 279.

large borrowings by European countries and Japan), and of the diminished "creditworthiness" of developing country borrowers.

The first half of 1974 was a period of record commodity prices. The primary-producing countries benefited from these prices, and the impact of the rise in oil prices upon their balance of payments was therefore less apparent. As of mid-1974, however, the possibility of a downswing in the business cycle in the industrial world cast doubt on the future of commodity prices. Although continuing world inflation obscured the trends of real output and made it difficult to estimate the size of a possible recession, there was a fairly strong probability that the majority of commodity prices would weaken significantly in the remainder of 1974 and in 1975.

Latin American countries which are net oil importers—indeed most developing countries—thus have to cope with a double problem: rapidly rising import costs, largely due to oil prices, and the slow growth or possibly even decline of export earnings.

Coping with the Immediate Problem

The possible courses of action open to the countries affected are limited. They can be summarized in three broad categories: measures which directly affect the consumption of petroleum, macroeconomic policies to reduce overall import growth and limit the deficit in the balance of payments, and compensatory financing, popularly known as "recycling."

In the next two or three years, the amount of reduction which can be

---

NOTES AND SOURCES FOR TABLE 2

*Estimates.

NOTES: Figures in Table 2 are rough estimates.

1. 1974 values are purely notional, assuming 1973 volume and a c.i.f. price of U.S. $10 per barrel, and an f.o.b. price of U.S. $9 in the case of exporters. A number of adjustments have been made, as explained in the notes below. Since the volume figures include derivatives, which have a higher price than crude, the value figures shown in the table for 1974 are underestimated; actual prices in mid-1974 were also about 15 percent higher, and possibly the average derived prices in 1974 will be about U.S. $11 per barrel instead of U.S. $10 assumed here.

2. Central American Common Market: Costa Rica, El Salvador, Guatemala, Honduras, and Nicaragua.

3. Includes imports for re-export.

COUNTRY NOTES AND SOURCES: All sources refer to 1973 volume, unless otherwise indicated. Argentina: Official statistics. Includes imports of natural gas from Bolivia equivalent to 9.1 million barrels of crude oil. Bolivia: Official statistics. Exports include sales of natural gas to Argentina. Crude exports based on January-October 1973 average. Brazil, Mexico, Panama, Peru, and Uruguay: Official statistics. Chile: Official statistics. Import volume figure is for 1972. Dominican Republic, Haiti, Jamaica: Estimates based on past trends and average import prices for 1973. Ecuador: U.S. Statistics for crude oil production. Volume and value of exports partially estimated. Trinidad and Tobago: Official statistics. Exports are on gross basis (i.e., include sales of refined products made from imported crude oil) and are partially estimated.

GENERAL NOTE: For somewhat different data on the same parameters, but within the same general orders of magnitude, see E. Walter Robichek, **The Payments Impact of the Oil Crisis: The Case of Latin America** in **Finance and Development**, IMF-World Bank, December 1974.

effected in petroleum consumption is very limited. About two-thirds of petroleum consumption in the net importing Latin American countries goes for industrial uses, public transportation, and thermal electricity generation. Forty-five percent of electricity generation in those countries comes from thermal sources, and is almost entirely dependent on petroleum-fired plants. A shift to domestically produced coal is expensive and possible in varying degrees only in Argentina, Brazil, Chile, and Mexico; the other countries do not have significant quantities of acceptable coal. As for the direct use of petroleum by consumers, it is unrealistic to expect the use of kerosene by lower income groups to be reduced, while gasoline rationing for automobiles, which clearly belong to upper income groups, would cut into the growth of the automobile industry. In Brazil in 1973 sales of automobile gasoline accounted for one-third of the total consumption of petroleum derivatives and the automobile industry, which produced 600,000 cars, accounted for about 8 percent of the gross value of industrial output.

Clearly, a number of countries will be forced to begin fiscal and monetary austerity programs designed to limit the growth of aggregate imports. The standard prescriptions are well-known, but so is the eventual result, a lower growth rate.[6] The popular idea of limiting luxury imports through prohibitions or high tariffs is unlikely to save much foreign exchange. In most countries "luxuries" are a modest proportion of imports, but they provide a significant proportion of import duty revenue; their disappearance from the market has in the past invariably triggered pressures for local assembly of such products,[7] a process which initially at least leads often to a greater outflow of foreign exchange than would have taken place without the prohibition, as foreign exchange payments for machinery, trademarks, licenses, etc., begin to take place.

All this is not to say that countries should not attempt to curtail import growth. They will be forced to do so, but at the same time they will have to be prepared to accept a lower rate of economic expansion. If the economic slowdown lasts for more than a short time, the resulting increase in the already high rates of open unemployment and disguised unemployment which prevail in most Latin American (and other developing) countries, combined with the existing unequal patterns of income distribution typical of that stage of development, can only result in strong social and political pressures.

The antidote most often mentioned against these dangers is that of "recycling." This means to channel money in the form of loans or grants from the surplus countries to the deficit countries. This process can take place at various levels: commercially through the international capital market, through international agencies, and by direct lending from surplus to deficit countries.

Some type of concessional assistance is clearly needed for obvious reasons. First, importing countries—assuming that most of the "recycled" funds come in the form of loans—will be borrowing for current consumption. This type of borrowing would most likely lead to the excessively fast increase of external debt. Second, Latin American oil importers have rapidly expanded their external debt in the last three years or so, mostly in the Eurodollar market, at precisely the time when their economies and balance of payments were in a strong position. Debt service on this borrowing will rise rapidly in the next couple of years. From the end of 1968 to the end of 1973, the outstanding external public debt (including undisbursed loans) of Latin American countries, excluding Venezuela, rose from $16.3 billion to about $34 billion; service on this debt in 1973 absorbed about $4.0 billion or 24 percent of merchandise export earnings, although the ratio was higher for the major economies in the region.[8] The high level of debt service, which will rise sharply in the next few years, and the deterioration in the balance of trade, are strong reasons for the Latin American oil importing countries to try to obtain as much capital as possible on noncommercial terms.

The chances of receiving large-scale assistance on concessional terms are slim, however, both in Latin America and elsewhere in the developing world. In the past the industrial countries contributed a very small proportion of their resources to the development of the Third World, whereas much greater demands are now being made on the "new rich" oil surplus countries. Several of these new surplus countries may feel that there is no equity in such a system.[9] Of course, the nature of the two problems is different: one is that of a long-term transfer of savings from rich to poor, and the other that of compensating a violent shift in the balances of payments of oil importers versus oil exporters. Still, general targets such as 0.7 percent of the gross national product as a target for "official development assistance"[10] have a way of backfiring. For example, if for the sake of argument the target were applied to government oil revenues of the major oil surplus countries (those listed in note 7), the amount to be transferred in 1974 would amount to about $500 million, a paltry sum in relation to the size of the deficit of oil-importing countries.

The oil-importing countries of Latin America have fewer chances of receiving substantial compensatory financing on concessional terms than the African and Asian countries, for which Middle East producers are beginning to mount various programs of direct aid. There is likely to be a "regionalization" of this type of financing. The only major surplus country in Latin America is Venezuela. The 1974 surplus for Venezuela was $4.5 to $5 billion. Of this sum, about $600 million has gone to repay various international loans. Of the remainder, a significant part is likely to be disbursed in the period from mid-1974 to mid-1975 in the form of assistance to international financial organizations. The Venezuelan Investment Fund, a specialized government agency, was created in May 1974 in order to insulate the economy from the pressures to monetize increasing international reserves and to invest the oil revenues into economic diversification. It has already made a number of large commitments, including the purchase of $500 million twelve-year 8 percent placement by the World Bank ($100 million of which was denominated in Bolivares), an as yet undefined sum of a similar magnitude out probably on concessional terms to the Special Fund of the Inter-American Development Bank, and promises in the $30 to $100 million range each to the Andean Development Corporation, the Central American Bank for Economic Integration, and the Caribbean Development Bank. The Central Bank of Venezuela was the first to make a firm commitment—of SDR 450 million, equivalent to about U.S. $540 million—to the Oil Facility of the IMF.[11] It is not yet known exactly how much of the Oil Facility will be channeled to the developing countries in the IMF, but it will be the largest part. The speed with which Venezuela's various contributions, totaling about $1.5 billion, are to be disbursed is not yet known, but it is clear that in 1974 and 1975 Venezuela will be contributing a high proportion of its current account surplus to "recycling," mostly to developing countries through international multilateral institutions. If the money were disbursed in one year, a not unlikely event, Venezuela would be contributing about 35 percent of its current account surplus in the form of Official Development Assistance to the Third World. The paradox is that this contribution comes from the country with probably the smallest relative balance of payments surplus among the major OPEC producers. At the same time, of course, it is recognized that Venezuela is also the most economically advanced of the OPEC countries.

So far, the only international mechanism specifically designed to help deficit countries bridge the portion of their balance of payments deficit due to oil is the IMF Facility. For the deficit countries as a whole, this recycling scheme falls short of meeting a substantial part of their needs. The facility, which will apply to all oil deficit countries that are Fund members, had available to it as of October 1974 the equivalent of U.S. $3.5 billion in loanable funds for the period 1974-1975. Of that sum, Latin American countries cannot expect more than $600 million, less than one-fifth of the additional cost of oil imports for the period mid-1974-1975 valued at January 1974 prices.[12]

Commercial channels are therefore likely to be sought as vehicles of major importance for recycling. Only a few Latin American countries—Argentina, Brazil, Colombia, Panama, Peru, and Mexico—have in recent years had significant access to medium-term general purpose external financing from commercial sources. Moreover, the commercial nature of the terms of this type of financing is likely to put a heavy burden on debt service. A number of other interrelated problems exist on the side of the supply of funds. First, the heavy demands of European countries in 1974 for medium-term loans have put serious strain on the Eurodollar market, which is the only segment of the international capital market to which selected developing countries—a minority of them—have hitherto had access in significant amounts. Second, the "creditworthiness" of most developing country borrowers has obviously been impaired, and in the course of 1974 it was already becoming more difficult for them to obtain medium-term credit in the market. Third, the oil surplus countries, which are well aware of the volatility of the balances of payments of key currency countries, have in general tended to invest their international reserves in the international money markets at unusually short terms—on sight, at 7 or 30 days; the borrowers want 5- to 10-year loans. In between stand U.S., European, and Japanese Eurodollar banks (and U.S. domestic banks). With their generally inadequate capitalizations these banks find it increasingly difficult to take the risk of converting funds borrowed at short-term into medium-term loans unless there is a big increase in the premiums to be received for this service. An obvious reason for the problem is that a handful of governments control a growing proportion of the deposits which are therefore potentially quite volatile, a very different situation from that to which financial intermediaries are accustomed.

There are thus a number of problems in "recycling." The balance of payments difficulties of Latin American countries are in general likely to be somewhat less than for other developing countries, but recycled funds cannot be expected to fill more than a modest part of the gap in the near term. Short of continued commodity export price boom, therefore, major internal fiscal and monetary adjustments will be needed.

The necessary domestic financial adjustments may take some time for certain countries, but eventually those with serious balance of payments problems will be forced to carry out fiscal and monetary policies designed to reduce the growth of aggregate demand and to limit the balance of payments deficit. Fiscal policies will no doubt involve some shift in expenditure priorities, probably away from current outlays such as education and health and toward heavier government investment in fields related to energy. Taxation will have to be increased, initially probably through increases in rapid-yielding sales taxes and other forms of indirect taxation. The degree of success of this type of fiscal policy will determine the extent to which countries will have to rely on contractionary monetary policies. In most Latin American economies in the past the extent of central bank financing of public expenditures has been by far the single most important variable in monetary policy. For several countries, however, changes in fiscal and monetary policy are unlikely to be enough to reduce the deficit in the balance of payments to manageable proportions.

LONGER-TERM IMPLICATIONS

The most obvious question for the future is whether and how long the balance of payments problem faced by net oil importers will continue. A great deal depends, of course, on the future of commodity prices and the trend of developing country export earnings other than oil, both of them factors difficult to predict. If petroleum prices stay anywhere near their 1974 levels, a likely event, there could be serious and persistent financial difficulties for several years until new policies affecting energy supply-and-demand produce tangible results. There are also likely to be repercussions of a social and political nature, including realignments in international relations.

Energy Supply and Demand

It is unlikely that Latin American governments will rely significantly on policies to cut energy demand. Economic growth in itself signifies an increasing use of energy per inhabitant. At present, the average per capita use of energy in Latin America is low, amounting to the equivalent of only 0.9 metric tons of coal annually compared to a world average of 1.9 metric tons. In a rapidly industrializing country such as Brazil the per capita consumption is still only about 0.6 metric tons; close to 20 percent of primary energy is provided by burning wood or bagasse; in Colombia, over one-third of primary energy comes from wood, and in the smaller less advanced economies the percentage is even higher.

In the "modern" sector of Latin American economies, oil provides by far the largest source of primary energy, accounting on average for about two-thirds of total supply to the sector. There are two areas where the growth in demand for oil might be cut. The first concerns shifting public utility sources of energy away from oil-fired thermal plants to coal-fired plants and to hydroelectric generation. Government policies for electric utilities in Latin America ought to be easier to implement than in some industrialized countries since virtually all electric generation and distribution systems in Latin America are owned by the governments themselves. The limiting factors are the domestic availability of coal (international prices of coal rose as much as petroleum prices from 1973 to 1974, although a downturn is probable) and the fact that some countries have a limited scope for shifting to hydroelectric power, because the bulk of their systems already rely heavily on hydroelectric power. For Latin America as a whole, hydroelectric power in 1972 provided 55 percent of total electricity generation; the proportions ranged from a high of 81 percent in Brazil to a low of 12 percent in Argentina. Only about 5 to 10 percent of the hydroelectric potential of the region has been tapped, and almost all countries still have a large, unexploited potential. The other possibility for cutting oil-demand is to diminish the proportion of fuel devoted to gasoline use by private automobiles by raising gasoline prices and taxes for car use and ownership. Large-scale price increases have already begun. In December 1973, Mexico—which depends only to a small, declining degree on imported crude[13]—raised the price of gasoline by an average of 70 percent and the prices of other petroleum products by similar percentages. A large increase in gasoline taxes was being discussed in October 1974. The Brazilian Government has begun a gradual increase of gasoline prices which will result in an almost threefold rise from a price of $0.55 per gallon of 95 octane gasoline in June 1973 to $1.50 at the end of 1974. Most of the countries which import all or a large part of their petroleum needs have raised domestic prices more or less in line with international prices. Despite the low price elasticity of demand for petroleum, at least in the short run, price increases of such a magnitude are bound to reduce demand.

Still, the bulk of the energy policy effort is likely to be directed at increasing the supply of oil and of hydro and nuclear electricity. Very large public investment expenditures will be made in electricity and public trans- port, including railway modernization and subways for the major cities of Latin America at present without them.[14] The financing of these very large projects will not be easy: the funds of international agencies which lend at concessional terms are limited, and governments—often at the urging of those agencies—have begun to look increasingly to the international capital markets in order to finance a major portion of those investments. The difficulties for developing countries in the international capital markets have already been mentioned. For the few Latin American countries which are still likely to be able to have access to these sources of funds, there will still be problems, such as maturity periods which are too short both for the projects in question and for the viable management of the external debt of the countries concerned. Some new type of financial arrangements will therefore have to be developed by the World Bank and the Inter-American Development Bank, perhaps along the principle sometimes used by the U.S. Export-Import Bank, under which private sector lenders are paid off first and the bank itself takes the later maturities.

The attitude of a number of governments toward petroleum exploration and production is likely to evolve away from heavy reliance on state-owned enterprises to more flexible arrangements with foreign companies. In several major countries, such as Brazil and Chile, petroleum output has stagnated, partly because of the insufficient exploration effort. The sensitive subject of relations between governments and foreign oil companies is obviously of key importance, since domestic state enterprises have rarely had the necessary expertise, dynamism, and financial backing. Peru began in 1970 to attract foreign companies with a scheme under which output would be shared by the state with the producing company (not as concessionaire of a state-owned resource but as manager) in lieu of tax payments. The scheme has undoubtedly been attractive to the companies. It may be an exception to the announced ideology of the regime on the exploitation of raw materials, but it has been basically successful and will convert Peru from a net importer to an exporter within the next three or four years. Multinational companies are likely to accept arrangements of this kind in new areas as their operations are gradually taken over in major producing countries (Kuwait, Libya, Saudi Arabia, and Venezuela, for example). For some countries, of course, these policy changes may lead to nothing, if there is no oil to be found.

The intensification of exploration efforts had already begun before 1974. As a result of prospecting begun several years ago, Petrobrás in 1974 brought into production new fields off the northeast coast of Brazil and made major strikes in the Campos field. With the higher world prices it has intensified its work (including the beginning of operations of a pilot processing plant) to extract oil from the very large deposits of shale in the state of Paraná. Still, Brazil is likely to continue requiring imported oil to meet much of its needs for a long time unless major new discoveries occur. The same is true in Chile, where ENAP, the state petroleum enterprise, is developing fields in the eastern part of the Straits of Magellan. The new output is expected to substitute declines from old wells, but is not sufficient to reduce the proportion of national needs which has to be met by imports. In Central America, the only significant discovery so far has been in northwestern Guatemala, but the commercial size of the field was not yet known as of this writing. The discoveries and developments in Mexico have already been alluded to; although still of uncertain size, they are likely to turn Mexico into a major net exporter. Moreover, there is a potential for larger discoveries. In general, the same is probably true about several Latin American countries which are not significant producers today, if large-scale exploration is begun as a result of the stimulus of the new level of oil prices.

The Social and Political Context

The higher prices for oil, the single most important commodity in the value of international trade even before the price increases, will have immediate and longer-range financial and economic consequences, and the latter in turn are bound to affect social and political dimensions. This will be true to some extent in all countries which rely on imported oil, but particularly so in the developing world. Within Latin America, the domestic economy of countries significantly dependent on oil imports is likely to be affected by three phenomena: lower real growth rates, higher inflation, and changes in the pattern of public investment, all of which in one way or another are likely to have social and possibly political repercussions.

The link between growth and improvement in income distribution has yet to be established for a relatively short historical period, although there is little doubt that over a long period of, say, fifty years, economic expansion has so far been invariably connected with an improvement in the relative welfare of at least a large part of the economic groups below the top. However, in the last decade or two, Latin American economic expansion seems to have been associated—at least in the larger countries—with an apparent deterioration in the relative distribution of income.[15] In practical terms, this reflects the fact that growth has taken place in the urban industrial sectors and in selected services, both of which have tended to be liberal in their use of capital (i.e., machinery or imported services) and economical in employment. As a result, the beneficiaries have tended to be a relatively small (but growing) class with earnings well above the national median. This group could be, or perhaps already is, potentially very strong in political terms. Lower growth rates could mean some improvement in the lower income groups' relative share of income in a stagnant national output, but this very stagnation would inevitably lead to the frustration of the hitherto economically dynamic class. Unable to keep up its rate of improvement, this group would become politically restless (as occurred, for example, in Uruguay in the second half of the 1960s). Moreover, the ambitions of those on the threshold of improved living conditions would be dashed. While there is no basis for painting a doomsday scenario, the dangers of slow or no growth in countries with rapidly expanding populations, especially in the cities, are fairly clear.

Inflation is a more complex phenomenon. With a young population, Latin American countries do not have large fixed-income or pensioner groups. Although such groups are affected by inflation, they are unlikely to be politically significant in most countries. However, inflation in the postwar period in Latin America has generally affected the farmer: in order to limit the squeeze of inflation on the most vocal groups in the population, which are in the cities, many Latin American governments in the last thirty years have resorted to a variety of devices—price controls, especially of food; overvalued exchange rates; favorable treatment of food imports; high protection for various industries—which have been unfavorable to agriculture. The renewed inflation which is evident in most Latin American countries since 1973, including oil exporting countries themselves, might lead to such reactions again. It is too early to tell whether this danger is real, but the temptation may be there, with its possible consequences on agricultural employment and incomes.

Most governments are going to devote a large proportion of their public investment to energy-related investment, most of which will be financed by the public sector itself. With possibly serious resource constraints, is it not a likely possibility that investments in the so-called social sectors—education, water and sewerage, health, public housing—will be held down? The evidence on whether the large increase in such investments in the last decade in Latin America has significantly improved the distribution of income is deficient, but partial evidence casts some doubt on the effect of this type of investment because of the magnitudes involved and bad distribution. (See, for example, Webb, 1973.) Still, a cutback in the amount of such investment per inhabitant is likely to exacerbate whatever political tensions are already latent.

Much of the above is speculation. There are few or no precedents. However, a situation which is likely to put the balance of payments of several countries in the region under serious strain and exacerbate already existing inflationary pressures is bound to strain the social and political health of the countries affected.

Finally, will the oil-rich help the oil-poor? In Latin America, of course, at present the oil-rich—those having a substantial exportable capital surplus—consist solely of Venezuela. By the balance of payments standards customary until 1973, the Venezuelan surplus is large. By the end of 1974, international reserves are projected to be around $6 billion, and, if petroleum prices stay at early 1974 levels, would reach $10 billion at the end of 1975. However, there are a number of reasons why Venezuela cannot be expected to become a large international lender of long-term funds during the 1970s. First, its surplus is much smaller in relative per capita terms than that of some of the Arab producers such as Saudi Arabia, Abu Dhabi, and Kuwait. Second, its internal needs for worthwhile domestic investments are large and will grow rapidly during the 1970s. Third, and most important, the known and measured oil reserves of Venezuela are low,[16] so that Venezuela will have to diversify its economy dramatically within the next decade or find new economical sources of petroleum output, or both. These tasks require huge investments. In the meantime, Venezuela will clearly invest its surplus in the international capital market, but at terms and yields which will provide the best available protection for its capital for the future.

Obviously, Venezuela will play an important role in hemisphere affairs in the coming years. Its influence upon international financial agencies will increase, especially in the case of the Inter-American Development Bank, whose headquarters Latin American shareholders might encourage to move from Washington, D.C., to Caracas. Venezuela could become an important voice in managing the bank. The Andean Common Market could receive a boost if Venezuela becomes a major financier of large projects in the area. However, it is improbable that Venezuela will finance more than a modest part of the deficits of other Latin American countries arising from the higher oil prices. Nor can a major contribution to Latin America be expected from the large oil exporters in the Middle East, either directly or through international financial agencies. With the high rixks posed by the inflated external debt of developing countries, these capital surplus countries will seek security as far as they can. The one exception might be capital inflows to Brazil. The smaller countries are thus the ones likely to be hit hardest if oil prices remain at or near their present levels.

Will these countries try to follow the example of Venezuela in OPEC? There are already signs that they will, such as the 1974 attempts of Central American countries to increase their revenues from the banana companies, and the somewhat more successful effort of Jamaica to do the same in the case of the bauxite companies. Whether efforts of this type will succeed is another matter. There are few commodities as essential as oil; the attempts at cartelization are coming at a time when commodity prices are falling and the members of the cartel are likely to be in a weakened position; few other products provide the level of rent which enables most oil-producing countries to reduce oil output without damaging their economies. Most countries therefore are likely to find that the bulk of the adjustment to the higher oil prices will have to be borne domestically.

NOTES

1. The figures used here are averages, since there is a wide range of export prices. In addition, export prices reflect differences in shipping distances and costs. The estimated market price of Saudi Arabian Light, a fairly representative crude, f.o.b. Ras Tanura (Saudi Arabia) has evolved as follows: $1.30 per barrel January 1970 (a price $0.63 below that of January 1955 in current dollars), gradually rising to $2.20 in January 1973, then to $2.70 in June 1973, $3.65 on October 16, 1973, and $8.18 on January 1, 1974. There were other smaller price changes between the main ones shown here. These average market prices are estimated from actual "posted" prices, which are the ones established by oil-exporting countries' governments for purposes of taxation.

2. No data are available as of this writing on terms of trade of the developing countries in 1974. For 1973, the available data show little change in relation to 1972 in the terms of trade of Latin America as a whole, even though the year was notable for extraordinary high commodity export prices. This was due to the very rapid increase in import prices in 1973, which continued at a faster pace in 1974. See both the UN and IMF data in International Monetary Fund, *International Financial Statistics.*

3. According to World Bank estimates published in the *IMF Survey* of August 19, 1974, out of an estimated $5,277 million of medium and longer-term Eurodollar loans announced in 1973 to non-OPEC developing countries (as defined in this chapter), $3,746 million went to Latin American borrowers (primarily Brazil, Peru, and Mexico) compared to $1,531 million to all other non-OPEC developing countries. The relative proportion of Latin American borrowings within the total for developing countries increased in 1974, after conditions for medium- and long-term lending in the Euro-currency markets tightened considerably.

4. Various indices of the vulnerability of the balance of payments of an economy

have been and can be constructed. Typically, they consist of a systematic presentation of the relationships between variables such as prospective export earnings; the commodity and geographic concentration of exports; the level and structure of, and prospective service on the external debt; and the size of international reserves.

5. For a recent summary of the sources and uses of energy in Brazil, see *Brazilian Economy–Trends and Perspectives,* quarterly review of Banco Lar Brasileiro, April 1974 issue. The data in the text have been estimated on the basis of various official sources.

6. For it to be otherwise, a downward shift would have to occur in the import coefficient (imports as a percentage of GNP, i.e., the import content of the economy), generally a lengthy process.

7. Part of the reason for this is the very high preference for such products as incomes rise. An obvious example is that of automobiles, the sales of which have risen rapidly in countries such as Chile, Colombia, and Peru despite prices which are very high in relation to the incomes of the majority of buyers.

8. Data derived in part from *1974 World Bank IDA–Annual Report,* which shows external public debt outstanding as of 1972 and projected external public debt service for 1973. Adjustment for exclusion of Venezuela estimated by the author on the basis of official statistics. Merchandise exports are taken from International Monetary Fund, *International Financial Statistics.*

9. Venezuela and Saudi Arabia, Iran, Iraq, Kuwait, Libya, Abu Dhabi, and Qatar; if they can mobilize their planning effort sufficiently, countries such as Algeria, Indonesia, Nigeria, and other Latin American net oil exporters (Bolivia, Ecuador, and Trinidad and Tobago) have immediate domestic requirements which are large enough to absorb most of their new financial resources.

10. Net disbursements of grants and long-term loans by the industrial to the developing countries, adopted as a goal by the United Nations for the "Second Development Decade" (of the nineteen seventies).

11. The facility was created in June 1974 for the period to December 1975. Its full title is "Facility to Assist Members in Payments Difficulties Resulting from Initial Impact of Increased Costs of Imports of Petroleum and Petroleum Products."

12. There is of course nothing automatic about the regional allocation of Oil Facility funds. The allocation is based on the special needs of each country and on the relationship between those needs and the quota of the country in the IMF. See *IMF Survey,* September 16, 1974.

13. Mexico's oil imports were substantial in 1973, amounting to U.S. $288 million, but imports declined in the first half of 1974 and had practically ceased by mid-year. The major new discoveries (at the Refoma field) in Chiapas will turn Mexico into a major net exporter.

14. Mexico and Buenos Aires have limited subway systems, Santiago, Rio de Janeiro and Sao Paulo are building networks, and Caracas is planning one.

15. See, for example, estimates shown in Chenery, and others, 1973: chap. 2. These estimates are of course subject to the qualifications pointed out by the authors.

16. About ten years of "fiscal" reserves at the rate of output of 1973. Although fiscal reserves, namely those which can be economically exploited at a given level of prices, underestimate total extractable oil, the additional oil which could be extracted (with secondary recovery and other techniques) would be costly, the profits lower, and the tax revenues accruing to the government also lower.

REFERENCES

Brazilian Economy –Trends and Perspectives (1974) Banco Lar Brasileiro (April).
CHENERY, H. B., and others (1973) "Redistribution with Growth," Oxford University Press, 1974.
International Monetary Fund, International Financial Statistics.
––– IMF Survey. September 16, 1974.
––– IMF Survey. August 19, 1974.
International Monetary Fund–World Bank, *Finance and Development,* December 1974, E. WALTER ROBICHEK, "The Payments Impact of the Oil Crisis: The Case of Latin America."
WEBB, R. C. (1973) "Government policy and the distribution of income in Peru, 1963-1973." Discussion paper No. 39. (June 1973). Research Program in Economic Development, Princeton University.

NOTES ON THE EDITORS
AND
CONTRIBUTORS

THE EDITORS

RONALD G. HELLMAN is Director of Public Affairs at the Center for Inter-American Relations and teaches political science at Brooklyn College. From 1970 to 1972 he was a visiting Professor at the Institute of Political Science at the Catholic University of Chile. Hellman also served in 1971 as a social science consultant to the Ford Foundation office in Santiago de Chile and held a National Institute of Mental Health fellowship during his graduate studies in political science at New York University. He is co-editor of a forthcoming book entitled *Ideology in Inter-American Politics.*

H. JON ROSENBAUM received his Ph.D. from the Fletcher School of Law and Diplomacy, and taught at Wellesley College and Tufts University before assuming his present post as an Associate Professor of Political Science at the City College and the Graduate School of the City University of New York. He is the co-editor of *Contemporary Brazil: Issues in Economic and Political Development* and *Vigilante Politics: Perspectives on Establishment Violence.* He has also written more than twenty journal articles, many of them concerned with Brazilian politics. Rosenbaum has been a fellow or guest scholar at the Brazilian Institute of International Relations, the Woodrow Wilson International Center for Scholars, Harvard University's Center for International Affairs, the Brazilian School of Public Administration, and Columbia University's Institute of Latin American Studies.

THE CONTRIBUTORS

ROBERT W. ANDERSON is a Professor of Political Science at the College of Social Science, University of Puerto Rico at Rio Piedras. He received his Ph.D. from the University of California at Berkeley. Anderson has been a consultant to various agencies and commissions of the Commonwealth of Puerto Rico and a Fulbright Lecturer at several Peruvian universities. He also has taught at the University of California and Brooklyn College of the City University of New York. He is the author of *Party Politics in Puerto Rico,* co-author of *Los Derechos y los Partidos Politicos en la Sociedad Puertorriqena,* and co-editor of *Public Administration in the Caribbean.* In addition, Anderson has contributed to numerous scholarly journals.

ALEXANDRE DE SOUZA COSTA BARROS is an Associate Professor at the Brazilian School of Public Administration of the Getulio Vargas Foundation and a Lecturer at the Instituto Universitario de Pesquisas do Rio de Janeiro. Barros studied as an undergraduate at the School of Sociology and Political Science of the Catholic University of Rio de Janeiro. He received his M.A. in political science from the University of Chicago, where he is currently a doctoral candidate. After completing his course work at Chicago, Barros taught at the University of Brasilia and served as an adviser to the Brazilian Foreign Ministry before assuming his current positions.

E. D. BROWN is Professor of Law at the University of Wales Institute of Science and Technology. Until recently he was Reader in International Law at University College of the University of London, where he also received his Ph.D. He is a member of the Board of Editors of the *Ocean Development and International Law Journal* and Secretary of the London Institute of World Affairs. Professor Brown has been a consultant in the international law of the sea for the United Nations, a fellow of the Woodrow Wilson International Center for Scholars, and Assistant Editor of *Current Legal Problems.* Among his publications are *Arms Control in Hydrospace, The Legal Regime of Hydrospace,* "The Conventional Law of the Environment," "Iceland's Fishery Limits," and "The Prevention and Control of Marine Pollution."

YALE H. FERGUSON earned his Ph.D. at Columbia University. During the course of his graduate studies, he participated in the Columbia International Fellows Program, was an intern in the Bureau of International Organization Affairs of the United States Department of State, and a Woodrow Wilson Dissertation Fellow. He is currently an Associate Professor of Political Science in the Newark College of Arts and Sciences, Rutgers University; an Associate in the Political Science Graduate Program at Rutgers—New Brunswick; and a member of the University-wide Latin American Institute. Ferguson has edited *Contemporary Inter-American Relations* and co-edited *Continuing Issues in International Politics.* His articles have appeared in the *Journal of Politics, Problems of Communism, International Organization,* and many other journals.

CARLOS FORTIN received his M.A. in political science from Yale University, where he is currently a doctoral candidate. He also has studied at the University of Chile Law School. Fortin has served as Associate Professor and Director of Studies at the Latin American School of Political Science and Public Administration in Santiago, Chile and Director of the Department of Political Science and Public Law of the University of Chile. In 1971 he was appointed head of the European Office of the Copper Corporation of Chile and during the same year was selected to chair the Inter-Governmental Council of Copper Exporting Countries (CIPEC). In July 1973 Fortin was designated by the Allende Government to become Ambassador to the United States and was awaiting confirmation from the Chilean Senate at the time of the 1973 military coup. At present Fortin is a Lecturer in Government and History at the University of Sussex in England.

IRVING LOUIS HOROWITZ is Professor of Sociology and Political Science at Rutgers, the State University, and was Founding Chairman of the Sociology Department at Livingston College. Formerly Professor of Sociology at Washington University, he has held visiting professorships at Stanford, Wisconsin, and California. He has also held a number of overseas positions including visiting professorships at the London School of Economics, the University of Buenos Aires, and the National University of Mexico. Professor Horowitz currently is at work on a volume tentatively entitled *Militarism and Legitimacy in Latin America.* He is Editor-in-Chief of *Transaction/Society,* a leading multidisciplinary periodical, and author of such works as *Israeli Ecstasies/Jewish Agonies; Sociological Realities: A Guide to the Study of Society; The Struggle is the Message: The Organization and Ideology of the Anti-War Movement;* and *Three Worlds of Development.*

PEDRO-PABLO KUCZYNSKI is a vice president of Kuhn, Loeb and Company International. He was educated in Peru and at Oxford and Princeton universities. Kuczynski has been a lecturer at the Economic Development Institute of the World Bank and the Pontifical Catholic University of Peru. He has held several positions with the World Bank, including those of Chief Economist of the Central America and Caribbean Department, Chief of the Policy Planning Division, Loan Officer and Economist in the Western Hemisphere Department. Kuczynski also worked with the International Monetary Fund. In his own country, Kuczynski has served as Deputy General Manager of the Central Reserve Bank of Peru, Director of the Compania Peruana de Vapores, an Adviser to the Banco de la Vivienda del Peru, and a member of several commissions and delegations.

EDWARD S. MILENKY received his doctoral degree from the Fletcher School of Law and Diplomacy and currently is an Assistant Professor of Political Science at Boston College. He has also taught at Albion College, Colby College, and the Universidad del Salvador and Universidad John F. Kennedy of Buenos Aires. Among the grants he has been awarded arè a Latin American Teaching Fellowship, a Woodrow Wilson Dissertation Fellowship, a Shell International Fellowship, and a Fulbright Travel Grant. Milenky is the author of *The Politics of Regional Organization in Latin America: The Latin American Free Trade Association*. In addition, he has contributed to such scholarly journals as *Comercio Exterior de Mexico* and *Inter-American Economic Affairs*.

ARTHUR SCHLESINGER, JR., received his A.B. from Harvard College and continued his education as a Henry Fellow at Peterhouse, Cambridge, and as a member of the Society of Fellows at Harvard. In addition, he has been awarded honorary degrees from the University of New Brunswick, the New School for Social Research, and several other institutions. Schlesinger has been a Professor of History at Harvard University and currently is Albert Schweitzer Professor of the Humanities at the City University of New York. Between 1961 and 1964 he was a Special Assistant to Presidents Kennedy and Johnson. He received the Pulitzer Prize for History in 1946 and a Pulitzer Prize for Biography in 1966 and also has been awarded the Bancroft Prize, a Guggenheim Fellowship, a National Book Award, and several other prizes. Among Schlesinger's many books are *The Age of Roosevelt; A Thousand Days: John F. Kennedy in the White House*, and *The Imperial Presidency*.

KALMAN H. SILVERT received his Ph.D. from the University of Pennsylvania and currently is Professor of Politics at New York University and Program Adviser for the Social Sciences at the Ford Foundation. Previously he taught at Tulane University and Dartmouth College and was a Staff Associate and the Director of Studies of the American Universities Field Staff. Silvert had been a Visiting Professor at Boston University, Brandeis University, Harvard University, and the University of Buenos Aires. In 1965 he became the Founding President of the Latin American Studies Association. Among Silvert's many published works are *The Conflict Society: Reaction and Revolution in Latin America; Chile Yesterday and Today;* and *Man's Power: A Biased Guide to Political Thought and Action*.

THOMAS E. SKIDMORE is a Professor of History at the University of Wisconsin in Madison. He received his Ph.D. from Harvard University, where he taught before moving to Wisconsin. Skidmore has been a Fellow of the

Latin American Centre at Oxford University and the Woodrow Wilson International Center for Scholars. His current research is being supported by a Guggenheim Fellowship. Among Skidmore's many publications are *Politics in Brazil 1930-1964* and *Black into White: Race and Nationality in Brazilian Thought*. Skidmore is a former President of the Latin American Studies Association.

BEN S. STEPHANSKY is Associate Director of the W. E. Upjohn Institute for Employment Research. He has had a long career in government service. Since 1945 Stephansky has served as First Secretary of the United States Embassy in Mexico, Labor Adviser for Latin America at the Department of State, United States Ambassador to Bolivia, Deputy Assistant Secretary of State for Latin America, Executive Secretary of the United States-Puerto Rico Commission on the Status of Puerto Rico, and Deputy United States Representative to the Organization of American States. Stephansky received his Ph.D. in economics from the University of Wisconsin and has taught at Sarah Lawrence College and the University of Chicago. He also has been a Federal Executive Fellow at the Brookings Institution and a Program Adviser on Latin America for the Ford Foundation.

ROBERT H. SWANSBROUGH received his Ph.D. in political science from the University of California at Santa Barbara and currently is an Assistant Professor at the University of Tennessee at Chattanooga. He also has taught at the College of William and Mary and served as a Congressional Fellow of the American Political Science Association. Swansbrough is the author of *The Embattled Colossus: Economic Nationalism and United States Investors in Latin America*.

What is Latin America's role in international relations today? What will it be in ten years?

Latin American scholarship—following the tradition of most earlier Third World research—has tended to concentrate on modernization within and among individual nations, rather than upon the roles of these developing nations, singly and as a body, in influencing world politics and economics. Hellman and Rosenbaum draw from commentary and scholarship on this too often neglected area of global political economy to present essays systematically dealing with the problems and challenges of Latin American nations as they develop their own spheres of influence in the Western hemisphere and in world affairs.

Specific areas explored in this volume include:

    —Domestic factors in inter-American foreign policy-making

    —inter-American relations

    —intra-American relations

These outstanding essays, by leading authorities in the fields of Latin American studies and world politics, will be invaluable to scholars interested in international relations, world economics, foreign policy, cross-national growth and development, and the place of Latin America in the modern world.